Harold B. Lee

Elder Harold B. Lee about 1959

Harold B. Lee
Man of Vision, Prophet of God

Francis M. Gibbons

Deseret Book Company
Salt Lake City, Utah

All photographs in this book are used courtesy of the Historical Department, The Church of Jesus Christ of Latter-day Saints.

© 1993 Francis M. Gibbons

All rights reserved. No part of this book may be reproduced in any form or by any means without permission in writing from the publisher, Deseret Book Company, P. O. Box 30178, Salt Lake City, Utah 84130. This work is not an official publication of The Church of Jesus Christ of Latter-day Saints. The views expressed herein are the responsibility of the author and do not necessarily represent the position of the Church or of Deseret Book Company.

DESERET BOOK is a registered trademark of Deseret Book Company.

Visit us at DeseretBook.com

First printing in hardbound 1993.
First printing in paperbound 2009.

Library of Congress Cataloging-in-Publication Data

Gibbons, Francis M., 1921–
   Harold B. Lee : man of vision, prophet of God / Francis M. Gibbons.
      p.   cm.
   Includes index.
   ISBN-10 0-87579-716-4 (hardbound)
   ISBN-13 978-1-60641-217-6 (paperbound)
   1. Lee, Harold B., 1899–1973.   2. Mormon Church—Presidents—Biography.
3. The Church of Jesus Christ of Latter-day Saints—Presidents—Biography.   I. Title
BX8695.L396G53   1993
289.3'092—dc20
[B]   93-2149
                                                                              CIP

Printed in the United States of America

10 9 8 7 6 5 4 3 2 1

To
Adeline Christensen Gibbons
Beloved Mother

Contents

    Acknowledgments   ix
1   The Progenitors   1
2   Childhood   12
3   The Student   29
4   The Teacher   38
5   The Missionary   46
6   Courtship and Marriage   76
7   Call as Stake President   86
8   Salt Lake City Commissioner   96
9   Shepherding the Flock   109
10   Managing Director of the Church Welfare Plan   122
11   The Newest Apostle   144
12   The Family behind the Man   157
13   The First Apostolic Years   165
14   Maturing in the Apostleship   191
15   Patterns of Change   214
16   The Centennial Year   236
17   A Peaceful Interlude   253
18   The Reins Change Hands   285
19   The Cycle Continues   313

Contents

20	Signs of Growing Influence	337
21	Grinding it Out	352
22	Family and Personal Trauma—South America	371
23	New Duties, Changes, and Challenges	386
24	The Ultimate Trauma Followed by Healing	393
25	A Family in Transition	404
26	The Church in Transition	411
27	Counselor in the First Presidency	419
28	President of the Church	458
29	The Prophet Passes On	496
	Bibliography	503
	Index	509

Acknowledgments

The author gratefully acknowledges his indebtedness to L. Brent Goates and Helen Lee Goates for their diligence and dedication in compiling the vast store of data upon which Brent's excellent biography of President Lee is based. The justification I offer for writing another full-length biography so soon after the prophet's death, if indeed one is necessary, is the different perspectives and insights provided by my service as the secretary to the First Presidency during the years President Lee served as a counselor in the First Presidency and later as the president of the Church. I also especially thank the First Presidency for making the personal diaries of President Lee available to me; the staff in the office of the First Presidency and the historical department, who were uniformly kind and cooperative; the many friends and associates who provided important insights; my research assistants: Ruth Stoneman, Ben Stoneman, and Sam Stoneman; the editorial staff of Deseret Book, especially Eleanor Knowles and Jack Lyon; and, as always, the Mentor.

Chapter One

The Progenitors

The philosopher Ralph Waldo Emerson once said, "It is impossible to make a silk purse out of a sow's ear." The nature of a product, therefore, depends largely on the quality of the materials available to produce it. Workmanship, of course, enters in to affect its appearance and its durability. But if good materials are lacking, no amount of skill or ingenuity can convert the product into something contrary to its basic nature. While the complex variables of human personality and potential create risk in making an unqualified application of the philosopher's analogy to people, still there are sufficient similarities to allow this generalization: For one to rise to eminence in any field during earth life requires inherent qualities of intelligence and character and an environment which will allow for a full flowering of one's native abilities. And what is said here generally applies specially to one who, in life, rises to prophetic status.

Such a one is the subject of this biography, Harold Bingham Lee. At his birth on March 28, 1899, he received as an earthly inheritance superior qualities of intelligence, devotion; and spirituality through ancestors of worth and good character, although none of his direct forebears achieved high reputation outside the small circles of family and village. There was a great uncle, Joseph W. McMurrin, his grandmother's brother, who had risen to become one of the General Authorities of The Church of Jesus Christ of Latter-day Saints, serving for thirty-five years as a member of the First Council of the Seventy. But, with this exception, the ancestry of Harold B. Lee is devoid of anyone who gained prominence of a kind which remotely resembled that which he attained. This lack, however, bears no relationship to the innate qualities they possessed and which were transmitted to him as a legacy by lineal descent.

It is interesting to study the characteristics of people and to trace them into the personality and conduct of their descendants. The solid integrity and reliability of Harold B. Lee, which inspired such confidence among his family and associates, is, in large part, a legacy from his British ancestors. The first Lee on his direct line to migrate to America was William Lee, who was born in Carrickfergus, Ireland, on August 15, 1745. At age 25, William, led by the lure of land and economic opportunity, migrated to America where, soon after arriving in Philadelphia in 1770, he married Susannah Chaffings. The fourth child born to this couple, Samuel Chaffings Lee, was Harold's great-great-grandfather. Not long after Samuel's birth, his mother, Susannah, passed away, leaving her husband, William, a widower with four young children.

At this time, the American colonies were caught up in their revolution against Mother England. Loyal to his adopted country, William Lee enlisted in the American Revolutionary Army, leaving his four children with friends. He almost paid the ultimate price for this loyalty, being critically wounded at the battle of Guilford County Courthouse, fought in the Carolinas in 1781. Afterward, William married the compassionate woman who nursed him back to health, Sarah McMullen, by whom he sired seven more children.

The Progenitors

Taught by his stepmother in an active family of eleven children, Samuel ultimately left home to marry. Moving westward where economic opportunities were more plentiful, Samuel Chaffings Lee settled in Wilmington, Ohio. It was here that Harold's great-grandfather, Francis Lee, was born on June 26, 1811. And it was through this ancestor that the destiny of Harold B. Lee's family first became intertwined with the destiny of The Church of Jesus Christ of Latter-day Saints.

Attracted by the clarity of the doctrines of the Church, and electrified by the existence of a living prophet who had seen and conversed with the Father and the Son, Francis joined the Church in 1832. Soon after, heeding the counsel of the Prophet Joseph Smith, twenty-one-year-old Francis Lee moved to Missouri to help strengthen the Church in what the Saints called "the land of Zion." This was the first of many moves the young convert would make at the direction of his leaders, or because of his commitment to the Church, moves which were never convenient, which entailed major turmoil in his living arrangements, and which were usually made with little or no advance notice. So far as is known, Francis Lee never complained about the inconvenience of these moves, about the upset they created in his personal and family life, or about the deterring effect they had on his ability to plan for the future. There can be little doubt that the dedication of Francis Lee to the cause of the Church was a strong incentive to the great-grandson, Harold B. Lee, to rise above mediocrity.

In Missouri, Francis met and married Jane Vail Johnson, a poised young lady, who had previously joined the Church and who shared his convictions about its divine origins. The nuptials took place on October 24, 1835, in Liberty, Clay County, Missouri, the site of the dreary jail where the Prophet Joseph Smith would later be imprisoned. The Lees, optimistic about the future, yet unaware of the impending tragedy that would overtake the Missouri Saints, established the foundations of their family in Liberty. Later, however, knowing that a temple site had been designated there and attracted by the character of the community, they moved to Far West where most of the principal leaders of the Church then resided. It was there in Far West, in 1838, that the world of Francis and Jane Lee and their two children seemed to crumble. Fueled by Governor Lilburn Boggs's order to exterminate the Mormons and by the spirit of mobocracy that ruled the day, the Lees and thousands of other Latter-day Saints were uprooted from their homes and were driven across the Mississippi River into Illinois.

At first, Francis and his family sought refuge in Payson, Adams County, Illinois. It was here, on January 8, 1840, that Harold's grandfather, Samuel Marion Lee, Sr., was born. Three years later, attracted by its prosperity and by the beautiful temple being constructed there, the Lees moved to Nauvoo, then the mecca of Mormondom. They had barely settled into their new home when the martyrdom of the Prophet Joseph Smith and his brother, Hyrum, shattered any dreams of peace and stability the Lees may have had.

Victims of the wave of anti-Mormon sentiment that washed over Illinois after the martyrdom, Francis and his family prepared to join the exodus of the Latter-day Saints. With a company of 225 other refugees, they crossed the Mississippi on February 14, 1845, and during the next four months, toiled their way across the plains of Iowa, arriving at Council Bluffs, Iowa, on June 14. The Lees remained at the temporary Mormon camps on the Missouri River for five years as they planned the second leg of their migration to the Rocky Mountains.

While there, by a quirk of fate, Francis was reunited with his father, from whom he had been separated for many years. His father, attracted by the reports of the gold strike, was on his way to California on foot. However, Francis persuaded him to join the Saints in their exodus, and upon arriving in Utah, persuaded him to remain there. He joined the Church in 1851 in Tooele.

The Progenitors

Tragedy struck the Lees in the summer of 1850 as their immigrant company prepared to leave for the Rockies. They were at the staging area on the Platte River west of Winter Quarters when cholera broke out. Several victims died. One of them was Francis and Jane's little boy, Jacob Edward. He was buried there in a lonely grave whose makeshift marker was later destroyed.

By this time, the trail westward was well marked and frequently used. The Lees' company made the tiring trip without incident, arriving in the Salt Lake Valley on September 17, 1850.

A spirit of enterprise and high expectation infused this new Mormon mecca when the Lees arrived in Salt Lake City. The Church leaders were directing an ambitious plan of colonization whose object was to settle Mormon families in all the valleys throughout the mountainous area. The Lees willingly followed the suggestion of the Brethren that they settle in the Tooele Valley, thirty miles west of Salt Lake City at the southern end of the Great Salt Lake. Here, during a period of twelve years, the Lee family put down deep roots, building a comfortable home while cultivating their fields, tending their animals, and enjoying the religious and cultural life of the close-knit Mormon community. It was the first time since their marriage that Francis and Jane had been allowed to remain long enough in one place to enjoy the fruits of their labors. They were ill prepared, therefore, for the bombshell that exploded at the general conference in April 1862. Without prior consultation, it was announced from the stand that Francis Lee and his family were called to move south to settle and to help build up an area popularly called "Dixie." No subsidy was offered to help them in the move, nor were they given assistance or advice in liquidating their holdings in Tooele. They were expected to use their intelligence and ingenuity to fulfill the "call," which had come from one whom they sustained as a prophet, so they went without complaint or remonstrance.

Arriving at St. George, which was the focal point of

5

the Dixie colonization, Francis was asked to settle in Meadow Valley to the west. The Mormon community that grew up there came to be known as Panaca, located in the territory, later the state, of Nevada.

The Lees' first home in this remote Mormon outpost was a dugout, gouged out of a hill. The front part of their dwelling was covered by timbers punched into the hill and covered with clay. Here fifty-one-year-old Francis Lee began to till the land, starting over at an age when most men of that day looked forward to retirement or to a reduced work load.

Samuel Marion Lee, Sr., the twenty-two-year-old son of Francis and Jane, had been left in Tooele to help wind up family affairs when his parents went south to Panaca. The following year, he married seventeen-year-old Margaret McMurrin, a perky and pretty lass, whose Scottish blood would add another vital ancestral strain to their future grandson, Harold Bingham Lee.

Margaret's father, Joseph McMurrin, was born in Crossmaloof, Scotland, while her mother, Margaret Leaing, was born in Glasgow. Joseph and Margaret were married in Glasgow in 1842, and their daughter Margaret was born there on May 13, 1846.

A few years after Margaret's birth, the McMurrin family migrated to the United States, presumably in search of greater economic opportunity. They found that, and much more. In their adopted country, they came in contact with The Church of Jesus Christ of Latter-day Saints, were converted to its doctrines, and, in 1854, were baptized. The following year the McMurrin clan, including nine-year-old Margaret, following the counsel of the Church leaders, migrated to Utah. They settled first in Tooele where Joseph plied his trade as a cooper. The McMurrins later moved to Salt Lake City, where they settled permanently, but not before daughter Margaret had married Samuel Marion Lee, Sr. About the same time, Margaret's sister, Mary, married Francis Lee, Jr., Samuel's brother.

Once the family holdings in Tooele had been closed

The Progenitors

out, Samuel and Francis Jr. and their wives moved to Panaca to assist the Lee parents in their pioneering effort.

The mission they had undertaken was fraught with difficulties. Starting from scratch, they had to break up and cultivate the virgin soil, prepare their own irrigation system, and go through a period of experimentation to determine which crops thrived best in that climate and the length of the growing season. Meanwhile, they were occupied in their "off" hours building permanent homes and Church buildings, performing their ecclesiastical duties, and mediating disputes with the surrounding Indian tribes. At one point the relations with the Indians, who were understandably irked by the intrusions of the settlers upon their ancestral lands, had become so volatile that the Mormon leaders authorized the Saints to abandon Meadow Valley and to move elsewhere. While at times that may have seemed to be an attractive alternative, and one which some of the other settlers opted for, the Lees did not take it. They toughed it out. The headstones of several generations of Lees found in Panaca's cemetery attest to the spunky durability and determination of the clan.

Francis and Jane Lee had ten children, seven sons and three daughters. During the early years of the Panaca settlement, most of the children who survived to maturity quite regularly added to the growing progeny of their parents, giving them grandchildren to dote upon and to spoil. The notable exception was Samuel and Margaret. From the time of their marriage in 1863 until 1875, they were childless. It was not that they did not want children or had not tried to have them. Indeed, during that period, Margaret had conceived eleven times, but her babies were either stillborn or lived for only a few hours. After ten failures, Margaret, who during most of her married life was very frail, almost despaired of having a child who would survive. But while on a trip to Salt Lake to visit her family, she received a remarkable blessing from Patriarch Abel Lamb who promised her, "you shall have a son and he shall be a mighty man in Israel and his name shall be the

7

name of his father." One can imagine Margaret's joy at receiving the blessing and yet her anguish when the first child conceived after she had received it was stillborn. But, the twelfth and last one, a son, survived, although the circumstances made it doubtful he would do so. The child, who was born prematurely on November 22, 1875, weighed only three-and-a-half pounds. Margaret, exhausted by the ordeal, lived only eight days afterward, then passed away. She was twenty-nine. Her miracle child was named Samuel Marion Lee, Jr., as the patriarch had decreed. He would become the father of the prophet, Harold B. Lee. Elements of Margaret's travail and Patriarch Lamb's blessing are reminiscent of Hannah's fervent prayers for a son, whom she received through the blessing of the priest Eli and who was also named Samuel. (See 1 Samuel, chapter 1.)

At the outset, there was serious doubt whether Margaret's son would grow to manhood. He was so weak and tiny, and after only eight days of life, he was also motherless. It was providential that at Margaret's death her sister, Mary, was nursing her own baby. She took Samuel into her home and, for six months, nursed him in tandem with her own child. However, by the spring of 1876, Mary was exhausted from the physical demands of nursing and caring for two babies. Out of family consultations came the decision to take Samuel to Salt Lake City to be cared for by Grandmother Margaret Leaing McMurrin. By then the baby was strong enough to endure the two-week trip to Salt Lake by horse and buggy.

What was originally intended as a place of temporary refuge for Samuel became his permanent home, at least until he was eighteen years old, when Grandmother McMurrin died. By the time his father had remarried and was able to provide a suitable family environment for him, Samuel had been fully integrated into the McMurrin household. All agreed at that time that the boy's best interests would be served by leaving him in the McMurrin home. Afterward the father visited his son as often as the long

The Progenitors

distance and the demands of pioneer living in Panaca allowed. And when Samuel grew into boyhood, he occasionally went to Panaca during the summer, where he was exposed to life on the farm and to his numerous Lee relatives who lived there.

It is inferred that an important reason why Samuel remained in Salt Lake was the educational and cultural advantages life in the city offered, advantages that would never exist in Panaca. The McMurrins lived on Sixth South and Main Street, only a mile south of Temple Square. For several years during his adolescence, Samuel's grandfather was in charge of the temple grounds. There the grandson witnessed the tedious process by which the majestic building was erected, stone by stone. Often he visited the unique, domed tabernacle on Temple Square, which by the time of his birth had been fully completed and in use for several years. Here he occasionally saw some of the high leaders of the Church, apostles and prophets, never imagining that one day his own son would stand as the chief living apostle and the prophet of the Church.

The McMurrin home was located within walking distance of both school and church. The family belonged to the Eighth Ward, where the grandfather served in the bishopric for many years. On February 1, 1876, a few months before Samuel came into the home of his grandparents to live, his uncle, Joseph W. McMurrin, who later became a member of the First Council of Seventy, left the family home to fill a colonizing mission in Arizona. The uncle was only seventeen years old at the time. He returned two years later and for a while lived with his parents before he married and established his own household. As he was only a baby at the time, Samuel undoubtedly had little awareness of these and of other events around his grandparents' home until later. As he grew older, however, he learned that his grandfather had taken a plural wife, Jeanette Irvine, whom he married in 1869 and by whom he sired nine children. These children were Samuel's aunts and uncles, as were the children of his Grandmother Margaret Leaing McMurrin, even though some of them were younger than he. So from his earliest days of remembrance, Harold B. Lee's father learned about the practical and the personal aspects of polygamy. He also learned about the trauma endured by some polygamous families when, during the 1880s, his Grandfather McMurrin was convicted of unlawful cohabitation and was imprisoned in the Utah penitentiary for six months. Samuel's sense of trauma was undoubtedly heightened during this period when his uncle, Joseph W. McMurrin, was shot twice in the abdomen by a trigger-happy officer who was trying to gather evidence of unlawful cohabitation. It was feared that these wounds would prove to be fatal. However, following an apostolic blessing given by Elder John Henry Smith of the Twelve, the uncle recovered and, as already mentioned, lived to become a General Authority of the Church.

These stressful times ended with the announcement of the Manifesto in 1890; and three years later the whole Church rejoiced when the Salt Lake Temple was dedicated by President Wilford Woodruff.

Margaret Leaing McMurrin lived only five months after this historic event. She died on September 4, 1893. Her passing marked another milestone in the life of Samuel Marion Lee, Jr. He was seventeen years old at the time, turning eighteen two months later. He might have returned to Panaca then had not his father died three years before. In mulling his options, Samuel decided to accept the invitation of his aunt, Jeanette McMurrin Davis, and her husband, Riley, to live with them and to help operate their farm at Clifton, Idaho. It was this decision that led Samuel into an acquaintance with the Bingham family, who lived in the upper Cache Valley, and more particularly with Louisa Emeline Bingham, who would become his wife. It was this unusual woman, whose roots also extended deep into Great Britain, who would provide the final ancestral mix for the son who became the President of the Mormon church.

For generations the Binghams had tilled the soil. Levi

The Progenitors

Perry Bingham, Harold B. Lee's great-grandfather, was known as one of the most careful and exacting farmers in the Cache Valley. He was born in Canada, joined the Mormon church as a teenager, and, after the expulsion of the Saints from Illinois, was swept up in the exodus. At age twenty he married Elizabeth Lusk at Council Bluffs, Iowa, while preparing for the trek to Utah. He farmed at Pleasant Grove and Payson, Utah, before settling in Clifton. While he lived in Pleasant Grove in 1857, his son Perry Calvin was born, the grandfather of President Lee. Perry Calvin, who learned farming from his father, moved with the family to Clifton, where he became established with his wife, Elvira Henderson of Kaysville, Utah, whom he married in 1875 at age eighteen. He later branched out into freighting and livestock brokering, was elected sheriff and assessor of Oneida County, and finally was appointed deputy warden of the Idaho State Prison at Boise. The second child of Perry Calvin and Rachel Elvira Bingham was Louisa Emeline Bingham, Harold B. Lee's mother. She was born at Clifton on January 1, 1879.

Louisa's older sister, Sarah, died when she was three years old. Because her mother was ill most of the time, almost to the point of being an invalid, Louisa had much of the responsibility to nurse her mother, to care for the household, and to supervise the younger children. Occasionally, when her father was away, she also had responsibility for some of the outside chores. Under this regimen, Louisa matured very fast. Indeed, it might be said that she never had the luxury of being a child.

Samuel worked on the Davis farm for several years, quickly learning the skills that were neglected during his growing-up years in Salt Lake City. In Clifton he met, courted, and married Louisa Bingham, who was four years younger than he. The couple travelled by horse and buggy to Logan, Utah, where, on May 13, 1896, they were endowed and sealed in the temple. The sealing ceremony was performed by Marriner W. Merrill, president of the temple and later a member of the Council of the Twelve.

Chapter Two

Childhood

Clifton, where Samuel and Louisa Lee made their home, lies on the west flank of the upper Cache Valley. Its name was derived from a high rocky cliff that towers over the community to the west. It is one of several string towns settled by Mormon colonists in the 1860s, including Oxford to the north and Dayton and Weston to the south, all of which are overshadowed by the mountains to the west. Several miles southeast of Clifton, in the center of the valley, is Franklin, Idaho, founded in 1855 by the Latter-day Saints. To the north of Franklin, on the east side of the valley, lies Whitney, the birthplace of Ezra Taft Benson, and Preston, the site of the Oneida Stake Academy. It was here that Harold Lee and "T" Benson, born only five months and several miles apart, would first become acquainted. In the north end of the valley is Red Rock Pass where, the geologists theorize, the walls of ancient Lake Bonneville were breached, allowing its waters to drain into the Snake River. The Great Salt Lake, it is also theorized, is the remnant of this vast inland freshwater lake.

Childhood

Because these communities had been founded of such recent date, they were very rudimentary at the time Samuel and Louisa set up housekeeping on a small farm in Clifton. They had no modern conveniences. There was no indoor plumbing, no electricity, and no central heating. At first, water was carried from a well or stream. Later when it was piped in, the water needed for laundering or personal hygiene was heated on the kitchen stove. Baths were taken in a washtub. Lighting was by kerosene or gas lamps. As electrification was introduced into the valley and as other modern conveniences were added, life became more comfortable. But it was never easy.

The high elevation of the Cache Valley greatly shortened the growing season, and late spring or early summer storms or freezes would sometimes blight the crops. There was ample fertile land available, but water was scarce. The farms were irrigated from the Twin Lake reservoir, which was fed by Mink Creek or from flowing wells that had been successfully dug. But there was seldom a surplus. Farming here was labor intensive, and before the Lee boys were old enough to do farm work, Louisa often pitched in to help with the lighter outside chores. She was an expert rider and had a pony named Maude that she rode often, either in helping Samuel or as a means of transportation. In addition to the crops needed to feed their cattle, the Lees had a truck garden and an orchard that provided vegetables and fruits for the table. Surpluses were bottled for use during the off-season. Chickens and a cow provided milk and eggs for their diet, and what meat they needed came from their own cattle and hogs. What little cash they had was derived chiefly from the sale of their cattle or surplus crops. A downturn in market prices could be as devastating as an unseasonable freeze.

While the Lees never went hungry, indeed they always had an ample diet, they, like other farmers in the area, lived frugally because of the lack of money to buy the things that could not be produced on the farm. This fostered a sense of ingenuity and resourcefulness to make do with what they had. So, notwithstanding a slender cash income, the Lee household presented an image of material abundance. This was in large part the result of Louisa's industry and skill as a homemaker. She was an expert seamstress, so most of the clothing of the children was the product of her needle and her treadle sewing machine. She had an innate artistic sense, which manifested itself in a flair for flower arrangements and in the careful selection of colors and fabrics to decorate the home. The years of her adolescence when she practically ran the Bingham household single-handedly had given Louisa a marvelous sense of competence and independence that was reflected in the orderliness of the Lee home and in the obedience of the children, which her positive and forthright character engendered.

Meanwhile, Samuel, the father, not only provided the brain and brawn necessary to make the farm produce a livelihood for his family, he also provided the kind of spiritual and intellectual leadership that imbued its members with a sense of purpose. Judging from the frequency with which he mentioned it, he was very conscious of the miraculous aspects of his birth. And judging from the intense interest he had in his ancestry, the father also seemed to sense that his line was destined to play an important role in the unfolding drama of the Church. Samuel's preoccupation with his family lineage was dramatized when he compiled 1,500 sheets of genealogical records. He then laboriously made copies of them by hand for members of the family, often with the approval of his employer, toiling over them while he supervised a night maintenance crew at Salt Lake's ZCMI department store. All this, added to his calm personality and his dignified bearing, created a patriarchal quality in Samuel Marion Lee, Jr., a quality that surfaced often. For instance, when sending Harold into the mission field, he told the son that he expected big things from him. And it surfaced again when, after Elder Lee had been called to the Twelve, the father gave him a special

Childhood

blessing as the apostle prepared to leave on an important assignment in the Pacific.

Samuel Lee, therefore, was a true patriarch in his family, a status that was enhanced by the many Church positions he held during his lifetime. His official Church career began shortly after marriage when he was made an assistant to the superintendent of the Sunday School in the Clifton Ward. Later, he became the superintendent, serving for five years. In that capacity, he had the responsibility to supervise gospel instruction for both children and adults in the ward, and thereby had the incentive to increase his knowledge of Church doctrine. Later he became a member of the ward bishopric, following which he was sustained as the bishop, a position he held for nine years, being released after Harold had completed his mission. So, from the moment of Elder Lee's birth until the time he left the family home, his father was heavily and continuously engaged in Church work. That influence carried into the home, where the principles and practices of Mormonism were a dominant factor. Family prayers and scripture study were a regular part of the daily routine, and the children saw in their parents' conduct a demonstration of how religious principles are applied to daily living.

In the Lee home there was a genuine concern for the welfare of others. Bishop Lee was a devoted shepherd of his flock, attending to the temporal and spiritual needs of the widows and others in his ward who required special attention. Louisa, who was skilled in nursing and midwifery, was often called on to comfort the sick or to preside at the delivery of a baby. And, of course, she used her healing arts in aid of her own family, applying the well-known home remedies of the day, chief among which were the clammy mustard plaster for chest colds, a hot onion or camphor for the earache, and cloves for the toothache. Because of the prevalence of pulmonary ailments and children's diseases in these rural communities, and because of the scarcity of professionally trained doctors, there was a greater reliance at the time than at present on priesthood administrations to heal the sick. Accordingly, Harold and the other children in the Lee home became witnesses at an early age of their father exercising his priesthood authority to bless the sick or to bring comfort to those who were troubled or who mourned.

They also became aware, when very young, of special spiritual qualities that their mother possessed. Louisa was prayerful by nature and frequently offered special, secret prayers for the welfare of her family. A notable example of this characteristic, handed down in family lore, was her earnest prayer for Harold's success in a school debate. With this habit of prayerfulness was an innate spiritual sense that prompted her to act instinctively in cases where members of her family were in peril. One such instance occurred in Harold's childhood when his mother, during an electrical storm at Clifton, suddenly, without warning or apparent reason, pushed him sprawling out of the doorway of the family home. Soon after a bolt of lightning flashed down the chimney and out through the door where Harold had been standing, scorching a huge gash in a tree that stood in the yard. Had not the mother acted with such promptness, it is likely the future prophet would have been killed. On another occasion, Louisa, moved by an impulse she could not explain, insisted that Samuel go in search of their son. The father found Harold in a pool of half-frozen mud where he had been thrown when his horse stumbled while crossing a stream. Louisa never attempted to define the source or the scope of this instinct, nor to elaborate on the sensations that accompanied its manifestations. It was sufficient that she felt impelled to take the action that the moment dictated, without preplan and without any consideration about the consequences of it.

This quality of spiritual sensitivity, so evident in Louisa Bingham Lee, was even more pronounced in her prophet-son. Of all the unusual qualities revealed in Harold B. Lee at the height of his powers, none was more pronounced nor more intriguing to witness than the sudden infusion of spiritual insights that he sporadically received. So confident was he of their source and of their validity that he acted upon them without hesitation in a manner not unlike his mother's impulsive action that sent him sprawling during the electrical storm in Clifton. It seems to have been this quality that caused many of President Lee's associates to refer to him as a "seer." And it was this quality that gave his leadership a special sense of immediacy and excitement. In the presence of Harold B. Lee, no one ever quite knew when the lightning would strike, when, because of a whispering or a spiritual impulse, an unforeseen chain of events would suddenly be set in motion. His actions on these occasions were reminiscent of the Prophet Joseph Smith, who, for instance, initiated the vast network of international proselyting by the Church merely by whispering to Heber C. Kimball in the Kirtland Temple about a spiritual impression he had just received, directing Elder Kimball to open the door to the preaching of the gospel in Great Britain. This same quality was manifested often during Harold B. Lee's apostolic ministry.

Other qualities in the character of Louisa Lee that, in varying degrees, were reflected in the personality of her famous son were a delightful sense of humor, extraordinary willpower, and a refreshing frankness. It was never necessary to wonder about Louisa Lee's meaning or about how one stood in her estimation. She spoke openly in words not to be misunderstood. So it was with her son. President Lee was forthright in all his conversations and dealings. He left no room for speculation about what he meant or how he felt. This induced an extraordinary sense of obedience and diligence among his associates and subordinates. To many of them, he was like the disciplined coach whom they wanted to please and to emulate. And, like his mother, he had extraordinary willpower. Louisa showed this quality when she summarily rejected the opinion of the doctors that her husband's death was imminent, checked him out of the hospital, and with the help of her sons, took him home. There she nursed him for a year before he died. Hints of a similar determination in the son will be seen in the way in which Elder Lee, in the face of doubts, carping criticism, and opposition, shepherded the welfare program through its infancy to the place of eminence it ultimately occupied.

While Samuel and Louisa Lee lacked opportunities for higher education, they were studious, enjoyed books, and cultivated a sense of scholarship in their home. This attitude was enhanced when, during the early years of their marriage, Samuel taught school during the off-season to supplement the income generated from the family farm. In such an environment, children were inclined toward intellectual and scholarly pursuits. Given this bent, the son Harold quite naturally gravitated toward a career in teaching during his earlier adult years.

Against this background, the home into which Harold Bingham Lee was born on March 28, 1899, was one characterized by religious conviction, intellectual interests, orderliness, and an overriding sense of urgency and uncertainty, which farm life induces. It was in this environment that he would begin to develop the skills, the capacities, and the qualities of character that would fit him for the prophetic office.

Harold was the second of six children born into the family of Samuel and Louisa Lee. The first child, Samuel Perry, was three years older than he. The other four, Clyde, Waldo, Stella, and Verda, would be born during the following ten years. Harold was a picture perfect baby—healthy, active, and appealing. As he grew into childhood, the most striking things about his appearance were his large, searching brown eyes and an abundant growth of dark, wavy hair. Perhaps betraying a secret hope that her second child would be a girl, Louisa insisted on letting the baby's hair grow; and when it was sufficiently long, she began to fashion it into long ringlets in the style of Little Lord Fauntleroy. In keeping with that image, Louisa spent long hours making clothes for Harold worthy of his hair: white shirts with ruffles in front, starched cuffs, and a

Childhood

Harold B. Lee (age four, right), with his brothers, S. Perry Lee and Clyde B. Lee, about 1904

white middy that was draped over the shoulder of a handsome coat, all set off with a large, flamboyant black tie. It is difficult to image such an outfit for a boy living in the rustic village of Clifton around the turn of the century. And Harold seems to have shared that view. When he went to school dressed like that and with his hair in ringlets, he naturally attracted wide attention. It was embarrassing and annoying when he became the butt of his classmates' jokes. He was angered when they pulled on his ringlets and taunted him for looking like a girl. Unwilling to submit meekly to these insults, Harold retaliated in kind, precipitating fist fights and wrestling matches. He apparently decided quite soon that this was no way to get an education and borrowing his mother's scissors cut off the front ringlets. This ruined the whole effect. Grandfather Bingham, apparently sympathetic to Harold's plight, finished the job, cutting off all the ringlets and shaping the boy's hair into a style that made him less conspicuous and more acceptable to his classmates. We get the idea that Louisa mourned over this, for she saved the ringlets. Years later when her father was the assistant warden at the penitentiary in Boise, she arranged with him to have one the prisoners, known for his skill in handicrafts, braid the curls into two attractive watch chains. One of these later became the prized possession of President Lee's first wife, Fern.

This incident occurred when Harold was only five years old, the age at which he started school. He was allowed to start early because he was very bright and because his mother had taught him some of the basics at home. This seemed to set a pattern that was repeated often throughout his life, a pattern that saw Harold B. Lee reach milestones at a younger age than his peers. He was ordained a deacon at age ten, was a school principal in his teens, became both a stake president and a Salt Lake City commissioner in his early thirties, was the managing director of the Church Welfare Department in his mid-thirties, and was ordained a member of the Twelve in his early forties. His precocity and maturity always belied his chronological age. His confident demeanor and bearing made Harold B. Lee seem older than he actually was. There was a certain dignity there, a certain sense about him, which conveyed the impression that he had always been an adult. It was an inherent quality whose roots seemed to extend back beyond the moment of his earthly birth. It was a spiritual quality that implied a pre-earth life where his character and personality had been molded and honed.

The rural school Harold and his brothers and sisters attended was located two miles from the Lee farm. In good weather, they could walk there along Clifton's one and only north-south road, which formed the spine of the town's street system. When the weather was bad, they used whatever mode of transportation ingenuity could devise: horseback, wagon, buggy pooling with neighbors, or sleigh when there was deep snow. If the weather was extremely bad, they stayed home. Like all rural schools of the day, scheduling was ordered around the demands of planting and harvesting so as to accommodate the labor needs on the farms. Fortunate, indeed, was the farmer who had sons who could help carry the heavy and continuing burden of work. And, notwithstanding Louisa's inordinate yearning for a girl, she and Samuel must have considered themselves fortunate that their first four children were boys. Each of the sons, in turn, as he became old enough and strong enough, took his place in the Lee's labor force to help carry on their family enterprise.

As already mentioned, in addition to the farm acreage, which consisted of a hundred acres of bottomlands, where their wheat and the feed for their animals were grown, the Lees had a garden, an orchard, cows, horses, pigs, and chickens. All these required special attention. Each member of the family had specified duties that spread the work load and, in the process, created in each one a sense of responsibility and self-worth. As indicated, money was scarce and came either from school teaching salaries, the sale of any surpluses, or from "hiring out" to neighboring farmers who lacked homegrown manpower.

But farm life was not all work. There were times, especially during the winter months, when the work slacked off, leaving time for leisure and the pursuit of personal hobbies or interests. At an early age, Harold developed a liking for music, especially the piano, although he also learned to play several wind instruments. His piano teacher was Sarah Gerard, a doughty Scottish lady, who would playfully rap Harold's knuckles at the sound of a sour note. The skill he acquired at the piano and organ was one which yielded rich rewards throughout his life, either in personal satisfaction or in the enjoyment he provided others. As a youth in Clifton, he often served as the accompanist at Primary and Sunday School. This skill followed him into the mission field where he was frequently called on to provide the music for various gatherings. It even followed him into the Quorum of the Twelve, where, for many years, he served as the organist at the weekly meetings of the First Presidency and the Quorum of the Twelve held in the upper room of the Salt Lake Temple. Indeed, he was still performing that function in the spring of 1970, but soon thereafter relinquished it to Elder Spencer W. Kimball, who continued as the official organist of the Brethren until after he became the president of the Church. Harold's skill with the horn earned him a spot in Mr. Cox's Clifton Silver Concert Band. This was his first experience with a musical group. As we shall see, it would not be his last.

Amidst work on the farm, school, and his music, Harold found ample time for the usual boyhood pleasures. He was an agile and well-coordinated athlete, enjoying the competitive sports of the day. Basketball was a favorite. There was fishing in the mountain streams. One of these fed what was called "Bybee Pond" located on property owned by Lester Bybee. It was in this pool that Harold was baptized by Lester Bybee on June 9, 1907. He was confirmed the same day, a Sunday, by his bishop, E. G. Farmer. It is inferred the baptism was postponed beyond Harold's eighth birthday because the water in the Bybee Pond was too cold. Indeed, in late March there could still have been ice on it, and at that elevation, the water was probably bracingly cold even on June 9. For whatever reason, the event made a lasting impression on him. Several decades later as Elder Harold B. Lee sat beside Glen L. Rudd at a Church meeting, Lester Bybee offered the invocation. Afterward, Elder Lee whispered to his companion: "That man baptized me."

"He what?" asked Glen Rudd in disbelief.

"He baptized me," Elder Lee answered.

Glen let that information seep into his brain during the meeting, and then afterward, to make sure he had it right, he asked Elder Lee again, "Did you say that that man baptized you?"

"Yes," came the answer, "is there anything wrong with

that?" Some time later when Glen Rudd, who was a long-time associate of his in welfare work, was with Elder Lee in Cache Valley, he persuaded him to drive to Clifton so he could see exactly where that extraordinary event took place. And it was an extraordinary event, marking the official entrance into the Church of one who was destined to become its presiding officer. (As related to the author by Glen L. Rudd.)

President Lee did not grow to maturity in Clifton without his share of trial, trauma, and testing. One of the most significant events that occurred there during this period introduced him to the realm of the spirit and demonstrated his obedience to spiritual promptings. It occurred when Harold had accompanied his father to Dayton, south of Clifton, where Samuel Lee owned a small forty-acre farm. While the father was busy with his chores, the son began exploring. Seeing the remnants of some old outbuildings, which had collapsed, Harold parted the strands of the wire fence to go inspect them. An audible voice warned, "Harold, don't go near that lumber over there." He heeded the warning and, frightened, turned back. He never knew whether danger lurked there or whether the warning was given merely to test his response to a spiritual prompting. The Prophet Joseph Smith occasionally tested the obedience of his followers by instructing them to do unusual things. And the breeders of thoroughbreds have been known to command a thirsty horse to "stay" before a stream of water to test the limits of its discipline. We shall never know whether such a purpose accounted for this spiritual warning to the boy, Harold Lee. One thing is clear, however. It demonstrated the obedient reaction, in a stressful situation, of one destined to fill a high place. The incident would have had little meaning for an omniscient God who knew beforehand how he would react. But it was doubtless an experience fraught with meaning for the young boy who thereby learned about the reality of the spiritual world and that there were beings there who were interested in protecting him.

Harold B. Lee

Judging from some of the experiences he had in Clifton, Harold needed protection. Without the protecting care of his mother and others in time of dire need, he would have been disfigured, or maimed, or would not have survived to adulthood. We have already seen how his mother's swift reaction saved him from instantaneous death by lightning. Later she saved him from a lingering death through the creative application of her nursing skills. Harold once lay gravely ill with pneumonia. Louisa first sought to reduce the congestion and to lower Harold's fever by applying a series of mustard plasters. They did nothing but turn his chest a fiery red. She then resorted to the ultimate remedy of the practical nurse in such cases. Slicing an apron full of onions into a pan of boiling water, she strained out the water and put the hot onion mass in a cloth sack which she then placed on Harold's chest. Then she prayed. By morning the patient was breathing more easily. That marked the turning point. He was soon healed. Typically, Louisa turned away compliments about her nursing skill, attributing her son's recovery to the blessings of God.

Another time, Louisa, in the process of making soap, had prepared a lye concoction that she had placed in a pan on a high shelf out of the reach of the little children. When she was ready to use the concoction, the mother asked Harold to help get it down. Standing together on a chair, they carefully lifted the pan off the shelf and were starting to lower it when it slipped. The pan flipped over, dumping the contents over Harold's head, face, and arms. Reacting immediately, Louisa held her son to prevent him from running away, kicked the lid off of a large container of beet pickles she had put up, and cupping her right hand, dipped out the pickle vinegar, which she splashed over the affected areas of Harold's body. The vinegar neutralized the lye, which prevented any scarring.

Years before when Louisa and her mother were bottling fruit, Harold drank from a cup he thought contained fruit juice. Instead, it contained a lye solution used to remove fruit particles caked in the pans. Immediately they grabbed him to pour olive oil down his throat, thereby averting injury or death.

Again, Harold accidentally caught his right hand in the milk separator, stripping the flesh from one of the fingers. At first, Louisa was so sickened by the sight that she was immobilized. Fortunately, Bishop Farmer stopped by at that moment and pulled the skin over the exposed bone. Regaining her composure, Louisa then bandaged the wound, which healed readily but left a jagged scar. However, it never prevented Harold from playing the piano.

Except for two memorable trips, the future prophet spent his entire childhood within a few miles of the house in Clifton where he was born. In company with his mother, Perry, and Clyde, he travelled to Boise, the state capital, to visit Louisa's parents. Harold and his brothers had never seen such a big place, although Boise at that time could not have had a population of more than ten thousand. Of the many new things they saw there, nothing seems to have impressed them as much as the penitentiary, where, as already noted, Grandfather Bingham was the deputy warden. In his maturity, Harold reflected on some of the things he saw during this visit. One Sunday his grandfather took him to a church service at the prison. He reported nothing about the program, but vividly described the impressions made upon him by the sight of hundreds of prisoners dressed in their striped uniforms. Even more memorable was the angry inmate cook who ran Harold and Perry out of the guard's kitchen with a butcher knife. Any argument of the cook that he only wanted to frighten the boys who had no right to be in his kitchen was unavailing. He got three days in solitary on bread and water.

The boys also witnessed the drama of an attempted escape. When a prisoner broke away from a work detail, Grandfather Bingham led a search and capture team that included bloodhounds. The baying of the dogs and the hurried excitement of their grandfather and his men as they armed themselves made a deep impression on the boys. However, their grandmother prohibited them from watching the climax of the drama. Concerned that the sight of the shackled prisoner, in his striped uniform, surrounded by the barking dogs and the armed guards, would leave a lasting and harmful impression on the minds of her grandchildren, Louisa's mother pulled down the shades of their house, which was adjacent to the prison, so Harold and his brothers couldn't see the end.

The second memorable trip took Harold to Salt Lake City with his father and Perry. Samuel wanted his sons to see where he was raised. More important, he wanted them to experience the excitement of a general conference of the Church. Louisa prepared a large basket of food for the travelers, which featured mounds of fried chicken, and saw them off to nearby Franklin where they caught the train to Salt Lake City. One who can remember his first ride on a steam engine train can imagine the excitement of Harold and Perry as the monstrous engine, spewing steam and smoke and sounding its shrill whistle, ground to a halt at the Franklin station. It was a busy time of the year for the railroad as many Latter-day Saints living in the upper Cache Valley and points north travelled to Salt Lake City to attend general conference. Boarding the train with other passengers who had waited at the Franklin station, Samuel and his two wide-eyed sons settled down for the three-hour trip. Passing through Logan they could see, on the crest of a hill to the east, the massive temple where Samuel and Louisa were married. Winding its way out of the Cache Valley, the train headed south, passing through the string of small communities, which, during the preceding sixty years, had been settled by the Latter-day Saints along the west flank of the Wasatch Mountains. At some of them, the train stopped to take on more passengers or to drop some off who were not destined for Salt Lake City.

Given the Mormon custom at that day of "doubling up" during conference, it is inferred that Samuel and his sons were guests in the home of one of their numerous McMurrin relatives. The family had gained wide promi-

Childhood

nence through the call of Samuel's uncle, Joseph W. McMurrin, to the First Council of Seventy in 1897, two years before Harold was born.

Samuel's sons had been told much about Salt Lake City. That their great-grandfather, Joseph McMurrin, had once supervised the maintenance of the grounds on Temple Square was a matter of family lore. To see these grounds in person brought to reality what they had been told about them or had seen in pictures. Here stood the imposing granite-walled temple, dedicated only a few years before, and the domed Tabernacle from whose pulpit all the presidents of the Church, except the Prophet Joseph Smith, had addressed the Saints. When Samuel and the boys went to Temple Square to attend a session of general conference, they found long lines queued up waiting to enter the Tabernacle. They had not arrived in time to find seating on the main floor and so were directed to the south balcony. From that vantage point, they had a close-up view of the holes in the ceiling of the building, used in the early days as apertures for ropes by which platforms were raised to the ceiling to clean or paint it. They also had a clear view of the huge organ in the west end of the building, which overshadowed the choir seats and the stands on which the General Authorities were seated. Here, for the first time, Harold B. Lee saw a prophet of God in person, President Joseph F. Smith. Tall, bearded, and austere looking, President Smith likely presented to the boy from Clifton an image similar to that of the biblical prophets. Seated on either side of President Smith were his counselors, John R. Winder and Anthon H. Lund, also bearded and also quite austere in appearance and demeanor. Harold never met and shook hands with President Joseph F. Smith. But on the stand that day were four future presidents of the Church, members of the Twelve, with whom he would later have an intimate acquaintance: Heber J. Grant, George Albert Smith, David O. McKay, and Joseph Fielding Smith. It was President Grant, of course, who, thirty-four years later, would call Harold B. Lee to the Twelve. Following

President Grant's death, Elder Lee would serve in that same capacity with George Albert Smith and David O. McKay, and when Joseph Fielding Smith became the prophet, Harold B. Lee would be called as his first counselor.

While Harold's attention would have been riveted on these men seated on the stand, it is undoubtedly true that none of them was aware of his presence, or even of his existence. Only the maturing of events in the years ahead would bring them into a personal relationship as special witnesses of the Lord Jesus Christ.

How often, as in this case, are adults oblivious of the potential and the coming eminence of the children in their midst? All of us, even the greatest of all, began as babies. Mark well, then, how you treat that rowdy, ruddy boy, or that little slip of a girl, so vulnerable and so dependent. Tomorrow may find them in positions of prominence, power, or prestige that you never thought possible, a status far beyond anything you could have conceived. We seldom know the true identity of those with whom we deal, especially among the young. In the same way, seldom do the young apprehend exactly who they are or what they may become. Such recognition usually comes only with maturity. So it is safe to infer that as the young Harold B. Lee gazed down upon President Joseph F. Smith from the south balcony of the Tabernacle that day, he had no inkling that one day in the future, he would occupy that place and would be invested with the vast authority and influence that inheres in the presiding high priest of The Church of Jesus Christ of Latter-day Saints. If the full truth were known, it is likely that at that stage of his development, Harold's modest goals and expectations did not extend beyond completing the requirements of the rustic school at Clifton or, perhaps, the Oneida Stake Academy, or beyond acquiring some competence with the piano or the horn.

Chapter Three

The Student

Harold Lee completed the eight grades of study at the Clifton school at age twelve. He had been a good student, admired by his classmates and a favorite of his teachers. That favoritism seems to have derived from an innate manliness he possessed, from a cooperativeness he always showed toward adults, and from the variety of his interests, which included music and athletics as well as his scholastic studies. Moreover, there was a certain presence about him that was enhanced by his abundant hair, wavy and dark, and by the steady gaze of his hazel brown eyes. So, Harold B. Lee was a standout, even though he was one year, and in some cases, two years younger than his classmates.

The next scholastic step for the graduates of Clifton's grammar school was the Oneida Stake Academy at Preston, Idaho, across the valley and south of Clifton. The academy was organized in 1888 under the direction of the Oneida Stake Presidency. Its first home was in Franklin, Idaho. It remained there until 1898 when it moved to Preston where a new two-story, cut-stone building had been erected for its use. Nine years later, a second building was added. In Harold's junior year, a well-equipped gymnasium was constructed. These buildings, with the nearby playing fields, comprised the campus of the academy. Here the new student from Clifton would spend four years, except during the summer months when he would return home to help on the farm. Here he would begin to reveal the qualities of leadership that would characterize all his adult years.

In his beginnings at the Oneida Academy, it is doubtful that young Harold Lee, soon to be called Hal by his friends, felt like much of a leader. He was the youngest student in his class and, therefore, the youngest in the entire school. Moreover, except for one other poor, benighted freshman, he was the only boy in the academy who still wore knee pants. While Louisa had yielded on the issue of Little Lord Fauntleroy outfits for her son, she had remained adamant that he wear knee pants. Had it not been for the protective guidance of Perry, who had preceded him at the academy, Harold's first days there could have been very rough, indeed. It is inferred that with urgent counsel from Perry, knee pants quite soon disappeared from the freshman's wardrobe.

The Lee brothers set up housekeeping at a large home across the street from the academy owned by Robert Daines. Eleven other male students were housed there, as was the principal, J. Robert Robinson, who had rooms on the main floor. On several occasions, the exuberance of the students prompted the principal to go upstairs to deliver pointed sermonettes to them about order and discipline. One can imagine Mr. Robinson's annoyance when, after supervising two hundred active students during the day, he had to endure the nighttime ruckus of the thirteen who lived above him. It may be more than happenstance that Mr. Robinson served as the principal of the academy for only the first two years of Harold's tenure there. He was replaced by Joseph A. Geddes, who apparently did not board at the Daines home. He lasted six years.

The Student

But while they were noisy, as young men of that age are inclined to be, especially when they are thrown together in such numbers, they were fine young men, clean and intelligent and highly motivated. For the most part, they were the sons of farmers, reared in orthodox Latter-day Saint homes, where they had imbibed from infancy the basic doctrines of Mormonism: that they were the children of God, that through obedience and discipline they could become like Him, that the glory of God is intelligence, and that any knowledge or abilities acquired during earth life would arise with them in the resurrection. These seminal ideas go far toward explaining the extraordinary spirit of scholarship, activity, and achievement that infused this remote rural school.

The curriculum at the academy included all of the basic courses taught in high school: science, mathematics, biology, business, history, and physical education, as well as special courses in domestic science, carpentry, music, and missionary work. In addition to taking all of the standard courses, Harold gave special attention to his music during the first two years. He played both the alto and the French horns and was a member of the academy band. Later, he took up the baritone horn and was good enough to be invited to join the Preston Military Band, directed by professor Charles J. Engar. This group performed for a fee at special civic and patriotic events held in communities throughout the area.

As he matured physically, Harold took a more active interest in sports. His favorite was basketball, which was the major sport at the school. In addition to playing, he was the athletic reporter for the school paper, *The Oneida*, during his junior year; and during his senior year, he was the student manager of all athletics. In this position, he accompanied all the school's athletic teams on their trips at school expense, handling the business affairs and travel arrangements. Like the executive who sweeps out the office, he also did some scouting of the school's opponents. Oneida competed with teams from Rexburg, Idaho, on the

Oneida Stake Academy Basketball Team, about 1915, with Harold B. Lee, manager, standing right rear

north to Ogden, Utah, on the south, including the college teams at Logan, Utah, with whom Oneida competed on par.

During his senior year, Hal Lee's school activities shifted into high gear. In addition to attending his regular classes, playing in the band, reporting for *The Oneida,* playing basketball, and managing the school's athletic affairs, he became heavily involved in debate. Each year, all the schools in the area engaged in round robin debate competition, addressing an assigned issue. This year the issue focused on was whether the Monroe Doctrine should be abolished. The two teams that made it to the final bracket were the Oneida Academy and the Fielding Academy at Paris, Idaho. Oneida had never before defeated Fielding in debate until this year when Oneida's team of Harold B. Lee, Sparrel Huff, Louis Ballif, and Irel Lowe defeated the Fielding team. Such was the novelty of this victory that when Harold and his teammates returned from Paris, an impromptu school assembly was held where the victors were lauded and lionized.

The Student

During his sophomore year, Harold had become acquainted with Ethel Cole of Fairview, Idaho, whom he dated intermittently, escorting her to school dances and other social events. This relationship continued throughout the remainder of his schooling at Oneida and, through correspondence and occasional visits, was perpetuated afterward until he entered the mission field. This appears to have been the nearest Harold Lee approached to having a steady girl friend until he married Fern Tanner following his mission. There were, of course, other girls with whom he socialized or was well acquainted, but his relationship with them was only sporadic and usually in group situations.

There was little resemblance between the young boy in knee pants who enrolled in the Oneida Academy in the fall of 1912 and the handsome, accomplished, and self-assured young man who graduated in the spring of 1916. Hal Lee had left his mark on the academy. There may have been other students who excelled him in one activity or the other, but it is doubtful there was anyone whose overall performance outshone his. He was not a one-dimensional student, pouring all his energies into one aspect of the school's curriculum. He sampled them all, and he was remarkably adept in everything he sampled. Yet, with all his prominence in athletics, music, debate, and the school's social and administrative affairs, Harold was still one of the boys, enjoying the high jinks so often associated with teenagers. He was very much part of the "ceiling cracking" episodes at the Daines boardinghouse that evoked Mr. Robinson's little sermonettes. And he was very much involved in the brawl that erupted between the senior and junior classmen during the founders' day celebration in 1916. Moved, perhaps, by feelings of nostalgia as their careers at Oneida wound down, the seniors fixed their class flag to the academy's flagpole. Then, in turn, each of them climbed the pole to kiss the flag as a symbol of class unity and loyalty. After singing together and giving the class yell, they retired, presumably in an expansive, mellow mood. That turned quickly to anger when they awakened the next morning to find that the juniors had removed their flag. These underclassmen discovered too late that what to them was a harmless prank was to the seniors a major affront to their honor. The brawl that ensued ended only with the intervention of the Preston police force. Since "T" Benson was a year behind Hal Lee at Oneida, we are left to wonder whether the two future prophets were arrayed against each other in the sound and fury of this meaningless brawl. If so, we can be assured that in later years, it afforded them many a good chuckle when the incident was put in proper perspective.

When Harold graduated from the Oneida Stake Academy in the spring of 1916, the Lee family was faced with major challenges. All agreed that Harold should seek further education. The issue was how to finance it. By then, Clyde was approaching the age when he could go to the Oneida Academy; and Waldo, the youngest son, was only eleven and therefore unable to perform heavy labor on the farm. The father had his hands full, especially because he had been called as the bishop of the Clifton Ward while Harold was in Preston. The decision was finally made that Harold would enroll at the Albion State Normal School at Albion, Idaho, for the 1916 summer session. Several factors appear to have driven this decision. First, the curriculum there was such that by attending through the summer, he could receive a second-class teaching certificate, which would qualify him to teach in the Idaho public schools during the 1916–17 school year. The second reason, it is inferred, was that the expenses at Albion were less than those at the college in Logan, Utah, where the students from Idaho would have been charged the higher out-of-state tuition fees. And third, it is assumed that a teaching certificate from a Utah school may not have satisfied Idaho's certification requirements. For whatever reason, the decision was made that Harold would go to Albion, some two hundred miles west of Clifton, rather than to Logan,

The Student

which was in the south end of Cache Valley, across the border in Utah.

But, it was not a foregone conclusion that Harold would be admitted to Albion, despite his having graduated from the Oneida Stake Academy. Idaho law required that admittance there would be granted only to those applicants who could pass a rigid examination in fifteen different subjects. Because so much rode on the outcome, Harold buckled down to a period of intense study immediately after graduating from the academy, during which he lost twenty pounds. The effort paid off when he passed the examinations with high grades.

The reason why Idaho has an Albion, which, of course, is the ancient name for Great Britain, is no more clear than the reason why it has a Paris and a Moscow. Certainly, Albion, Idaho, bears no physical resemblance to its namesake. It is a tiny town, nestled in a remote valley, off the main thoroughfare. That the State Normal School was established there in 1894 is a testimonial to the political adroitness of a group of influential citizens in south central Idaho, led by J. E. Miller of Burley, Idaho, some thirty miles northwest of Albion. The assumption is that those who persuaded the Idaho legislature to establish the Normal School there reasoned that it would be a powerful magnet, which, in the wake of the students, would draw a host of business interests needed to sustain the school, its faculty, and student body. When Harold arrived at Albion in 1916, this formula seemed to be working. Everything in the small town gravitated around the school with its student body of three to four hundred students who came from different parts of the state. But Albion's remoteness doomed the school to a temporary existence. Several decades later, schools at Twin Falls and Pocatello siphoned off students who otherwise would have gone to Albion, which resulted in its abandonment. It exists today only in the empty, solid brick buildings on the old campus, in the minds of its former students, and in the reflected distinction of some of its alumni like Harold B. Lee and David B. Haight.

Harold B. Lee

The remoteness and the setting of Albion were conducive to scholarship. There were no diversions in the town itself to distract the students. Downtown consisted solely of a few businesses scattered along a two-block area with wooden sidewalks in front of them to protect pedestrians from the mud during periods of bad weather. And there were no towns nearby where the students could find entertainment. Any yen for entertainment, therefore, had to be satisfied on campus. This consisted of a cluster of five redbrick buildings located on a grassy knoll, dotted with shade trees, on the north end of town. The buildings included a men's dormitory, Miller Hall, presumably named in honor of the patron, J. E. Miller, who spearheaded the effort to establish the Normal School at Albion. It is also assumed that the women's dormitory, Hansen Hall, was named after another of these skillful boosters. There was a large brick building that housed the school's administrative offices, an auditorium, a library, and lecture rooms. Also there was a gymnasium that included a hardwood basketball court, a cork-covered running track, and game and locker rooms. The fifth structure was a model elementary school building for children in the area where the Normal School students could receive teacher training in a practical setting. And nearby, of course, were the outdoor playing fields.

It was here that the new student from Clifton settled down for what was perhaps the most intensive period of study of his entire lifetime. Here he encountered an atmosphere and an attitude unlike anything he had experienced at Clifton's rural school or at the Oneida Academy. Albion had been settled in the 1870s by a group of non-Mormons. The Latter-day Saints came later, attracted by the fertile land of the Marsh Valley, which extends six miles south from the townsite toward the towering Goose Creek Mountains, which are part of the Sawtooth National Forest. The primacy of the non-Mormon influence put a stamp on Albion unlike anything Harold had experienced in the Mormon communities of the Cache Valley. Moreover, both the

The Student

student body and the faculty included many who were not members of the Church. The curriculum, which was devoid of religion classes, included subjects that were entirely new to Harold, subjects like educational psychology and political science. In a sense, it was his first real exposure to the outside world, and he seemed to enjoy it and to be motivated by it.

For reasons never fully explained, Harold elected not to live at Miller Hall. Instead, during both summers at Albion, he lived with a Latter-day Saint family, the Burgesses. On first arriving at Albion, he was only seventeen years old. Since it was his first foray into the world, so to speak, it is likely that his parents urged him to live off campus with members of the Church so as to minimize the affect of any adverse influences there. A ward had been organized in Albion in 1887, which, until 1916 when Harold first arrived, was housed in a rustic log cabin. During 1916, however, a modern building was constructed for the Albion Ward Saints who lived in town and out in the valley. It included a chapel, amusement hall, and seven classrooms. We may be assured that the bishop, Thomas Loveland, enthusiastically welcomed the new student from Clifton and promptly utilized his many musical talents.

During his first summer at Albion, Harold, apparently preoccupied with the challenges of his new environment and the expanded curriculum of the school, completely immersed himself in his studies to the exclusion of any extracurricular activities. This changed during his second summer when he played in the Albion town band under the direction of Lee M. Lockhard; and on campus, he played on the school's baseball team.

Chapter Four

The Teacher

After completing the requirements for his second level teaching certificate in the summer of 1916, seventeen-year-old Harold B. Lee was prepared for his first professional teaching assignment. Negotiating with the local school board, he contracted to teach at the Silver Star School during the 1916–17 academic year. Located five miles south of Weston, this one-room country school included about twenty-five students in grades one through eight. In negotiating the contract, the new teacher wanted sixty-five dollars a month and the school board wanted to pay him sixty. They flipped a coin for the difference and Harold lost. However, he was given an additional fifteen dollars a month to cover his room and board with the family of Lars Rasmussen. The fifteen dollars also paid for feed for his horse. Each Friday afternoon at the end of the week, Silver Star's teacher would ride his horse to Clifton where he would spend the weekend with his family. He would then return to Weston in time for his classes the following Monday morning.

The wide age spread of his pupils placed a heavy bur-

The Teacher

Silver Star School, Weston, Idaho, where Harold B. Lee served as principal, 1916–1917

den of preparation on the new teacher. When the schoolbell rang in the morning, he had to be ready to take charge so as to prevent chaos in the classroom. Then he had to have enough ammunition to keep things going on an even keel throughout the day, satisfying the special needs of all the students ranging from his lone first grader, an adventuresome little boy named Vassal, to those in the advanced classes. So anxious was Harold to succeed, and so concerned was he that each child receive proper training, that he spent long hours outside the classroom in preparation. This included not only a mastery of the subject matter for each level and a plan on how to roll it out effectively, but also frequent prayers for divine guidance. Never before had Harold been faced with such a challenge of self-discipline. And never before had he faced a task better calculated to show the need for help beyond his own powers. In reflecting on this experience in later years, the mature Harold B. Lee concluded that in that little one-room school, he had learned some of the most important lessons of self-mastery of his entire life.

Ordinarily, classes at the Silver Star school commenced at 9:00 A.M. But if in counting the heads of those playing on the school grounds the teacher found that everyone was present, he would ring the starting bell early. We infer he did this because he felt the need for extra time to get the heavy teaching job done and because he was concerned about possible injury on the playground. The school board had cautioned him to keep the children off the picket fence that enclosed the school yard. We gather this caution was given because the fence had been the source of previous injuries. Imagine, then, Harold's horror one day when he looked up to see Vassal standing on his head atop the fence. He couldn't resist snapping a picture of the spectacle with his Kodak so as to be able, tongue-in-cheek, to show the school board how he had been enforcing their policy. Judging from the frequency with which his name was mentioned, we gather that Vassal was Harold's most unforgettable student.

The one-room Silver Star school also served as a community center for Weston and the surrounding area. It was a favorite place for town dances. When one was held there, the student desks were arranged around the walls, leaving space in the center for the dancers and providing seats for the watchers. The music was by a three-piece combo of violin, banjo, and portable organ. These were usually all-night affairs. Near midnight, there would be an intermission when refreshments were served. The menu implies that the dancers either were not active Latter-day Saints or that the restraints of the Word of Wisdom had not yet taken hold in the area. The women served coffee with their cakes and sandwiches inside, and outside some of the men drank beer and whiskey brought from Utida on the state

The Teacher

Oxford, Idaho, District school where Harold B. Lee became principal at age eighteen, 1917–1918 (he and two teachers are standing in front of the school)

line. After the intermission, the dance would usually continue until daylight.

Harold turned over to his father most of the salary he earned during the year he taught at the Silver Star school. He also did that when he transferred to the school at Oxford, continuing to do so during the three years he taught there. This was a godsend to Bishop Lee, who constantly struggled to obtain the means to maintain his family and to educate Harold's younger brothers and sisters.

This new employment marked a major increase in Harold's responsibility and prestige. At Oxford he was the principal of a school whose faculty included two other teachers: Velma Sperry and Tressie Lincoln. Because of the added administrative responsibilities, the principal's salary was set at ninety dollars a month, a 50 percent increase over what he had received at Weston.

The Oxford district school was housed in a two-story stone structure, the most impressive-looking building in town. Here Harold's teaching responsibilities were less complicated as his assistants took over the younger students. This was offset by a challenge he did not face at Weston. At Oxford, a few of the students were older than he, and some of the boys were bigger than he. These boasted that the new eighteen-year-old principal wouldn't last long. Harold's athletic ability, self-confidence, and inherent dignity came to his rescue. He immediately began to teach the older boys to play basketball. During the noon hour, he would put on basketball togs to train them and to play with or against them. This soon dissolved any antagonisms toward the new principal or any effort to try to drive him out of school. Indeed, Harold B. Lee became a vast favorite of the students at Oxford and the relationships and loyalties formed there would endure throughout life. Moreover, he quite soon became a vital force in the community. His involvement in school athletics led to the organization of the Oxford Athletic Club, whose membership was open to anyone in the community regardless of age. Harold played forward on the club's basketball team, which competed regularly with teams in neighboring communities. The fiction that basketball is a noncontact sport existed even then, and Oxford's principal later bore permanent scars of the rugged games his teams played.

But Harold's intense activity in sports, both at the school and in the community, did not inhibit his keen interest in music. He provided piano or organ accompaniment at both school and church events. And during the Oxford period, his musical skills led him into two new artistic outlets. He organized and trained a women's chorus, and he became heavily involved in a dance orchestra. The chorus was comprised of ten young ladies who sang at various school, church, and civic functions. Since there were few entertainments in Oxford and the surrounding rural communities, a chorus such as this was doubtless very much in demand. So grateful were the members of this group for Harold's efforts in bringing them together and training them, that when he left for the mission field they gave him a gold ring as a remembrance of their association.

The Teacher

Harold B. Lee and the ladies' chorus he conducted, about 1919, before his mission

The orchestra Harold joined was organized by Dick and Chap Frew, whose parents purchased a ranch at Oxford while he was the school principal. The brothers had earlier been members of an orchestra that performed at the Lagoon Resort near Farmington, Utah, Dick playing the violin and Chap the drums. In organizing what they called the Frew Orchestra, the brothers conducted auditions for musicians who could play the cornet, piano, and trombone. They found their cornet and piano player in Marion Howell and Reese Davis. The only trombonist who auditioned lacked the necessary skill. Learning of Harold's musical background, the Frews invited him to to try out. Although he had never before played the trombone, his experience with other wind instruments, which he played in the bands at Clifton, Preston, and Albion, enabled Harold to play the trombone readily in what became Frew's Orchestra. After practicing together for a time to become acquainted with each other's styles and skills and to synchronize their instruments into a whole, and after developing a wide repertoire of catchy dance tunes, the Frew

Orchestra went public. It did not take long for the group to catch on.

This period, immediately before and after World War I, saw the emergence of a whole new concept of ballroom dancing. It was a time that also saw the emergence of the so-called liberated woman, the flapper, with her bobbed hair, her short skirts, and her saucy attitudes. This spawned a set of new dance steps, among which were the Charleston and the Black Bottom, which gave energetic expression to the mood of the times. It was during this period that various temperance societies, with widespread public support, were able to shepherd through Congress the wartime Prohibition Act, passed in November 1918, and to obtain ratification of the Prohibition Amendment to the United States Constitution in January 1919. This in turn gave rise to the prevalent use of "the flask" by nonabstainers in which to carry their forbidden liquor about with them.

This, then, was the character of the era during which the Frew Orchestra and its members, including the trombonist Harold B. Lee, acquired a wide reputation in an area that extended from Logan, Utah, on the south to Pocatello, Idaho, on the north. Once its reputation had been established, it was not uncommon for the orchestra to play for dances two and three nights a week. This became a rich source of extra income for Harold and the other members of the orchestra, and made it possible for him to turn over to his father the entire amount of his school salary. But this also became a source of concern for Harold's parents. They disliked the idea that their son was repeatedly thrown into an environment that fostered attitudes and practices contrary to the standards of the Church. Their concerns were intensified by the knowledge that some members of the Frew Orchestra were known to drink and to engage in other conduct unbecoming a Latter-day Saint. While they had confidence in the integrity of their son, still they knew he was not immune to temptation. Harold later expressed the feeling that during this period, his parents "held their breath" out of fear that he might succumb to the enticements that surrounded him. And, they were concerned about his health. When the orchestra had a midweek engagement, Harold would have little sleep during a period of thirty-six hours. If, for instance, the musicians were scheduled to play on a Wednesday night, after working at school all day Harold would leave Oxford as soon as he could break away in the late afternoon. There would then be a long ride over a rough, unsurfaced road to the town where the dance was to be held. Usually these lasted well into the early-morning hours. After packing instruments and riding home, it would be nearing the time when Thursday's workday would begin. With the duties facing him at school that day, he could not hope to get any sleep until Thursday night, except for a short nap he might steal during the day. If this were a week, as often happened, when the orchestra also had commitments on Friday and Saturday nights, the musicians could look forward to little rest over the weekend, except on Sunday. And, as we shall see, Harold's Sunday commitments left little room for leisure on that day. With such a heavy schedule, it is small wonder that Harold contracted a serious case of pneumonia during this period. His mother, ever solicitous over his well-being, carefully nursed him back to health. We can be assured that when the son recovered, Louisa admonished him to reduce his work load and to be more conscious of the need to guard his health. There is no evidence that he did this, and judging from the tendency toward overwork that Louisa's son exhibited throughout his adult life, it is unlikely that he slowed down.

During this period, Harold was also called as the president of his elders quorum, whose members were drawn from the Clifton, Oxford, and Dayton wards. His counselors were Walter Hatch and William Hardwick. This was the first significant priesthood calling of Harold B. Lee's career in church service. He no doubt devoted to it the same disciplined attention he gave to the many callings he later received, so that there would have been little time on Sundays for other than church work.

Chapter Five

The Missionary

Harold's career as the principal of the Oxford School ended in the summer of 1920. He had just turned twenty-one. By that time, he had been a professional educator for four years, with a proven track record both as a teacher and as an administrator. His extensive involvement in athletics and music, and his position as the elders quorum president, had enhanced his reputation and prestige among the residents of the upper Cache Valley. All this, with his solid educational background, his innate dignity, his drive, and his handsome good looks marked him as a young man of great promise.

At that stage of his development, a crucial decision was made. In consultation with his father, who was then the bishop of the Clifton Ward, it was decided that Harold would be recommended to serve as a missionary for the Church. It was not an easy decision to make, either for the son or for his parents. At the time Harold was an adult in every way. He was mature physically, well educated, emotionally stable, and possessed of a rare spiritual instinct. He was of marriageable age and had the training and the skills that would have enabled him to comfortably support a wife and children. If he had settled down at the time into domestic life, one could have predicted a rewarding future for him as a pillar of strength in his local community and church, while enjoying all the blessings of married love and family life. It was not an easy thing, therefore, for Harold Lee to turn away from that prospect toward two years of austere and demanding missionary service during which he not only would be unable to earn an income, but would be a financial burden on his already overburdened father. As for the parents, they knew that with the loss of their son's income, with the need to regularly send money to him in the mission field, and with the obligation to finance the education of the younger children, they would be financially strapped as never before. Yet, there was never a serious question that their second son would willingly accept a call to serve, and that they would support him fully.

The call came in September 1920 in the form of a letter from Heber J. Grant, the president of the Church. It directed Harold to come to Salt Lake City in early November to be set apart and from thence to go to his field of labor, the Western States Mission, with headquarters in Denver, Colorado. If Elder Lee was disappointed in being sent next door, as it were, rather than to some exotic mission overseas, he never let on about it. He accepted the call with enthusiasm and made preparations to leave. Later events suggest that there was a divine purpose in Harold B. Lee being called to that mission at that time.

Elder Lee's preparations included fitting out his wardrobe; speaking at his farewell in the Clifton Ward chapel; saying good-bye to his family, friends, and associates; and arranging to receive his temple endowment. This last event took place at the Logan Temple on November 6, 1920. His father accompanied him there. The mother, whose presence was urgently needed in Clifton to perform midwifery duties, was unable to go. Louisa's deeply spiritual nature

Harold B. Lee

Harold B. Lee as a missionary, about 1920

gives assurance that she offered fervent prayers for his safety and success as he left.

At the Logan Temple, the missionary was introduced to aspects of his religion that until then had been withheld from him. What he saw and learned comprised what Harold B. Lee later referred to frequently as the training provided by the "University of the Lord." There he gained further insight into his relationship to Deity, learned about the marvels and purposes of the Creation, was taught the plan of salvation, was shown the exaltation he might obtain through obedience and diligence, and was put under solemn covenant to observe basic laws of morality and godliness. With all this, he became obligated to wear a new garment, night and day, bearing symbolic markings that were to remind him of his identity and of the covenants he had made. Judging from the intense interest he later showed in temples, and from the frequency with which he taught the significance of temple ordinances, especially to young people, it is reasonable to assume that the experience young Elder Harold B. Lee had in the Logan Temple that day had a profound influence on his mission and on his later life.

From Logan, Elder Lee travelled by train to Salt Lake City. It was his first visit since his father took Perry and him there when they were little boys. While Utah's capital was then looked on as little more than a western hick town by the metropolitan centers in the East, compared to Clifton and the other string towns on the west side of the upper Cache Valley, Salt Lake City was *big*. It then boasted the ornate Hotel Utah across the street east of the temple and the large and modern Newhouse Hotel, which anchored the south end of Main Street's business district. In between were several large office buildings that had been constructed since Harold was last in the city, and along with these were a variety of shops, stores, and restaurants. The streets were lighted by electricity and an efficient streetcar system linked the city together. Aside from the massive granite-walled temple and the adjacent Tabernacle and Assembly Hall, which he had seen before, the building in Salt Lake that most interested the young elder likely was the comparatively new Church Administration Building at 47 East South Temple. It was here on November 9, 1920, that Elder Lee first saw a group of General Authorities assembled in a setting other than a general conference. On that day, he attended a meeting in the auditorium on an upper floor of the Administration Building where members of the Quorum of the Twelve and the First Council of the Seventy were present. Also present were other missionaries who had been called to serve in various missions of the Church. During an hour meeting, the missionaries were given instruction by some of the General Authorities present about their work and about their conduct in the mission field. This was the extent of the pre-mission training given to missionaries at that day.

At the end of the meeting, the missionaries were assigned by name to go to the offices of designated General Authorities where they were to be set apart. Harold was assigned to the office of Brigham H. Roberts, a member of the First Council of the Seventy. In the blessing setting him apart, Elder Lee was promised that he would go to his field of labor and would return in safety. Before leaving Salt Lake City, he also received a second patriarchal blessing, this one under the hands of the Presiding Patriarch of the Church, Hyrum G. Smith. That blessing contained this significant promise: "And, if thou wilt honor the Holy Priesthood which has been given thee, thou shalt be advanced therein in due time, and be called into positions of trust and responsibility and leadership, and shall have an influence for good among thine associates."

Having been instructed and authorized and blessed by the General Authorities of the Church, and with this admonition of Bishop Lee ringing in his ears, "Your father and mother are looking for big things from you," Elder Harold B. Lee boarded a train at 5:30 P.M. on November 10, 1920, destined for Denver, Colorado.

There was an unusually heavy crush of people at the Union Pacific Depot on this occasion. In addition to the normal traffic expected at any departure, there were many relatives and friends there to say good-bye to other missionaries on that same train who were going to different missions in the East. Their animated voices, added to the general hubbub that reverberated through the cavernous depot, punctuated at intervals by the rumble of baggage carts, the loud voices of the red caps, and, from the outside, the hissing, squeaking, and chugging of the trains as they entered and left the depot, created an atmosphere of great excitement. It was quite unlike anything the elder from Clifton had experienced before. Nothing he had seen at the depots at Franklin and Logan could compare with it. In a sense, it was Elder Lee's initiation into a new and alien world that bore little resemblance to the sheltered farming community where he was born and raised. It was the first of innumerable trips he would take as an authorized representative of The Church of Jesus Christ of Latter-day Saints.

The Missionary

Elder Lee's companion on the train was Elder Owen H. Martin of Salt Lake City who was also going to the Western States Mission. The trip, which today takes an hour by jet, took the elders eighteen hours. Seated uncomfortably in a chair car, which lurched and rocked its way to their destination, it probably seemed longer than that to the elders.

They arrived in Denver at noon, November 11, Armistice Day. Rumpled and much in need of a shave, a shower, and a change of clothing, they were met at the Denver depot by their mission president, John M. Knight, and members of the mission office staff. This man would play an important role in the development of Harold B. Lee, not only during his mission, but afterward. He was a seasoned leader, forty-nine years old, who was not only the mission president, but was also a counselor in the Ensign Stake Presidency in Salt Lake City. When the Ensign Stake was organized on April 1, 1904, as part of the breakup of the original Salt Lake Stake (a breakup that also saw the creation of the Pioneer and Liberty Stakes), John M. Knight was called as the second counselor to Stake President Richard W. Young, who was a son of Brigham Young. Under a practice that was followed often in years past, when John Knight was called to preside over the Western States Mission, he retained his position in the Ensign Stake Presidency, which he actively resumed when he was released as mission president.

The new elders were taken immediately to the mission home, which was adjacent to the LDS chapel located on the corner of Seventh Avenue and Pearl Street in Denver. They first witnessed a baptismal service that was in progress at the chapel font when they arrived. Later, they were able to freshen up and to have a bite to eat before being assigned to their fields of labor.

At the time, the Western States Mission extended from North Dakota on the north to New Mexico on the south and from western Colorado to eastern Nebraska. There were then no organized stakes within this vast area. As a result, President Knight not only directed the proselyting work of the elders and sisters assigned to the mission, but he also presided over and directed the activities of the members who lived in the districts and branches within the mission. The missionaries who served under President Knight occasionally were given responsibilities in these units. This provided the few who were given this opportunity with excellent training in Church administration, which was quite apart from their role as proselytizers. As we shall see, Harold B. Lee was one of these.

The new missionary from Clifton, Idaho, was assigned to work temporarily with Elder Daniel Peterson who had responsibilities in the Denver Branch. Their first task was to visit members of the local Relief Society to teach them and to encourage their active participation in the affairs of the branch. Very soon, however, Elder Lee was permanently assigned to labor in the Denver area with Elder Willis J. Woodbury of Salt Lake City. Their main proselyting tools were tracting, street meetings, and cottage meetings. Harold's introduction to tracting was discouraging. At the first house, the woman who answered the door abruptly closed it before the elders were able to explain their purpose. The entire tracting harvest for the day consisted of conversations with eight people at the door, six of whom accepted literature and one of whom agreed to attend church at the Pearl Street chapel. Not once were they invited in so they could begin to engage in meaningful teaching. In time, however, the two elders devised a novel means of getting beyond the threshold of a door. Elder Woodbury, who was a cellist, had brought his instrument with him into the mission field. When he learned that Harold played the piano, he insisted that they practice regularly at the chapel. After the companions had acquired some skill in playing together, Elder Woodbury began to take his cello along when they went tracting. The instrument, of course, became an unusual conversation piece. When householders learned that these nice-looking young men weren't selling cellos but wanted to serenade them, they were invited in with increasing frequency. If a home had a piano, the elders would make it a duet. If not, they would sing to the accompaniment of the cello. Elder Lee reported with a sense of triumph that this approach, on an average, gained them admittance to three homes a day, breaking down barriers, creating friendships, and laying the groundwork for solid gospel teaching at cottage meetings.

There was hardly any way the elders could be creative in holding street meetings. It was simply a matter of finding a street corner where there was a good flow of pedestrian traffic, singing a song, offering a prayer, then speaking at the top of your voice on a gospel subject of your own choice. While one of the missionaries was speaking, his companion would circulate around, engaging bystanders in conversation, distributing tracts, and endeavoring to set up teaching appointments.

A favorite location for street meetings of the Denver conference was at the corner of Nineteenth and Welton Streets. Of his first street meeting there, Elder Lee wrote, "I thought I would surely faint until I got started, then somehow I forgot myself, and everyone else, I'm afraid." Then with becoming self-deprecation, he added, "I think if I keep on finding out how little I know, by the time my mission is over, I will be convinced I don't know anything."

High among the things the elder from Clifton knew was how to work. Once he had overcome the normal feelings of apprehension and inadequacy, which most new missionaries feel, Harold began to focus on his duties with the same concentrated effort he had previously bestowed on his schooling, his teaching, his athletics, and his music. "If ever I felt like working, it is now," he wrote after seven months in the field, "when I am just beginning to appreciate the responsibility that rests upon me." By this time, he had been instrumental in the conversion and baptism of several and had tasted the sweet fruit of missionary service. "I am praying," he added, "that I will always be kept just a 'high private in the rear ranks' so that I can continue to do the work I am beginning to love."

Harold B. Lee's chief orientation and skill was that of a teacher. Those who knew him well observed that he seldom, if ever, missed an opportunity to teach a lesson to his associates. He was always on duty, as it were, and therefore took advantage of the moment to drive home a lesson regardless of the time or place. Read in this light, the last quoted statement takes on special meaning. It seems to tell us that he did not want to be burdened with administrative responsibilities but would prefer to be left alone to do what he most loved to do—to teach. This dominant interest surfaced intermittently throughout his life. During the early 1930s, for instance, while he was a Salt Lake City commissioner and the president of the Pioneer Stake, heavily involved in caring for the temporal needs of his people, he took time to teach early-morning seminary classes at Salt Lake's South High School. And as a member of the First Presidency, nothing seemed to please him more than to go to the Salt Lake Temple to teach groups of young missionaries about the importance of the temple endowment. These were special moment when ideas or ideals were planted in the fertile minds of his listeners, setting in motion events whose consequences might extend forever. Only in this way could one hope to exert an influence upon people and events beyond his own life. Brother Lee hinted at this idea in the sermon he delivered after he had been sustained as the president of the Church. Said he, "The only true record that will ever be made of my service in my new calling will be the record that I may have written in the hearts and lives of those with whom I have served and labored, within and without the church." (Conference Report, Oct. 1972, p. 19.) It was in such a way, through his teachings and example, that Harold B. Lee's ideal, the Savior, exerted strong influence upon others after his death.

After nine months, Elder Lee was called to preside over the Denver conference, the strongest, most productive conference in the mission. Ordinarily such calls were given to missionaries who had served a year or longer. That the appointment came to him after only nine months shows again a familiar pattern in Elder Lee's life, which saw him reach important milestones before his peers.

As the conference president, he supervised the proselyting of thirty-five missionaries who served in an area extending from Littleton, Colorado, south of Denver, to the Wyoming border on the north and thence east to the Nebraska border. The western boundary of the conference generally followed the eastern flank of the Rockies. He also presided over the Church units and the members within that area, which included branches in Littleton, Denver, Boulder, Greeley, and Fort Collins. Because Elder Lee's headquarters were in Denver, close to the mission office, he had frequent contact with President Knight. As this relationship developed, President Knight began to give Elder Lee assignments beyond his duties as conference president, which, in effect, made him an assistant to the president.

It is easy to see why John Knight called Elder Lee to this important position after only nine months. Harold was then twenty-two years old, a little older than the average missionary. His years as a professional teacher and school administrator had given him a reputation that would lend authority to his role as conference president. He had proven himself to be a dedicated worker who was wholly reliable. And, perhaps more important, he was a producer. That is, he had the ability to both teach the gospel and lead his investigators to baptism. It is a truism that 20 percent of the missionaries account for 80 percent of the baptisms. A few missionaries have a special knack or skill, rooted perhaps as much in will and determination as in technical ability, which enables them to convert investigators into members. Harold B. Lee was one of the few. Serving at a time and in a mission where conversions were not prolific, he baptized forty-five converts. Their prior religious affiliations covered the spectrum. They included former members of the Salvation Army, Methodists, Baptists, Lutherans, Christian Scientists, and Catholics. Eight of them had no prior religious affiliation. Some of them retained a close relationship with Elder Lee during the remainder of his life. These qualities, and others less tangible and definable, equipped Harold to provide effective leadership during the remaining sixteen months of his mission.

President John M. Knight was a shrewd leader. Upon extending the call to Elder Lee, he goaded him by saying, "I am just giving you a chance to show what is in you." The implication was that the elder from Clifton, while showing some promise, had not yet arrived. Few things would have been better calculated than this to have motivated a person of Harold B. Lee's native ability and record of achievement. Later in his career, Elder Lee was known to use the same device. When, for instance, thirty-eight-year-old Dallin H. Oaks was interviewed as a possible choice to become the new president of the Brigham Young University, President Lee told him that if he were called it would not be because of what he had accomplished but because of what he might become. (Author's diary 1971, pp. 88–89.)

The new president of the Denver conference accepted the call with an admirable spirit. There was no sense of pride or vainglory in his attitude. "Only nine short months since I arrived in Denver," he wrote, "and when I think back on all the wonderful experiences that have been mine in that time, I feel as though it had been but a dream, but I thank the Lord continually." He then added a statement that would typify all the remaining days of his Church service, in whatever capacity. "The crying necessities of today," wrote he, "wake me up to the fact that I must be working always if God is to accomplish anything through me." In this same entry, Elder Lee noted, "I know now I have gained what I'm sure Father would call 'big things' — the confidence of President Knight."

Harold's first companion after he became conference

president was Elder Vernal Bergeson of Cornish, Utah. They settled into quarters at 740 Grant Street and went to work. Elder Bergeson's assignment to labor with the new conference president produced a revolution in his personal habits. A principal change was in his living costs. Accustomed to spending eighty to ninety dollars a month, "Berg" had to cut these in half to conform to Elder Lee's austere budget. This reduction in spending was offset by an increase in work output. Street meetings were accelerated to two a week. Tracting was intensified, and with that came an increase in cottage meetings. The end result was a significant increase in baptisms. Elder Lee reported seventy-two baptisms through the first nine months of 1922, one more than during the entire previous year.

Although Harold knew that missionary success could not be measured exclusively in terms of baptisms, yet this was a vital aspect of the work. "I almost feel as a little kid today," he wrote several months after becoming conference president, "and I cannot help but be happy. If all those who have promised to be baptized appear, there will be twelve or fourteen new members of the church after our baptismal service today. Of course, many have experienced the satisfaction that comes when you are able to measure the effectiveness of your work by converts. Although success can't possibly be measured in that way, yet therein is the fascination of missionary work." The essence of that fascination was to see the changes made in the lives of people through the teaching of the missionaries.

The significant increase in convert baptisms in the Denver conference can be laid in large part to Elder Harold B. Lee's leadership style. In the first place, he led by example. He did not expect the missionaries to do anything he had not done himself or was not prepared to do. He also took time to give specific training to the missionaries. "I had a fine day tracting," he recorded of an outing with Elders Kelsey and Allred. "I sent them alone and when I got around the block I found them sitting under a tree utterly disgusted because they couldn't talk at the homes. After I preached 'Mormonism' to them for fifteen minutes to give them an idea what to say, they started out and had a very successful time, some of the conversations lasting half an hour." In addition to leading by example and properly training the missionaries, Elder Lee deliberately introduced a spirit of competition among them as a means of stimulating the work. "There is a healthy spirit of competition among the Elders here now," he wrote in a letter home, "the very condition I have wanted to see; and as a result the pace is fast and furious and all will be well if someone doesn't weaken." Yet, he was acutely aware of the danger inherent in this strategy should it result in a sense of individual pride rather than in a selfless feeling of joy in the overall success of the work. Confiding this concern to his journal, he wrote, "I'm happy, despite the vying of the elders for credit for baptisms, as though it were I who had brought the proper pressure to bear to bring about their conversions, and I rejoice that I am able to erase my own selfish desires and to push loyally for the success of the entire conference—that anyone's success is a big boon to my individual appreciation." He then added this sentence, almost as a postscript, which casts some light on the inner drives that impelled him: "I'm going to live up to the expectation made of me to the end that patience and strength will prevail." It is inferred that a chief influence, which goaded the elder from Clifton to a supreme effort of achievement, was the high expectations of his parents. His later reference to it shows that he never forgot his father's parting words that he and his mother expected "big things" from him. And the challenge of his mission president to demonstrate what he had in him could not have failed to motivate one such as he whose competitive fires burned with such obvious intensity. We see this quality reflected in entries such as this: "When the president selected me as conference president, he told me he was giving me a chance to show what was in me. He certainly has played fair with me, and if I fail it will be because I wasn't a big enough man for Denver."

Whatever the motivation, its effects were as evident in Elder Lee's work with the members and the local unit leaders as in his relationship with the proselyting missionaries. He was intimately involved in the selection, the training, and the supervision of branch and district officers. He also assumed the overall responsibility for the periodic teaching and counselling visits to the homes of the members. Because of an apparent lack of local priesthood strength, he involved the missionaries in this work, although he looked forward to the time when this responsibility could be shifted entirely to the local brethren. "We are gradually working in a few of the local members of the priesthood," wrote he, "and some day I hope to be able to step out and leave the visiting entirely to the branch officers." Elder Lee was also heavily involved in counselling the local members about their personal affairs, in blessing them, in performing their marriages and priesthood ordinations, and in conducting and speaking at their funerals. His maiden effort in speaking at a funeral was a scary experience. "Although I felt pretty shaky in the knees," he wrote, "everything went all right and without a hitch."

By this means, Elder Lee became acquainted with every aspect of the work at the grass-roots level. His knowledge of Church administration and procedure was not theoretical, but was precise, practical, and personal. The lessons he learned in Denver would be invaluable as, in the years ahead, the scope of his responsibilities widened to an extent he could not then have conceived.

Along with the basic leadership skills of organization, delegation, motivation, and discipline that developed during the Denver experience, there emerged a quality in Elder Lee's character that overshadowed all these and would be a dominant feature of his future leadership. This was a feeling of genuine love and concern for his co-workers, a feeling reflected in many entries made in his private journal. "Many times have I prayed that God would make me worthy to be a leader among such fine people," he noted on one occasion. And in recording the events of a conference held in November 1921 after he had been in the field a year, Harold wrote: "When conference finally arrived I was as happy as a little child, so much so, in fact, that when my turn came to talk it was nearly impossible. Through sheer joy I could hardly speak. Never before have I been able to appreciate real people who are doing their best to help in God's great work, and words fail me in expressing my love toward them."

A manifestation of that love was an insistence by Elder Lee that the missionaries strictly adhere to the rules of the mission. When missionaries in the Denver conference violated mission rules and Elder Lee learned about it, he was prompt and direct in speaking out. A notable incident illustrating this quality involved a sister missionary, Harriet Jensen (later Woolsey). The incident occurred in September 1922, three months before Harold's release. Sister Jensen and her companion went to a fashion show in downtown Denver one evening instead of to a choir practice. The next morning Elder Lee asked, "Where were you two last night?" When they told him he merely said, "Don't let it happen again." There were no preachments or chastisements, only this five-word instruction, that's all. At least, that is all that was said. Actually there was much more than this involved. Sister Jensen explained: "As I looked at him, I wished the floor would swallow me up. His look said more than words and made me feel like I had committed a huge crime." At the moment, the offending sisters did not feel too kindly toward their leader. In time, however, these feelings changed. "Later," she added, "we came to appreciate and respect the high standards that he held for all of us." (*He Changed My Life,* p. 193.)

In the years that followed, many others would receive instructions or reproof from Harold B. Lee. Judging from the known instances when it occurred, it is safe to say that his looks and demeanor always conveyed as much or more meaning than his words. There was some indefinable something in the man, which spoke out by means other than words. It lay in the spiritual realm beyond normal, human understanding. Perhaps another experience Sister Jensen had with Elder Lee will shed some light on this enigma. It occurred one night while, by invitation, he was explaining Mormon doctrine from the pulpit of another church. "It was while Elder Lee was speaking that night," wrote Sister Jensen, "that I saw a hallowed light encircle his head. The light was much brighter around his head than was the surrounding light, and it was mingled with several beautiful colors. His head was framed in a half circle from the top of one shoulder to the other." Such was the impact of this extraordinary experience on her that after the meeting Sister Jensen went to the speaker and said: "Elder Lee, you are going to someday be the president of the church." His modest reply was, "Sister, I won't be worthy enough to be the president." Sister Jensen added, "But from that day on, I was convinced that he would become our Prophet." (Ibid., p. 194.)

This was not the last time such an aura would be seen surrounding or hovering over Elder Lee. "Stewart Mason and his wife drove me in their car over to Boise," he recorded in his diary on March 23, 1942, "where I was to board the train for Salt Lake. Sister Mason told me she had witnessed an 'aura' as she called it, surrounding me as I spoke." In the same entry, Elder Lee noted, "Fern had previously seen the same thing in the First Ward."

Sister Fern Tanner, Elder Lee's first wife, like Sister Harriet Jensen, was also a missionary in the Western States Mission when Elder Lee was there. She arrived in Denver two weeks before Elder Lee. They met for the first time on November 14, 1920, three days after his arrival. At the time, Fern was the junior companion of F. Elinor Johnson, an older sister who was a graduate of the Brigham Young University and who, at the time, served as the "matron" in charge of the work of the sister missionaries in Denver. These sisters lived in an apartment across the street from the chapel and mission home and offices, and because Elder Lee and his companion, Elder Woolley, were often there in the line of duty, they became well acquainted. Although there was no romantic involvement between Elder Lee and Sister Tanner at the time, there seemed to have been a strong affinity between them from the beginning, which, months after Elder Lee's release, blossomed into love and finally marriage. Of his acquaintance with Sisters Johnson and Tanner during the first months of his mission, Elder Lee reported: "Among the three of us there was formed a 'trinity' that 'sat in judgment' on most of the affairs of the mission." This trinity was broken up when Fern was transferred to Pueblo, Colorado, where she spent most of her mission. During that interval, she and Elder Lee retained their platonic relationship through occasional correspondence. She was transferred back to Denver near the end of his mission, where she served for a short while under the direction of her conference president, Harold B. Lee.

When Sister Tanner was transferred back to Denver, Elder Lee's success as conference president was just beginning to crest. By that time the initiatives of organization, delegation, training, and discipline he had put in place were beginning to bear significant fruit. There was an optimistic attitude among the missionaries, which, in no small part, could be traced to the inspired, energetic leadership of their conference president. It was about this time that Elder Lee received one of the special bonuses of his mission. It came in the form of a visit by Elder James E. Talmage of the Quorum of the Twelve Apostles. It was the first time the elder from Clifton had ever associated with a member of the Twelve on a personal basis. He, of course, had been in a special meeting with some of them while he was in Salt Lake prior to leaving for the mission field. But then, he had only seen them from a distance. Now, over a period of two days, February 18–19, 1922, he was directly involved with the great man.

Elder Talmage arrived at the Pearl and Seventh Avenue

chapel on Saturday, February 18, during a baptismal service that was under the direction of Elder Lee. With him was President Knight. Not being too familiar with Church protocol at the time, Elder Lee went forward with the service without consulting Elder Talmage. During the baptism, Elder Talmage stepped forward to the edge of the font and carefully watched what went on. When the confirmations started, the apostle again stepped forward, uninvited, and said, "Here, I will confirm this one." In performing the confirmation, he deliberately reversed the order and first said, "Receive ye the Holy Ghost," and then he confirmed the candidate a member of the Church. After the ceremony, when they were alone, Elder Talmage said, "Elder Lee, you did a splendid job, but . . ." and then proceeded to point out his error in not recognizing the presiding authority and in not checking with him before he proceeded. He also emphasized that there was no special way to confirm someone a member of the Church. (Author's diary 1973, pp. 334–35.)

There is little doubt that those present at the meetings on Saturday and Sunday, especially the missionaries, were practically awestruck by the depth of knowledge and the eloquence of this extraordinary man, Elder Talmage. His extemporaneous remarks, so precise and closely reasoned, sounded like a carefully crafted sermon he might have toiled over for hours, or days. Such was the reputation of the man for gospel scholarship, gained chiefly through his major works, *The Articles of Faith* and *Jesus the Christ*, that some members of the Church slavishly sought to emulate his style, to speak and to write like James E. Talmage. It is likely there were some of those among the Denver missionaries on this occasion who faithfully recorded his words and sought to incorporate them into their own vocabulary. While Elder Lee never sought to emulate the speaking or writing style of James E. Talmage, the experience at the baptismal service made a profound impression upon him. Later when he became the president of the Pioneer Stake, Elder Lee occasionally consulted with Elder

Talmage about matters of policy and procedure in addition to matters of doctrine. He considered that one of Elder Talmage's greatest strengths was in the realm of Church administration.

It is obvious that Elder Lee did not take offense at the counsel given to him by Elder Talmage. On the contrary, he seemed to appreciate it and to profit from it. This quality of being teachable seems to have been one of the main things that attracted President Knight's interest in the elder from Clifton. His early success as a teacher and school administrator had not given Harold an exaggerated idea about his ability or his importance. Therefore, notwithstanding his father's prediction of "big things" for him, he had entered the mission field with a cooperative, submissive attitude, anxious to do the work in whatever capacity, even as a "high private in the rear rank." This attitude doubtless inspired a sense of confidence in President Knight and was a chief factor in Elder Lee's appointment as the president of the most prestigious conference in the mission after only nine months in the field. As that attitude persisted after his appointment, and Elder Lee's leadership abilities were more clearly revealed, the mission president continued to show preference to him and to give him special assignments, which, in effect, made him a counselor or an assistant to the president. For instance, he was invited to accompany President Knight to Pueblo, Colorado, to inspect the damage caused by a devastating flood and to direct reclamation efforts among the Saints there.

The Mormons had had a presence in Pueblo since the mid-1840s when infirm elements of the Mormon Battalion and Latter-day Saint immigrants from Mississippi had wintered there in 1846–47. On arriving in Pueblo, President Knight and his young companion faced a scene of terrible devastation. An unusually heavy snowpack on the upper reaches of the Arkansas River and a late, rapid thaw had sent torrents of water cascading through the Royal Gorge and other deep, narrow, rocky canyons to the plain below, inundating Pueblo and its surrounding farms. This overwhelming volume of water had been augmented by an unusually heavy runoff on Fountain Creek, which converges with the Arkansas River at Pueblo. So sudden and unexpectedly heavy was the flooding that the townspeople were caught unaware and an estimated fifteen hundred of them were drowned. Property damage was estimated at thirty thousand dollars, a large sum for that day. As he was the presiding priesthood authority in the area, President Knight took the lead in efforts to comfort and to care for those who had lost loved ones or whose homes had been destroyed and to reclaim, as far as possible, their damaged properties. The Denver conference president witnessed at firsthand how, in an emergency, the priesthood, the Relief Society, and the other resources of the Church could be marshalled to alleviate suffering and to provide a glimmer of hope to those caught up in adversity. It is likely that some of the lessons Elder Lee learned at Pueblo were useful years later when he struggled to find solutions to a different kind of emergency that faced the members of the Pioneer Stake.

Later President Knight took Elder Lee with him on a tour of conferences in the eastern part of the mission. Everywhere they went, meetings were held where Harold was called upon to share the pulpit with his mission president as they taught and motivated the missionaries and members. More important, perhaps, for the training of a future prophet than these experiences was the opportunity the trip afforded Elder Lee to spend hours alone with his mission president as they travelled from place to place, or as they shared accommodations along the way. To kneel in prayer and to converse in an informal, relaxed way with a man of such broad experience in the Church undoubtedly provided the young elder from Clifton with insights and perceptions that would be of great value in the years ahead.

There was still another aspect of this trip that was of special significance to Elder Lee. As the tour drew to a close, President Knight, either on an impulse or on authorization from his supervisors, travelled into an adjoining mission to visit some of the Church's most important historic sites. At Nauvoo, Illinois, he and Elder Lee walked the streets of the once beautiful city on the east bank of the Mississippi River, which the Latter-day Saints, led by the Prophet Joseph Smith, had built upon what was once a swamp. While at the time of this visit Nauvoo was a mere shadow of its once thriving condition, with its buildings largely unoccupied, its gardens untended, and its tree-lined streets showing signs of careless disuse, still there was sufficient evidence there to enable the visitor to reconstruct in his mind's eye the original grandeur of the place. Here was the Mansion House, the Prophet Joseph Smith's stately, federal style, two-story home where his body lay in state after the martyrdom. Across the street and to the south was the rustic cabin in which the Prophet and his family had first lived in what was originally called Commerce, later renamed Nauvoo. And on the grounds of this cabin were found the grave sites of the Prophet Joseph Smith and his brother Hyrum. Across the street to the east was the foundation of what was originally projected as a luxury hotel of that day; and not far away were the substantial brick homes of Brigham Young, John Taylor, Wilford Woodruff, Heber C. Kimball, Bishop Vinson Knight—the bishop of the Prophet's ward—and others. On an eminence above the main residential area the visitors inspected the barren site of the once beautiful temple, which had commanded a panoramic view of the orderly neighborhoods below and the majestic river that snaked its way around the once swampy promontory on which the city had risen. As Elder Lee walked these streets with his mission president, reflecting on the events that had transpired there long ago, he could not have failed to remember that his great-grandfather, Francis Lee, and his family had lived in Nauvoo during its heyday and had been forcibly driven from it across the river to Montrose, Iowa, on the Mississippi's west bank and from thence had struggled forward to the valleys of the mountains. Here were some of Harold B. Lee's earliest Mormon roots, which extended in an unbroken line to Winter Quarters, to Tooele, to Panaca, to Salt Lake City, and finally to Clifton.

If Elder Lee was exhilarated by his visit to Nauvoo, he was probably depressed by his visit to nearby Carthage. Here he and President Knight inspected the dreary, forbidding jail where Joseph and Hyrum were slaughtered by a mob with painted faces. As the pair stood in the upper room where the murders had occurred, what earthly wisdom could have foretold that the dark-haired, earnest young man who stood there with his mission president would one day stand as number eleven in a line of modern-day prophets that began with the enigmatic Joseph Smith who was martyred there. That Harold B. Lee's visit to Nauvoo and Carthage had a profound effect on him is evidenced by the frequency with which he referred to it and by the detailed description he made of it.

President John M. Knight had still another special experience in store for his young protégé. In November 1922, a few weeks before Elder Lee's release, President Knight assigned him to conduct a conference in Sheridan, Wyoming, which the president could not attend during the first two days of it. In making the assignment, the president gave the ultimate accolade of confidence when he told Harold "there was no one else he would rather trust." Since he had no time to prepare in advance, Elder Lee spent the time on the train arranging his thoughts as to what he would do. Judging from his established habit, we can assume he prayed fervently for help.

Located in northern Wyoming near the Montana border, Sheridan, named for General Philip Henry Sheridan of Civil War fame, is the trading and cultural center of a wide area of farms and cattle ranches in the vicinity of the Bighorn Mountains. It was seventy miles north of here when, in 1876, General George A. Custer made his last stand at the battle of Little Bighorn. Sheridan was founded a few years later and soon attracted Latter-day Saint settlers who plied their farming and ranching skills to help build the community. In many ways, therefore, Sheridan was not unlike Clifton, Idaho, where Harold was born and raised, which gave him much in common with the members of the branch there.

Despite this, we can safely assume that the members there were not thrilled to see him get off the train. They were expecting the mission president, not this unknown elder. Their attitudes soon changed, however, when they found he was a triple threat man. He preached the gospel with eloquence and played the piano and conducted the music with equal competence. And between meetings on Sunday, he mediated disputes between members with wisdom beyond his years. We can gauge the impression he made on the members at Sheridan by this comment made by Elder Lee on Monday, after President Knight arrived: "When President Knight arrived on Monday, Elder Scadlock insisted that I talk again, but I graciously declined and played the part of wisdom." That Harold's mission president shared this high opinion of him is suggested by this entry in Elder Lee's diary: "While there, the President took me into his confidence more than he has ever done before and took me with him wherever he went." Reflecting on the impact this experience had upon him, Elder Lee wrote that it made "[me] more appreciative and humble in the responsibility that is mine—to determine whether or not I can make good among strangers."

Despite his achievements, it should not be assumed that Elder Lee's missionary service was crowned only with success. He had his off days, his times of failure, and his times of despondency. During his early service in Denver, Elder Lee seriously bungled the anointing of a little girl, entirely forgetting the wording and fumbling around in confusion. Afterward his companion, Elder Woodbury, after being assured Harold wouldn't "get sore" about it, said, "For Pete's sake, don't ever do it like that." Later, when he returned to a house where he had first received a warm reception, the woman wouldn't even answer the door. "I sure thought I had a convert there," wrote a wiser elder. And at another home, a woman slammed the door in his face while he was quoting a scripture, ordering him to "go on down the street."

These and other similar experiences were the normal fare for missionaries of that day and were usually passed off with a certain lightheartedness. But, there were other times when negative events piled up to create real despondency. "Felt pretty blue all day," he wrote some time after being called as conference president, "because of many griefs and complaints brought by the missionaries and from different Saints. Felt as incapable as a babe and sure acted like one too." However, bouts of despondency such as this, arising from his work, were not of frequent occurrence and were soon brushed off and forgotten. There was another cause of concern, however, which was external to the work and which was so persistent that it could never be entirely submerged. This was Elder Lee's constant struggle because of having so little money. We have already seen how his first companion, after he became conference president, had to halve his spending to accommodate Elder Lee's slender budget. The money pressures grew worse near the end of his mission. Indeed, doubt existed he would be able to finish. But, he was buoyed up by a letter of August 27, 1922. "I received a most encouraging letter from father," he wrote, "who told me they would never ask for my release and would only pray God to increase their crops so I can stay until released." He was further encouraged to receive a forty-dollar check from his sixteen-year-old brother, Waldo, who "wanted some credit too." The missionary did not take these gestures of generosity for granted. "I am so appreciative of my people at home," wrote he. "I could cry when I think of it all, and my prayer is that God will make me humble so that I shall not disappoint them when I go home."

President Knight hoped Elder Lee would be able to serve until the spring of 1923. When he learned about Harold's pinched finances, however, he decided to release him at the conference in early December 1922. As it drew near, the elder from Clifton seemed determined to make it the best conference ever. He "declared a housecleaning day and cleaned the church from top to bottom." All the woodwork was scrubbed and oiled as were the chairs. Nor were the floors neglected. "I crawled up and down the floor on my knees," he explained, "until my knees were calloused and my back ached." His other preparations were equally demanding. Not only was he to conduct and to speak at the meetings, he was also to sing in a mixed quartet and a male quartet and to play accompaniment for the congregational singing. With all planning and rehearsals completed, everything was in readiness for the opening session of the conference on Saturday, December 9, 1922. This was a missionary report and testimony meeting, which went on for eight hours. Each of the twenty-eight missionaries present was allowed to speak without a time limit. "When my turn came to speak," wrote Elder Lee, "after all the others had talked, I found I was up against a hard proposition. I was finally able to control myself after a time, and then say what I wanted." President Knight, who was the concluding speaker, "experienced the same difficulty when he attempted to speak." We gather this show of emotion by the mission president reflected both a sense of personal and institutional loss at the departure of one so able and dedicated. "When the president announced that I was released," wrote Elder Lee, "he said that it would bankrupt the English language to tell how much he thought of me and said that I had been on the firing line from the time I had arrived in Denver." At this meeting, sixty-two-year-old Andrew Hood was appointed to succeed Elder Lee as the president of the Denver conference. And the missionaries in the conference joined to give their outgoing president a beautiful watch chain as a token of their love and appreciation.

Thus ended Harold B. Lee's first major Church calling. While it is easy to record the significant events of that assignment as we have done here, it is difficult to assess their impact upon his emerging personality and character. There can be little doubt that the unusual skills in Church organization and administration that would be reflected in President Lee's later career traced their origin in large part to his experiences in Denver. It was there that his ability to organize and to motivate followers to work toward a common goal first surfaced in a significant way. The depth of his gospel knowledge and his spirituality were enriched while there, and his teaching skills were honed and broadened. But more important, perhaps, than any of these was the acquaintance he made there with Fern Tanner, an acquaintance that would later ripen into love and marriage and, in turn, would bring about the genesis of his eternal family.

In appraising the impact of Elder Lee's missionary experience upon his future career, we must not ignore the influence of his association with John M. Knight. He characterized his mission president as "a fearless fighter" in missionary work and as a leader who was "always on the go, visiting the various divisions of the mission." He owed much to this man who gave him the chance to demonstrate his inherent abilities and who provided special opportunities for travel and varied experiences outside his conference.

But President Knight's influence on him did not end with Elder Lee's release from the mission. Commitments at home made it necessary that John Knight return to Salt Lake City in December 1922. He and Elder Lee travelled to Salt Lake together in company with Sister Harriet Jensen, who was going there for special surgery. This trio received a rousing send-off when missionaries, members, and friends gathered at the Denver train depot to say goodbye. Among those present was Elder Lee's first convert, Mabel Hickman, who would retain a friendly relationship with him and his family through the years ahead. Indeed, Mabel Hickman and her maiden sister were almost like members of the Lee family. They, with other guests, were staying at the Lee home during the April general conference in 1941 when Elder Lee was sustained as a member of the Twelve. Mabel, who was seated beside Sister Lee when her husband's name was read as the new member of the Twelve, noted how the knuckles of Fern's hands turned white as she gripped the seat in front of her.

The long train ride back to Salt Lake City offered ample time for thoughtful reflection, interspersed with quiet conversation. Elder Lee's private reflections most likely centered largely around a concern he had expressed shortly before his release. "To think that I have caused my parents worry and hardship makes my heart ache," he had written. "Never again, if I know it, will my folks be in the position they are in today. What I shall do in the future is dark and uncertain; my prayer to God is that things will happen for the best." Herein we see a Nephi-like quality in his character, which surfaced often during Elder Lee's life. It was clearly evident during the dark days of the depression as he struggled to care for the needs of the members of the Pioneer Stake and later as he wrestled with the complicated problems faced in establishing the Church welfare plan. And it was seen dramatically at a press conference held shortly after he was ordained as the eleventh president of the Church. There a reporter asked about the prophet's plans for the future of the Church. He answered, in substance, that he had no specific plans but that he would go forward like Nephi of old, taking one step at a time, confident in the knowledge that when he had taken that step, the next step would be made clear to him. Inherent in this attitude, of course, was the assumption that the Lord would guide him along, day by day, through the mists of darkness that occasionally obscured his view.

While Harold's view of his future may have been dim at the time, the same was not true of President John Knight. He foresaw a distinguished future in Church leadership for his young protégé, although his view of the exact nature of that leadership role was somewhat skewed. "While talking to President Knight about my next mission," Elder Lee recorded in his diary under date of December 15, 1922, "he said that someday I would be sent to preside over one of the missions." What John Knight saw in this young man

The Missionary

was something many people saw in him over the years. That was a vast, indefinable capacity for leadership. A vague sense of the impression he made on others is seen in an appraisal made of Elder Lee by a Brother Smart who had served under him as the president of the Denver branch. "When he left me," wrote Elder Lee, "he told me he respected me and was glad for the opportunity of working with me, saying I was a hard one to say that about, because of the peculiar qualities that were distinctly mine that kept people long in the dark as to superior abilities that I might possess." That Elder Lee himself was not quite sure exactly what President Smart meant is suggested by this concluding entry: "That one fact of my makeup has caused me more misgivings as to my ability to succeed than any other. I wish someone would give me a recipe of instruction so I might overcome."

While the road ahead seemed dark to Elder Lee, and while President Knight saw a distinguished but vague leadership career ahead for him, their travelling companion, Sister Jensen, had seen Harold B. Lee's destiny clearly from the beginning, a destiny that would lead him to the prophetic office.

One of the things that had drawn President Knight to Salt Lake City at this time was a quarterly conference of the Ensign Stake scheduled on Saturday and Sunday, December 21–22, 1922. He invited his protégé to accompany him to the Sunday sessions, which were held in the Assembly Hall on Temple Square. The Ensign Stake, in whose presidency John M. Knight had served for almost twenty years, included the neighborhood on the north bench of Salt Lake City in which many General Authorities lived, including President Heber J. Grant. Indeed, so many of them lived there that it seldom happened that several of them were not in attendance at each stake conference. Sunday, December 22, 1922, was no exception, especially because Christmas was only three days away. It was quite extraordinary, therefore, that even with so many distinguished leaders present yet still an unknown missionary from a rural ward in remote Clifton, Idaho, was called on to speak for ten minutes. The reason, of course, was that his mission president, as a member of the stake presidency, had given Elder Lee still another opportunity to show what he could do. It was the first time Harold B. Lee had spoken from this pulpit, or from any pulpit on Temple Square. It would not be the last.

Earlier in the week, Elder Lee had officially reported his mission to Harold G. Reynolds, the mission secretary of the Church, who for many years had worked in the missionary department helping to prepare outgoing missionaries and to receive returning missionaries, arranging for their transportation, visas, steamship passage, and railroad transportation, etc. Later, President Knight took his protégé on a tour of the Church Administration Building, introducing him personally to some of the leaders, including President Charles W. Penrose—first counselor in the First Presidency—and Elders Joseph Fielding Smith and Richard R. Lyman of the Twelve. From President Penrose, Elder Lee obtained a recommend to enter the Salt Lake Temple, where he later went through an endowment session. At one of the offices they visited during their tour, President Knight introduced Elder Lee to one of the secretaries as the next president of the Western States Mission. That Harold was only twenty-three years old at the time suggests the mature image he projected, notwithstanding his youth.

During the week Elder Lee spent in Salt Lake City, he also paid courtesy calls on several former missionaries and their families. Two of these warrant special mention. He visited Freda Jensen, the girl friend of his missionary companion Elder Murdock. The expected marriage between this pair never materialized. Indeed, Freda Jensen never married until she became the second wife of Harold B. Lee following the death of his first wife, Fern Tanner. The other special contact he made was, of course, with Sister Tanner, who would become his first wife and the mother of his children. From the time they first met shortly after Elder

The Missionary

Lee arrived in Denver in November 1920, there was a marked affinity between him and Fern. In the beginning, the relationship was nothing more than a friendly association between two people who shared common convictions and aspirations. Their acquaintance in Denver was notably brief, but was kept alive by periodic correspondence after Fern was transferred to Pueblo. Then following her release in July 1922, the frequency of their correspondence increased. So, despite the brevity of their personal contacts before then, by the time Harold arrived in Salt Lake City in December 1922, he and Fern were well acquainted with each other at the intellectual and spiritual level. Elder Lee was anxious to expand that acquaintance. He therefore called Fern by telephone; she was living with her parents on Salt Lake's west side. Observing the proprieties expected of those whose acquaintance was first formed in the mission field, she contacted her brother, Bud, and his wife, Ethel, who drove her to meet Elder Lee at the Kenyon Hotel downtown. The four of them then went to the Tanner home at 1310 Indiana Avenue, a home the Lees would purchase from Fern's parents, Stuart T. and Janet Tanner, several years after their marriage. Here the well-chaperoned couple spent several hours together, reminiscing about their days in the mission field, discussing their mutual acquaintances, and sharing the moments of triumph or disappointment they had experienced. From the events that followed a few months later, it is clear that this brief encounter was sufficient to convince both of them that they wanted to extend their relationship beyond mere friendship.

Chapter Six

Courtship and Marriage

Harold caught the train for Franklin, Idaho, on Monday, December 23, 1922, the day after the Ensign stake conference. Members of his family were waiting there to drive him across the valley to Clifton. It was a joyous reunion. The patriarch's promises that Harold would be "called into positions of trust and responsibility" and would "have an influence for good" among his associates had been literally fulfilled. And the fact that he had presided over the largest conference in the mission for sixteen months, had served as the unofficial assistant to the mission president, and in the process had become his close confidant, seemingly fulfilled the expectations of his parents that their son would accomplish big things in the mission field.

Aside from the joy of again being in the heart of his family where he was loved and admired, there were the last-minute preparations for Christmas, which absorbed Harold's attention. And the renewal of acquaintances with friends and neighbors and the prospect of reporting his mission to the members of the ward undoubtedly aroused feelings of happy anticipation. Underlying all this, however, was a vague sense of anxiety. Harold found that the financial condition of his father was much worse than he had imagined. In order to maintain his son in the mission field, Bishop Lee had incurred heavy indebtedness, which, in view of the depressed farm conditions of the day, he had no prospect of repaying. "I thank the Lord that my parents didn't tell me all their difficulties," he wrote on learning of the financial peril they faced. Had he known earlier, it is likely he would not have remained in the mission field. Yet, the discouraging financial prospects facing the family were temporarily submerged in the festivities of the season. "I believe there has never been a time when there was more of the real Christmas spirit," he wrote.

Once the excitement of Christmas and homecoming had worn off, Harold was faced with difficult decisions. He was torn between the responsibilities owed to his family and his personal career plans. It seemed apparent that his future did not lie in Clifton. Even if he had an interest in farming as a career, which he did not, there could not have been a worse time to become involved in it. Like his father, most farmers in the area were mired in debt, and depressed market conditions had spread a cloak of gloom over the valley. Harold's interests and his training lay in the field of education, but it was midseason and a teaching contract for the balance of the year was not available. Moreover, if he hoped to teach at the high school level, increasing accreditation standards would require that he obtain more education. So, for the moment, the returned missionary was locked into a catch-22 situation from which there was no immediate escape. Matters were worsened when he was caught up in a post mission letdown, which afflicts most missionaries. For two years he had been strung taut with the responsibilities of his calling, which had kept him fully occupied during most of his waking hours. During most of his mission, his calling as the conference president had stretched his capacities to the limit and had given him a status and prestige he had never known before. Now at home he had reverted to the obscure role as one of the six children of Bishop Samuel Lee and his wife Louisa, without employment and without any immediate prospects of obtaining any. It was a most stressful time for one as able and creative as he. In these circumstances, Elder Lee put the best possible face on a bad situation. He busied himself about the farm, helping to tend the animals, to chop wood, and to perform other chores. He enjoyed visiting with his family and friends, sharing his missionary experiences and his convictions about the Church. While this was enjoyable and aroused fond memories, it had its down side. The fact is Harold was disappointed at the lowered level of spirituality and commitment he found among the members at home compared to those in the mission field. He had noticed this the first Sunday after returning from Denver when he attended services in a Salt Lake City ward, and he had noticed the same thing in Clifton. So, while recalling incidents in the mission field evoked pleasant memories of the past, it caused feelings of regret that those days were gone. He therefore welcomed an assignment to teach a class in theology in his home ward. It was absorbing to prepare his lesson, delving into the scriptures, which he loved. He enjoyed the challenging interplay between teacher and students in the classroom. Here Harold was in his proper element. He was a natural teacher, born to the task, as it were. His intelligence, his spirituality, his eloquence, and his genuine love for people combined in a classroom setting to provide ideal conditions for sharing knowledge and for kindling testimony and resolves to improve. Yet, in a sense, Harold B. Lee never left the classroom. He was always teaching wherever he went and in whatever circumstance he found himself. O. Leslie Stone, for instance, deceased member of the Seventy, recalled a casual conversation he had with Elder Lee as the two of them rode together toward the chapel where Elder Stone was to be presented as the new stake president. "Les," said Elder Lee, "you want to begin thinking now about what you will do when you are released." (As related to the author.) It would be impossible to calculate the impact on Elder Stone of that lesson on foresight taught by his friend, or the impact upon others with whom Elder Stone shared the incident. Nor could one tabulate the number of times that same sage advice has been given to others as they faced a Church calling, advice whose origin traces back to a master teacher, Harold B. Lee.

In addition to this teaching assignment, Harold was called again to preside over the elders residing in the Clifton, Oxford, and Dayton wards. He travelled across the valley in January 1923 to attend the quarterly conference of the Oneida Stake at Preston where he was set apart. This was a demanding assignment, which called into full play his genius for organization and motivation. It was a calling that, in some ways, was more challenging than his call as the Denver conference president. The main difference lay in the higher level of commitment and discipline among the full-time missionaries who devoted all their waking hours to the Church. At home, however, the members of Harold's elders quorum spent most of their days at work or in school, leaving little time for family life or Church assignments. Their quorum duties, therefore, were a relatively low priority item, which imposed heavier burdens on their leader. Despite this, Elder Lee appreciated the assignment as providing a much needed outlet for his energies and a vehicle to help recapture the sense of purpose and the spirituality that had typified his service in the mission field. But, it was not the same, and his role as the elders quorum president, while being much appreciated, suffered by comparison.

Beyond the love for his family, his teaching and quorum assignments, and his menial duties around the farm, there was nothing at Clifton to attract and to hold the interest of one whose views of life's potential had been so vastly broadened as had those of Harold B. Lee. It seems apparent, therefore, that he knew his future lay elsewhere, especially because of the bonds between him and Fern

Tanner, which grew ever stronger through their frequent correspondence, and which seemed to attract him magnetically toward Salt Lake City.

Meanwhile, Elder Lee marked time as best he could. He became involved with Perry in producing a minstrel show, and he took a special interest in the young members of his family: Clyde, who was then twenty, Waldo, seventeen, Stella, fifteen, and Verda, twelve, all of whom admired and sought to emulate him. Clyde, who by this time had developed into a basketball player of some note, pleaded with his missionary brother to join him and others in a pickup game. Harold, whose athletic toughness had been weakened during his mission, unwisely agreed. The results were disastrous. During the game, which was marked by rough physical contact, he was knocked to the floor where he lay, writhing, until he was carried off with a severely wrenched back. This injury further aggravated a hernia that had developed in the mission field. When his condition worsened a few weeks later, surgery became necessary. He travelled to Utah for this purpose, where in February 1923 the operation was performed in a Salt Lake City hospital. Afterward, he gladly accepted the invitation of Fern's parents to stay at their house while he convalesced.

It was during this period that Harold and Fern decided on marriage. The affinity they seemed to have had from the moment of their first acquaintance had ripened into a fast friendship, and that, in time, had developed into an enduring love. Neither of them, apparently, could identify a moment in time when it had become clear to them that they wanted to be man and wife. Indeed, it seemed in retrospect that their union had been foreordained. Whatever the process by which it had occurred, they both were confident, indeed were eager about their desire for marriage. They were less confident, however, about the economic realities that would make marriage possible. Those realities became ever more pressing when Harold received a sobering letter from his mother, which advised that his father had been released as bishop and which hinted that they were overwhelmed with financial chaos. This put all plans for marriage on hold, and Harold left immediately for Clifton to lend support to his family. "Father and Mother have gone through a veritable hell," he wrote after arriving home, "and appear to have aged years since I last saw them." For the first time, Harold learned of the full extent of his parents' financial difficulties and of the way they had masked them so as not to upset him while he was in the mission field. "I could cry," he wrote, "when I think that in the midst of all their trouble and grief, they have placed uppermost the spiritual values, and in their great stress, have found peace and rest through the gospel."

Out of a Lee family council came the decision that Harold return to Salt Lake City "to work to get ahead financially." That decision removed any lingering doubts about whether Harold B. Lee's future lay in Clifton, Idaho. He would never return except for occasional nostalgic visits.

On returning to Salt Lake City, Harold decided his future lay in education, but to teach school in Utah required more certification than he had obtained at Albion. More schooling required money for tuition, books, and his personal needs, money that he lacked. The financial crisis of his parents meant he would have to bootstrap it, looking only to his own resources.

He obtained part-time employment at the Paris Department Store on Broadway (Third South), between Main and State Streets. This generated enough money to enable him to enroll for the summer quarter at the University of Utah. By continuing to work through the summer, he survived, but not in luxury. And a full academic load greatly limited his social life. He did spend some time on Sundays with Fern as they planned their nuptials in the fall. This was the extent of his leisure activities. Such a crowded schedule did not seem to create a sense of deprivation in them. Their youth, their love, and their self-confident attitude that together they could surmount any obstacle produced a happy buoyancy, which marked all their relationships.

After he received certification to teach in Utah, Harold negotiated a contract to teach and to serve as the principal at the Whittier School in the Granite School District at $135 a month. With an assured income, he and Fern made definite plans to marry. The wedding took place on November 14, 1923, in the Salt Lake Temple where Elder George F. Richards of the Twelve performed the ceremony.

The newlyweds were fortunate to rent a modest home at 1538 West Eighth South owned by Fern's parents, and by borrowing eleven hundred dollars, they purchased furniture and a used Ford automobile. Considering that Harold's contract was for nine months, it is apparent the indebtedness they incurred about equalled his total income for the school year. But by paying on installments and with a modest rate of interest, they lived comfortably and happily, now fully launched on their exciting voyage of matrimony.

The Lees' first home was located in the Poplar Grove Ward of the Pioneer Stake. It was here they planted their marital roots, deep and firm, roots that grew into an extraordinary life career in the coming years. One wonders what life would have been like for the Lees had they lived in some other part of Salt Lake City or in some other city. So many critical things occurred to them along the path that led to the presidency of the Church, which had their roots in the Pioneer Stake, as to suggest that establishing their home there was based on some divine purpose. That Elder Lee was the president of the Pioneer Stake, leading out in welfare work, and a city commissioner representing the west side of Salt Lake, were key factors that led him into significant involvement at Church headquarters. And that, of course, put him on the path that led him into the Council of the Twelve and ultimately into the prophetic office.

Incidents that occurred shortly before Harold and Fern

set up housekeeping at 1538 West Eighth South support this speculation. On January 1, 1922, Paul C. Child was called as the new bishop of the Poplar Grove Ward. Some time after Bishop Child was installed, he and his counselors began to pray fervently that the Lord would bring into their ward persons who would provide good leadership for its members. In not too long a time after this, both Harold B. Lee and S. Perry Lee and their wives moved there. (As related to the author by Glen L. Rudd.) As we shall see, Paul C. Child later became Brother Harold Lee's counselor in the Pioneer Stake presidency and played a key role in the development of the stake's welfare plan.

Bishop Child lost little time in harnessing the talents of the newcomers from Clifton. Very soon after the Lees moved into the Poplar Grove Ward, the bishop called Harold as the M-Men instructor. At the time, there was an able but dispirited group of young men in the ward whose activities had no sense of direction due to a lack of leadership. In only one year, this same group, who had previously enjoyed the reputation of being the doormats in stake competition, led out in basketball, debating, male quartet, and public speaking. We see here the skills in which Elder Lee had excelled while he was a student at the Oneida Stake Academy and at Albion, skills that he had honed while teaching at Weston and Oxford. While the technical skills Elder Lee taught were vital to their success, it is undoubtedly true that new attitudes of self-confidence he instilled in his M-Men were equally if not more important. This quality was evident in every position of leadership Harold B. Lee occupied. It was certainly true during his second year in Poplar Grove Ward when he served as the superintendent of the Sunday School. His previous experience as a teacher and principal in Idaho and his everyday employment as a teacher and principal at Whittier enabled him to instill a sense of professionalism and commitment in the Sunday School faculty.

By this time, the leaders of the Pioneer Stake had become aware that there was an extraordinary young man at work in the Poplar Grove Ward who would bear watching. When they saw the revolution, which had been effected almost overnight in the M-Men and the Sunday School organizations of the ward, they called him the next year as the superintendent of all religion classes in the entire stake. Here again, a "complete rejuvenation and reorganization" took place. Such was Elder Lee's success in this position that the next year, 1927, his stake responsibilities were enlarged when he was called as a member of the Pioneer Stake high council at age twenty-eight. He was set apart to this position by Elder Richard R. Lyman of the Twelve.

In the meantime, during this five-year period while he was gaining prominence as a leader in the Pioneer Stake, Elder Lee was making steady progress toward his professional goals and in establishing the foundations of his family. His summers during this period while school was in recess were actually periods of accelerated activity. The minimal salary he received at the school, and the heavy indebtedness incurred at the time of his marriage, made it mandatory that Harold find supplemental employment in the off-season. So, he was alternately employed selling meats and produce for Swift and Company, pumping gas at a service station, and checking out equipment at the Salt Lake City Streets Department. Later he sold Nash automobiles and worked as a clerk in the grocery department of ZCMI. While handling these summer jobs, Harold juggled his schedule to enable him to take summer school classes at the university or by correspondence in order to maintain his teaching certification. Also, during this period he switched from the Whittier to the Woodrow Wilson School in the Granite School District. Here he also served as the principal and taught as well.

Brother Lee's family grew apace with his stature as a Church leader and a professional teacher. The first few months of their marriage were idyllic for Harold and Fern Lee. Indeed, the husband referred to them as a "glorious honeymoon." Harold had good employment, their house

Courtship and Marriage

was nicely furnished, and they had a car, which gave them mobility. Since Samuel and Louisa had moved to Salt Lake City from Clifton, both sets of parents were nearby, as were brothers and sisters from both families. Moreover, in a short time the Lees had developed a circle of close friends from among their neighbors and the members of the ward and stake. In this environment their love flourished as they found that the spiritual and intellectual affinities that had first attracted them to each other were matched by the physical attraction of romantic love. They seemed to lack nothing to make their joy complete, except children. That culminating joy came soon when, several months after they were married, Fern conceived. Their first child, Maurine, was born on September 11, 1924, in the Latter-day Saint Hospital in Salt Lake City. Her arrival brought about a major change in the routines of the Lee household. In the first place, the baby and all her gear soon made it mandatory that larger quarters be found. Fortunately, there was a larger, better appointed place available next door at 1534 West Eighth South, to which they moved with little upset.

Sister Lee conceived a second time within a few months after Maurine's birth. This news was received with some concern because of the serious problems connected with Fern's first pregnancy and childbirth. Then she almost lost her life because of serious bleeding. Their concerns were affirmed when the mother spent sixty hours in intense labor before the second daughter, Helen, was born on November 25, 1925. Helen, too, was born in the Latter-day Saint Hospital, a facility her future husband, L. Brent Goates, would later direct as its administrator. The Lees would not be blessed with other children, a lack that was compensated for in part by the handsome grandchildren these two daughters would later bear.

Chapter Seven

Call as Stake President

The year 1928 was a banner year in the life of the Lee family. It saw major changes in Elder Lee's occupation and Church responsibilities. And for the first time, the Lees became home owners. In the fall of 1928, Harold resigned his position with the Granite School District and accepted employment as a salesman with the Foundation Press, Inc. This company, which was headquartered in Denver, Colorado, published and marketed a set of classic books called the "Master Library." Brother Lee's supervisor in Salt Lake City was Mr. L. A. Ray, who had recruited and hired him at a fixed salary of fifty dollars a week, plus a percentage bonus on all sales made by those whom Harold might employ and train. His territory included not only parts of Utah, but also Idaho, Wyoming, Colorado, Washington, and Oregon. It was a unique opportunity for Elder Lee since the guaranteed salary exceeded the amount he received from teaching school, and the bonus arrangement held out the prospect of significant additional income. Moreover, the product he sold was one he could endorse without reservation. During the several years Elder Lee worked with the Foundation Press, he travelled extensively throughout his territory, often taking Fern and the girls with him. This employment significantly increased his income and elevated him to an economic level he could never have attained as a school teacher and principal.

There is little doubt that Fern's subtle influence was a vital factor in her husband's career change. "Fern was never content that I should remain in the school teaching profession," wrote Harold. That discontent was not expressed in a nagging, critical way. Nor, presumably, was it generated by any desire for increased wealth or social status. It rather would seem to have been caused by a sense that teaching was a blind alley insofar as the full flowering of her husband's vast potential was concerned. It was apparent, therefore, that once this idea had taken root in Fern's mind, she pursued it quietly, adroitly, and persistently. Elder Lee once characterized his wife as being quiet, unassuming, sensitive, and impressionable, yet "vigorous in her denunciation of unfairness and calumny." This vigorous quality was also evident in all matters pertaining to her husband and their family for whom she felt a responsibility in helping to chart their career paths.

But, aside from this important aspect of Fern's contribution to the growth and development of her husband and her daughters, the most significant role she played was that of homemaker. Wherever the Lees lived, Fern maintained a home of culture and refinement whose appointments reflected the level of Harold's income and whose routines were well ordered and free, insofar as she could control it, from unnecessary pressures and from distracting outside influences. It was to this sheltered place that her family could come for comfort, for refreshment, and for renewal. And as her husband's outside activities became more demanding and, in some instances, hectic, this haven of rest and relaxation became ever more important to him and to the family. As already noted, it was during 1928 that Harold provided his wife with a home she could call her own. It was a home that had special significance for Fern as she had been raised there. When during this year the Tanners moved to Granger, Utah, to live with their daughter Emily where they could get better care in their old age, the Lees bought the family home at 1310 Indiana Avenue.

This purchase firmly anchored the Lees on Salt Lake City's west side and more particularly in the Pioneer Stake. During 1928, Elder Lee's rapid rise to leadership in the stake took a quantum leap. Prior to the October quarterly stake conference that year, Elder Lee had been released as the stake superintendent of religion classes and had been called as the stake superintendent of the Sunday Schools, replacing T. T. Burton. He had selected Edwin Bronson and E. Albert Rosenvall as his counselors and had expected that their names would be presented for sustaining vote at one of the general sessions of the conference. As Harold entered the Assembly Hall on Temple Square on Sunday, where the general sessions of the conference were held, he had no inkling of the surprise that awaited him there. Instead of hearing his name presented as the new stake superintendent of the Sunday Schools, he was presented to the conference as the new second counselor to President D. E. Hammond in the stake presidency. The other counselor sustained was Charles S. Hyde, who replaced J. A. Hancock as the first counselor. The unexpected action taken this day elevated twenty-nine-year-old Harold B. Lee to a place of visible prominence among the seven stakes in the Salt Lake Valley, a place comparable to that which his mission president John M. Knight had occupied six years before when Harold was released from the Western States Mission.

The men with whom Elder Lee was thus brought into close association in the stake presidency were men of ability and wide experience. Datus E. Hammond, who was forty-one years old at the time, was a professional scouter who had served as a missionary in England, who was educated at the University of Utah, and who was a veteran of World

Call as Stake President

War I where he had risen to the rank of first lieutenant. President Hammond was called as the president of Pioneer Stake in 1925, and after his release in 1930, he was called as a member of the general board of the YMMIA. His long experience in Scouting reflected an intense interest in the youth of the Church. President Charles S. Hyde, the first counselor, who was forty years old at the time, had served as the president of the Netherlands Mission. In addition, he had served there as a missionary when he was a young man. He was called into the presidency of the Pioneer Stake in 1925. President Hyde, whose father, Charles H. Hyde, had also served in the presidency of the Pioneer Stake, was a member of the staff of the Presiding Bishop's office.

The stake over which these men presided took its name from Pioneer Square, which was within the stake boundaries, the place where the Mormon pioneers first camped upon entering the Salt Lake Valley. It included ten wards, a Mexican branch, and a population of over ten thousand members. The eastern portion of the stake included much of the industrial section of Salt Lake City and on the western boundary of the stake were many homes of humble character. In between were neighborhoods of typically middle-class quality. Also included in the stake were homes of a more substantial nature, some of which had been built by pioneer families bordering or near the Jordan River, which flows through the stake. Among these was the Cannon family, which included Sylvester Q. Cannon, a son of President George Q. Cannon, who was released as the president of the Pioneer Stake in 1925 when he became the Presiding Bishop of the Church.

President Lee's tenure as a counselor in the Pioneer Stake presidency was short-lived. In October 1930 the stake presidency was reorganized under the direction of Rudger Clawson, president of the Twelve, assisted by Elder George Albert Smith of the Twelve. On the Friday before the conference, Brother Lee was invited to the office of President Clawson where he was told he had been approved by the

First Presidency and the Twelve to serve as the new president of the stake. He was shocked. As he groped for words to respond, Elder Lee said he would rather serve as a counselor to Charles S. Hyde who was much more experienced than he. Harold was promptly disabused of that idea when Elder Smith pointedly told him he had not been invited there to give counsel about a new stake president but to determine whether he was willing and worthy to accept the call. When put in those terms, he accepted with alacrity.

This was the second time the young Harold B. Lee had been given direct counsel by a member of the Twelve, the first being when Elder James E. Talmage had corrected him in Denver about the way he had conducted the baptismal service. He did not take offense at being corrected by these brethren. Indeed, he seemed to appreciate having the miscues called to his attention and to profit from the direction he received, but unsolicited or questionable directions from others were not received with the same deferential attitude. Elder Lee was very much his own man. If he felt he was right on a given issue, and if it had moral implications, he would adhere to it regardless of who stood in opposition. But in instances like the two cited here, he yielded immediately when it was apparent he was in the wrong.

Once he had accepted the call to serve, Elders Clawson and Smith raised the question about Harold's counselors. He asked if they had suggestions about whom he should select. Their answer, presumably, was as shocking as was the call itself. He was told they had two men in mind, but did not intend to identify them. That decision, he was told, was his responsibility and that if he was guided by the Spirit, he would select the ones whom they had in mind. With such a pointed challenge to the depth of his spirituality, it hardly needs mentioning that he spent a fitful night. It was a night alternately divided into periods of wakefulness and troubled slumber. While it wore on, he reflected on different combinations of ten or twelve men whom he visualized serving as his counselors. As he did

Call as Stake President

so, drifting in and out of sleep, he could foresee obstacles and misunderstandings that might impede the work, clearly indicating that certain men should not be given consideration. When dawn came, he had, by this process of elimination, reduced the number under consideration to two: Charles S. Hyde, the incumbent first counselor in the stake presidency, and Paul C. Child, the bishop of the Poplar Grove Ward. When he informed the apostles of his decision, "they smiled their approval," indicating he had selected the ones they had in mind.

That night after the priesthood meeting, Elder Lee went for a long ride with Charles Hyde. He told him of the call he had received and of his desire that his friend continue to serve as the first counselor in the stake presidency. Brother Hyde was "thunderstruck" at the idea. He refrained from answering until he had thought about it and had counselled with President Clawson. It is a mark of Charles Hyde's maturity and dedication that he accepted the call to serve the one who had been his subordinate, who was much younger than he and whose credentials in Church leadership were far less impressive than his own. As for Bishop Child, he received the same treatment Harold had received when he was called as the second counselor and was unaware of it until his name was read from the pulpit. It is safe to say that the bishop was thunderstruck, but in a different way.

What took place in the Assembly Hall that day undoubtedly created a stir among many members of the Pioneer Stake. They had just sustained the youngest stake president in the Church, one who had been jumped over the first counselor, the scion of one of the oldest and most distinguished families in the stake. While President Lee had lived there for seven years and was well known and highly respected, still he was a comparative newcomer to many whose ancestral roots in that area reached back more than three-quarters of a century to the very beginnings of the Latter-day Saints in the Salt Lake Valley. Although such as these would have raised their hands in support of the new leaders, some of them undoubtedly did so with a "wait and see" attitude. This attitude was evident during the first months of Elder Lee's ministry as stake president, even among some in the inner circle of leadership. In time, however, when they saw this extraordinary man at work, it is doubtful that anyone in the Pioneer Stake harbored negative feelings toward Harold B. Lee, except those who may have been motivated by jealousy instead of skepticism. It is safe to assume that upon taking the helm of the Pioneer Stake, Elder Lee had feelings akin to those he had when President Knight called him as the president of the Denver conference. Was he "big enough" for the job? The two apostles had given him still another chance to show what he could do, to show his generalship under difficult circumstances.

At the threshold of his administration, President Lee was faced with numerous problems of organization. It became necessary to reorganize the bishopric of the Poplar Grove Ward because of the call of Bishop Child to the stake presidency. Since the bishops of the Cannon and the Thirty-Second wards had been called to the high council, the reorganization of the bishoprics of these two wards was also required. In addition, changes were necessary in the leadership of the high priests quorum and the Genealogical Society. All these required extensive interviews and prayerful consultations, and, in the case of the three new bishops, it was also necessary to obtain the approval of the council of the First Presidency and Quorum of the Twelve. Over a period of several weeks, all these changes were effected, which seemed to position the stake leaders to begin to grapple with the many substantive problems with which they were faced. It was then that a bombshell was dropped on President Lee which would divert his attention from these problems, would create rancorous feelings of long-lasting effect, and would present a serious challenge to his leadership.

In the audits that were conducted as part of the change in the leadership of the three wards, serious shortages were

Call as Stake President

uncovered in the tithing and building fund accounts of one of the bishops. As there was no convincing explanation that justified these discrepancies and because of incriminating evidence that the former bishop had deliberately misappropriated the funds, it became necessary for the new stake president to convene a high council court. Added to the normal circumstances that make disciplinary councils unpleasant and disruptive were the stressful facts that the former bishop was then a member of the high council and there were intertwining personal relationships between him and his family and various members of the stake, which had been forged over a period of many years. These circumstances created an atmosphere of extreme tension when the court was convened and the former bishop stood accused before his brethren of the high council. What made it especially difficult for the thirty-one-year-old stake president was that he had never before presided over a high council court. He was, therefore, apprehensive about following the court procedures while subjected to the personal anguish of having to sit in judgment on a dear friend and co-worker. The trial was long and wearing, lasting from evening until four o'clock the next morning. After the detailed evidence developed by the audit was introduced showing a pattern of dishonesty and misappropriation, the accused was allowed to respond with evidence by way of mitigation or in justification for what he had done. Then followed the customary procedure when half of the high council spoke in favor of the accused and the other half spoke for the court. President Lee then retired with his counselors to prayerfully mull over the evidence and to discuss the complex ramifications of the trial and the consequences of any decision to be reached. At length, President Lee decided that the circumstances required that the accused be disfellowshipped from the Church, and being supported in that decision by his counselors, returned to announce it to the high council. To his surprise, the high council refused to sustain it. We can only imagine the consternation of the young stake president to be rebuffed in that way by his high council in the first real test of his leadership. In this stressful situation, President Lee merely announced for the record that the decision of the stake president, concurred in by his counselors, was not the decision of the high council. He then adjourned the hearing. However, when it was reconvened the following Sunday morning, the high council reversed itself and unanimously sustained President Lee's decision. It is apparent that upon reflection, the members of the high council concluded that the evidence fully justified the decision of the stake president, and that perhaps they had been swayed by their emotional attachment to the accused who was one of their own.

It is not difficult to appraise the impact and the significance of this decision upon the members of the Pioneer Stake. It assuredly conveyed the message that high position in the Church would not insulate one from the consequences of misconduct. And the way in which the young and inexperienced stake president had adroitly brought about unanimity in the court undoubtedly enhanced his leadership role in the stake. Here was a man of strong mind and purpose who showed qualities of leadership and judgment far beyond his years. These qualities, and the confidence they engendered in his followers, would be of vital importance in the years ahead as Harold B. Lee and his associates forged an instrument for the relief of their people and infused it with an extraordinary enthusiasm and sense of purpose.

The judicial machinery of the Pioneer Stake seems to have fallen into disuse prior to Brother Lee's call as stake president. The common judges apparently had closed their eyes to all transgressions, allowing disobedient members to go their way without restraint or warning. This condition had created widespread indifference in the stake, blurring the meaning of what it meant to be a Latter-day Saint. This in turn weakened the incentive to live up to the high standards of the Church. This situation was radically altered with the call of President Harold B. Lee. Following the

Call as Stake President

high council court that disfellowshipped the erring bishop, a series of other Church courts followed, which disciplined members for a variety of transgressions including adultery, fornication, polygamy, apostasy, and dishonesty. It is inferred that this had a bracing effect on the members of the stake, awakening them to the duties of membership and reminding them of the aim of the Church to lead its members toward perfection. It is also assumed that this revival of the judicial system caused some disobedient members to change their ways voluntarily, thereby eliminating the need for formal Church discipline.

Chapter Eight

Salt Lake City Commissioner

At the time of Elder Lee's call as stake president, his mission president, John M. Knight, was a member of the Salt Lake City Commission, responsible for Public Safety. A controversy had arisen out of Commissioner Knight's administration, which had drawn much public criticism. One of the critics was Elder Richard R. Lyman of the Twelve, who aired his views at a public meeting held in the Pioneer Stake. In doing so, Elder Lyman made accusations that impugned the commissioner's integrity. Oblivious of the source of these charges and of the consequences of speaking out, President Lee defended his friend in a public meeting by questioning the accuracy of Elder Lyman's charges. Anyone seeking evidence of Harold B. Lee's boldness and independence need only consider this astonishing incident. How many thirty-three-year-old men, with no powerful friends or relatives to support them, would publicly oppose a member of the Twelve Apostles? It is true that as a stake president Elder Lee had significant influence in the Salt Lake Valley. But, he had been in office for only two years and therefore was a relative unknown. The conventional wisdom would have suggested that he not speak out publicly against someone as prominent and as powerful as Elder Lyman. However, to him it was not a question of what was politic or popular. Still less was it a question of whether it would enhance or diminish his reputation. It was rather a question of whether he would remain silent while his mentor was wrongly attacked. It is safe to say that if Harold B. Lee had not previously appeared on the scope of the General Authorities, his opposition to Richard R. Lyman assuredly put him there. To have the youngest stake president in the Church speak out in opposition to a member of the Twelve was unusual, to say the least. Actually, it was unprecedented. The content of any discussions the incident may have touched off within the leading councils of the Church never seeped out to the public. Whether individual members were appalled or whether they secretly admired the young man's spunk and loyalty, they were all undoubtedly aware that something new and unusual had been added to the leadership on the west side of Salt Lake City. This would become even more abundantly clear with the passage of time.

Not long after the public meeting where President Lee had defended John M. Knight, he went to the commissioner's office to discuss the incident with him. During the conversation, the recent death of Salt Lake Commissioner Joseph H. Lake was mentioned. He had been elected from the west side of the city. In the discussion, John Knight asked whether President Lee would accept the appointment to fill the vacancy in the commission were it offered to him. "It was the furthest thing from my mind," wrote Elder Lee. Once the subject had been broached, however, he asked what the chances were that he could receive the appointment. "He said he thought I had all the chance in the world." With only a tacit indication that Harold would accept the appointment if it were offered to him, Commissioner Knight immediately began to make contacts to gather support for the candidacy of his protégé. As President Lee left the commissioner's office, he met his brother-in-law, Clarence Cowan, a city employee, who suggested that he seek the appointment to fill the vacancy in the commission. And later in the day, when he visited the offices of the Presiding Bishopric on business, his counselor Charles S. Hyde, who worked there, and Frank Penrose said they had just been discussing the possibility of President Lee being appointed to fill the vacancy. At day's end, Brother Lee considered the coincidence of these three separate but similar events to be "rather startling." Having decided to try for it, he obtained Fern's less than enthusiastic approval and began to take positive steps toward obtaining the appointment. "It seemed that I was shoved from this place to the other," he wrote, as he sought the support of influential people whose voices might be heeded by the Board of City Commissioners as they made their decision. In the forefront of those who took up his candidacy and made it their own cause were Joseph H. Preece, E. C. Davies, Jack Findling, and Lee Lovinger, in addition to those already mentioned. In the process of drumming up support, President Lee met numerous other new friends who, in the future, would play important roles in his brief political career. Chief among these was John F. Fitzpatrick, who managed the widespread interests of the powerful Kearns family and who was the publisher of the *Salt Lake Tribune* and the Salt Lake *Telegram*. Historically, these newspapers had shown a consistent and sometimes bitter anti-Mormon bias whose roots traced to former United States Senator Thomas L. Kearns. It was he who had locked horns with the Mormon apostle Reed Smoot in the battle to deny Elder Smoot his seat in the United States Senate, and repeatedly thereafter, the Salt Lake *Tribune* had attacked various Mormon leaders and policies, often in the most blunt and vitriolic language. A favorite target in the past had been President Joseph F. Smith, whom Senator Kearns had characterized as "the ruling Monarch" of a dangerous monarchy, which, he charged, fed on the tithes of the people, covertly allowing its leaders to live in polygamy. Four days before his term in the United States Senate ended, Mr. Kearns berated President Smith on the floor of the Senate, saying in conclusion: "It is the duty of this great body—the Senate of the United States—to serve notice on this church monarch and his apostles that they must live within the law; that the nation is supreme; that the institutions of this country must prevail throughout the land, and that the compact upon which statehood was granted must be preserved inviolate." (*Congressional Record.* 58th Cong. Vol. 39, pt. 4, p. 3613.) Later blasts at President Joseph F. Smith and other leaders were more explicit and abusive than this, creating a bitter relationship between the Church and the owners and management of the Salt Lake *Tribune.* Now to have a harmonious rapport with the publisher of this paper boded well for the young stake president who sought to become one of the political leaders of Salt Lake City.

Elder Lee's efforts to receive the appointment proved successful when the city commission unanimously designated him to fill the vacancy effective December 1, 1932. An editorial that appeared in Mr. Fitzpatrick's *Tribune* the following day set the tone for the new commissioner's relationship with the press and the public during his brief political career. "The commission is entitled to public commendation for its wise and happy selection," it read. "The Tribune extends its congratulations to the new commissioner and commends the remainder of the commission for an appointment so promising of sound public service." The editorial also referred to President Lee's youth, his vigor, his courage, and to his keen interest in public affairs, notwithstanding a lack of experience in politics. The editorial announcing the appointment, which appeared in the Church-owned *Deseret News,* elaborated on this interest. "He has been prominent in civic organizations, particularly those interested in building up and improving the west side of the city. He has been the leader in battles before the city commission for the maintenance of adequate public transportation for west side residents." The *Tribune* editorial also emphasized the new commissioner's connection with the city's west side, suggesting that this was the key factor in his appointment since his predecessor had been elected from that area. President Lee's ecclesiastical role in aiding the Latter-day Saints living on the west side further underscores the significance of the decision he and Fern made to put their roots down in that area following their marriage.

While President Lee was lauded publicly and privately for it, there was a down side to his appointment. Most troubling was the reaction of some of Elder Lee's close friends to his entrance into politics. They felt it would be "disastrous" to his character and to his standing in the community. He apparently had similar concerns as he pursued the appointment. But, these seem to have left him as the result of a conversation he had with his counselor Paul Child. President Child told Elder Lee that he had "placed the matter before the Lord" and that if the appointment should materialize, it would be because the Lord wanted him there. Elder Lee noted that this "defined" his own feelings "very clearly." Therefore, the new commissioner had no concern about his reputation being tarnished if this was the place where the Lord wanted him to be. Moreover, this aspect of the appointment likely would have mitigated any concern he may have had over the financial consequences of his decision. By this time Elder Lee had become the intermountain manager of the Foundation Press with offices in the McIntyre Building in Salt Lake City. While the effects of the great depression had touched his business as they had all others, he had basic confidence in his ability to survive while building a solid base for future success. Politics, with its minimal compensation and all its uncertainties as to tenure, did not hold out any substantial hope for the financial security of his family. Still, as indicated, this and other drawbacks to a political career seem to have been swallowed up in his overriding feeling that this was the place where the Lord wanted him to be. Subsequent events demonstrated the soundness of this impression as Harold B. Lee's dual role as the president of the Pioneer Stake and a member of the Salt Lake City Commission representing the west side provided essential ingredients in the successful development of the welfare plan.

The timing of Elder Lee's appointment could not have been worse from the standpoint of his new duties. The budget for his department for the year 1933 had to be completed by December 15, which gave him only two weeks in which to do it. This heavy responsibility, added to the normal duties of administering the affairs of a sprawling department with which he had no familiarity, required the new commissioner to work almost around the clock during these first few days. His job was aggravated by the diminished funds available to the city because of the depression, notwithstanding the need for services continued at the same if not an increased level.

We get the sense in reading his account of this period that Elder Lee was exhilarated by the challenging complexity of his new assignment. It is also inferred that during this period he developed to a high degree his ability to keep many balls in the air at the same time and to do it with poise and grace. His duties as stake president were, as we shall see, especially demanding at this time as he and his brethren struggled to stem the tide of economic disaster that had engulfed their people. His family duties continued unabated as he fulfilled the needs of his wife and their maturing daughters, while taking care of the yard work and other chores around the home. In addition to all this, the new commissioner taught an early-morning seminary class. He had taken on this responsibility in 1931 when the Church organized a seminary at the then new South High School in Salt Lake City. There he was associated with Merrill D. Clayson, a full-time employee of the Church Education System, who supervised the overall curriculum and the activities of the students. These activities, Elder Lee recalled, "ranged from bonfire parties to dancing and Sunday night programs." Here Harold B. Lee, teacher and principal of schools in Idaho and Utah, was in his natural element. He revelled in his association with young people, enjoying the challenge of leading them toward personal testimony and commitment to the Church. In teaching the youth, he would often say to them in substance, "If you don't yet have a personal testimony of the truthfulness of the gospel, use mine for a while." Of his association with the seminary students at South High School, Elder Lee said, "This association to me was life at its best." And his students reciprocated that sentiment. Years afterward they reflected with a mixed sense of pride and awe on their relationship with their seminary teacher who ultimately became the prophet of the Lord. Many of them counted it as a badge of honor that he later performed their marriages in the temple. One of these, Allen H. Lundgren, whom the apostle sealed to his wife, Ruth Horne Lundgren, remembered the special rapport Elder Lee had with his students and the genuine interest he showed in their personal development. Another of Elder Lee's students at the South High seminary was D. Arthur Haycock, who later became President Lee's personal secretary when he was the president of the Church. Arthur remembers the notable day when Elder Lee called on him to pray in seminary. As he closed his eyes and began to speak, Arthur felt movement in his body and in the floor beneath him. Amazed that his prayer had such powerful impact, he opened his eyes to find the class scurrying for cover from an earthquake that had struck the valley.

Elder Lee's special interest in teaching and motivating young people never waned. In later years he compensated for the loss of a connection with the seminary students by giving special instruction to missionary groups about the meaning and significance of the temple ordinances. This practice continued even after he became a member of the First Presidency. On one occasion he took the author with him to such a meeting of newly called missionaries held in the Assembly Room in the Salt Lake Temple. He asked that a verbatim report be prepared of his preliminary com-

Salt Lake City Commissioner

Salt Lake City Commissioner Harold B. Lee, about 1940

ments and of the questions and answers that followed. His purpose was to have this transcribed and edited with the aim of preparing an outline, which could be used by others in instructing young people about temple ordinances. His unexpected death prevented this project from reaching fruition.

Once the new commissioner had completed his budget and had gotten through the Christmas holidays with their happy agenda of family and Church responsibilities, he was prepared to buckle down to the challenging task of directing the Salt Lake City Streets Department. It was not an enviable job. The area's cold and wet winters, with alternate freezing and thawing, played havoc with Salt Lake City's surfaced streets. As water filtered into cracks in the streets and then froze, damage was caused as the expanding ice opened up fissures in the pavement. Auto traffic often expanded these fissures into chuckholes, which endangered the safety and raised the anger of motorists. Public complaints aggravated by nagging news articles and editorials made the job of streets commissioner one of the most visible and miserable in the city. Added to the continuing problems of street maintenance was the problem of snow removal during the winter months. This work was more demanding on the bench areas of the city where the hills required that after the snow had been removed the streets had to be salted to prevent the buildup of ice. In addition to these duties, the Streets Department was responsible for garbage and sewage disposal.

The heavy and continuing work of the department required a force of 250 workers and extensive equipment with maintenance shops and material depots. Except for Public Safety, the Streets Department employed more workers than any other city department. The budget crunch caused by the depression made it necessary that the new commissioner pare down the size of his administrative staff. As a result he discharged the supervisor of streets and the office manager. However, he kept the laborers in the department on the job. The former supervisor of streets was so angry when he was discharged that he threatened the new commissioner and swore to defeat him at the election in 1933. As a condition to accepting the appointment, Harold B. Lee had agreed to be a candidate in that election. Later events proved the former supervisor's threat to be an idle boast.

Through budget economies and careful supervision, the new commissioner managed the Streets Department on $145,000 less during 1933 than was spent during the previous year. He did this while employing more laborers but without reducing the wage scale.

As the streets commissioner looked toward the election, he created an organization to help insure victory at the ballot box. In doing so, he showed a flair for organization, which would be revealed repeatedly in the future.

Salt Lake City Officials, 1938–1939. Seated left to right: George D. Keyser, Commissioner, Water Department; Ethel McDonald, City Recorder; Harold B. Lee, Commissioner, Streets Department; Mr. Finlayson, City Auditor; William Murdock, Commissioner, Public Finance; and Salt Lake City Mayor E. B. Erwin

He began by enlisting the support of the workers in his department. Since most of them were not on civil service, their continued employment depended on the success of Commissioner Lee. He was not content with their personal support, but organized them into precincts and then began to hold meetings with them. He explained it, "To become better acquainted, to outline plans, to define my position on various questions, to prepare them to answer complaints, and to meet opposition that might come." Meanwhile, he was busy making personal contacts outside the department among both members and nonmembers of the Church. He was driven toward success in the election, not only because of the commitment he had made but to protect the financial security of his family. In accepting the appointment as city commissioner, Elder Lee had turned away from the Foundation Press and from teaching. The deepening depression had made steady jobs extremely scarce. The tip-off as to the scarcity of jobs was the slate of twenty candidates for the city commission at the primary election in the autumn of 1933.

As election day drew near, Commissioner Lee and his supporters moved into action. In addition to organizing and training the members of his department, he appointed an advisory committee consisting of Joseph H. Preece, Clarence Cowan, E. C. Davis, and Lauren W. Gibbs. The campaign manager was Parley Eccles. Limited funds greatly restricted the quantity and variety of the campaign literature. It consisted of simple flyers that briefly listed his personal and professional background, his achievements as commissioner, and named his principal supporters. These flyers were widely distributed by the campaign workers who were organized into teams given specific neighborhoods to cover.

One of the flyers emphasized the candidate's youth as a point in his favor. Yet this was the very thing that caused the political professionals to predict his defeat. Traditionally, the Streets Department was considered to be worthless as a political base. The professionals thought Commissioner Lee was so young and inexperienced that he did not realize this and that therefore he was doomed to certain defeat. It came as a rude shock that this rank newcomer polled 13,336 votes, far outdistancing all the other candidates. By contrast, J. Fields Greenwood, who had sworn to defeat his former boss, polled fewer than five hundred votes. It was this remarkable showing by a young political neophyte in Utah's largest city that sent Harold B. Lee's political star into orbit. The outcome suggested that the public had witnessed the birth of the state's political luminary of the future. It was the extraordinary appeal he demonstrated in this election that caused politicians to approach Elder Lee repeatedly after his call to the Twelve, pleading with him to become a candidate for governor or for the United States Senate. He routinely turned these offers aside, advising that he would become a candidate only if he were directed to do so by the First Presidency.

The four top candidates for city commissioner in the primaries qualified to run in the general election held two weeks later. Because the proposed repeal of the Eighteenth Amendment to the Constitution was a hot political issue nationally, with public sentiment strongly favoring repeal, and because Commissioner Lee was known to oppose it, his opponents sought to inject this issue into the campaign. He first took the position that the issue was irrelevant in Salt Lake's municipal election since it would have to be decided at the national level. While this position was logically correct, the issue, nevertheless, was thrust into the campaign when a local newspaper demanded that each of the four candidates publicly state his position on it. Trading on his friendship with him, Elder Lee asked John F. Fitzpatrick how his statement should be worded. The *Tribune*'s publisher suggested a nebulous statement to the effect that while the candidate was not "satisfied" with conditions as they existed under prohibition, he certainly could not sanction "the old saloon conditions of the past." While this was an obvious attempt to skirt the issue, the voters apparently saw through the effort to skewer Commissioner Lee who was a known dry, but who could have been damaged politically had he forthrightly said that. As expected, his opponents attacked the statement for its lack of clarity, but the effort to derail his candidacy failed as Commissioner Lee outpolled his three opponents, gaining 29,336 votes.

At this point in his life, Elder Lee's future appeared to trend toward a career in politics and public service. On this account, he "kept minute records of election returns, district by district, as they were reported in the public press." As a politician, he knew the value of statistics of this kind, which could be important in future campaigns as showing areas of strength or weakness and therefore suggesting strategies that could increase support or minimize opposition. The successful candidate also showed his political acumen by personally contacting influential voters after the election to express appreciation for support or to guarantee his willingness to work cooperatively with all groups as a means of improving the quality of his service to the community.

Among those whom Elder Lee contacted was the First Presidency of the Church. At the time, however, the only member of it available was President Anthony W. Ivins, first counselor to President Heber J. Grant. The commissioner told President Ivins that he would be pleased to counsel with the First Presidency about any matters of public interest in the city as to which the Brethren had any concern. President Ivins responded that the only counsel he had was that the commissioner take those actions that he thought were right. "I would ten times rather a man would make a mistake while doing that which he thought was right," Elder Lee quoted President Ivins as saying, "than to do right just for policy sake." To avoid any implication that the newly elected city commissioner intended to be controlled or unduly influenced in his decisions by the General Authorities of the Church, he paid similar courtesy calls on other prominent persons in the city who were not members of the Church, making the same offer to them. His obvious purpose, aside from cementing personal relationships, was to receive input from a wide spectrum of his constituency so as to improve the effectiveness of his administration. This attitude typified Harold B. Lee's performance as a Salt Lake City commissioner. While the high-profile nature of his department and his meteoric rise as a political force attracted his share of criticism, his reputation for sound, efficient, and honest dealings was never questioned. And he reciprocated the kindly feelings others had toward him. "My work brought me in contact with the leaders in every field," wrote he of his experiences as a Salt Lake City commissioner, "and I have formed friendships that wouldn't be possible otherwise."

Chapter Nine

Shepherding the Flock

At the time of his election as Salt Lake City commissioner in the fall of 1933, Elder Lee had been the president of the Pioneer Stake for three years. During that period, he and his associates had set in motion important initiatives intended to alleviate the dire economic want of their people, which the deepening depression had produced. These efforts had been watched with avid interest by the General Authorities who were searching for remedies for similar ills that affected the entire membership of the Church to one degree or another. Already there appears to have developed a special affinity between Elder Lee and President J. Reuben Clark, who became the second counselor in the First Presidency in April 1933. Because of the need to be out of town on election day, President and Sister Clark went to the City and County Building before leaving to cast their votes. While in the building, they stopped at the office of Commissioner Lee to wish him luck in the election. It is apparent that at this early period, J. Reuben Clark had his eye on this promising young leader. In time, their relationship would almost be that of a father and son. Meanwhile, several years and many demanding challenges would intervene before this pair would be brought into almost daily personal contact as they labored, side by side, in helping to lay the foundations of what became known as the Church welfare program.

This program traces its beginnings to Pioneer Stake and other stakes in the Salt Lake Valley. As the depression took hold following the market crash in November 1929, unemployment became widespread as businesses folded and as confidence in the economy plummeted. By 1933, the national jobless rate had risen to 24.9 percent, but a survey of the seventy-three hundred members of the Pioneer Stake revealed that more than half of them were dependent on assistance outside the family for their livelihood. As President Lee and his associates in the leadership of the Pioneer Stake appraised this problem, they set on a course of action that would be a model for the entire Church in the years ahead. Basically, it consisted of determining needs and resources and then of matching the two. The needs were apparent from a survey that revealed about forty-eight hundred members of the stake needed help from outside the family in providing for their food, clothing, and shelter. The main resource available in the stake to fill these needs was idle manpower. The challenge, therefore, was to put the manpower to work to fill the needs. After long hours of study, fasting, and prayer, President Lee appointed a committee to take the leadership in meeting this challenge. It consisted of his counselor Paul Child as chairman, with C. O. Jensen, Thomas E. Wilding, Alfons J. Finck, and Fred J. Heath as members. The strategy, as outlined by President Lee, was to negotiate contracts with farmers in the area to harvest their crops in exchange for a percentage of the harvest. The produce obtained from these contracts was then to be gathered in a central place for distribution to needy members of the stake, with the surplus to be canned for future use. The implementation of the strategy involved these essential steps: obtain a facility for the warehousing and distribution of commodities, organize a staff to manage this facility, negotiate contracts with farmers to harvest their crops, and organize and supervise the harvesting crews. The first step was taken when the central committee obtained, without cost, a warehouse at 333 Pierpont Avenue, which was within the boundaries of the stake and which was owned by the Browning family of Ogden, Utah. Jesse M. Drury, bishop of the Fifth Ward, who was then unemployed, was appointed as the manager of the storehouse. Alfons J. Finck of the committee was selected as the bookkeeper and office manager, while Gladys May became the office secretary and stenographer. Three other unemployed bishops in the stake, C. E. Davey, R. F. W. Nickel, and James Graham were appointed to contact farmers in the surrounding area to negotiate harvesting contracts. They and others were then involved in recruiting and supervising the volunteer harvesting crews drawn from the membership of the stake. In anticipation of the flood of produce that would be garnered at harvest time, the storehouse crew was fleshed out to include numerous people who received, merchandised, and distributed the produce and who canned the surplus for use in the off-season. The storehouse organization also came to include many sisters who were productively involved in mending or making clothing and bedding for the use of the needy in the stake. In time, the stake contracted with local industries to provide work parties to help in times of emergency or seasonal overload. As this vast self-help organization was perfected, there developed with it an extensive network of volunteers and patrons, many of whom were not members of the stake, who donated items of clothing or equipment necessary for the successful operation of the system. As the work projects got into full swing, a system of welfare entitlement was perfected. Those who performed direct services, whether in the field-work crews or at the storehouse, were given "pay" slips that could be presented at the storehouse to obtain food or other commodities they needed. The needy in a ward who could not render services in the program could go to their bishop, who, with the aid of the ward Relief Society

Bishops' Storehouse, Pioneer and Salt Lake Stakes, 333 Pierpont Ave., Salt Lake City, Utah, one of the first bishops' storehouses in the Church

president, would determine worthiness and need and would then issue orders on the storehouse for designated items of food and clothing or other commodities. In exchange for this assistance, recipients were expected to render some kind of charitable service of which they were capable, thereby removing any stigma of a dole or a mere handout.

Eventually, an executive committee comprised of the eleven bishops in the stake was appointed to oversee the work of the storehouse, with Bishop Joseph H. McPhie of the Twenty-fifth Ward as the chairman. Later still, the neighboring Salt Lake Stake was invited to join with the Pioneer Stake in the operation of the storehouse, and its members thereafter were entitled to receive commodities from it on the same basis as the members of the Pioneer Stake.

It comes as no surprise that when this elaborate yet simple mechanism for supplying the needs of the poor in the Pioneer Stake became fully operative, it attracted widespread, favorable notice. John F. Fitzpatrick of the *Tribune* went to visit the Pierpont Avenue storehouse and was so intrigued by what he found that he assigned a reporter to prepare a feature article for his paper. "For the past month," the reporter wrote, "unemployed carpenters, painters, and other workmen have been working on the building, which includes a storage basement, a mezzanine sewing department for renovating old clothes, a main floor for canned goods and groceries and a second floor for dry goods and groceries." The article also reported that trucks had been donated to the program for transporting goods and workers and then described the procedure followed in fulfilling work assignments. "As many as twenty men a day are being sent out," the reporter explained, "to pitch hay on Salt Lake County farms, or to pick peas in American Fork, or cherries and apricots in Bountiful and other towns." The reporter then characterized the system as a form of barter in the tradition of the pioneer west, explaining, "No charity is involved and the unemployed person works strictly on a no wage basis, receiving goods and food necessary for his immediate needs."

But, the notoriety of what was being accomplished in the Pioneer Stake to solve the nagging problems of the depression extended far beyond the state of Utah. "Several Eastern men came to visit our projects," Elder Lee explained in his records, "among whom was a Mr. Pearmain from Washington, who was connected with government relief; Mr. Mackey, a friend of President Clark's from New York; and a brother of the Reverend Webb, who years ago wrote 'The Case Against the Mormons.' " As to the reaction of these visitors, President Lee wrote: "Each was the same in saying without hesitation, 'We dream of these accomplishments being possible in the east, but never hoped to have it worked out as practically as you have it here.' "

It is apparent from what has been said already that the welfare program as it was worked out in the Pioneer Stake was not a one-man show. President Lee did not feel it was necessary for him to be personally involved in every aspect of the work. He conceived it as his task to set the course, to develop overall strategy, to call able people to positions they were qualified to fill, to define their authority and responsibility, and then to let them do their job. With all this, he provided a mechanism of accountability so that those who served under him had the opportunity to report on their work and to receive any overall direction he considered necessary. This quality of leadership is best illustrated in the first committee he organized to supervise the welfare work in the Pioneer Stake. As already indicated, he appointed Paul Child as the committee chairman. When matters involving this committee were discussed in stake council meetings, he always called on President Child to take the lead in discussing the work. He received regular reports from his counselor, at which point he gave any necessary instruction or counsel. There was never a misunderstanding in the stake as to who held the ultimate authority and responsibility with respect to welfare or any other matters in the stake.

As a member of the Twelve, and later as a member of the First Presidency, Elder Lee was particular in training stake presidents about the key role they played in the administration of the stake affairs and of the void created when they stepped out of that role. He would occasionally illustrate the point with this story he once shared with the author: Not long after Elder Lee was called to the apostleship, he accompanied a senior member of the Twelve to a multi-stake meeting in an outlying area. On arriving at their destination, the two apostles went to the home of the host stake president to check on the final plans for the conference. The stake president's wife answered the door and when they asked to see her husband, she explained he was at the stake center setting up chairs for the meeting. On their way to the chapel, the senior apostle said to Elder Lee: "Well, if we have a stake president here who wants to fill the role of a deacon, we had better release him to do that and call a man who will fill the role of stake president." Within a year, that is what happened.

The wisdom of giving Paul Child wide latitude in directing the work of his committee is seen from the profusion of other initiatives President Lee originated as a means of helping the members of the Pioneer Stake. Very soon after the storehouse was acquired and renovated and the headquarters staff and committees were organized, a stake garden was prepared. It was located on a large vacant lot on South Second West (now Third West) within the stake boundaries. The owner made the lot available to the stake without cost. Here members of the stake of all ages and both sexes gathered to prepare the ground, to plant, to water, to weed, and to harvest. The produce from the garden was handled and distributed in the same way as the produce obtained from the work contracts the stake negotiated with farmers in the area. The garden became such a showplace that when President Lee took John F. Fitzpatrick on a tour to show him what the stake leaders were doing to help their people, a visit to the garden was one of the highlights.

Another highlight of the tour was a visit to the Pioneer Stake Gymnasium, located on South Eight West (now South Ninth West), which was then under construction. As President Lee and his brethren surveyed the resources of the stake, they found a large pool of unemployed artisans—bricklayers, carpenters, masons, painters, and laborers—who wanted to work but who could not find employment. Again, President Lee's ingenuity found a way to match resources with needs. The result was the construction of the Pioneer Stake Gymnasium. The first step was to organize. T. T. Burton was appointed as the overall superintendent of the project, and Fred J. Heath was called to recruit and to direct the laborers. Much of the material for the gymnasium was obtained from old buildings that the stake workers demolished with the approval of their owners. What little money was needed for new materials came from a donation of the First Presidency, forty-five hundred dollars, and from the sale of surplus commodities realized from the operation of the stake storehouse. The workers on the gymnasium were compensated by receiving "pay slips," which could then be used to purchase food, clothing, and other commodities at the storehouse. When completed, the building had an appraised value of thirty thousand dollars. After its completion, an opening social was held in the building on June 16, 1933. Honored guests were President Heber J. Grant and Presiding Bishop Sylvester Q. Cannon, a native of the stake and a former president of the Pioneer Stake.

As would be expected, President Lee then appointed a committee to operate the gymnasium and to schedule the athletic and cultural events held in it. During the first winter of its operation, it was in use every night except Sunday from 6:00 P.M. until 11:00 P.M., the events often drawing from four hundred to seven hundred spectators. Later the building was the focal point of a program devised by President Lee "to provide fully for the spiritual, physical, educational and recreational needs of every member of Pioneer Stake." To control the use of the facility and to provide funds for its maintenance, annual "budget tickets" were sold to families at a nominal cost, which admitted holders to all events held in the building. Those who lacked the means to purchase these tickets could obtain them without charge from their bishops.

As the economic crisis deepened during 1932, President Lee sought and received permission to use tithing funds collected in the stake to help care for the needy, but, as will be seen, by the fall of that year, even that added source of revenue was insufficient. It was at this point that the Pioneer Stake leaders were faced with a major crisis. They had promised the members of the stake that their needs would be met within the resources of individual families and of the Church without resorting to government aid. However, during the last months of the administration of President Herbert Hoover, the Federal Congress passed a measure that created what was known as the Reconstruction Finance Corporation through which vast sums were made available for loans to businesses as well as for direct relief to the needy. Some Church leaders outside the stake had authorized the Saints to resort to the RFC for relief funds. This put pressure on President Lee and his associates to follow suit. To have done so, however, would have violated a basic premise of the Pioneer Stake's welfare plan—that of caring for their own—and, in their view, would have represented a breach of faith with their people. In these circumstances, a meeting of the stake's central welfare committee was convened to discuss the matter. As the bishops asked what counsel they should give their people about accepting RFC aid, Paul Child, chairman of the committee, said: "We want you to see that every one of your people is taken care of. We don't know where the money will come from to pay the bills, but our people must be provided with their needs." President Lee, who had attended the meeting and who reported President Child's remarks as having been "moved by the spirit," heartily endorsed what he said but privately wondered about the source from which the help would come. Within days the answer was given. Through the influence of President Lee, who by then was a Salt Lake City commissioner, the Pioneer Stake storehouse was designated as a temporary county auxiliary storehouse. The government then purchased all the produce and other commodities on hand at market value. The proceeds from this sale were then distributed among the bishops for use in caring for their people.

Despite these vigorous efforts made by President Lee and his associates to provide for their people, they found they still needed additional aid. It was then they turned again to the General Authorities for help. President Lee and his counselors first went to the Presiding Bishopric, who turned them down. They then sought an audience with the First Presidency, where they outlined what they had done to solve their problems, failing which they had come to them for help. When they had finished, the prophet asked his counselors, Anthony W. Ivins and J. Reuben Clark, if they agreed with him that the Church should care for the needy. After receiving an affirmative response, he pounded the table with his fist for emphasis and according to President Lee's record said, "This is the decision of the Church of Jesus Christ of Latter-day Saints: If necessary we will close every seminary, and church school, and temple, and take care of our people if it takes the hide off the church." The First Presidency then made additional funds available for the Pioneer Stake welfare program and President Lee was told if in the future more supplemental help was needed, he was to come directly to them.

Meanwhile, President Lee and his brethren continued to use their initiative to try to solve their own problems. Another one that surfaced at this time arose from the decision of the Presiding Bishopric to reduce the amounts allocated to local units for the maintenance and operation of Church buildings. In an attempt to find a source for funds to replace those lost because of the Presiding Bishopric's decision, President Lee and the presidents of the other five stakes in the city banded together to seek a solution. They created an organization called the Six Salt Lake Stakes Associated, which sold scrip certificates intended to be used as a medium of exchange. In redeeming the certificates, the association realized a two percent override, which was then distributed to the bishops of the sixty-six wards in the six stakes on a pro rata basis. This plan, which was approved by President Anthony W. Ivins while President Grant was away, and prior to the time President J. Reuben Clark became a member of the First Presidency, very soon met with widespread opposition. When President Grant returned, he rejected the plan as smacking of an attempt by the stakes to get something for nothing. So President Lee and his associates—President Wilford Beesley and the Salt Lake Stake, chairman of the association; Bryant S. Hinckley of the Liberty Stake; Winslow Farr Smith of the Ensign Stake; Hugh B. Brown of the Granite

Shepherding the Flock

Stake; and Joseph J. Daynes of the Grant Stake—dissolved the association and redeemed all the outstanding scrip certificates at their full value.

All of these activities took place in an atmosphere supercharged with tension and uncertainty. The economic chaos that followed the market crash was matched by violent political turmoil, which seemed for a time to threaten the very foundations of government. As the major parties geared up for the 1932 presidential election, emotions ran high and occasionally spilled over into violence. Agitators who aimed for the overthrow of democratic government sought to capitalize on the political and economic unrest by creating incidents that would inflame public opinion. One of these, reported by President Lee in his annals, occurred on the steps of the Salt Lake City and County Building where he had his office. A group of communists and communist sympathizers gathered there to try to prevent the sheriff from conducting the sale of property whose owners were delinquent in the payment of taxes. When these agitators physically prevented the sale and forced the sheriff and his deputies into the building, the officers retaliated by spraying them with a fire hose. When the rioters wrested the hose away, the officers resorted to throwing tear gas bombs at them, which were as promptly thrown back. Aided by the surprise and the determination of the attack and by their overwhelming numbers, the agitators at length took control of the building, forcing the sheriff and his deputies to take refuge in their offices. Once having achieved their objective of stopping the sale and of demonstrating their dominance, the rioters withdrew. Encouraged by this success, they then began a campaign of terror and vilification against government officials, demanding concessions that, if granted, would have effectively placed them in charge. The crowning act of their rebellion occurred when, led by an alien revolutionary, Oscar Larson, they marched on the State Capitol while the legislature was in session, demanding to be heard. Wishing to avoid another violent confrontation like the one at the

City and County Building, the legislators acquiesced. The radical demands of their spokesman, and their rude and unruly behavior, finally convinced the government officials that strong countermeasures were necessary to combat this rebellion. They convened a secret meeting of the American Legion at the armory, where the legionnaires were deputized and provided with truncheons. The following day, learning of another planned assault on the City and County Building by the agitators, the beefed-up police force assembled early, positioning themselves at all the entrances to the building. This massive show of force deterred any attempt by the rioters to occupy the building. Mass meetings held throughout the city during the day, where officials discussed strategies to quell the rebellion and to try to meet the economic crisis in a rational, orderly way, rallied public support behind the government. These initiatives effectively stalled the rebellion. The subsequent arrest, conviction, and deportation of the ringleader, Oscar Larson, eliminated the threat.

The high-profile positions of Harold B. Lee during these and other events connected with the depression, and with efforts to combat it, suddenly vaulted him to a place of eminence in the community. His youth, his energy, his courage, his creativity, and his bedrock integrity created an aura of excitement about him and a sense that what he had shown thus far was mere prelude. A sign of Elder Lee's growing reputation was a lengthy article about him that appeared in the *Deseret News* under date of October 24, 1934. The article, which appeared under the caption "Personality Portraits of Prominent Utahans," traced his life from birth, emphasizing his home life, his education, his teaching experiences in Idaho and Utah, his mission, his business experience, and his roles as stake president and city commissioner. The photograph of the thirty-five-year-old leader, which accompanied the article, showed a side view of Elder Lee, silhouetting his ample, dark, wavy hair and his strong, manly features. Asked about the extraordinary achievements of one so young, he modestly answered: "Anything I have done has been possible through my splendid associates." Then he made a statement that seemed to give expression to the widely held view that Harold B. Lee was a young man on the move who would bear watching in the future. Said he, "I have more ahead of me to do than I have ever done."

Another lengthy article about Elder Lee appeared in the November 23, 1935, issue of the *Deseret News* under the caption "One Administrative Unit of the Church Shows How Christian Living Brings Results," written by Dr. Francis W. Kirkham. The article cited a recent gathering of farm, industrial, and scientific leaders in Dearborn, Michigan, hosted by Henry and Edsel Ford, which concluded that "continued enforced idleness and the dole in a land of plenty . . . will eventually destroy those personal qualities of character upon which this country has been founded." It then outlined in detail the plan of self-maintenance being carried out in the Pioneer Stake. It also reported that "the person quietly directing and guiding the plan is Harold B. Lee, one of the five city commissioners of Salt Lake City."

Chapter Ten

Managing Director of the Church Welfare Plan

What Dr. Francis W. Kirkham did not know was that several months before his article about Harold B. Lee was published in the *Deseret News,* Commissioner Lee had become involved, behind the scenes, in plans to launch a Churchwide welfare program. On April 30, 1935, he had been invited to meet with the First Presidency to discuss a Church welfare plan whose focus would be on self-reliance rather than on a direct relief, or a dole, formula. Held on a Saturday, this turned out to be a half-day session with President Heber J. Grant and his second counselor, President David O. McKay. President J. Reuben Clark, the first counselor, was out of the city at the time but was aware of the meeting and had previously approved the purpose of it and also the assignment given to Elder Lee at the conclusion of it.

At the invitation of President Grant, Elder Lee explained the details of the welfare plan as it had been developed in the Pioneer Stake. Most of this was already known by the First Presidency, but the explanation of it by the young stake president filled in any gaps of knowledge they may have had and also served as a point of discussion of alternative approaches in handling the massive welfare problems in the Church. The result of that meeting was explained by Elder Lee in his journal: "I left the First Presidency's office about noontime," he wrote, "with an assignment to work out a program of relief for the entire church based upon my experience with the relief problem in the Pioneer Stake, where, perhaps, the greatest problem of unemployment in the entire church was to be found." It is difficult to imagine the weight of anxiety and responsibility thrust upon Harold B. Lee by this assignment. Less than a month before this meeting he had celebrated his thirty-sixth birthday. At the October general conference in 1972 when he was sustained as the eleventh president of the Church, President Lee endeavored to describe the feelings this incident aroused in him. "There I was," he told the conference, "just a young man in my thirties. My experience had been limited. I was born in a little country town in Idaho. I had hardly been outside the boundaries of the states of Utah and Idaho. And now to put me in a position where I was to reach out to the entire membership of the church, world wide, was one of the most staggering contemplations that I could imagine. How could I do it with my limited understanding." (Conference Report, Oct. 1972, p. 124.)

In such a dilemma, Elder Lee emulated the example of the Prophet Joseph Smith whose anxiety over a perplexing question had led him to the Sacred Grove. There, through an astonishing spiritual manifestation, the restoration of the gospel was begun. In like manner, Elder Lee sought spiritual direction to help in fulfilling the heavy responsibility he had received. He got in his car and drove up City Creek Canyon, whose mouth is only a few blocks from the Church Administration Building. Driving through Memory Grove, which is near the canyon's mouth, he wound his way upward alongside the stream, which at that time of year would have begun to increase in volume as the snow on the high watersheds melted. Arriving at what was called Rotary Park, which was then the terminus of the canyon road, he parked his car. Elder Lee's journal describes what then happened: "I got out and walked up through the trees, seeking a secluded spot, where I knelt in prayer and sought the guidance of an all-wise God in this mighty undertaking. I asked the Lord to guide me to conclusions dictated by his will, and that, for the safety and blessing of his people, I must have his direction." As the Prophet Joseph Smith had a specific question as he kneeled in the Sacred Grove, "Which church is right?", so also Elder Lee had a specific question, which he asked in his prayer: "What kind of an organization should be set up in order to accomplish what the Presidency has assigned?" While the answer to his question did not come to Elder Lee in the same extraordinary way as it had to his predecessor, Joseph Smith, it came through a spiritual "prompting," which was no less explicit and inspiring. "It was as though something were saying to me," he explained in his journal, " 'There is no new organization necessary to take care of the needs of the people. All that is necessary is to put the priesthood of God to work.' "

Some have erroneously thought that this was the beginning of welfare work or a welfare plan in the Church. President Lee certainly never considered it as such. It was merely a spiritual response to an urgent current need, which revealed an age-old, even an eternal, remedy for the ills that beset us. From the earliest days of the restored church, the priesthood has been invoked to help resolve serious problems of temporal need. So, in the early days at Kirtland, Ohio, Newel K. Whitney and Edward Partridge were called as bishops by the Prophet Joseph Smith and were given the charge to care for the hundreds of poor and needy who were flocking into Kirtland in response to the revelation that the Latter-day Saints should "assemble together at the Ohio." (See D&C 37.) The "welfare plan" Bishops Whitney and Partridge devised to care for the needy of the Church at that time differed markedly from the "welfare plan" that came into existence a century later because of vast differences in needs and resources, which the passage of time had produced. But, they were the same in that they were priesthood directed.

Elder Lee's role in developing the Church's welfare plan in the 1930s followed other initiatives that had taken place before the First Presidency asked him to outline a plan based on his experience in the Pioneer Stake. His record of the meeting with the First Presidency on April 20, 1935, makes this clear. "I was astounded to learn," he explained, "that for years there had been before them, as a result of their thinking and planning, and as a result of the inspiration of Almighty God, the genius of the very plan that was waiting and in preparation for a time when, in their judgment, the faith of the Latter-day Saints was such that they were willing to follow the counsel of the men who lead and preside in the church. My humble place in this program at that time was described."

The main initiatives looking toward the creation of a churchwide welfare program in the 1930s took place in 1933. President J. Reuben Clark was sustained as the second counselor in the First Presidency at the April general conference in that year. Soon after, at the direction of President Heber J. Grant, the new counselor began to sketch out the organization and philosophy of a Church welfare program. This was outlined in a pamphlet entitled "Suggested Direction for Church Relief Activities," completed in July 1933, three months after President Clark took office. Thereafter, the bishops were asked to make a survey to determine the extent to which the members of the Church were in need. The responses to this request were sporadic and incomplete. Meanwhile, President Clark, who had played the key role in laying the groundwork for the welfare plan, became heavily involved with President Grant's approval as the chief counsel to Secretary of State Cordell Hull at the Seventh Pan American Conference at Montevideo, Uruguay, and with the Foreign Bondholders Protective Council. These responsibilities entailed frequent, lengthy absences from Salt Lake City with the result that decisive action in developing the Church welfare program lagged. When by 1935 President Clark's outside commitments had not diminished, President David O. McKay was asked to assume the principal responsibility for the welfare plan. It was in that role that President McKay took the leading part at a special meeting of the First Presidency, the Twelve, and the Presiding Bishopric held just before the last general session of the April 1935 general conference. At that time, preliminary approval was given to develop a churchwide welfare program. It was two weeks later, on April 20, 1935, that President Heber J. Grant and President David O. McKay met with Elder Harold B. Lee to request that he sketch out a suggested plan based upon his experience in the Pioneer Stake.

In the weeks after April 20, 1935, Elder Lee, who continued to serve as a member of the Salt Lake City Commission and as president of the Pioneer Stake, worked diligently to fulfill the assignment given to him by the First Presidency. He not only reviewed his records about the development of the welfare program in his own stake, but he consulted many knowledgeable people to get their input about welfare principles and procedures. These included Elder Reed Smoot of the Twelve, a former United States Senator; John M. Knight, Salt Lake City Commissioner and Elder Lee's former mission president; Stringham Stevens; Lester Hewlett; Campbell Brown; and of course Paul C. Child, his counselor in the stake presidency and chairman of the Pioneer Stake welfare committee. Based upon this preparation, Elder Lee made a report that outlined "a preliminary program together with a chart showing the various agencies to participate in a churchwide relief program." This was submitted to the First Presidency about June 1, 1935. When this report was circulated among the General Authorities for review and comment, some negative reactions were generated to developing a churchwide welfare program based on Elder Lee's proposals. These created uncertainty in the mind of President Grant, who hesitated in going forward. "In the face of this indecision and opposition," Elder Lee noted in his record, "President McKay felt incapable of taking the initiative without the personal support and backing of at least one other member of the First Presidency." Since President Clark was not available to get involved, Elder Lee's plan lay dormant with no action being taken on it. However, between June 1, 1935, when the plan was submitted and the October 1935 general conference, Elder Lee met periodically with President McKay to discuss welfare principles. As a result of these meetings, preliminary steps were taken toward establishing a Church welfare plan (originally called the Church security plan) when in September 1935 a church-wide survey was initiated to determine the welfare needs of the members of the Church. In the ensuing months, a close follow-up was made to insure that these data were gathered and submitted to Church headquarters. Also, at the general priesthood meeting on October 5, 1935, the First Presidency developed themes that became fixtures of the Church welfare plan as it was rolled out. The brethren, for instance, were admonished to get out of debt and to stay out of debt and to be faithful in paying their tithes and offerings. As to the latter, President McKay said, "We have in the church one of the best systems in the world of aiding one another—the fast offerings. Our young people should be taught from their youth; our older people should practice it and set a proper example."

The survey of welfare needs commenced in September 1935 was completed in February 1936. At that time, Elder Lee and Campbell M. Brown were invited to meet with the First Presidency. According to Elder Lee's record, they were instructed "to study the results of the survey and in light of its findings, submit a revised report for further consideration of the presiding brethren." During a three-week period, when he worked at all hours of the day and night, Elder Lee "prepared a graph to show clearly the findings and, counselled by Brother Brown, revised, simplified and extended" his original report. "On March 15,

1936," Elder Lee recorded, "we read over the program carefully with President McKay. After the conclusion of the reading, he slapped the table with his hand and exclaimed, 'Brethren, now we have a program to present to the church. The Lord has inspired you in your work.' " Nine days later, President McKay met alone with Elder Lee to further discuss and analyze the report and recommendations in preparation for a special meeting of General Authorities, stake presidencies, bishoprics, and mission presidents to be held in the Assembly Hall following the last session of the general conference on April 6, 1936. At their private meeting, President McKay advised Elder Lee that President Grant wanted him to go to Fresno, California, to participate in a conference of the Farm Chemurgic Council. During this conference, held March 26–27, whose main focus was on the use of farm products for commercial purposes, Elder Lee sketched the outline of the Pioneer Stake's welfare activities in a talk billed as "Finding Our Way Out."

Following the morning session of the general conference on Monday, April 6, a special meeting of all General Authorities was held when the "security plan" was presented and approved. At the meeting held in the afternoon with the General Authorities, stake presidencies, bishoprics, and mission presidents, President Grant called on President McKay to make the presentation. He first referred to the survey conducted after the October 1935 general conference, which revealed that 17.9% of the entire Church membership, or 88,460 persons, were receiving some form of relief. To help in providing for the needs of the poor, a fast offering goal of one dollar per member per year was set. Tithing faithfulness was encouraged. Each bishop was urged to accumulate, by the following October general conference, enough food and clothing to provide for every member of his ward during the coming winter. The principle of performing services in exchange for assistance was emphasized. All members then employed on WPA projects were to be asked to continue but were admonished to do an honest day's work for a day's pay. It was announced that while the direction and coordination of this effort would be in the hands of the Presiding Bishopric, the First Presidency would appoint a Church relief committee to assist the Bishopric. In concluding his remarks, President McKay, echoing the spiritual direction Elder Lee had received as he prayed in City Creek Canyon, told the brethren that the organization necessary to accomplish the goal—the organization of the priesthood—was already in place. He reminded them that this organization had been established by divine revelation and that all that was necessary for success was "to turn on the power and to start the wheels in motion."

On April 15, 1936, nine days after this historic meeting, Elder Lee was again asked to meet with the First Presidency. At that time, he was called to serve as the managing director of the Church security plan and to launch it churchwide among the organized stakes. This entailed his resignation as a Salt Lake City commissioner. He was also advised at that time that a central security committee would be organized under which he would serve in a manner like a board of directors. Because of the sensitivities this central committee would create with the Presiding Bishopric, which historically had principal authority and responsibility for temporal matters, he was also told that a member of the Twelve would be designated as the chairman of the central committee so as to give it authority over any objection raised by the Presiding Bishopric or by priesthood leaders in the field. Soon after, Elder Melvin J. Ballard of the Twelve was designated as the chairman of the central security committee, with Elder Lee and Mark Austin as members. Within a few months, Campbell M. Brown, Stringham Stevens, Henry D. Moyle, and William E. Ryberg were added to the committee. Once this central organization had been put in place and the general and local leaders had been advised of its existence and of the scope of its authority and responsibility, Elder Harold B. Lee had a track to run on and, as the managing director of the

Harold B. Lee as managing director of the Church Welfare Program, 1937, with secretary Ted DeBry

churchwide security plan, was in a position to begin to implement the welfare program he was so instrumental in formulating.

Elder Lee set up shop in an office provided for him in the Church Administration Building. In addition to necessary clerical help, he was provided with a secretary, Theodore M. DeBry, who also served as the secretary to the central committee. He was of vital assistance to Elder Lee as he began to work with local leaders in implementing the plan. For ease and efficiency in administration, the stakes of the Church were divided into regions. In each region, a stake president was designated as the regional chairman, with all the stake presidents in the region serving as an advisory regional council. There was a security council at the stake level, and the bishops of the wards in a stake were organized into a stake bishops council, with one of the bishops being designated as the chairman of the council. In an article he wrote, published in the April

Managing Director of the Church Welfare Plan

1937 issue of the *Improvement Era*, Elder Lee further sketched the existing Church priesthood and auxiliary organizations, which became part of the vast machinery of the Church welfare plan. "Reaching into every corner of the church," wrote he, "are organized quorums of the priesthood: 118 High Priests quorums with 20,214 members, 220 Seventies quorums with 13,621 members, 611 Elders quorums with 53,198 members, 850 Priests quorums, 820 Teachers quorums, 1351 Deacons quorums with a total membership of 79,953 — a mighty army of 167,000 'soldiers', organized and officered and supported by an equal army of Relief Society sisters whose ordained mission is to 'provoke the brethren to good works in looking after the wants of the poor in each quorum, and searching after objects of charity.' " (*Improvement Era*, Apr. 1937, pp. 209-10.)

Once he had been called into full-time service as the managing director of the Church security plan, Elder Lee lost little time getting into the field to organize and instruct the regional councils. The first such meeting he held was at Ogden, Utah, on April 21, 1936, six days after his call. From then until May 4, 1936, he held thirteen regional council meetings in the states of Utah, Idaho, California, and Arizona. At each one of these, a regional chairman and vice-chairman were appointed from among the stake presidents in attendance and instructions were given about how the program would roll out. In order to lend authority and support to the young managing director, Elder Melvin J. Ballard attended most of these meetings, introducing Elder Lee and then leaving to him the detailed instructions and training. Also, President Heber J. Grant attended a few of these meetings in order to give the authoritative endorsement of the First Presidency to what was being done. And, on a few occasions, Sylvester Q. Cannon participated in order to demonstrate the cooperation and the relationship between the Presiding Bishop and the welfare department of the Church. At some meetings, in addition to the usual instructions about welfare principles and organizational matters, there was discussion about production assignments that had already been given and about possible welfare projects. So, at a meeting held in Provo, Utah, on April 23, 1936, there was discussion about promoting truck garden projects and about acquiring an old sugar factory that could be converted into a cannery. At Nephi, Utah, on April 27 there was discussion about a wheat growing project and about the creation of a farmers cooperative. The next morning at Richfield, Utah, commercial fertilizer and lumber mill projects were considered while that evening at St. George, Utah, the local brethren talked about growing beet seed and semi-tropical fruit. May 1, 1936, found Elder Lee, Elder Ballard, and Bishop Cannon in Oakland, California, where there was discussion about organizing a storehouse to serve as a distributing point for Utah and Idaho produce.

It was here at Oakland that Elder Lee found the first signs of a phenomenon that had cropped up during the early days of the Pioneer Stake welfare effort. "Elder Ballard was disappointed," wrote he, "that opposition continued among a few in high places." Undoubtedly this was not the first place where those attending a welfare meeting had had some lingering doubts about the program, nor would it be the last. It was, however, the first place where the doubts had surfaced openly and where they had been expressed by persons who sat "in high places." While Elder Ballard was disappointed at this discovery, he most likely was not surprised by it. Indeed, it likely would have surprised the brethren had everyone accepted the plan without doubt or hesitancy. There seems to be an inertial quality in people that causes them, almost instinctively, to resist change, especially change as far-reaching as that which was contemplated by the security plan. This inertial quality finds an analogy in the law of physics that a body at rest tends to remain at rest unless acted upon by an external force, a concept that provides the basis for Sir Isaac Newton's first law of motion. The germ of the same idea is found in Lehi's instruction to his son Jacob that "it must needs be, that there is an opposition in all things." (2 Nephi 2:11.) Thus, the opposition to the security plan, which surfaced at Oakland, was not surprising, but it was disturbing. And this opposition was not limited to prominent persons in outlying areas but included some at Church headquarters.

In late April 1936 just before Elder Lee went to Oakland, he learned while in Salt Lake City that a story had been widely circulated that the welfare costs in caring for needy members of the Pioneer Stake had been much larger than those incurred in the adjoining Salt Lake Stake. The damaging effect of this story was spiked by compiling and publishing detailed statistics that revealed that almost twice as many persons were assisted in the Pioneer Stake as in the Salt Lake Stake at about one-half the per capita cost. This did not end the opposition, however, but only altered its focus. Because of his relative youth, Elder Lee became the target of some critics who characterized him as a boy wonder whose minimal experience as a high church leader did not qualify him to spearhead such a vast churchwide undertaking. Such criticism could have been devastating had not the First Presidency wisely installed a member of the Twelve as the chairman of the general committee and had they not given Elder Lee their unqualified support.

That support was dramatized at the October 1936 general conference. Until that time, the security plan had been implemented through priesthood channels without much general publicity. That changed at the first session of the conference held on October 2, 1936, when, in his keynote address, President Heber J. Grant read a message from the First Presidency, explaining and endorsing the security plan. It described the formation of the general committee of the plan, whose members were later identified by name in a report presented by President David O. McKay. It also explained that the functions of the general committee "were to represent the Presiding Bishopric in the detailed administrative work of coordinating and supervising the labors of the various regularly established church organizations in their large and important security operations." The message also explained the foundation upon which the plan rested and which, ever since, has been regarded as the basic charter of the Church welfare program. "Our primary purpose," it read, "was to set up, insofar as it might be possible, a system under which the curse of idleness would be done away with, the evils of a dole abolished, and independence, industry, thrift, and self-respect be once more established amongst our people. The aim of the church is to help people help themselves. Work is to be re-enthroned as the ruling principle of the lives of our church membership." (Conference Report, Oct. 1936, p. 3.)

In his remarks during the conference, President J. Reuben Clark stressed that as the security plan rolled out, its object would be twofold: To provide sustenance for the needy and to emphasize the overriding role of work in the plan of earth life. As to the latter, he said work "is the law of the earth." He added, "I wish it were within my power, as I know it is not, to express what is in my heart regarding this great plan, and to say how I feel about the dignity and honor of work." President Clark specifically commended the general committee, whose members were named, for "getting this security plan started." (Ibid., pp. 112–13.)

President David O. McKay's major conference sermon focused on another more pervasive and enduring facet of the plan. Said he, "It is something to supply clothing to the scantily clad, to furnish ample food to those whose table is thinly spread, to give activity to those who are fighting . . . the despair that comes from enforced idleness, but after all is said and done, the greatest blessings that will accrue from the church security plan are spiritual. Outwardly, every act seems to be directed toward the physical: remaking of dresses and suits of clothes, canning fruits and vegetables, storing foodstuffs . . . all seem strictly temporal, but permeating all these acts, inspiring and sanctifying them, is the element of spirituality." (Ibid., p. 103.)

Managing Director of the Church Welfare Plan

The preliminary reports of the various security projects made at the October 1936 general conference showed that significant progress had been made. These revealed that almost three hundred thousand cans of fruits and vegetables had been accumulated, along with large quantities of wheat, beans, dried fruit, flour, potatoes, and shelled corn. Also twenty-three thousand articles of men's, women's, and children's clothing had been accumulated, along with more than two thousand quilts.

Realizing this was but a start, Elder Lee and his associates, heeding the admonition of President Clark, "There is still work to do," aggressively continued their task of training and motivating local leaders. This entailed extensive travel into various parts of the western states where welfare projects were inspected and where council meetings were held to iron out problems of procedure and to answer questions about the plan.

As the end of the first year of the Church security plan approached, Elder Lee was asked to prepare an article for the *Improvement Era*, explaining its purpose and objectives, its accomplishments, and its future needs. It appeared in the April 1937 issue of the *Era* and was provocatively entitled "Church Security, Retrospect, Introspect, Prospect." In defining what the plan was, Elder Lee wrote, "By now it is clear to the minds of most people that the Church security plan is not something new to the church; neither does it contemplate a new organization within the church to carry out its purpose; but rather it is the expression of a philosophy that is as old as the church itself, incorporated into a program of stimulation and cooperation to meet the demands of church members in the solution of present day economic problems." (*Improvement Era*, April 1937, p. 204.) The format of the article seemed to be designed not only to explain the plan but to strengthen the hand of Elder Lee in administering it. The author was identified as the "Managing Director of the Church Security Plan and President of the Pioneer Stake." A large picture on the first page showed him seated at the side of President Heber J. Grant, and below this large picture were inset pictures of Presidents J. Reuben Clark and David O. McKay. On the second page were pictures of Elder Melvin J. Ballard and other members of the general committee on Church security: Mark Austin, Campbell M. Brown, Stringham A. Stevens, Henry D. Moyle, and William E. Ryberg. The third page contained pictures of the Presiding Bishopric: Sylvester Q. Cannon, David A. Smith, and John Wells. And on the fourth page were pictures of the general Relief Society presidency: Louise Y. Robison, Amy Brown Lyman, and Kate M. Barker. Also included were numerous pictures of food and other commodities produced and stored in various regional and stake storehouses and pictures of many chapels built or remodeled in connection with the program. The article also listed twenty-eight categories of projects that had been undertaken. These included canning or drying fruits, vegetables, and meats; sewing; farming; shoe manufacture and repair; logging; coal mining; the manufacture of temple and other garments; and making cement building blocks, sorghum, molasses, furniture, toys, mattresses, and disinfectants. As the author looked forward to the unfolding of the plan, he foresaw these five steps as being essential to its success: the elimination of idleness in the Church, developing a spirit of self-sacrifice, mastering the art of living and working together, practicing greater brotherhood in priesthood quorums, and acquiring the courage to meet the challenge of current problems. In these steps are seen the philosophical basis of what came to be known as the Church welfare plan—work, sacrifice, cooperation, brotherhood, and courage. This underscores why Elder Lee and others repeatedly said that there was nothing really new in the plan. It merely involved the application of age-old principles to help solve the problems of the day, and it will be readily seen that these basic principles could be called into play to solve other than temporal problems. So, challenges in the realm of intellect or spirit will as readily yield to these principles as will the challenge of economic want. It is apparent, therefore, that those who at the time, or later, viewed the plan only as a response or reaction to then current political or economic pressures missed the mark. Equally in error are those who failed to recognize the revelatory impetus that caused President Heber J. Grant to invoke these basic principles in helping to solve the economic crisis brought on the Latter-day Saints by the Great Depression. Those closest to the event have left their explanation as to how it occurred. "But there is still another way in which revelation comes," said President J. Reuben Clark, "and that way is through the ministration of the Holy Ghost. . . . Now I say unto you, that that kind of revelation, revelation of the Holy Ghost, did come to President Grant. Not only in this case, but in others. And through that revelation, inspiration if you wish to call it, from the Holy Ghost, President Grant launched this great welfare plan." (Address to Central Utah Welfare Regional Meeting at Brigham Young University, August 3, 1951.) In the same vein is this statement of President David O. McKay made at a meeting of the Salt Lake Welfare Region in February 1937: "That Church Security Plan has not come up as a mushroom over night. It is the result of inspiration and that inspiration has come from the Lord." Later, one of the principal actors in developing the welfare plan, Marion G. Romney, added his testimony to the others: "I believe I have made a rather complete study and I now testify to you that I do know beyond any doubt, by the same power that Peter knew that Jesus is the Christ, that the Church Welfare Plan in its inception was and now is inspired of the Lord; and that the great principles implemented by it are eternal truths, which the Saints of God must abide if they are to purify and perfect themselves as the Lord has commanded." (Conference Report, Oct. 1945, p. 156.)

As the security plan developed, much ingenuity was shown. Local leaders, anxious to develop projects that would fit into the overall plan, came up with creative ideas, some of which were approved. Others were turned down. Two that were rejected surfaced shortly after Elder Lee's article appeared in the *Improvement Era*. On April 29, 1937, he accompanied President McKay and others to Layton, Utah, to see a demonstration of the Bonham Brothers tractor. It had been proposed that the Church manufacture and market these machines under a franchising agreement. While they were impressed with the tractor, the security committee, after study, rejected the proposal as being infeasible. Not long afterwards, Elder Lee went to Tooele, Utah, with members of the committee to consider a proposal to divert water from Tooele Valley to Salt Lake Valley by means of a tunnel in order to irrigate fertile land on the east side of the Oquirrh Mountains. Again, the idea was rejected as being infeasible. Despite the lack of merit of these and other proposals, no attempt was made by the central committee to dampen the enthusiasm of the local leaders. All ideas to advance the work were given respectful consideration. Many were accepted and implemented; and others, like these two, were rejected. In this manner, step by step, and sometimes by trial and error, the Church welfare program developed.

Meanwhile, Elder Lee and other members of the central committee continued to teach welfare principles at every opportunity. On July 2, 1937, he participated in a meeting presided over by President David O. McKay. All General Authorities and all members of general boards were instructed there in the principles of Church welfare and were asked to support and to promote them. Despite this and notwithstanding the frequent expressions of support of the program by the General Authorities and the frequent visits of Elder Lee and other members of the central committee into the regions where welfare principles were taught, there continued to be much opposition to the plan.

This caused Elder Lee moments of discouragement and occasionally some apprehension. His appointment as the managing director of the plan had placed him in an awkward position. His duty to train local leaders in welfare principles and to supervise the development and operation of welfare projects intruded on responsibilities traditionally thought to belong to the Presiding Bishopric. This awkwardness was increased because the Presiding Bishop at the time was a former president of the Pioneer Stake, whose welfare program, developed under Elder Lee, was the prototype of the churchwide security plan. The fact that President Lee's first counselor in the stake presidency was also the chief staff assistant in the office of the Presiding Bishopric created another layer of concern. All this, added to the voices of opposition that were raised, placed the managing director of welfare under great personal stress. Had it not been for the unqualified support of the First Presidency, it is questionable whether Elder Lee could have withstood the pressure.

By 1937, the outside commitments of President Clark had been largely fulfilled so that he had begun to play the most active role in welfare among the members of the First Presidency. This had placed him into more frequent contact with Elder Lee, who had begun to regard the older man as his mentor. In turn, President Clark had begun to regard Harold Lee as a protégé and almost as a son. As this relationship developed, Elder Lee sought direct counsel from President Clark more frequently, a practice President Clark seemed to encourage. After their friendship had matured, President Clark began, in private, to address Elder Lee as "kid." On one occasion, during this period, Elder Lee had gone to President Clark for counsel when he expressed concern about the opposition he faced. After hearing him out, President Clark said, "Look, Kid, you continue to follow the course and it won't be long before they will all want to jump on the bandwagon." (As related to the author by President Lee.)

Buoyed up by the encouragement of President Clark, the other members of the First Presidency, and of Elder Ballard, the chairman of the central committee, Elder Lee struggled through the seemingly endless problems the security plan encountered. One of these involved the difficulty the owners of small homes had in complying with the recommendation to accumulate a store of food and clothing for future use. Some members lived in such cramped quarters there was no room for storage. Elder Lee raised this problem in one of his meetings with President Clark, who suggested that an old warehouse be obtained on the west side of Salt Lake City and that space be allocated in it to families whose homes lacked storage room. As they discussed this suggestion, which seemed to have some merit, it was decided to present it to the central committee for consideration. President Clark, anxious to learn how the committee would react, decided to attend the meeting where the proposal was to be considered. Knowing that if it were presented as his idea the members likely would be reluctant to express their true feelings, President Clark suggested that Elder Lee present it without divulging its source, which he did. The reaction was quite unexpected. Several members of the committee branded it as impractical if not foolish. During the entire discussion, President Clark sat quietly, never hinting that it was his brainchild being gored. Afterward when they were alone, President Clark said to Elder Lee, "Kid, you can see how lacking in imagination are those who trashed this idea and how soon the program would founder if they were in charge." (As related to the author by President Lee.)

In April 1937, a company was organized named the Cooperative Security Corporation, which handled the legal and financial transactions of the Church security program. Later that year, the federal social security legislation was passed. Out of concern that this might cause confusion, the name of the Church security program was changed to the Church welfare plan at the April 1938 general conference. Other significant changes made at that time had impact on the Church welfare plan and on Elder Lee's role as the managing director. Presiding Bishop Sylvester Q. Cannon and his counselors were released and were replaced by LeGrand Richards and his counselors, Marvin O. Ashton and Joseph L. Wirthlin. Also, about this time, Henry D. Moyle was appointed as the chairman of the general Church welfare committee and Elder Melvin J.

Managing Director of the Church Welfare Plan

Ballard, John A. Widtsoe, and Albert E. Bowen of the Twelve were designated as advisors to the general committee.

With intermittent changes in personnel, this welfare organization provided the leadership for a literal explosion of projects and facilities during the ensuing years. By 1964, the Church welfare plan included hundreds of enterprises located throughout the United States. Among these were over five hundred farming projects that produced soybeans, peas, hay, beans, sugar beets, peanuts, pineapples, cotton, grapefruit, oranges, and other crops. There were also numerous canneries that handled and processed these crops, as well as ranches or farms that produced cattle, hogs, and sheep. Along with these projects, numerous storehouses were constructed, which warehoused and distributed the foods and other commodities the welfare plan produced. In the process, there were developed companion enterprises designed to provide job opportunities and to improve work skills. Early on, Deseret Industries was organized, whose purpose was to repair, renovate, recycle, and resell used furniture, clothing, and other commodities donated to the system. Toward this end, factories were established where these commodities were renovated or renewed. They were then marketed through Deseret Industries retail stores. This creative system provided gainful employment for numerous people, many of whom would otherwise have been unemployable because of advanced age or physical disabilities. There also grew up an employment arm of the welfare plan, whose object was to help train and place the unemployed or to upgrade the skills of those who sought to improve their status. Later as the plan evolved, it came to embody the concept of "provident living," which embraced every aspect of human life, whether physical, mental, emotional, or spiritual. All of this grew out of the initiatives that were begun during the depression of the 1930s and were based upon timeless principles enunciated and reinforced by prophetic inspiration.

Harold B. Lee

Working under the direct supervision of the First Presidency, and later within the framework of the formal organization that came into being, Harold B. Lee was the key player in this extraordinary effort. It was he who, as the president of the Pioneer Stake, first demonstrated practically how the ageless principles of work, self-help, and cooperation could be applied on a large scale to help satisfy the economic wants of the people. It was he who, under assignment of the First Presidency, first designed the basic structure used to implement the goals of the Church security, later the Church welfare plan, and who formulated the basic job descriptions of the principal leaders. And it was he who, over the first formative years, provided the executive drive and acumen that overcame the initial inertia and opposition to the plan, established it on a firm foundation, and kept up the momentum as it continued to grow and strengthen.

As one reflects on the origin and the development of the Church welfare plan and on President Harold B. Lee's role in it, several things stand out. The first is the wide gulf between what it was at the beginning and what it became. The extraordinary growth that took place over the years illustrates an eternal principle that operates in every earthly endeavor and is succinctly stated in a revelation received by the Prophet Joseph Smith on September 11, 1831, which states in part: "And out of small things proceedeth that which is great." (D&C 64:33.) The second is the way in which the seed, which grew into the full-blown welfare plan, was planted in the minds of the First Presidency and Harold B. Lee. He explained the process in a talk given at the general priesthood meeting of the general conference when he was sustained as the president of the Church: "It was as though something were saying to me, 'There is no new organization necessary to take care of the needs of this people. All that is necessary is to put the priesthood of God to work.' " (Conference Report, Oct. 1972, p. 124.) The revelatory process, which this incident illustrates, lay at the root of Harold B. Lee's extraordinary

Managing Director of the Church Welfare Plan

personality and achievements. He repeatedly relied on such "illumination" or "whisperings" to chart his life's course.

The third thing that stands out is the disciplined and determined way in which he pursued the objective shown to him by revelation.

Chapter Eleven

The Newest Apostle

On February 9, 1941, Elder Reed Smoot of the Quorum of the Twelve Apostles passed away in St. Petersburg, Florida. He was seventy-nine years old at the time and had served as a member of the Twelve for almost forty-one years. During that period he had also served for many years as a United States Senator, representing the state of Utah. Elder Smoot had not been well for some time and had gone to Florida to get away from the cold of a harsh Utah winter and to try to regain his health. His passing, therefore, was not entirely unexpected, but it still was a great shock to his family and friends and, for that matter, to the entire Church.

Those who comprise the Quorum of the Twelve Apostles occupy a position of special importance in the minds and hearts of the Latter-day Saints. These are the special witnesses of the life and ministry of Him for whom the Church was named and of His divinity as the Savior and Redeemer of the world. Aside from that special role played by these men, they hold a special fascination for Church members because the induction of a person into

The Newest Apostle

that body holds out the prospect that he may one day become the prophet of the Church. This is so because of the principle of apostolic seniority that has become firmly imbedded in the government of the Church. Under that principle, upon the death of a Church president, the senior surviving apostle immediately becomes the de facto head of the Church due to his status as the president of the Quorum of the Twelve Apostles, which is then, because of the dissolution of the First Presidency at the death of the prophet, the presiding quorum of the Church. That de facto status is later confirmed and made official by his ordination under the hands of the other members of the Twelve, thereby investing him officially with the keys of authority necessary to direct the Church. These keys were conferred upon him in a suspended form at the time of his ordination as an apostle and his induction into the Twelve. So the prospect that a newly ordained member of the Twelve may one day become the president of the Church creates an unusual sense of anticipation among the Latter-day Saints as to the identity of the one to be called to fill a vacancy in the Twelve.

The passing of Elder Smoot, therefore, touched off the customary speculations about who would be called to fill the vacancy. There were many able men around whom these speculations centered, men who had served as stake or mission presidents or who had distinguished themselves in business, in education, or in the professions. The youngest among the potential candidates, and the one ultimately selected, was Elder Harold B. Lee, former stake president and Salt Lake City commissioner and the incumbent managing director of the Church welfare department. Elder Lee's call was probably a surprise to some because of a perception that the Brethren might not want to upset the smooth flow in the development of the welfare plan. However, this would not have been of critical significance to President Heber J. Grant, who made the decision and extended the call. The thing of significance to him would have been a spiritual witness or confirmation attesting that

Harold B. Lee was the one the Lord wanted to fill the vacancy. While we are left to wonder precisely when the spiritual witness, or confirmation, came to President Grant, we know that it came to Elder Lee the morning of April 5, 1941. "Before I arose from my bed," he wrote under that date, "I received a definite impression that I would be named a member of the Quorum of the Twelve." Elder Lee was no stranger to impressions of this kind. Indeed, they were experiences of frequent occurrences, similar to the one he had as a little boy when he was warned to stay away from the fallen barn. Repeatedly thereafter, he received other spiritual impressions, or whisperings, which came to him by way of warning, or encouragement, or foreknowledge, or to point out what he should or should not do. These were the spiritual illuminations that lighted his way and by which he governed his conduct. So when he received this impression as he lay in bed that Saturday morning, he had confidence it would occur. Yet, the impression was not sufficiently explicit to confirm that he would be called to the Twelve to fill the vacancy created by the death of Elder Smoot. So, it is inferred that Elder Lee's anticipation was tinged with some uncertainty as he arose to prepare for the day.

There was much stirring that morning, which prevented Elder Lee from dwelling at length on what had been revealed to him. The house was brimming with guests, a customary condition at conference time. Harold's cousin, William H. Prince, and his entire family were visiting from St. George. Also, Mabel Hickman, a long-time friend of the family, whom Elder Lee had been instrumental in converting in Denver twenty years before, was staying with the Lees. This, together with the presence of two teenaged daughters, whose meticulous grooming standards, even without company, strained the limits of the family bathroom facilities, prompted their father to rise early to shave and shower and, after a light breakfast, to leave the home. After checking at his office at 47 East South Temple to see if any urgent matters had surfaced, Elder

The Newest Apostle

Lee went to the Tabernacle for the Saturday morning session of conference.

The general conference had convened the day before with two general sessions and was scheduled to continue through Sunday, April 6. According to the usual pattern, it was expected the General Authorities would be presented for sustaining vote on Sunday, the anniversary of the organization of the Church. However, it was not uncommon for the Brethren to deviate from the usual routine when special circumstances required it. Therefore, no one except those in the inner circle knew for certain when the General Authorities would be presented for sustaining vote. And because there had been cases when calls to the Twelve had been made from the pulpit without prior notification, Elder Lee was in a quandary as to whether his name might be read out as the new member of the Twelve at either the morning or afternoon session on Saturday. When this did not happen, the tension increased with the knowledge that the matter would be resolved one way or the other on Sunday.

Neither by word nor by intimation did Elder Lee receive a hint from the Brethren throughout Saturday that he was to be called to succeed Elder Smoot. However, at the end of the general priesthood meeting held in the Tabernacle Saturday night, April 5, an announcement was made that Harold B. Lee was to confer with Bishop Joseph L. Wirthlin on the stand. There was nothing unusual in this to alert Elder Lee as to what was afoot because he was in frequent contact with Bishop Wirthlin on welfare matters. However, when afterwards Joseph Anderson, the secretary to the First Presidency, told Elder Lee that President Heber J. Grant wanted to see him in the General Authorities room behind the pulpit, he knew instantly that something unusual was about to happen. "It amazed me," he wrote, "and I immediately sensed that there was something more than just a social visit that President Grant had in mind." When the two of them were alone, the eighty-four-year-old prophet told his young friend, who was only half his age, having turned forty-two just nine days before, that he had been chosen to fill the vacancy in the Twelve caused by the death of Elder Smoot. "Oh, President Grant," Elder Lee responded, "do you really think I am worthy of such an exalted calling?" The old prophet's answer must have been reassuring. "If I didn't think so, my boy, you wouldn't be called."

In that brief moment, Harold B. Lee was elevated to a place of eminence reached only by a select few. It placed him within a small circle of men who, under inspiration, chart the earthly destiny of The Church of Jesus Christ of Latter-day Saints. And, it put him in the chairs, so to speak, which in the normal course of events would lead him to the prophetic office President Grant then occupied. That, in turn, would invest him with vast authority as to people, property, and programs all around the world. Yet, with that would come correlative responsibilities of crushing weight as the master of all would become the servant of all. In this process, Elder Lee would discover a fine irony — that the modest living allowance provided for General Authorities (which, incidentally, is not paid from tithes but from the income of Church-owned companies) was less than the salaries earned by some Church staff personnel. This reality would serve to underscore the dominant spiritual aspects of the apostolic calling as compared to those of a temporal nature.

The Harold B. Lee who left the Tabernacle that Saturday night was hardly the same man who entered it earlier. Outwardly it would have been difficult to detect a difference, except, perhaps, for a certain air of distracted nervousness that a careful appraisal of him might have revealed. Inwardly, however, a major revolution had undoubtedly taken place. While it is impossible for us to know precisely what went on in Elder Lee's mind as a result of this call, his later conduct, comments, and writings enable us to make a reasonable estimate. He knew that the course of his life had been irrevocably changed and that things would never be the same. He knew, also, that his life and that of his family would thereafter be subjected to the most intense scrutiny both by the loving, supportive members of the Church and by the critics and detractors of the Latter-day Saints. And he knew that his elevation to the highest echelons of Church leadership would radically alter his relationship with friends and associates he had known and with whom he had worked over the years. He had been around long enough to know of the idealized perception held toward members of the Twelve and of the tendency to defer to them and generally to ascribe to them superior qualities of knowledge and judgment in all matters. And he knew that these attitudes might tempt him to arrogate special qualities of character to himself, forgetting that such adulation is largely directed toward the apostolic office, not toward the individual who occupies it.

While it may be that any such thoughts were not formulated with completeness or coherency at the time but existed there only in a vague, amorphous state, there was one thought that, it is inferred, was crystal clear and upon which he acted promptly. That was to share what had happened to him with his family. Arriving home, he found Fern and Helen entertaining the house guests and making preparations for the next day's menus. On learning that Maurine had called asking to be picked up at a friend's home, Elder Lee volunteered to go get her, but insisted that Fern and Helen accompany him. Since it was after ten, they thought this strange but complied, as Helen explained it, "because of his serious manner and insistent voice." Alone in the car, he told them what had happened. He acted "very quietly and obviously more subdued in manner than I ever remember my father being before . . . ," Helen explained. (*Harold B. Lee, Prophet and Seer*, p. 159.) Later Maurine was informed of what had happened. Returning home, the four of them had a private family prayer in the parents' bedroom before retiring.

In a sense, the events of the next day were anticlimactic as far as Elder Lee and the members of his immediate family were concerned. By then, the shock of his call had subsided, and he and Fern and the girls had adjusted their thinking to the reality of what had happened and of what lay ahead. However, among the audience assembled in the Tabernacle on Sunday morning, April 6, 1941, there was an air of great expectancy. The Saints had gathered with the knowledge that a new member of the Twelve likely would be sustained. When the name of Harold B. Lee was announced, a quiet murmur spread through the audience, caused perhaps by a combination of surprise and approval. Because of his visible role in Church welfare during the preceding six years, Elder Lee was widely known in the Church and was admired for his administrative skills, his spirituality, and his eloquence. However, for the reasons already mentioned, he was not generally regarded as the prime candidate for the call along the Mormon grapevine. When the new apostle was invited to take his place on the stand, the sense of surprise among the audience was accentuated. Daughter Helen captured the essence of this historic moment in these words: "It created a lasting picture when my father went up and sat by the side of Brother Cannon, who had snowy white hair. When the audience stood up during the rest break midway in the two-hour session, I remember how startled I was to see all of the members of the Council of the Twelve standing in their places before us. The contrast was graphic. There stood Brother Cannon, tall and stately with his beautiful, white hair, and next to him was my father, who was much shorter, with his black hair, which gave him a youthful appearance. He almost looked like he didn't belong, for he was so much younger than the next youngest of the men who were then members of the Council of the Twelve. It came as a new and rather surprising realization to me to consider how much younger he was than the other brethren." (Ibid., pp. 161–62.)

Helen's perception was most likely shared by the entire audience. The average age of the other members of the Twelve was seventy-one years, twenty-nine years older than Elder Lee. The oldest of them was eighty-four-year-old Rudger Clawson, the president of the Quorum, who was born in 1857, only a decade after the Saints arrived in the Salt Lake Valley. The youngest, next to Elder Lee, was Stephen L. Richards, age 62. But differences in chronological age and the color of her father's hair were not the only factors that may have caused Helen and others to feel that Harold B. Lee "didn't belong" in that group. It included one member, Rudger Clawson, who was ordained to the apostleship a year before Elder Lee was born; two university professors, John A. Widtsoe and Joseph F. Merrill (Elder Widtsoe also having served as a university president); a historian, Joseph Fielding Smith; and three lawyers: Stephen L. Richards, Charles A. Callis, and Albert E. Bowen. Cumulatively, these eleven men represented 239 years of apostolic service, years during which they had borne the principal burden in the direction of the Church. They, with the members of the First Presidency, were chiefly responsible for its recent growth and development under divine inspiration. Elder Lee's diary entry for that day hints that he, too, may have entertained some feelings of inadequacy in joining that distinguished body. Wrote he, "I was sustained before the general conference at the ten o'clock session by President J. Reuben Clark, Jr., after which I was invited to a place on the stand 'at the foot of the ladder,' as he expressed it, a member of the Twelve."

But despite his youth, Elder Lee brought special distinctions to the Twelve, which few, and in some respects, none of his brethren possessed. Except for Elders Clawson and Cannon, none of them had served as a stake president as he had done; none of them had held elective office as he had done; none of them had had such wide experience in welfare matters as Elder Lee; and, except for Elders Lyman, Widtsoe, and Merrill, none of them could match his experience as an educator, whether in teaching or administration. A special distinction Elder Lee brought to his new calling, which he shared in common with all the other members of the Twelve, was a personal, spiritual testimony and witness that Jesus Christ lives and is the

Savior and Redeemer of the world and the head of the earthly Church that bears His name.

This general conference was also notable because five other Brethren were added to the roster of General Authorities when Marion G. Romney, Thomas E. McKay, Clifford E. Young, Alma Sonne, and Nicholas G. Smith were sustained as Assistants to the Twelve. This was a new category of General Authorities, ordained high priests, who would be able to relieve some of the burdens on the Twelve in ways the First Council of the Seventy were unable to do because of limitations under which they then served. Through his service as the managing director of the Church welfare plan, Elder Lee had become well acquainted with all of these brethren, but he had a special relationship with two of them, Elders Romney and Smith.

Some time after Elder Lee became the managing director of Church welfare, he and Elder Joseph Anderson, who was then the secretary to the First Presidency, and Elder Nicholas G. Smith, who was then serving as the acting Patriarch to the Church, organized a Church history study group comprised of these brethren and their wives, who met regularly to study Church history and to socialize. In time, others were added to this group, including Marion G. Romney and Hugh B. Brown. Five days after Elders Lee, Romney, and Smith were sustained in their new callings, their study group met in the home of Roscoe and Irene Hammond, where the three new General Authorities were honored. Elder Lee commented on that gathering in his diary under date of April 11, 1941: "There was an excellent spirit in the gathering," wrote he, "in no small part due to the splendid attitude manifested by Hugh B. Brown who had been prominently mentioned for appointment to fill the vacancy in the Quorum of Twelve." This unusual group, whose membership included Elders Lee, Romney, and Brown, who were ultimately elevated to the Twelve and then to the First Presidency; Elder Lee, who became the president of the Church; Elders Smith and Anderson, who became Assistants to the Twelve; and Elder

The Newest Apostle

Anderson, who became a member of the First Quorum of the Seventy when that quorum was reconstituted, also included other distinguished members like Heber Meeks, a prominent political leader who later became the president of the Southern States Mission and the first general manager of the Church's large ranch near Deer Park, Florida, and John Wahlquist, distinguished educator who became the president of a university in California. The wives of these brethren, who in their own right possessed qualities of intelligence and character equal to their husbands, added a vital element to this group that met intermittently over the years to share knowledge and testimony about the Church and its doctrines, to socialize, and to compare notes about raising children and nurturing grandchildren. Aside from their immediate families, this group appears to have exerted a more powerful and enduring influence on the personal lives of its members than almost any others.

The day before these new General Authorities were honored by their study group, Elder Lee enjoyed one of the crowning experiences of his life when he was ordained to the apostleship and set apart as a member of the Quorum of the Twelve Apostles. Earlier in the week, on Tuesday, April 8, 1941, Elder Lee was briefed by his mentor on what to expect in the upper room of the temple. "I went to lunch with President Clark," he noted in his diary on that day, "where he gave me careful and detailed explanations of the procedure on Thursday, where I was to be ordained an Apostle in the temple and accept a charge from the President of the Church as to my duties, obligations, and responsibilities as a member of the Quorum of the Twelve."

On the appointed day, Harold B. Lee entered the fabled "upper room" of the Salt Lake Temple for the first time. No picture or description of the room could have prepared him for the impact the experience would have upon him. The mystique that has built up around the room over the years because of frequent, veiled references made to it and to things that have taken place there, cannot fail to create a sense of wonder, or even awe, in one who enters it for the first time. Aside from this, the actual appearance of the room conveys a clear visual impression of its purpose, its historical significance, and the reason why it bears the name "council room." Arranged in a sweeping semicircle are twelve large easy chairs, facing the west side of the room, and so positioned that each member of the Twelve seated there can see all the others. Facing this semicircle is a desk, behind which, against the west wall, are positioned three other matching, upholstered chairs intended for the First Presidency. To the right and south of the First Presidency's desk and chairs, adjacent to the semicircle, stands a second desk for the use of the secretary. The only other pieces of furniture in the room are a third desk, standing against the south wall beyond the semicircle of chairs, which holds scriptures and reference books, a small bookcase in the southeast corner of the room, a movable altar used during prayer circles, a sacrament table with an upholstered stool for use by the one offering the kneeling sacramental prayer, and an organ with its bench, used to accompany the singing, which stands in the northwest corner of the room. It would not be long before Elder Lee's skill at the organ would earn him the role of "official" organist for the meetings of the Council of the First Presidency and Quorum of the Twelve, a role in which he would serve for almost thirty years, and which he would relinquish to Spencer W. Kimball only after he became a member of the First Presidency. On the walls of this unusual room hang portraits of all the former presidents of the Church, as also a portrait of the martyr Hyrum Smith, and three paintings of the Savior depicting him calling his disciples at the Sea of Galilee, on the cross, and at the tomb standing before Mary after his resurrection. The heavy carpeting in this isolated room, which produces a quiet hush on it, and the furniture, arranged as explained, create an atmosphere conducive to careful and deliberate council by the apostolic brethren who direct the worldwide affairs of The Church of Jesus Christ of Latter-day Saints. The

The Newest Apostle

imposing presence of the portraits and paintings described conveys the impression that all the deceased modern prophets, as well as heaven, are looking down and listening in on the deliberations going on there.

The deliberations of Thursday, April 10, 1941, were of special significance, not only to Elder Lee, but also to the entire Church. To him, they once and for all time placed him in a select circle of distinction from which he would never be removed, except by death or misconduct. Throughout the remainder of his days, he could look forward to returning to this room, again and again, to counsel with his brethren, to report his activities, and to be renewed in his spirituality and in his resolve to serve with diligence and discipline until the end of his life. This continual, unending routine, laden with the diverse joys and traumas of the conflict between light and darkness, has been called the "imperious mandate." To the Church, these deliberations meant that another distinguished name had been added to the select list of special witnesses of the divinity and mission of the Savior, Jesus Christ, and that the newest apostle had been set on a path whose tortuous and testing course could lead him ultimately to the prophetic office.

The procedure followed in the temple this day was one whose origin extended back to the dawn of the restored church. After the preliminaries of song and prayer, and after the newest member had taken his place anchoring the north end of the semicircle, the aged, bearded Prophet Heber J. Grant turned toward Elder Lee and, in slow, measured words, delivered the apostolic charge to him. Once this charge had been given by the prophet, Elder Lee was asked to respond to it, and then to express himself. With quiet humility, he accepted the charge without qualification, and then shared things of a personal, sacred nature.

After this part of the ceremony had been completed, a chair was placed within the circle. When Elder Lee had been seated there, the other members of the council surrounded him, placing their hands on his head. With President Grant acting as voice, he was then ordained an apostle and set apart as a member of the Quorum of the Twelve. In the ordination, he was given all the keys and authority necessary to lead the Church, although at the time, these were only in a suspended form and were to become operative only upon the happening of future events—that he survive to become the senior, living apostle, and that he then be ordained as the prophet of the Church by the united action of the other living apostles.

When this procedure was completed, Harold Bingham Lee had officially taken his place as the sixty-first apostle inducted into the Quorum of the Twelve Apostles in this dispensation. He was then finally launched on the voyage, sometimes turbulent and sometimes placid, which would ultimately bring him to the prophetic office to which he had been foreordained before the dawn of time.

Chapter Twelve

The Family behind the Man

Harold B. Lee was the same man after April 10, 1941, as he was before. Yet he was different. The difference lay largely in his self-perception and in the way others perceived him. His youth, his spirituality, and his achievements created a widespread perception that he would one day be the president of the Church. This and the normal reaction of the Saints toward one newly elevated to the Twelve produced an outpouring of love and congratulations that was astonishing. "In the days to follow," Elder Lee confided to his journal, "I was able to do little else than to receive telephone calls and letters of congratulation from many friends on my appointment as a member of the Council of the Twelve. It was pleasing that many of these were from those who were not members of the Church, with whom I had associated in politics or in business." This flood of excitement spilled over to affect the entire Lee family. "I remember that we had never been so busy," wrote youngest daughter, Helen, "with people coming to the home and calling on the phone. These were beautiful, warm memories. It was a tremendous time in our lives. We heard from people that we hadn't heard from for years and years." (*Harold B. Lee, Prophet and Seer,* p. 163.)

One effect of Elder Lee's call was to place the entire family on a pedestal where their actions were under the most careful scrutiny. He was fortunate in that there were no chinks in the armor of his inner circle. His wife, Fern, possessed a character and personality ideally suited for one who was the companion of a person such as he. She was quiet and unassuming, spiritually sensitive, and a gracious hostess. The home she had created was one of refinement and culture, tastefully decorated and immaculately maintained. Yet, it was not of such an appearance as would make one feel uncomfortable for fear of disturbing or breaking something. It was a home to be lived in and enjoyed, not only by the immediate family but also by the numerous relatives, friends, and associates who came there.

While the role Fern played as the genial and gracious hostess of this home and the catalyst of the order and peace that prevailed there was vital, her role as her husband's sweetheart, counselor, and confidant was of far greater significance. There was no one whose judgment or counsel Harold Lee was more willing to accept than that of his wife Fern. She was blessed with the gift of discernment, which enabled her to detect any signs of insincerity or deviousness in those who sought association with her husband or her daughters. And behind her demure and gentle exterior, which was not feigned but was inherent and habitual, lay a willpower of the most determined and inflexible kind. Anyone who thought this retiring, inoffensive lady was an easy mark, or was one who could be easily manipulated or controlled, was due for a rude awakening.

The influences that Fern Lee exerted upon her husband were subtle and were hardly discernible by outsiders. She was four years older than he, and this, added to the faster maturation rate of women and their greater tendency toward spirituality, provided a bulwark of strength and support for Harold B. Lee that cannot be minimized. It is apparent that Fern's influence was paramount in Elder Lee's decision to leave the safe and secure niche he had carved out in education. It was her unqualified encouragement, too, which helped him toward success in the business world. While she had some misgivings when her husband entered politics, once he became involved, she was a wise advisor, who gave sound counsel about critical issues, about his political plans, or about any political ally or opponent she perceived as posing a danger to him. As for Harold B. Lee's role in the Church, it is clear that from the beginning of their acquaintance, she felt instinctively he was destined for greatness. This vague, yet powerful, impression was affirmed repeatedly as she saw her husband steadily rise in the ranks of Church leadership and as she saw the results of his creative initiatives.

There is one additional aspect of the relationship between this pair that deserves special mention. Alongside his loving, kindly nature, there was an impetuous quality in Elder Lee's personality, tinged with a certain combativeness. It was a compelling quality that, it is believed, contributed significantly to the high achievements he attained. Yet, Fern's gentle but firm nature seems occasionally to have laid a mild restraint on her husband's conduct, smoothing ruffled feelings and minimizing any negative fallout.

This quality in Elder Lee's character, and Fern's influence on it, is best described by daughter Helen. "My father's personality," wrote she, "was one of being very quick, moving ahead into a situation, making a decision and taking action promptly, regardless of whether the given situation was in church work, employment, or in a family setting. He needed the influence of a wife who would say to him, as Mother would, 'Now, dear, you need to think about this and you must not fail to look at the other side of the situation.' " It is significant, however, that this appraisal, made from the perspective of a young daughter during the early years of her father's maturity, differs from the characteristics seen in the fully mature Harold B. Lee after more than three decades of apostolic service. By that time, there were few people who were more calm, deliberate, and careful in looking at all sides before making a decision than was he. In this change is seen good evidence of President Lee's capacity for growth.

It is noted, parenthetically, that this quality, which was more evident in Brother Lee's younger years, can be discerned in the lives of other notable leaders. Consider Peter's impetuous action in jumping into the sea to walk on water toward the beckoning Savior. Or think of the instances in Brigham Young's life when he boldly attacked his enemies or chastised his brethren, conduct he had occasionally observed in his mentor, Joseph Smith.

These contrasting yet complementary characteristics of Harold and Fern Lee, added to their mutual love and their shared qualities of compassion and concern for others, combined to create a favorable environment for their daughters, Maurine and Helen. Separated in age by only a few months, these girls were almost like twins in size and appearance, but were different in personality. From their earliest years, they were taught to do things together and to look out for each other. This relationship continued throughout their growing-up years and followed them into the university, where they shared sorority activities and where it was not uncommon for them to double date. Early on, through the encouragement of their parents, they were introduced to the pleasures and the discipline of music. Maurine was trained in piano and Helen in the violin. These musical skills, with those of the parents, added a special, cultural tone to the home as music became a routine part of family gatherings. As the girls matured, these skills, their close relationship, and the wise encouragement of their parents made the Lee home a favorite place for gatherings of young people. Here the Lee girls and their friends were sure to find a welcome mat out for dancing on the patio, for refreshments, or for visiting with Elder Lee who always made himself available to talk to and to counsel

The Family behind the Man

Elder Harold B. Lee with his wife Fern Tanner Lee and daughters, Helen and Maurine

and to motivate young people. Frequently when the girls hosted gatherings at their home, their father would spend many hours beforehand manicuring the yards, painting and fixing up, and arranging the lights and furniture. Also, he would sometimes pitch in during the party to barbecue the meat, flip hamburgers, or otherwise make himself useful so the young people could enjoy themselves.

At the time Elder Lee was called to the Twelve, the place his family called home was located at 1208 South Eighth West (now Ninth West). It was a large, two-story, brick home, set on a big lot, whose backyard extended to the Jordan River. In the front yard were large shade trees, shrubbery, flower beds, and a wide expanse of lawn. In the backyard, which Elder Lee landscaped, were found more lawn and flowers, as well as fruit trees and, in season, a vegetable garden. Until the time the Lees sold this home in the late 1940s, Elder Lee did most of the work maintaining the yards and the exterior of the house. He also did most of the interior painting and was Fern's chief assistant during the annual spring housecleaning, which was a truly major undertaking. When Elder Lee's car needed washing or polishing, he did it himself, although when his daughters provided him with sons-in-law, they sometimes did it if they were available.

Because he did not engage in recreational sports, Elder Lee's work around the home was his recreation. But because there was so much of it to do, given the large size of his house and yard, and because there was so little time in which to do it because of his many outside duties, he had to hustle to get it done. We are again indebted to daughter Helen for this revealing insight: "He moved like lightning," she wrote in explaining how he was able to handle the heavy chores at home. "His movements were always very quick, and I suppose that as he became busier, and his life became more complicated, he compensated by just running at top speed to accomplish everything. This was especially true of the case demanded by the big yard around our home. He could cut a lawn faster than any man I ever knew, including our young, vigorous sons. He'd just tear back and forth, up and down, and if you had to deliver a message to him or say something to him, you would have to run along with him back and forth across the lawn, because he never stopped. Even mother had to do this if it was necessary for her to report a telephone message to him." (*Harold B. Lee, Prophet and Seer*, p. 128.)

At the time of Elder Lee's call to the Twelve, Maurine was seventeen and Helen sixteen. By then they were accomplished musicians who were frequently invited to play piano and violin duets at church and other gatherings. As word of their skill first spread when they were younger, they received invitations to play in different parts of the city. Before the girls learned to drive, it was not uncommon for their father to chauffeur them to their engagements if he were available. It was a service he enjoyed rendering as it provided him with a chance to visit his daughters and also to hear them perform, something he never tired of doing.

As Maurine and Helen matured, especially after entering the university, they had questions about the doctrines of the Church, raised by teachers or classmates or by their own inquisitiveness. Invariably they would pose them to their father, whom they considered to be an inexhaustible fount of knowledge. But being the skilled teacher he was, Elder Lee seldom answered outright but responded either by adroit questioning or by direct reference to the scriptures where the girls could read the answers for themselves. He was never abrupt with them or condescending on these occasions, but he treated them with the respect and dignity he would give to an adult.

It must not be inferred that the Lee household always functioned on an unbroken plane of peaceful accord. There were times of upset and disagreement, which most often arose from scheduling conflicts or dating practices. But these were not of a serious, persistent nature but were only occasional and, actually, quite trivial.

In essence, therefore, the family of Harold B. Lee was one characterized by love, scholarship, unity, and industry, which functioned in a gracious, well-ordered environment where music was frequently heard and where service to others and to the Church were dominant themes. It was, accordingly, a family that could be held up to the Church as a model for others to emulate. In this fact, Elder Lee found one of the most potent sources of strength and justification in his apostolic ministry.

Surrounding this inner core of family were a few other relatives who were frequently brought into special family events and celebrations. These were his parents and his youngest sister, Verda; and, after Verda married in 1946, her husband, Charles J. Ross, fondly called Uncle Chick by the girls, was added to the group. There was, of course, a congenial relationship with other members of the extended family, but contacts with them were less frequent and were not of the same intimate nature as were those with the ones just named. Later, as we shall see, when the daughters married, their husbands and the grandchildren occupied places of special favor in Elder Lee's estimation.

Beyond the scope of those related by blood or marriage were a select few who were drawn into the Lee family orbit, occupying a special status there. These are typified by the Hickman sisters, especially Mabel, whose relationship with Harold and Fern extended back to the missionary days in Denver. And, of course, in the years ahead, after Fern's passing, Joan Jensen Lee came into Elder Lee's life to play a vital role of love and companionship during the later apostolic years and during the years he served in the First Presidency.

Chapter Thirteen

The First Apostolic Years

Once Elder Lee was ordained to the apostleship and was set apart as a member of the Twelve in April 1941, he immediately began to function in this new and intimidating role. It was intimidating, in large part, because of the high expectations the Saints have for members of the Twelve and the First Presidency who are in a class apart from all other leaders of the Church. These are the special witnesses of the Savior who bear responsibility to testify about His divinity and His atoning sacrifice in all the world.

The magnitude of this responsibility seems to have created a sense of inadequacy in Elder Lee during the first weeks of his ministry. His first assignment as an apostle was to accompany Elder Charles A. Callis to the conference of the Salt Lake Riverside Stake over the weekend beginning Saturday, April 12, 1941, two days after his ordination. Since the Riverside Stake was adjacent to the Pioneer Stake, where Elder Lee had presided, one would have thought he would have been at ease there among Saints who knew him well. It was not so. "I had extreme difficulty expressing myself," he noted in his diary. "Things I said seemed to lack spirit and enthusiasm." The following week found him at a stake conference in Vernal, Utah, where he had a similar experience. "Somewhat disappointed at my difficulty in gaining the freedom of speech necessary for a satisfying feeling." Over a month later, he experienced the same thing when on May 25 he delivered the graduation address at Snow College, located in Ephraim, Utah. "Dissatisfied with my efforts," he wrote of the event.

Soon after this, however, he seems to have gotten rid of these negative feelings about his public addresses and began to get into a satisfying rhythm. He had great freedom, accompanied apparently by a sense of satisfaction, in delivering the baccalaureate address at Brigham Young University on June 1, 1941.

Elder Lee's call to the apostleship shed a light of distinction over the Cache Valley and surrounding areas where he was born and raised. It at once marked him as one of its most distinguished alumni and caused him to become an object of great demand by those living there who wanted to honor him. Elder Lee accepted as many of these requests as he was able to fit into his schedule. On May 30, he spoke at a special service in Wellsville. With him were Fern and the two girls and his parents. Afterward, they drove on to Clifton, visiting the old farm where Harold was born and raised and other places of interest, both in Clifton and in the neighboring towns of Dayton and Oxford. He was the honored guest and speaker at the annual "Idaho Days" celebration at Franklin, Idaho. Also present to honor him was Idaho Governor Chase Clark. Of the occasion, Elder Lee wrote: "At the celebration were many of those whom I had known as a boy." A month later, Elder Lee was a special guest at the July 24 Pioneer Celebration at Bancroft where, again, he was lauded and lionized as the Church's newest apostle and as a native son of Idaho.

Such was his newfound notoriety that old friends and neighbors sought to rekindle their relationship by inviting

The First Apostolic Years

him to speak at funerals or other special meetings, or by paying courtesy calls to reminisce about the old days before he became famous. So on June 27, Elder Lee travelled back to Clifton at the urgent request of the family of the deceased to speak at the funeral of a well-known townsman called "Uncle Joe Howell" by one and all, whether or not they were related by blood. Several days earlier, Elder Lee's former debating coach, A. D. Erickson, came to discuss old times and to remind him of incidents when the apostle was his student.

These incidents reveal a phenomenon experienced by anyone raised to a position of public prominence. Like moths attracted to a flame, or filings to a magnet, many seek to connect themselves with a person in the public eye, whether to bask in reflected glory or merely to express support and congratulations. The phenomenon, while flattering to the one experiencing it, carries the deadly danger of attributing the public attention strictly to personal qualities rather than to the prominence of the new position. It was a danger of which Elder Lee was fully aware and with which he struggled with notable success throughout his ministry.

Soon after his ordination, Elder Lee began to perform temple marriages, an activity that, in the future, would occupy an ever-increasing amount of his time. "Performed my first temple marriage," for John P. Gleave, Jr., and his bride, he noted on April 12, 1941. "Doctor John Gleave is the father of the bridegroom."

The second temple marriage he performed united Glen L. Rudd and Marva Sperry, two young people from the Pioneer Stake. The bridegroom would later be associated with Elder Lee in welfare work and would look to him as a mentor. Many years after Elder Lee's death, Glen Rudd would be called as a member of the Seventy.

Numerous couples, attracted by his youth and spirituality, sought a special relationship with Elder Lee through the distinction that he had performed their temple sealing. When it was learned he was accommodating, many flocked to him, though they often lacked any significant personal relationship. The counsel Elder Lee gave to newlyweds usually focused on mutual love and consideration, obedience to the commandments, and cleanliness of thought, word, and action in their marital relations.

Doctor Gleave mentioned above was the patriarch of the Bonneville Stake and was seated in the Tabernacle beside his stake president, Marion G. Romney, when, without previous notice, Brother Romney was named as the first Assistant to the Twelve. It was a source of mutual satisfaction that Elder Romney was appointed to serve as the assistant managing director of the welfare department under Elder Lee.

Thus began a close relationship between these two powerful men, which would extend over more than thirty-two years. It would end with President Lee's death in December 1973, eighteen months after the prophet had called Marion G. Romney as his second counselor in the First Presidency.

Actually, this acquaintance began in the early 1930s when Harold was the president of the Pioneer Stake. They first met in a grocery store on Thirteenth East in Salt Lake City. The store manager, who was Elder Lee's brother-in-law, introduced the pair. "He was dressed in striped coveralls," Elder Romney recalled in his sermon delivered at President Lee's funeral. "His left hand was on his breast, and he reached out his right to shake my hand. Captivated by his magnetic presence, I felt I had found a friend." That friendship grew into a personal relationship when, a few years later, they and their wives and others became associated in a study group. When Marion G. Romney was called as the president of the Bonneville Stake in 1938, he acquired an ecclesiastical relationship with his friend through Elder Lee's role as the managing director of Church welfare. That loop was closed in 1941 when, as noted, Elder Romney, newly called as an Assistant to the Twelve, became Elder Lee's assistant in welfare.

During his first years in the Twelve, Elder Lee's principal headquarters duties centered around his responsibilities in welfare. The far-flung and rapidly burgeoning welfare projects created vast and ever-changing problems of administration. It was big business with farms, ranches, fruit orchards, dairies, processing facilities, manufacturing plants, and distribution centers to oversee. The supervision of accounting practices and personnel policies, added to the ongoing process of recruiting and training local welfare leaders, were constant challenges.

In time Elder Lee's headquarters duties multiplied, despite the increasing load in welfare. The assignments that came to him along the way included the chairmanship of the servicemen's, music, and general priesthood committees; advisor to the general board of the Primary association; and member of the publications, garment, and expenditure committees. In addition to these duties were those arising directly out of his membership in the Twelve, in the Council of the First Presidency and Quorum of the Twelve, and in the Council on the Disposition of the Tithes. Beyond these fixed and continuing duties, of course, were the intermittent, though heavy, ones of counselling and comforting members; setting apart missionaries as they went into the field; speaking at funerals, graduations, and sacrament meetings; performing temple marriages; and serving on the boards of directors of Church-owned or other corporations.

The sheer volume of these duties was overwhelming. It required the juggler's art to keep all the balls constantly moving in the air. What amazes, however, is that over the weekends, when most working people have a chance to enjoy some leisure, the apostle, like his brethren, was usually involved in conducting stake conferences. And if the stake were located at a distance from Salt Lake City, the travel time spilled over into the "work" weeks that preceded and followed the conference. At this day, the practice has been set that the General Authorities may, if they wish, take off on Mondays following stake conferences, thus providing a break in the routine and allowing islands of free time to take care of personal needs. It was not so in the early days of Elder Lee's apostolic service. It was the practice then that if, for example, a General Authority attended a stake conference out of state over a weekend and arrived home Monday morning after spending the night on a sleeper, he would usually go home to freshen up and would then proceed to his office to handle any matters that had accumulated since the previous Friday when he had had to leave early in order to arrive at his destination for the weekend meetings.

Yet, for Elder Lee, and, undoubtedly for other General Authorities, there was a certain exhilaration in getting out into the field to mingle with the Saints, to teach them, and to bear testimony to them, which was renewing to mind, body, and spirit. On this account, Elder Lee genuinely looked forward to his conference assignments. An added attraction in the early years was that the Brethren travelled in pairs when it was possible to do so. This provided a rare opportunity, during the hours of travel, or at free moments over the weekend, to share insights into their work or to build up each other through testimony.

His first assignment out of state was to attend a conference in northern Arizona in late August. Because there was no train service there, he and his companion travelled by automobile. En route, a leak drained out all the oil from the motor. The crisis came when they were between towns and with no service station in sight. They hailed a passing motorist who had no spare oil but who had compassion. He pushed Elder Lee's car twenty-eight miles to the next town, where the leak was fixed and new oil added. When compensation was offered to the motorist for his generous service, he refused it.

The following day at their destination, Elder Lee and his companion found a different spirit. Two prominent local brethren were feuding over water rights. Neither was willing to yield anything to the other until the visitors counselled with them. Elder Lee noted with satisfaction that their differences were resolved amicably and the controversy was laid to rest. This was the first of many similar situations Elder Lee would encounter over the years. He found that most faithful Latter-day Saints were amenable to the counsel given by a General Authority, and especially by a member of the Twelve.

On the return trip, the visiting Brethren offered a ride home to Oscar A. Kirkham, a scout executive who had been counselling in the area. Elder Lee was impressed by the "human interest and faith promoting stories" shared by their passenger and confided to his diary that Oscar A. Kirkham was a likely candidate to fill the vacancy in the First Council of the Seventy created by the death of Rulon S. Wells on May 7, 1941. Five weeks later, on October 5, 1941, Elder Kirkham was sustained as the forty-first member of the First Council of Seventy at the semiannual general conference.

Two days after returning home from Arizona, Elder Lee experienced another conspicuous first when he was asked to lead the Council of the First Presidency and Quorum of the Twelve in their prayer at the altar in the upper room of the Salt Lake Temple. This was a ritual to which he attached great significance. He frequently attested to the spiritual power generated by these prayers, bringing solace, healing, and comfort to those remembered. Often through the years he would add names to the prayer list, placed on the altar during the prayer circle, confident that through the exercise of faith and the power of God, miracles could occur in the lives of men and women.

On September 12, 1941, Elder Lee left Salt Lake City for Chicago, Illinois, where he had been assigned to preside at a stake conference. It was the first time he had travelled that far east. Unlike the days when he was a missionary, or when he travelled in the interests of the welfare department, he was booked into a Pullman sleeper. This enabled him to move about and to have the room and facilities for study and reflection. He was impressed by the golden crops in Nebraska, Iowa, and Illinois ready to be harvested. On the return trip, he spent many quiet hours "reflecting on the relationship of the present welfare plan to the United Order as revealed." This was a subject that would often engage his interest over the years. He seemed to feel that the essential qualities that would have to characterize those who could successfully live the United Order were absolute faith and self-discipline. He was heard to say that the ultimate challenge of the Latter-day Saints was to learn to live at peace from day to day without fear of what the morrow might bring.

Elder Lee prepared thoroughly for the October semiannual general conference held during the first week of the month. Yet, he did not feel satisfied with his talk. "I was conscious of my limitations," he wrote, "and did not speak with the freedom I hope to be able to enjoy after more experience." Over the years, he did, in fact, through wide experience, gain more "freedom" in speaking from the Tabernacle pulpit. Yet, until the very end, he seems to have approached each speaking assignment with a certain trepidation.

A week after the conference ended, Elder Lee, accompanied by Elder Marion G. Romney, travelled to the Gila Valley in southeastern Arizona to give on-the-ground counsel about relief efforts there, made necessary by a disastrous flood that had stricken the area two weeks before. Elder Lee first learned of the disaster on October 1 when he received a telephone call from Stake President Spencer W. Kimball of Safford, Arizona. At that time, tentative plans for relief through the welfare system had been formed. Meanwhile, President Kimball had gone forward to assist his people, many of whom had been financially ruined by the devastating flood whose waters had covered their fields and farms, drowned their animals, and wrecked their homes. The main devastation was near Duncan, Arizona, where the Gila River had overrun its banks, converting pleasant farmland into a lake. Now the main executives of the welfare plan were on the ground to help the local leaders assess their needs and to furnish resources beyond their own ability to provide.

The First Apostolic Years

This was the first major test of the welfare plan in a disaster situation. Therefore, the attention of the whole Church was riveted on the Gila Valley. Articles in the Church publications kept the Saints everywhere advised of what was going on there. Three main figures stood out in this glare of publicity: Elder Lee; his assistant, Marion G. Romney; and the young, energetic stake president, Spencer W. Kimball, who seemed to be everywhere at once as he rallied his people to rise to the challenge of the disaster. This was the first time the unusual leadership qualities of Spencer Kimball had come to the attention of the presiding brethren in Salt Lake City. That they were impressed is suggested by the fact that within two years, he would be called to the Twelve to take his place in the circle at the right hand of Elder Harold B. Lee. There for twenty-seven years this pair would sit, side by side, as they slowly moved up in apostolic seniority toward the prophetic office, which both were destined to fill. Their leadership styles present an interesting study in contrasts that stand out against the background of the Gila Valley flood.

On the one hand was Elder Lee, the consummate planner and delegator, whose genius was chiefly responsible for the development of the Church welfare system. He had the capacity to formulate plans of broad scope and to marshall the energies and the talents of numerous people to bring his vision to fruition. As he stood in Duncan, there were at his command vast resources, developed in large part through his skill, which could be called upon to alleviate the suffering of the Gila Valley Saints. On the other hand was Brother Kimball, whose chief role in this disaster was to lift the morale of the people and to set them to work, fighting off the flood and repairing the damage once the wasting waters had subsided. We can see him in that setting, hustling to put a sandbag in place, to lead a crew in rescuing a householder marooned on his housetop, or to bring food, clothing, and bedding to a family who had lost all to the angry waters of the Gila. Such qualities of leadership were showcased on a world stage when, as the president of the Church, he activated a whole people through his nonstop industry and his admonitions to the Saints to "do it," to "lengthen your stride," or to "quicken your pace." Meanwhile, quietly, persistently, and deliberately over the years, Elder Lee would put in place an intricate system of correlation and coordination in the Church whose impact and importance would survive him and would influence the direction of the Church for decades. He would also revamp the headquarters machinery of the Church to introduce more modern methods of preparing and distributing instructional and other materials and of facilitating public communications. If Harold B. Lee was more adept at designing and building an intricate vehicle, with all the planning, delegation, and follow-through that entailed, Spencer W. Kimball could demonstrate novel and daring ways to drive it. The contrasting leadership styles of these two unusual men would appear repeatedly during the long years of their association.

Shortly after returning from the Gila Valley, Elder Lee found another way to publicize and popularize Church welfare. In late October, representatives of *Look* magazine came to Utah to prepare an article about author Maurine Whipple and her book, *Giant Joshua*, which had a Utah setting. At the insistence of President Clark, Elder Lee went to St. George, Utah, to meet with them and the author in order to provide background information about the Church and its people. Back in Salt Lake City, he ushered them through Welfare Square to explain the purposes and procedures of the plan and to arrange for appropriate photographs of the facility for inclusion in the article. He also took them to Temple Square where he arranged for pictures of the temple and its grounds and the Tabernacle, especially of the baptistry. This enabled him to explain basic doctrines of the Church, tying them to what the visitors had been shown at Welfare Square, as indicating the concern of the Church for both the temporal and spiritual welfare of its members. Elder Lee's comparative youth, his natural eloquence, his detailed knowledge of Church doctrine and the development of Church welfare, and his inherent missionary focus made him an ideal host for visiting groups such as this. President Clark, especially, was anxious to put prominent visitors into the hands of Elder Lee, knowing that he would portray the Church and its purposes in the best possible light. So, during the several days the visitors from *Look* magazine were in the state, he stayed close with them to provide them with necessary information and to help form their itinerary.

These same qualities in Elder Lee, added to the magnetic attraction he had for young people, drew him to an activity during these early months of his service in the Twelve that would claim his avid interest throughout his apostolic ministry. Don B. Colton, director of the mission home, invited him to instruct the missionaries then in training about the temple ordinances. Before going to the temple, Elder Lee conferred with President David O. McKay, who had performed the same function over the years, to get his counsel. Thus authorized and prepared, he went to the Assembly Room on the fifth floor of the temple where a large group of missionaries awaited him. For an hour, in a quiet, informal way, using the scriptures extensively, Elder Lee explained the purposes and the symbolisms of the temple ordinances in language his young friends could not misunderstand. In this sacred setting, he was in his natural element, doing the thing for which he had been professionally trained and for which he was best qualified—teaching. His method, especially with young people like these missionaries, was usually Socratic. Questions he put to the group, and the responses, or questions volunteered from the audience were a tip-off to the things that were bothersome or as to which there was only a fuzzy understanding. Then, like the skilled physician who has diagnosed a patient's illness, he would apply the remedy, which might be a key scripture, an insightful comment, or perhaps follow-up questions that would help to clarify and to bring understanding. The set of scriptures

Elder Lee used in teaching was one of a kind. Over the years he had inserted into them thin leaves containing explanatory comments, analogies, significant cross-references, or historical or anecdotal material. These added a richness and depth to his teaching, which could never have been attained by the mere citation or reading of a scripture.

There can be little doubt that interludes such as this, where he could discern flickerings of understanding or conviction in his listeners, were a tonic to Elder Lee, which helped to bridge over the less enjoyable aspects of his ministry. One must understand that apostolic service does not entail an unbroken skein of happy, enjoyable experiences. There is a down side, usually caused by human imperfection or the clash of personalities. Only nine days after his mountaintop experience in the temple, Elder Lee learned of a deep-seated rift between two key members of his staff in the welfare department. One of them had come to him complaining about the "somewhat domineering attitude" of the other, which, Elder Lee speculated, was "born of jealousy." Concerned that this would cause serious disruption in the work if it continued, Elder Lee counselled about it with Henry D. Moyle, who was then the chairman of the general welfare committee. Working together, they adroitly attempted to resolve the conflict.

Even Elder Lee's relationship with Brother Moyle was not always placid. Notwithstanding the deep love and respect they always had for each other, there were times when differences of opinion on policy or procedural matters evoked strong opposition or dissent. They were much alike. Both were strong-minded with opinions they did not yield easily. Both were self-confident. Both had ably served as stake presidents during the 1930s when the welfare plan was born. Both were spiritual by nature, although practical and analytical in administration. Both had political aspirations at one time and were well known and respected among nonmembers. Yet, they were unlike. Ten years older than he, Henry Moyle was six years Elder Lee's junior in apostolic seniority. The son of James H. Moyle, an affluent Salt Lake attorney, businessman, and politician, who once served as the assistant secretary of the U.S. Treasury, Elder Moyle was heavily subsidized by his family while being educated in engineering and law at major universities in Europe and the United States. Meanwhile, Elder Lee struggled financially to obtain primary and secondary teaching certificates at Albion Normal and afterwards turned over most of his teacher's salary to his parents until he entered the mission field. Finally, Elder Lee's early years of married life and Church service were spent in a modest neighborhood near an industrial area on the west side of the city, while Henry Moyle, himself a prominent attorney and businessman like his father, lived in an exclusive, affluent neighborhood in the southeast part of the Salt Lake Valley. So, their perceptions about the poor and the needy were vastly different. For Elder Lee, it was a matter of personal knowledge, having been raised in an environment where money was always in short supply. As the president of the Pioneer Stake, he had witnessed at firsthand poverty of the most abject kind. For Elder Moyle, however, poverty and economic want were largely abstractions. In essence, he seemed to approach welfare work as involving merely the solution of economic or legal problems.

One other difference between these two men should be noted: Having early on come under the powerful influence of President J. Reuben Clark, and being so disposed by nature, Elder Lee was inclined to follow policy guidelines with exactness. Elder Moyle, on the other hand, was inclined to cut through what he considered to be red tape in order to achieve an end that he considered to be proper and desirable. This occasionally brought them into conflict when they outspokenly opposed each other. But these occasional conflicts never permanently marred a relationship that continued on a congenial basis throughout their lives. Both were acquainted with the rough-and-tumble state of politics and debate, and therefore never allowed these periodic conflicts to color their personal relationship.

A mark of their maturity and congeniality is shown in their cooperative relationship in welfare work over many years while Elder Moyle served as the chairman of the committee that directed Elder Lee's work as general manager, even though Elder Moyle was junior to Elder Lee in the apostleship, and, indeed, though for several years of that relationship, he was not a General Authority.

In addition to incidents such as these, which injected occasional controversy, there were other facets of the work that made Elder Lee's service in the Twelve less than ideal. On an almost daily basis, he was exposed to the trials and trauma, the sad tales of woe, of those who came to him for counsel and solace. There were also those whose lives hung in the balance, or who had grave physical or emotional problems, who came to be healed or comforted. Concern or empathy for these inevitably invaded his own feelings, causing sorrow or apprehension he otherwise would have avoided. Finally, Elder Lee's calling entailed almost constant travel by automobile or train, with awkward schedules, and sometimes with less than suitable housing facilities or diet. Sometimes, trips were undertaken when he was not well or was weary, or perhaps was troubled about Sister Lee's health, which was never robust. Yet, when duty called, he went regardless of his own feelings or convenience. So, like life itself, Elder Lee soon found that service in the Twelve was a mix, that there were happy times, and there were sad times, that there were sweet and peaceful experiences, and there were stressful experiences.

There were also times when Elder Lee's sense of humor shone through his diary entries, which ordinarily were very terse and factual. On November 14, 1941, for instance, which was his and Fern's eighteenth wedding anniversary and Fern's forty-sixth birthday, he wrote, tongue-in-cheek: "For her celebration, she went relief society block teaching, was a guide at the Lion House in the afternoon and she assisted in the MIA road show act from the ward." In between these events, Elder and Sister Lee enjoyed a rare privilege when, in celebration of their wedding anniversary, President and Sister Heber J. Grant called to take them for a ride up the canyon. This was a favorite pastime for the prophet and his wife, who would usually take members of their family or friends with them to enjoy the scenery and their conversation. A week after celebrating their wedding anniversary and Fern's birthday in this way, the Lees gathered for their Thanksgiving feast, of which Elder Lee wrote appreciatively: "I enjoyed this lovely association with my little family, an opportunity not often afforded me."

The day after Thanksgiving, Fern drove her husband to the depot where he boarded the train destined for Oakland, California, where he had a stake conference assignment. On the train he made the acquaintance of two government officials engaged in defense work. Of his conversation with them, Elder Lee noted: "I found them wholly in support of the idea that nothing short of complete participation in the war would suffice for the present situation." At the time, the United States government was providing heavy support to the war effort of the allies in Europe through the so-called Lend-Lease Act. It was that conflict about which the remarks of Elder Lee's travelling companions were directed. Only a few days later, the attention of all Americans suddenly shifted from Europe to the Pacific following the Japanese attack on Pearl Harbor. On December 7, 1941, Elder Lee was attending the conference of the Grant Stake in Salt Lake City. "Received word over the radio," he wrote on that date, "that Japan had attacked at Hawaii and the Philippines with heavy losses." The next day, he noted that all cities along the Pacific Coast were blacked out for fear of air attacks and that unidentified planes had been reported in the vicinity of San Francisco. With the formal declaration of war against both Japan and the Axis powers, Germany and Italy, which followed soon after Pearl Harbor, the United States was plunged into a terrible war that would dominate its action, devour its resources, and destroy the flower of its youth for four stressful years. The conflict had a heavy impact upon the Latter-day Saints, altering plans, imposing burdens, and creating anxieties. For some, its impact was devastating. "Talked with President J. Reuben Clark," Elder Lee wrote on December 10, "and he just advised me they had heard definitely that their son-in-law, Mervyn Bennion, had lost his life at Pearl Harbor." President Clark, who harbored deep-felt pacifist views, was terribly shaken by this news, so much so that he excused himself from the temple meeting so he could mourn with his bereaved daughter.

Because of the shocking suddenness with which America had been plunged into the war, the devastation at Pearl Harbor, and the reports of unidentified aircraft on the west coast, the whole country became jittery to the point of paranoia. Fear of bombing attacks gripped most of the western United States. Even in remote Salt Lake City, the street lights were turned off at night and windows were shrouded. Trains travelling to Salt Lake from the West Coast at night regularly curtained their windows. And local officials began to organize for war. "Was asked by President Clark," Elder Lee wrote on December 19, "to submit names of leading younger men for membership on air raid committees now being organized for the city." And the following day, the Brethren received the disturbing news that some Church members, panicked by news of the war, had begun to hoard food in the wall partitions of their homes.

In these circumstances, the Christmas festivities were quiet and austere and hardly joyous. A highlight was the preparation of thirty-five hundred Christmas baskets at Welfare Square for the needy of the city. And on a personal basis, Elder Lee saw another evidence of the liberality of his friend Henry D. Moyle from whom he received a hundred shares of stock in the Wasatch Oil and Refining Company as a Christmas present, along with a dividend check for $250 and a dividend note for $450.

In reflecting on the significant events of the year 1941,

Elder Lee confided these thoughts to his diary: "In my call to the apostleship, I have experienced the most intense schooling and preparation of any similar period. I have known the terror of the evil tempter and, in contrast, the sublime joy of the inspiration and revelation of the Holy Spirit. My wife and family have been a constant source of encouragement and happiness and despite the terrors of world war, the peace of God seems to be with us."

At the request of President Franklin D. Roosevelt, the Latter-day Saints joined in special prayers for the nation on January 4, 1942, the first Sunday of the year. In the morning, the Lee family attended a prayer meeting in the Cannon Ward; and in the evening, Elder Lee spoke at a sacrament meeting in the Garden Park Ward, where he experienced "considerable difficulty" in speaking. He attributed this to a lack of responsiveness on the part of the audience, which included "the governor . . . business leaders, etc." Throughout his ministry, Elder Lee found that his "freedom" in speaking depended largely on the spiritual receptivity of his audience. When that was lacking, he always felt a sense of letdown or disappointment as he did on this occasion.

The effects of the war very soon began to be felt in every aspect of the work. On January 14, 1942, Elder Lee participated in setting apart eighty-three missionaries who left later in the day for their various fields of labor. Called before Pearl Harbor, this would be the last large group of young missionaries to be sent out until the war ended. Stringent requirements of the draft thereafter limited mission calls to sisters, older men, and the physically disabled. A series of events in early February revealed some of the other significant changes the war had wrought: The nation went on what was then called "war time," later called daylight savings time, which set the clocks ahead an hour in the spring as a means of conserving energy; plans to construct a $126,000,000 steel plant in Utah Valley near Provo, Utah, were announced; Elder Lee registered for the draft; and the Brethren cancelled the June conference and decided that only certain priesthood leaders would be invited to the April general conference.

Meanwhile, Elder Lee and the other General Authorities continued to attend stake conferences on assignment. Indeed, these meetings took on new significance as they provided a means of welding the Church together in a time of crisis and enabled the Brethren to make sure there was uniformity of doctrine and procedure throughout the Church. So, during the first months of the year, Elder Lee attended stake conferences in San Bernardino, California; Blackfoot, Preston, Nampa, Paris, and Rigby, Idaho; Woodruff, Millard, Ogden, Delta, and Richfield, Utah; and Snowflake, Arizona, among others. En route to San Bernardino, California, all the shades on the train were drawn as it neared Barstow, presumably to prevent sightings by Japanese aircraft or to thwart the activities of Japanese snipers along the way. Later in passing through California en route to Snowflake, Arizona, Elder Lee saw army pickets on guard at all bridges, presumably to prevent their being blown up by Japanese saboteurs. Such was the paranoia brought on by the war, that in Salt Lake City members of the Veterans of Foreign Wars were assigned to guard the facilities at Welfare Square. During this period, Americans of Japanese descent were herded into "Relocation Centers," which in reality were concentration camps. One of these named Topaz was established not far from Salt Lake City in the spring of 1942, only a few months after Pearl Harbor. While in retrospect these precautions seem incredible, those living today who did not experience it cannot begin to understand the pall of uncertainty and fear that permeated the United States because of the shocking surprise attack on Pearl Harbor. These apprehensions were fed by incidents of the kind reported by Elder Lee on February 24, 1942, as he returned from his stake conference assignment at Snowflake, Arizona. "As the train left Los Angeles," wrote Elder Lee, "the radio station KFI went off the air and we learned later that a submarine had shelled a steel company plant near Santa Barbara. I think but little damage was done." Although such incidents were only sporadic and had no serious consequences, they achieved the apparent objective of the Japanese—to stir up anxiety among the people and to keep them wondering about what to expect.

When Elder Lee returned from this trip, he found that Fern was "in a highly nervous state," apparently caused by concern about the war and about her husband's frequent absences from home. While his heavy headquarters assignments limited the time he could spend with her, Elder Lee assisted his wife in her duties as often as he could. If available, he always pitched in to help with the spring cleaning and other household chores. His aid on these occasions was more than perfunctory. He got right in the middle of things, doing the heavy, physical work while leaving the more delicate touches to his wife. And he helped her with other things. "I spent this morning," he wrote on March 14, "helping Fern getting her costumes and other paraphernalia from the ward following her three act drama." These activities were a relaxing outlet for her energies as were her periodic guiding duties at the Beehive House and Lion House. They helped keep her mind off the loneliness caused by the frequent absences of her husband and off the dreary news of the war.

Beginning in mid-August 1942, Elder Lee commenced a war-related activity that would occupy him off and on for many years. On the fourteenth he left for Los Angeles with Elder Albert E. Bowen of the Twelve and Hugh B. Brown to visit defense facilities and LDS military personnel on the West Coast. Brother Brown had previously been appointed as the coordinator of LDS servicemen and the two apostles were to assist in indoctrinating him in his duties. They first inspected defense installations in the area before participating in a stake conference over the weekend. The next day, Monday, they met with the presidencies from the nearby stakes "to discuss problems of finding and caring for young men in the military or in defense work."

From Los Angeles, the Brethren went to San Diego

where the same procedure was followed as at Los Angeles. In addition, they conferred with the Chief of Chaplains at the sprawling Naval Training Station and had dinner with a number of LDS servicemen at Fort Rosecrans. It soon became apparent that the most pressing problems of servicemen were loneliness and fear of what the future held for them. They concluded that the main antidotes for these were regular communications from home, Church-sponsored social activities near the military bases, and spiritual nourishment to be gained from private prayer, scripture study, and group worship services. These needs and the perceived remedies later gave rise to an aggressive campaign to encourage families and Church leaders at home to correspond frequently with their servicemen, to create an intricate Church network to identify and locate servicemen and defense workers, and to organize an ongoing program of LDS social gatherings and sacrament and testimony meetings among them. To foster private devotions, the Church later distributed to military personnel pocket-sized editions of the scriptures, which could be easily carried on their persons, and which, therefore, were readily available at any time.

At Camp Roberts near Paso Robles, California, Elder Lee and his companions witnessed a phenomenon that usually occurred at stops along the way. Word of a hurriedly called meeting with the visitors spread throughout the camp like lightning via the efficient Mormon grapevine, bringing most of the Latter-day Saints to the appointed place on time. Once they were assembled, a chorister, a pianist, and those to pray and to administer and pass the sacrament were called up from the audience, who functioned with an efficiency and reverence that implied hours of careful preparation. Talks by the visitors were followed by testimonies from the audience. Such impromptu participation by the Latter-day Saints was always a source of amazement to non-Mormon chaplains who could not understand how such able and willing service could be obtained from lay people on such short notice.

Similar inspirational meetings were held at Fort Ord and at military installations in the vicinity of San Francisco. At a meeting in Oakland, with servicemen destined for combat duty in the Pacific, Elder Lee was overcome with emotion as he realized that some of these young men would not return.

While in the Bay Area, the Brethren visited war and defense installations in addition to conferring with military officers at the Presidio, the site of the pioneer fort at the mouth of San Francisco Bay. At Portland, Oregon, they were poignantly reminded of the grim aspects of war when Brother Brown received a copy of the memorial service held for his son who had been killed while flying for the Royal Air Force in Great Britain.

As a temporary diversion, the Brethren played a round of golf at Portland. This was a diversion in which Elder Lee engaged only infrequently. Indeed, following his mission, and during the remainder of his life, there were very few occasions when he participated in sports of any kind. This is an anomaly considering the active role he played in sports as a student and teacher. The explanation seems to lie in the vigorous life-style he adopted following his mission. With the time constraints imposed by working full time while completing his education, struggling to get ahead in the business world, meeting the constant demands of a political career while moonlighting as a stake president, supervising the development of a Church-wide welfare program, and, finally, confronting the constant demands of his apostolic calling left little time for competitive sports. Elder Lee's main physical activity after marriage was yard work, either at his own home or at the home of his daughter Helen. And, as already noted, he attacked his yard work with vigor so that it provided a good physical outlet for his energies. But, this was a seasonal activity, and even in season it was sporadic due to the complications of his travel schedule. It did not, therefore, provide the kind of consistent, year-round, physical activity essential to the maintenance of robust health. One must wonder, then, whether the frequent colds and intermittent stomach disorders Elder Lee suffered with over the years can be explained, in large part, by the absence of an ongoing exercise regimen. And the deterioration in his health this lack of exercise fostered could well have shortened his life.

While Elder Lee's active participation in sports was minimal during his married years, he remained an avid spectator until the end. He especially enjoyed football and basketball. After Helen's marriage, her husband, L. Brent Goates, frequently accompanied his father-in-law to sporting events.

The day following the round of golf in Portland, Elder Lee and his companions visited the huge army base at Fort Lewis, Washington, where they found a homesick group of Mormon GIs who hungered for more news from family and friends. It seems to have been here that Elder Lee became confirmed in his belief that there was nothing more vital to the emotional stability of a serviceman than the lifeline of letters from home. And during the many years of his involvement with military affairs, he laid great stress on this critical need.

The three brethren completed their tour of facilities in the Pacific Northwest by visiting the naval base at Bremerton, Washington. There the war assumed an aspect of greater immediacy for them when they saw the battleship *Nevada*, bristling with its guns and armor, which was undergoing repairs for the damage it sustained at Pearl Harbor.

Following a district conference in Spokane, Washington, on the last weekend in August, the two apostles headed for home while Hugh B. Brown remained in the Northwest to work with local leaders in completing the organization to track and to help servicemen. En route home, they stopped briefly at the Bay View military camp near Coeur d'Alene, Idaho, to visit LDS servicemen. Among them was a young man, Grant W. Lee, whom

Elder Lee identified as a great-great-grandson of his own direct ancestor, Samuel Lee.

During the trip home, the two apostles reviewed their tour analytically, discussing the direction they felt the work with servicemen should go. They concluded that Hugh B. Brown should be given General Authority status as an Assistant to the Twelve in order to strengthen his hand in dealing with stake and mission leaders. While that suggestion did not materialize at the time, his status and authority were enhanced when, on October 9, he was appointed to serve on a three-man general Church servicemen's committee, chaired by Elder Harold B. Lee. (The other member was Elder John H. Taylor of the First Council of the Seventy.) This began a long association between these two old friends in the interest of Latter-day Saint servicemen. And over ten years later, the role Elders Lee and Bowen had envisioned for their associate became a reality when, on October 4, 1953, Hugh B. Brown was sustained as an Assistant to the Twelve.

Back home, Elder Lee was assigned to reorganize the presidency of the New York Stake, which entailed another long trip before the October general conference. He boarded the train at 6:30 P.M. September 9 and arrived in New York three days later. En route he stopped in Chicago long enough to visit Fern's cousin, Richard Tanner, who was studying medicine there. Through a miscommunication, no one met Elder Lee at the New York depot. Undeterred, he simply caught a cab to the Eastern States mission home, which he used as headquarters during a three-day stay in the city.

As he began the interviewing to find a new stake president, Elder Lee was inclined toward the young bishop of the Manhattan Ward, Howard S. Bennion. However, questions had been raised about him by prominent local men because of his relative youth, which had created some doubt in Elder Lee's mind. That doubt was removed in the early morning hours of September 13. "Had a remarkable demonstration as I awoke this morning," he noted on that day, "as to divine direction in showing Howard S. Bennion to become the new stake president, despite the objections that had been raised." This impression was confirmed when the man who was most prominently mentioned by the local brethren later made a "sarcastic remark" in a setting, which "conclusively" showed to Elder Lee that he was not the man.

The instantaneous way in which his preference was swung toward one man and away from the other reveals a key quality in the makeup of Harold B. Lee. Although he possessed superior analytical powers, which he used with significant effect, as in the slow and measured development of the welfare plan, these always yielded to the impromptu flashes of insight or revelation like those he received in reorganizing the New York Stake presidency. It was this quality, more than any other, which prompted so many of his associates to refer to Elder Lee as a "seer." It was this quality, also, which introduced an element of unpredictability in any dealings with him. Those close to him came to expect those sudden impulses, which would divert him from a course of action and take him away on a tangent toward something he had not originally aimed for. Such an instance occurred on his return home after reorganizing the New York Stake presidency. During a layover in Chicago, on September 15, he learned that a former member of the Pioneer Stake lay gravely ill in Lafayette, Indiana, a distance of ninety miles from Chicago. This was Theodore M. Burton, who was working on his Ph.D. at Purdue University. Theodore had undergone an appendectomy in June. A postoperative infection resulting in empyema caused his diaphragm to rupture and the infection spread to his body cavity. Then followed several operations that unsuccessfully sought to locate the source of the infection. By the time Elder Lee arrived in Chicago in mid-September, Theodore had lost so much weight he was little more than skin and bones. The doctors had decided on a final operation that involved removing part of some ribs so as to provide access to the chest cavity for a flushing procedure that might eliminate the infection.

Elder Lee learned of Theodore's peril from the mission president, Leo J. Muir, who was headquartered in Chicago. At the time, Charles S. Hyde, Elder Lee's former counselor in the Pioneer Stake presidency, was auditing the mission records. "Charlie," said the apostle to his friend, "I understand that Theodore T. Burton's son, young Theodore, is down in Indiana fighting for his life. I feel impressed that we should go down and give him a blessing." (See *He Changed My Life*, pp. 233–36.) Accompanied by President Muir, they went to Lafayette, arriving at the hospital just as the patient was being wheeled toward the operating room on a gurney. Elder Lee asked that it be wheeled back to the room so they could give the patient a blessing in private. What happened then is best told in the words of Theodore M. Burton. "Brother Hyde anointed me with consecrated oil. Then those three men placed their hands on my head, and Elder Lee, as mouth, sealed the anointing and gave me a blessing. I don't remember all he said, but one idea stays in my memory. He did not bless me to get well as the others had done. He *commanded* me to get well and said that my work on earth was not yet finished. He *commanded* my spirit to take over the healing process and, through me, blessed the doctors who were about to operate that they would know what to do to restore me to health." (Ibid.)

A Catholic sister, misunderstanding why the three brethren were there, later chastised Theodore's wife, Minnie, for inviting the "Mormon Priests" to administer the last rites to her husband. "I believe he can live until tomorrow," said the sister, "perhaps for another day, but now he knows he is going to die and all hope is gone." When Minnie explained that the blessing her husband had received was for life, not death, the sister knowingly observed: "My dear, it is well to have faith, but you must face up to reality. He cannot live, and you will only hurt yourself further by keeping up an impossible hope." That hope was fulfilled when, six weeks later, the patient was discharged from the hospital to return home. Less than twenty years later, the earthly mission for which Theodore M. Burton's life had been spared emerged when, on October 8, 1960, he was sustained as an Assistant to the Twelve.

Chapter Fourteen

Maturing in the Apostleship

Shortly before the October 1942 general conference, Elder Lee was assigned to conduct a conference in the Ensign Stake. Twenty years before, he had attended a conference there shortly after his release from the Western States Mission. He had been intimidated then when he was called on to speak briefly because it was the stake in which President Grant and other General Authorities lived. That sense of intimidation had not entirely left when he attended the conference there on this occasion. He always had a deferential feeling toward President Grant and toward President Clark, who also lived in the Ensign Stake, not only because of the positions they occupied in the First Presidency, but also because of their business and professional achievements. It was, therefore, a sense of relief to him when the conference was over, and he could concentrate on his less conspicuous assignments in connection with the general conference.

It was at this general conference that Joseph F. Smith was sustained as the Patriarch to the Church. In his remarks responding to the call, the new patriarch, who had been a professor at the University of Utah, said his colleagues there had derided him for giving up his academic career in order "to pray" the rest of his life. While there is no indication it was intended as such, Elder Lee's conference address could have served as an answer to these critics. In it he focused on spirituality and its importance as an anchor in the lives of the Latter-day Saints.

On October 14, 1942, he left Salt Lake City by automobile with President J. Reuben Clark. Fern and Sister Clark accompanied them. The two-week trip ahead would take them to southeastern Arizona and back. Along the way, they would hold meetings with members and leaders. It was the only time during their association that they travelled together as companions over such a long period.

The crisp, clear weather, good roads free of snow and ice, and the congenial, relaxed conversation made the trip through the autumn splendor of southern Utah and Arizona's Kaibab Forest an idyllic experience never to be forgotten. Their first meetings were at Snowflake, a remote Mormon outpost in northeastern Arizona, settled in part by descendants of Silas Smith, the Prophet Joseph Smith's uncle. Here President Clark focused on obedience in his preaching, while his companion discussed the baptismal covenants and their implications.

The travelers were met at Snowflake by Levi S. Udall, president of the neighboring stake, who led them to nearby St. Johns. En route, they visited the Painted Desert and the Petrified Forest, ancient tokens of the earth's generative and erosive forces. As they teamed up to speak at St. Johns, President Clark talked about the power of prayer, while Elder Lee discussed the value of adversity in a world where it was foreordained that there would be an opposition in all things.

Driving south across the Mogollon Rim, where they saw some of the most ruggedly beautiful and heavily forested terrain in all of Arizona, the travelers reached Safford in the Gila Valley, the home of Spencer W. Kimball, then the president of the Mount Graham Stake. This energetic young stake president, whose leadership capabilities were magnified during the previous year's flood, was President Clark's cousin through the Woolley family. It had been said of a distinguished member of this clan that if his body were to be thrown in the river at his death, it would float upstream. The quality of persistence this story implies would be repeatedly reflected in the life and ministry of Spencer W. Kimball after his call to the apostleship less than a year following the visit of these guests.

Led by President Kimball, the visitors were taken to Duncan, Arizona, and Virden, New Mexico, where still could be seen evidence of the ravages wrought by the flood. At one of the meetings held on this side trip, President Clark made comments about Elder Lee, which had special meaning to him and which he recorded in detail. "He was very kind to me," wrote Elder Lee. "He related my experience in the welfare plan, and in politics, and told the people he was confident that if I had remained in politics, I would have been in the United States Senate. He said he loved me as his son and that . . . I reciprocated that love as a son to a father. He said, further, that while he was not prophesying, that in the providence of the Lord, because of my age, I would one day become the president of the church." These words, spoken analytically, and not by revelation, expressed the views of most Latter-day Saints who were knowledgeable about Church history. There was a widespread assumption among them that because of the age differential between Elder Lee and the other apostles he would in time become the senior living apostle and, therefore, the president of the Church.

After parting with President Kimball, the travelers went to Tucson and thence to Phoenix, holding meetings in both places. While at Tucson the Brethren also conferred with Church institute teachers at the University of Arizona, admonishing them to teach sound doctrine and to avoid delving into controversial philosophies. This counsel seems to have been prompted by reports that in some classes at the institute, things had been taught that had questionable relevance to accepted Church doctrine.

Also, since they were so close to the border while at Tucson, the party traveled to Nogales and, crossing into Mexico, enjoyed a meal of Mexican food, which the Clarks had grown to love while they lived in Mexico City while President Clark served as the United States Ambassador there.

The travelers had hoped to visit the Boulder (Hoover) Dam near Las Vegas, Nevada, on the way home, but were unable to do so because of the tight security imposed by the war. This evoked strong comments by President Clark, deploring the war, which he said was needless, and predicting that it would not end until the nations that had caused it had been "humbled."

A week after completing this trip in the comfort of a private automobile, Elder Lee boarded a crowded, cluttered chair car, which reeked of tobacco smoke and echoed with the boisterous talk and laughter of the numerous servicemen who were aboard. He was en route to Austin, Texas, where he would begin a tour of the Texas-Louisiana Mission. The servicemen were destined for military camps. The transportation crush, caused by frequent troop movements, had made it impossible for Elder Lee to get a Pullman reservation out of Salt Lake City. However, he was able to transfer to one out of Denver, so he traveled in greater comfort and privacy during the last leg of the trip.

The two-week mission tour commenced in Austin on November 8, with a public meeting and a training session with Mission President William L. Warner and his missionaries. The next day, the party, which included Elder Antoine R. Ivins, who had joined Elder Lee at Austin, drove southwest to San Antonio, the site of the famed battle of the Alamo. Here, in addition to the public and missionary meetings like those held in Austin, Elder Lee dedicated a new chapel to accommodate the rapidly growing Mormon population in that city. Then followed a motor marathon that took the party, in succession, to Houston,

Texas, and in Louisiana to Lake Charles, New Orleans, Albany, Baton Rouge, Many, Monroe, and Shreveport. Returning to Texas, the Brethren held meetings in Kelsey, Kilgore, Dallas, and Fort Worth. At each stop, in addition to the meetings already mentioned, Elder Lee conducted private interviews with each missionary, conferred priesthood blessings on the many who requested them, counselled with local leaders, and met with media and government representatives. This hectic schedule, added to the long distances between stops, left little time for relaxation. The only exception was at New Orleans when Elder Lee took several hours to visit the places of historic interest, including the massive Catholic Cathedral, the depiction of the Battle of New Orleans, and the French Quarter with its quaint shops and restaurants. Here he bought some French perfume as a gift for Fern. At the state capital in Baton Rouge, Elder Lee was impressed with Huey Long's "masterpiece," the twenty-seven-story capitol building. And at the meeting in Many, Louisiana, where another new chapel was dedicated, the apostle was introduced to the sister of Huey Long, who was investigating the Church. Here the visitors also enjoyed a southern specialty, "dinner on the grounds," featuring mounds of fried chicken, "greens," and banana pudding for dessert.

At Kelsey, Texas, and the neighboring communities of Gilmer and Tyler, Elder Lee found the nucleus of a Mormon colony that had been established more than fifty years before. Originating in the deep South, the pioneers of this group, who had planned to migrate to the mountainous west, were impressed by the moderate climate, the lush vegetation, and the fertile soil of the area and decided to put down roots here. It was the first large Mormon community established in the state of Texas. It may have been this background that prompted some of the Saints at Kelsey to ask Elder Lee whether, in view of the war, they should go to the Rocky Mountains for safety. In answer, Elder Lee's public sermon used the text, "If Ye are Prepared, Ye Shall Not Fear." The essence of his message was that real peace and safety must be found within, despite the stresses of outside pressures.

The tour ended with meetings in Dallas and Fort Worth. At Fort Worth, a city where today the Church is firmly rooted, with thriving stakes and wards and a nearby temple, Elder Lee met with a handful of Saints in a rented Knights of Pythias Hall. The vigorous growth that occurred in the interim resulted from the wise policies of Elder Lee and his brethren, the industry of the numerous missionaries who served under them, and the blessings of heaven.

Elder Lee boarded a train for Denver, Colorado, soon after the meeting in the Knights of Pythias Hall ended. It was also filled with military personnel and tobacco smoke. He was met at Denver by Western States Mission President Elbert Curtis who took him to the mission home Elder Lee knew so well at 538 East Seventh Avenue. After freshening up, he counselled with the missionaries laboring with President Curtis, who could not have failed to recall that only two decades had elapsed since the apostle had labored where they then served.

Elder Lee's Salt Lake bound train was delayed for several hours to make way for a special troop train that was given the right of way. "Spent the afternoon," he wrote on November 24, "getting cleaned up from the tobacco smoke and grime of travel."

This mission tour was typical of the many Elder Lee made during his service in the Twelve. While the tight schedules, the long distances traveled, the irregularity and sometimes the inadequacy of meals, and the constant changes in sleeping accommodations were inconvenient and wearing, these were more than outweighed by the pleasure he had in counselling with the young missionaries, mingling with the Saints, visiting new places, and feeling the thrill of the Holy Spirit working through him. Therefore, he always received with enthusiasm any assignment from the president of his quorum to tour a mission.

The same was true of his assignments to attend stake

conferences. These, of course, came with greater frequency—on an average of three a month—and took him throughout the Church. The fixed meetings of a stake conference included welfare, priesthood leadership, and general sessions held over Saturday and Sunday, interspersed occasionally with special missionary and youth sessions. Aside from these meetings, he was usually heavily involved in between them, counselling with leaders and members, giving priesthood blessings, interviewing prospective missionaries, and setting apart officers. Because in the early days of his ministry, only members of the Twelve could ordain or set apart stake presidencies, bishoprics, high councilors, and patriarchs, it often happened that brethren from adjoining stakes would travel to the place where the conference was being held so Elder Lee could do it. This meant that from the time he arrived in a stake, usually about noon on Saturday, until he left Sunday night or Monday morning, he was on duty practically all the time with little opportunity to rest or to eat. When he did eat, it was usually a sumptuous meal that the sisters had lovingly prepared to fete him, which ordinarily included their most delectable and caloric dishes. Thus occupied and stuffed, sitting down during most of two days, it is little wonder that early in his ministry Elder Lee developed stomach problems. These would stress him intermittently throughout the remainder of his life and would even contribute to his comparatively early death at age seventy-four.

As a prelude to the significant events of the following year, Elder Lee ended 1942 on a quiet note. He had only two stake conference assignments during December, both close to home. One was at the Bonneville Stake in Salt Lake City. His major address during the conference mirrored the tensions and frustrations of the time. It was titled "How to Find Peace in the Midst of Great Trial and Trouble." As if to underscore the uncertainty of the times, Salt Lake City had its first air-raid warning the following night, which ironically was on December 7, 1942, the first anniversary of Pearl Harbor. Word received from Portland, Oregon, indicated that planes, presumably Japanese, were on their way toward Salt Lake City. The city was blacked out for forty-five minutes before the "all clear" was sounded. So jittery was everybody that no one seemed to question the fantastic idea that the Japanese could mount an air attack on an inland city like Salt Lake.

Also on Pearl Harbor Day, 1942, Elder Lee was contacted by "an old German brother," who told him his sermon at the afternoon session of the Bonneville Stake conference "was too long." The apostle noted agreeably, "I thought so too."

Elder Lee enjoyed an interesting change of pace during the first few months of 1943. Beginning on February 25, he gave a series of six lectures at the Lion House, which focused on the subject, "Finding Oneself in the World." As he so frequently did, the speaker emphasized the key role of spirituality in life, which would safely anchor one to eternal principles, which, if lived, would insure a return to God's presence. The last lecture was given on April 1, of which Elder Lee wrote: "There has been an attendance of from 200 to 250 at each lecture. They presented Fern with a bouquet of flowers. They called on Father to dismiss the meeting and he seemed very tender toward me in his expression." The father, the child of promise, saw in the achievements of his son an affirmation of his own self-worth and a fulfillment of some of God's purposes in the miraculous preservation of his own life.

The general conference, which convened a few days after Elder Lee's last Lion House lecture, passed without incident. However, following the conference, an official action was taken, which Elder Lee considered to be of major importance. "A most historic meeting was held of the Twelve and the First Presidency," he recorded on April 8, "in which it was decided that hereafter the tithes of the church would be disbursed by a council composed of the First Presidency, the Twelve and the Presiding Bishopric instead of by just the First Presidency and the Presiding

Bishopric as in the past. This will contemplate also the Twelve giving approval to the financial budget each year." This change brought Church procedure into harmony with the revelation given July 18, 1838, which designated the First Presidency, the Twelve (referred to as the "high council"), and the Presiding Bishopric (referred to as "the bishop and his council") as the body authorized to dispose of the tithes of the Church. (See D&C 120.) The significance of this change to Elder Lee and his brethren of the Twelve was incalculable. It gave them a vital voice in one of the most important aspects of Church administration. At the same time, it added significantly to the weight of their responsibilities.

A responsibility Elder Lee had in welfare took him to Washington, D.C., a week after this historic meeting. His purpose in visiting the capital was to seek an exemption for the welfare department from the government's food rationing policy. Enlisting the aid of this boyhood friend, "T" Benson, who was then the executive secretary of a national farm cooperative, Elder Lee met with officials of the Office of Price Administration. The results of the meeting was inconclusive. There was hope that commodities distributed to the needy from bishops storehouses would be exempt from rationing. Elder Lee left for home on April 18, asking Brother Benson to follow through in meeting with the O. P. A. officials to resolve the rationing issue. Little did these two old friends know as they bid goodbye at the Washington depot, that unforeseen events in the near future would bring them together as colleagues in the Quorum of the Twelve.

Elder Lee's return trip was on the new streamliner, a bullet-shaped train with a diesel engine. He marvelled that it took only fifteen and one-half hours to get home. Because it was his first experience with this "train of the future," in a sense it opened up a new world of transportation for him and the other General Authorities. A few years later, the widespread use of airplanes would completely revolutionize their travel habits. Ironically, they would find this hardly reduced their work load. It simply enabled them to do more and more, faster and faster.

Not long after Elder Lee returned home from this trip to Washington, events began to unfold that led to the elevation of his friend Ezra Taft Benson to the Quorum of the Twelve. On May 29, 1943, Elder Sylvester Q. Cannon of the Twelve passed away at the comparatively young age of sixty-five, creating a vacancy in the quorum. He had served as an apostle for only five years, and during that entire time he was in frail health so that his passing was no great surprise. Then on June 21, 1943, Rudger Clawson, president of the Twelve, died at the ripe age of eighty-six, creating a second vacancy in the quorum. However, President Clawson had completed forty-five years of apostolic service and enjoyed the distinction of being the only man in the history of the Church who had been sustained as counselor in the First Presidency, but who had never been set apart to that office. On October 6, 1901, at the age of forty-four, he was sustained in general conference as the second counselor to President Lorenzo Snow. Since President Snow died four days later and since President Joseph F. Smith did not select Elder Clawson as a counselor, he was never set apart.

Soon after President Clawson's death, President Heber J. Grant set in motion the process for filling the two vacancies in the Quorum of the Twelve by asking his brethren to submit nominations for his consideration. On July 1, 1943, Elder Lee spent an hour visiting at the home of President J. Reuben Clark when the subject of filling the two vacancies came up. Of that interview, Elder Lee wrote: "We discussed the names of Spencer W. Kimball and Ezra Taft Benson. . . . I was pleased to know that President Grant had already decided to appoint one or the other of these two, or probably both, inasmuch as they had both been in my mind as the logical men to appoint." That Elder Lee was "pleased" with this knowledge likely derived from his admiration for these two men with whom he had had recent, favorable contacts and from a sense of comfort that

Maturing in the Apostleship

his impressions coincided with those of the prophet. Significantly, in this conversation with President Clark, Elder Lee mentioned Mark E. Petersen as a third possibility to fill one of the vacancies. Months later, when the excommunication of Richard R. Lyman created still another vacancy, Mark E. Petersen would be called to fill it. As Elder Lee prepared to leave his study, President Clark kissed him on the cheek and complimented him on the "wonderful work" he was doing. Revealing the admiration he had for his mentor, Elder Lee wrote: "I told him that there was nothing more I desired than to please him and my Heavenly Father."

Soon after this elevating experience with President Clark, Elder Lee had a depressing experience when he was called on to cast out an evil spirit. There was a stultifying feeling in the room that oppressed the apostle as he laid his hands on the woman's head and, through priesthood authority, rebuked the evil spirit in her. The terror that the incident produced is hinted at in Elder Lee's diary. "I trembled like a leaf," wrote he, "and my hair seemed to almost be as pin pricks." This seems to have been the first time in Elder Lee's ministry when he was directly exposed to the power of the adversary. It was not an imaginary thing, but was something real and powerful and beyond his individual ability to control. Intermittently during the remainder of his ministry, Elder Lee was exposed to the power of Satan, revealed in changing forms and in different degrees of intensity. It was a power that he detested but, at the same time, he respected because of the dangerous influences it exerted.

At the meeting of the Council of the First Presidency and Quorum of the Twelve held on July 8, 1943, George Albert Smith was set apart as the president of the Quorum of the Twelve, replacing President Rudger Clawson. At the same meeting, Spencer W. Kimball was approved as a new member of the Twelve. And two weeks later, Ezra Taft Benson was approved to fill the other vacancy. Because both men were serving as stake presidents, the reorganization of their stakes was necessary before the October general conference when they would be presented for sustaining vote. Elder Lee was assigned to reorganize President Kimball's stake. In early September, he traveled to Safford, Arizona, by train via Los Angeles for this purpose. Assisted by Brother Kimball, Elder Lee interviewed the leaders of the stake until 1:00 A.M. on Saturday the eleventh when, by analysis and spiritual confirmation, J. Harold Mitchell was selected as the new stake president. At the general session on the twelfth, there was an outpouring of love for Elder Kimball, who was presented with gifts and mementoes to remind him of his Arizona flock. Those present doubtless did not perceive the historical significance of what took place when Harold B. Lee, a future president of the Church, released as stake president the man who would succeed him as the prophet.

Elder Lee remained in Safford for two days after the conference, setting apart and instructing the leaders and counselling with his new colleague. It was a difficult time for Elder Kimball, whose children faced the trauma of being uprooted from the place they loved and of moving to a city where they were unknown. "He had arisen at 4:45 A.M.," Elder Lee noted on September 14, 1991, "and had written them a long letter pleading for their cooperation and support." Often unnoticed is the way Church callings have severe impact on family members, through sacrifices and difficulties they experience in supporting their father or husband.

En route home, Elder Lee stopped again in Tucson to check into reports about questionable teachings at the Church institute at the University of Arizona and to participate in a community worship service on campus. He stayed in the home of his cousin Sterling W. McMurrin, whom he counselled about "the importance of keeping foremost in his mind the responsibility of stimulating the faith of the institute students." At the community service on Sunday, September 19, where a thousand students were present, Elder Lee "spoke on the value of religion in the solution of individual and world problems."

As the October 1943 general conference approached, Elder Lee met privately with Elders Kimball and Benson to brief them on what to expect as they went through the process of sustaining and ordination to the apostleship. This likely was done at the behest of President J. Reuben Clark, who in the future would occasionally refer to Elder Lee as "the dean of the younger men." Because he had been a member of the quorum for two and a half years and, before that, had worked for five years at Church headquarters where he was constantly in contact with the Church leaders, Elder Lee was in a position to give them tips on protocol and procedure, which would smooth their way into the Church hierarchy. Elder Lee especially focused on the procedure to be followed at the time of their ordination by President Grant. But, he went further than this, giving advice about matters that would help them to avoid needless difficulties or embarrassments. He suggested to Elder Benson that he not make too much out of the reduction in income he had suffered by leaving the employment of the farm cooperative in Washington. "He was somewhat taken back," wrote Elder Lee, "but like the good soldier that he is, I am sure he will be wise." The incident reflects, again, a salient quality of Elder Lee's character and leadership. He seldom failed to teach a lesson regardless of the time, the place, the circumstances, or the person involved. He took every opportunity to plant an idea, or to stimulate faith, or to lay a remonstrance upon someone, whether gentle or firm. He seldom, if ever, engaged in small talk. What he said had meaning and purpose. And a wise stake president would have done well to listen carefully to his words at the pulpit which though ostensibly addressed to the audience may well have been intended especially for him. It was not uncommon for him to speak "over the heads" of an audience to a specific person or persons. This reflected an interesting aspect of Elder Lee's makeup. There were few leaders of his day more plainspoken than he. Yet, if the circumstances required it, he could be indirect and remote, accomplishing a desired result by finesse and adroit maneuvering rather than by direct speech. Occasionally, he would induce obedience by his silence.

Ordinarily, new members of the Twelve are ordained in the upper room of the Salt Lake Temple. However, because of President Heber J. Grant's physical disabilities, this procedure was not followed in the case of Elders Spencer W. Kimball and Ezra Taft Benson. Instead, for the prophet's convenience, a special meeting was convened in the First Presidency's council room, located at the north end of the main floor of the Church Administration Building. Here, after the usual preliminaries, the aging prophet, lacking strength to stand, invited the new brethren, in turn, Elder Kimball being first, to kneel before him. He then invited his counselors and the members of the Twelve to stand round in a circle, joining him in laying hands on the head of the one kneeling before him. Acting as voice, the prophet then ordained each one to the apostleship and set him apart as a member of the Twelve.

"Today marked a new chapter in church history," Elder Lee wrote of the occasion. "The two new members of the Council of the Twelve, Spencer W. Kimball and Ezra Taft Benson, were ordained apostles by President Grant in a special meeting of the Twelve and the First Presidency held in the office of the First Presidency." The historical significance of the event was apparent to all because both were direct descendants of men who had held the apostleship, Elder Kimball being a grandson of Heber C. Kimball and Elder Benson being a great-grandson of the first Ezra Taft Benson. It was historically significant, too, that both were ordained on the same day and that at the time of their calls, both were serving as stake presidents. However, future events would add further historical significance to this day: Both would live to serve as the president of the Church, something which had never happened before to men ordained on the same day, and the induction of this

Maturing in the Apostleship

pair into the quorum began an astounding turnover in the makeup of the Twelve, unprecedented in the history of the Church. In the decade from 1943 to October 1953, ten vacancies were created in the Quorum of the Twelve, caused either by death, by calls to the First Presidency, or, in the case of Richard R. Lyman, by excommunication. As already noted, President Rudger Clawson and Sylvester Q. Cannon passed away in the fore part of 1943. Later that year, Elder Lyman was excommunicated. Then in 1945, George Albert Smith left to become the president of the Church, Charles A. Callis died in 1947 as did George F. Richards in 1950, Stephen L. Richards became a counselor in the First Presidency in 1951, John A. Widtsoe and Joseph F. Merrill died in 1952, and Albert E. Bowen passed away in 1953. These departures and their replacements advanced Elder Lee in seniority in the quorum so that in October 1953 when Elder Richard L. Evans was called to the Twelve, Elder Lee was its second ranking member, junior only to President Joseph Fielding Smith. President Smith and the members of the First Presidency, David O. McKay, Stephen L. Richards, and J. Reuben Clark, who were also senior to Elder Lee in the apostleship, had an average age of over seventy-eight years. Since Elder Lee was then fifty-four, the perception that he would one day be the president of the Church was even more pronounced than it was in 1941 when, as the newest member of the quorum, he stood at the end of the long line of white-haired men who were senior to him. The magnitude of the changes that occurred in the decade 1943 to 1953 is better understood by the fact that for seven years from 1963 to 1970, Elder Thomas S. Monson was the junior member of the Twelve.

Less than a month after the ordination of Elders Kimball and Benson, Elder Lee was assigned by the First Presidency to work with President Joseph Fielding Smith to investigate charges that had been made against Elder Lyman. This resulted in his excommunication, which took place on November 12, 1943. By any measure, it was the most stressful thing that occurred to Elder Lee as part of his apostolic service. "It was a most saddening experience," wrote he, "with most of the Twelve in tears as Brother Lyman was asked to leave the meeting and shook hands in parting."

The following weekend, Elder Lee and Elder Kimball were assigned to attend the stake conference together in Parowan, Utah. They found that the sense of shock and disbelief with which the Twelve had faced the reality of the excommunication had extended there. "I sought to strengthen the faith of the people in my sermon," wrote Elder Lee, "by showing the evidence of continuing warfare between the forces of good and evil and the power of the gospel in meeting every crisis in life."

The epilogue of this tragedy had already begun to be written before the excommunication took place. Earlier, Mark E. Petersen, managing editor of the *Deseret News*, had a vivid dream, which was a rarity for him. In it he saw a headline in the *Deseret News*, "Lyman R. Richard Dies." In the dream, it was also shown to him he would be called to the Twelve to fill the vacancy. On awakening, he was troubled as much by the glaring error in the headline as by the personal implication of the dream. He sent the Church reporter, Henry A. Smith, to 47 East South Temple to inquire about the health of the Brethren; he returned to say everyone seemed to be well. It was some time later that Elder Petersen was informed of the excommunication and instructed to publish a notice of it in the news. In early April 1944 when he was called to the prophet's office and told he was to fill the vacancy, Elder Petersen said: "President Grant, I have known for some weeks that this was coming." After hearing the account of the dream, President Grant said the Lord had given him "the right impression." (*Mark E. Petersen, A Biography,* p. 86.) The call of Elder Petersen confirmed the impression Elder Lee had received about him the previous year when there were discussions about filling the vacancies created by the deaths of Sylvester Q. Cannon and Rudger Clawson.

As part of the 1944 April general conference, the Twelve held their quarterly meeting. These meetings, which usually last for several hours, convene in a room on the fourth floor of the Salt Lake Temple. At these meetings, each member of the quorum is at liberty to express himself at length as to any subject of his choosing. At the quarterly meeting held on April 5, 1944, Elder Lee discussed a subject that to him was vital. It was summarized in his diary when he expressed the hope that "we would never discourage the relating of faith promoting experiences in testimony bearing." This was prompted by comments he had heard expressing the contrary view. It was difficult for Elder Lee to understand this attitude, given the aim of the Latter-day Saints to be led constantly by the whisperings of the Spirit. This was a reality for him. Seldom did a day pass but that he received spiritual direction from the Lord. It was his lifeblood. And the thought that he should not mention these faith-promoting experiences in bearing testimony was incomprehensible. Therefore, whenever the circumstances were appropriate, Elder Lee never failed to share spiritual direction or insight he had received. In doing so, he bolstered the faith of many who, seeing how the Lord had revealed to him, were anxious to receive similar spiritual direction. In this practice, Elder Lee emulated the Prophet Joseph Smith, whose repeated testimonies about heavenly visitations and other extraordinary phenomena have provided spiritual nourishment for generations of Latter-day Saints.

During this period, Elder Lee's family went through a crisis. Fern, the heart of the home, was ill. Always frail, she had begun to tire more easily and lacked the energy to care for their large two-story home. Yet her compulsive nature dictated that the house undergo its annual cleaning. On May 18, Elder Lee "helped Fern get the house cleaning started." He was around for two days to assist but was then on the road to a conference in the San Juan Stake in southern Utah. The following week found him in Gridley, California. And prior to the July break, he attended stake conferences or other special meetings in Ogden, Utah; Salmon, Idaho; and Provo, Utah. Of course, the girls helped their mother, and Elder Lee assisted with the work as his crowded schedule allowed. But, the heaviest burden rested on Fern. These exertions, added to her natural frailty, put Fern in bed. By mid-July, the doctor decided major surgery was necessary. She was admitted to the hospital on July 21, and four days later, Doctor A. C. Callister performed abdominal surgery on her, removing several tumors. Fortunately, none was malignant. "She was colorless throughout the day," wrote Elder Lee the day of the surgery. During the next twelve days, the harried husband haunted the hospital at every opportunity, anxiously monitoring his wife's recovery. "Fern miserable with gas pains," he wrote the day following the operation. Thereafter, he watched carefully for any change in her condition, whether for better or for worse.

Elder Lee was stressed as he tried to keep all the balls in the air at the office, at home, and at the hospital as he comforted his wife. Before the surgery became necessary, the girls had planned two major social events at the home. Unable to reschedule them, or to transfer them to another home, their father stepped into the breach to help. Four days after the operation, he spent several hours working in the garden and beautifying the yards for a party the following night. This was sandwiched in between duties at the office and visits to the hospital. The next night, he presided at the grill, barbecuing hot dogs for a large group of young people who came to the Lee home. Four days later, he returned to his yard work, between visits to the hospital, preparing for a party of the Alpha Chi sorority for which the girls were hostesses.

The next Sunday, the crisis ended. "Fern was like one released from prison," wrote Elder Lee on August 6 after bringing his wife home from the hospital. "Everything seemed beautiful and lovely to her." Several weeks of convalescence lay ahead for the patient as she recovered from her ordeal. The girls, who had part-time summer work, pitched in on their off hours and this, with their father's help when he was home, made it possible to maintain the home and to help Fern in her recovery without outside assistance.

Toward the end of August, Elder Lee counselled with Maurine and Helen about their courses at the University of Utah for the coming year. However, when their father dropped a hint they might be able to accompany their parents on a trip to Mexico in the fall, their plans changed. They decided to drop out of school for a year to work and to go to Mexico, if the opportunity to do so came. It did. After the October general conference when Elder Lee's itinerary firmed up, the family began to plan for their once-in-a-lifetime trip. It would be the only long trip they would take together while the girls were single. And even before they left Salt Lake, Helen's single status was in jeopardy. "Helen went out last night with Brent Goates," Elder Lee recorded on October 29, "whom I met as a missionary in Fort Worth, Texas, two years ago; and they seemed to be immediately in love with each other. Each had seemingly been admiring the other at a distance and hardly daring to confess their real (feelings) to each other. He is leaving in ten days for the Merchant Marine service; and they will have their love put to a real test." Later events revealed that Helen and her young man met that test since on June 24, 1946, Elder Lee performed their temple sealing. By this act, the apostle received into his family a son-in-law who, in every respect, filled the role of the natural son he had never had.

The family packed their things in Elder Lee's Buick and left Salt Lake City early on November 3, 1944. Driving south through Price, Moab, and Monticello, Utah, they bent eastward into southwestern Colorado, passing Cortez and thence proceeding south to Albuquerque, New Mexico. They spent the night there before driving on to El Paso, Texas, on the border of Old Mexico. With their two vivacious daughters in the car with them, drinking in sights they had never seen before and bubbling over with youthful exuberance, the time passed quickly for the travellers. Amazingly, that enthusiasm hardly lagged during the five weeks they were together, despite wearing travel in a foreign land where the language, the customs, and the food were different from anything they had previously known.

At El Paso, the travellers were met by President Arwell L. Pierce of the Mexican Mission who would be their guide and host. Although born in Utah, President Pierce was raised in the Mormon colonies in Old Mexico, spoke Spanish as fluently as English, and with the insight of a native, understood the culture of the people his guests were to visit. Moreover, he had served as the first bishop of the El Paso Ward, whose membership included many Mexicans, so that he had had extensive grass roots experience in administering Church affairs among these people. All this, added to his buoyant, positive personality and the fact that his middle name was Lee, made President Pierce the ideal guide and companion for Elder Lee and his family.

During the two days the travellers remained in El Paso, getting their identification papers in order and organizing for their trip into the heart of Mexico, Elder Lee and President Pierce crossed the Rio Grande into Cuidad Juarez where they organized a branch of the Church. The branch president told the brethren that the action taken "fulfilled a vision" he had received eight years before when he was baptized. This experience typified the high level of spirituality Elder Lee found among the Mexican people during this tour, and which he would find years later as he toured throughout Latin America. The high level of poverty among them and their reliance on divine influences for help in battling life's problems tends to make many Latin Americans more spiritually attuned than those who enjoy material abundance.

The travellers left El Paso on November 6 for the three-day trip to Mexico City. The first part of their journey, through the states of Chihuahua and Durango, treated them to landscapes similar to those they had seen in Texas and New Mexico north of the border. Lying on a plateau between the Sierra Madre Occidental and the Sierra Madre Oriental, the area travelled was marked by broad and distant vistas, dotted with rugged mountains and carpeted with desert grasses and plants. Here lay winter ranges for cattle. Occasional green valleys appeared, surrounding villages, whose existence depended on variable water resources. As the travellers moved further south, the terrain and the climate changed, becoming more mountainous and tropical as they came nearer to the equator. They arrived in Mexico City on November 9, feeling, no doubt, the effect of the city's seventy-four-hundred-foot altitude, three thousand feet higher than Salt Lake City.

The visitors spent three weeks in and around Mexico City. The apostle, joined by President Pierce, held meetings with members and missionaries. He also conducted special training sessions with local leaders. A pressing problem at the time arose from the militant activities of a group of dissidents called the Third Convention. The members of this group became disaffected because they resented Anglo leaders from the United States and insisted that their leaders be selected from among Mexican members. Later they added other planks to their platform of dissent, including a demand that the Church resume the practice of polygamy. At meetings held in Mexico City and Ozumba, the apostle explained in detail the status of those involved in the Third Convention and the points of doctrine and policy underlying the controversy. This rebellion, which ultimately resulted in the excommunication of eight of its ringleaders, simmered for two more years, when it was largely quelled during a personal visit from George Albert Smith in 1946, the first president of the Church to visit Mexico during his prophetic tenure. The third prophet to do so was President Harold B. Lee, who attended an area general conference in Mexico City in August 1972, a month after he was ordained the eleventh president of the Church.

Elder Lee held additional meetings with members and missionaries at Puebla, Toluca, Cabrerra, San Marcos, San Pedro, Martin, Guereiu, and Santiago in the Mexico City area. In between, he joined his family in visiting historic sites. Within the city itself, the Lees were most interested in the National University, the National Museum, and Chapultepec Park, including the Chapultepec Castle. Outside the city, the main attractions were the pyramids and other archaeological sites at San Juan Teotihuacan, remnants of an ancient civilization that once flourished in the area. While it was not possible to precisely identify the builders of these structures with peoples named in the Book of Mormon, the mere existence of these buildings, revealing the kind of intelligence and skill possessed by the people who built them, added powerful credence to the story told by Joseph Smith about the origin of the Book of Mormon.

The travellers began their meandering return home on November 28 when they left Mexico City at 4:40 A.M., destined for Uruapan to the west. Because of gas shortages caused by the war, Mexican motorists were allowed to drive their cars only on certain days of the week. However, Brother Periu, a branch president, was able to obtain a special permit, which enabled the Lees to travel every day. After leaving Uruapan, the party veered northwest toward Guadalajara, Mexico's second largest city. En route they passed an active volcano, Paricutin, where they rented saddle horses in order to obtain a better view of the surroundings. What they saw was graphically described by Elder Lee. "With the intermittent rolling and ground shaking, the molten rocks and lava, with smoke and dust belching forth, and (with) the miles of red lava flowing, a most impressive and soul stirring spectacle was presented, one never to be forgotten."

The usual meetings were held in Guadalajara, in between which was a visit to the Plaza Mayor, the heart of the old city. Here are found the three-hundred-year-old cathedral and the state capitol, called the Palacio del Gobierno. The nearby shops contain a wide variety of the items for which Guadalajara is noted—pottery, clay figurines, leather goods, and glassware of various hues: green, amber, and blue—and which are alluring to visitors. Elder

Lee did not make note of any purchases made there by his wife and daughters. But, it is difficult to imagine that these three, who took such pride in the decor of the home, could have wholly refrained from sampling these wares.

After spending a day at San Luis Potosi, northeast of Guadalajara, which is in the heart of Mexico's cattle, wheat, and corn country, the travelers went to Monterrey, located in the foothills of the Sierra Madre Oriental. In this area, at an elevation of sixteen hundred feet, the Lees found a moderate, balmy climate, not unlike that of southern Arizona, with palm trees and an abundance of citrus fruit. Here Elder Lee held a two-day conference on Saturday and Sunday, December 2 and 3. And, it was here that they encountered the only really inclement weather of the entire tour when a storm of cloudburst proportions hit the area.

Leaving Monterrey, the visitors reentered the United States at Laredo, Texas, on December 4. Travelling through Eagle Pass; El Paso, Texas; Albuquerque, New Mexico; and Moab, Utah, Elder Lee and his family negotiated the last leg of their journey, arriving home December 9. They were as happy to return as they had been to leave. Indeed, they may have been even happier to return because Fern had contracted an annoying head cold during the last part of the tour.

The images and impressions created by this tour—the vastness, the variety, and the beauty of Mexico, the warmth and the spirituality of its people, the vigor of the Church that was beginning to gain a foothold there, the enthusiasm and the dedication of its young leaders, and the lingering reminders of an extinct civilization, mirrored in the crumbling ruins of its gigantic buildings—all these, and many more, would remain securely stored in the memories of the members of the Lee family, to provide moments of quiet reverie in the days ahead or the grist for future sermons, lessons, or leadership counselling.

Chapter Fifteen

Patterns of Change

The year 1945, and those immediately following it, brought many changes in the life of Elder Harold B. Lee and the Church that he served. By this time, he had been a member of the Twelve for four years, during which he had grown in stature and in personal influence and maturity. His increasing stature among the Brethren was reflected by an assignment he received during the first half of 1945, when he was asked by the First Presidency to give a series of talks on Sunday evenings over radio station KSL in Salt Lake City. During this time, he was excused from attending stake conferences in order to have adequate time to prepare and to deliver these talks. Because of Elder Lee's youth, compared to most of the other General Authorities of the Church, and because of the extraordinary influence he had with young people, he was asked to focus his talks on the youth. Thus, the series was given the title "Youth and the Church." Later, the talks were compiled in a book bearing the same title. Still later, after Elder Lee became the president of the Church, the talks, as modified, were published again, this time under the title *Decisions for Successful Living*.

Patterns of Change

It is clear Elder Lee found his main laboratory for studying and counselling young people at home. "When this material was first prepared," he wrote in the preface to *Decisions for Successful Living,* "my own daughters, Maurine and Helen, served as representatives of the modern youth of the day, and were my chief critics and consultants in the preparation of these chapters." In addition, of course, he relied on the experiences he had had as a teacher and principal of youth in the public schools, as a seminary teacher in the Church Education System, and as a tutor of young missionaries about the temple ordinances as they prepared to enter the mission field. All these experiences had given him a keen insight into the problems and challenges of the youth of the Church and a special rapport with them. He addressed them as a friend and a confidant, not as a scolding schoolmaster, and as one genuinely interested in them and their future. They reciprocated in kind, taking him into their confidence and regarding him as one of their own.

The titles of a few of the twenty-six talks delivered in this series give a flavor of Elder Lee's approach: "Why The Church?," "Your Search for Truth," "Ideals," "The Worth of a Human Soul," "The Rapture of a Moment or the Peace of Years," and "Toward Happy Homes." Undoubtedly, the impact of these talks was a chief factor that caused so many young people to flock to Elder Lee, requesting that he perform their temple sealings. Although a couple may never have met him personally, nor have had even a remote connection with him through family or friends, they felt no reluctance to invite him to perform their sealing, apparently because of a sense that there was a bond between them. And ever after, they could point with a sense of pride to the fact that Elder Lee, their "special friend," had sealed them in the temple. We gain some insight into the magnitude of the added administrative burden this placed on the apostle from the fact that during a nine-day period in June 1946, he performed twenty-one temple sealings. It is not known that he ever declined a request to do this, except for illness, absence from the city, or a conflicting appointment. We infer that this was not a mechanical thing for Elder Lee, because he would not merely record that he had performed, say, seven sealings on a given day in June, as he did on June 12, 1946, but he recorded the full names of each couple.

Major changes occurred in the hierarchy of the Church during the year 1945. The First Council of the Seventy was most significantly affected when two of its members passed away on successive days, Rufus K. Hardy on March 7 and Samuel O. Bennion on March 8. They were replaced by Elders S. Dilworth Young and Milton R. Hunter at the following April general conference. At that time, President Heber J. Grant was grievously ill, suffering from a debilitating stroke he had suffered several years before. The end came for the eighty-eight-year-old prophet on Monday, May 14. Elder Lee was advised of President Grant's passing by Elder Joseph Fielding Smith at 7:00 P.M. that night, only twenty-five minutes after the prophet died. Elder and Sister Lee immediately went to the Grant home, high on the avenues in Salt Lake City, to pay their respects to President Grant's widow, Augusta. There they joined in a kneeling prayer with members of the Grant family and others who had assembled.

The following morning, a special meeting of the Council of the Twelve was held where the funeral arrangements were discussed and where Elder Lee was assigned to prepare a tribute from the Twelve to the prophet. Three days after the funeral, a special meeting of the Twelve convened in the upper room of the Salt Lake Temple to consider the reorganization of the First Presidency. Following the established precedent, it was decided that the reorganization should not be delayed because of the pressing need to have a functioning First Presidency in place. President George Albert Smith was then unanimously approved to replace President Grant, and he selected the same counselors President Grant had had, J. Reuben Clark and David O. McKay. Elder Lee joined with the other apostles present to place their hands on the head of Brother Smith to ordain and to set him apart as the eighth president of the Church, and George F. Richards was approved and set apart as the president of the Twelve.

This was the first of four times Elder Lee was to witness this formal transfer of prophetic authority to a new president of the Church. The fourth and last time, of course, was when in July 1972 he was ordained, in the same manner, as the eleventh president of the Church, with Spencer W. Kimball acting as voice in the ordination. On each occasion, he was struck by the simple, orderly way in which the transfer of such vast authority was effected, without dissent or controversy, and without any divisive "campaigning," which often accompanies changes in ecclesiastical or other leadership.

The last change in the general officers of the Church during 1945 occurred at the October general conference when Matthew Cowley was chosen to fill the vacancy in the Twelve created when George Albert Smith became the president of the Church.

These significant changes in Church leadership during the period of a few months corresponded with major changes in world affairs, which occurred at the same time. In early March 1945, World War II still raged both in Europe and in the Pacific. The terrible effects of this conflagration were being felt in communities around the world. Elder Lee's journal entry of March 18, 1945, reflects the grim consequences of war. "I received a call from Wm. E. Ryberg," he wrote on that date, "saying 'Harold, my boy is gone.' He was killed in Italy." Elder Lee immediately went to the Ryberg home to console the grieving parents and to give them a blessing. Later, he was the main speaker at memorial services for the Ryberg boy. Later he performed the same service for the Gold family, whose son, Oscar, had been killed in Germany. Fortunately, events that followed not long afterward signalled the end of the war and of sad experiences like this. By early May 1945, both Germany and Italy had been defeated. And by that time, the Okinawa campaign pointed the way toward victory in the Pacific, which became a reality the following August after the atomic bombs were dropped on Hiroshima and Nagasaki.

Once it became clear the end of the war was near, Elder Lee and his brethren moved promptly to prepare for the changes that event would produce. Elder Lee convened a meeting of the military relations committee to consider the steps to be taken to help returning servicemen smoothly reenter civilian life. Also it was decided Hugh B. Brown would return to England to remain for a year to help coordinate the return of LDS servicemen from the European theatre.

When this meeting was held, it was uncertain how long the war in the Pacific would last. The Japanese were fighting tenaciously and apparently had the will and the resources to continue the struggle into the indefinite future. It was under these circumstances that Elder Lee received an assignment to go to the Hawaiian Islands to hold a series of meetings with members and missionaries and to check on the LDS servicemen's facilities at Honolulu. Because he would be travelling into areas where he might be exposed to enemy fire, his father, as already noted, wanted to give him a special blessing. "He reminded me of my lineage," the son reported in his diary, "rehearsed my life, and blessed me for the trip to Hawaii."

The first leg of the journey, from Salt Lake to San Francisco, was taken in high style. President J. Reuben Clark, who was travelling to the coast on business in a private car of the Western Pacific Railroad, invited his protégé to go with him. "It was luxury class," Elder Lee reported, "with modern bedroom accommodations and a private chef and steward." His accommodations on the last leg, from San Francisco to Honolulu, suffered badly by comparison.

After spending twelve vexing days in the bay area, the apostle was finally able to book passage on a dumpy old freighter, whose unkempt and tired appearance hardly inspired visions of a classic voyage on the blue Pacific. Elder Lee and twenty-three other travellers boarded this nameless old tub on July 9 and were assigned to the four ten-foot by twelve-foot cabins reserved for passengers. Elder Lee chose an upper bunk nearest the entryway "so the tobacco smoke would not be too obnoxious." After stowing his gear and making the acquaintance of his cabin mates, Elder Lee went on deck to watch with fascination as the ship eased out of its berth, maneuvered through the bay, and passing under the Golden Gate Bridge, headed into the Pacific toward Hawaii.

It was Elder Lee's first voyage. Therefore, every aspect of it was new and exciting. As the freighter breasted the heavy ground swells off the California coast, he was pleased to find that the motion of the ship did not nauseate him. This enabled him to enjoy the sights, the sounds, and the smells of the open sea to the fullest extent. Since the weather was clear for the entire seven-day voyage, he spent many hours on deck, watching the albatross, which glided effortlessly behind the ship, or the flying fish, which occasionally were seen alongside. After dark, he was treated to a dazzling view of the heavens, unobstructed by clouds or pollution and undimmed by man-made lights. And standing at the rail at night, he was fascinated by the phosphorescent particles in the water, which sparkled like tiny flecks of light, a phenomenon that had intrigued mariners through the centuries. During the day when he was not gazing at the sea, the apostle spent his time profitably, reading, writing, and preparing for the meetings to be held in the islands. The only distractions to this enjoyable routine, aside from his smoke-filled sleeping compartment, were the vulgarities and profanities of the crew, a motley bunch who made no effort to accommodate or to defer to the passengers, whom they regarded as an annoyance and an impediment to their work. Here was none of the glitz and glamor found on a luxury liner, whose sole objective is the comfort and pleasure of its passengers.

On Sunday, nine of the twenty-four passengers joined

for an ecumenical worship service. Elder Lee offered the opening and closing prayers; a Catholic, connected with the USO, read a scripture; and a Korean minister gave an impromptu speech.

On arriving at Pearl Harbor, the apostle was met by Stake President Ralph E. Woolley and his son and Bishop Jay Qualey. The absence of a jovial group of Hawaiian members at the pier to greet and to sing to the visitor and to load him with leis resulted from the deadening effect of the war on this sprawling harbor, which bristled with fighting ships and bustled with work as crews from the base toiled around-the-clock to repair or to outfit the ships and to load them with munitions.

The day after his arrival in Honolulu, Elder Lee, accompanied by LDS chaplain Lt. Commander John W. Boud, visited the military cemetery where Naval Captain Mervyn Bennion was buried. Here, at the grave site of President Clark's son-in-law, the apostle paid symbolic respect to all LDS servicemen who had fallen in the war. From there, he and Commander Boud visited the LDS Servicemen's Center near downtown Honolulu. Located in an old home, the center was a focal point for all LDS servicemen who passed through Pearl Harbor, destined either for the mainland and rehab leave or for the shooting war in the Pacific. Here a lonely GI could find a place to relax, to visit with those who shared his values, or, perhaps, to locate a friend from home. To facilitate this, the center maintained a registry in which visitors were invited to record their names, homes, and military billets. A large bulletin board, plastered with messages and greetings, scrawled on paper snippets of different sizes and colors, provided a means of communication between buddies passing through Pearl. Elder Lee spent time at the center to counsel with those in charge, to thank them for their service and to make sure that everything possible was being done to care for the Mormon GI's.

During his two-week stay in the islands, Elder Lee, in addition to the island of Oahu, on which Honolulu is located, visited the islands of Maui, Kauai, Hawaii, and Molokai, where he held meetings with members and missionaries. At Molokai, he also visited the leper colony at Kalaupapa, where fifty-two members of the Church lived. The apostle and Mission President Castle E. Murphy descended to the colony by mules over a steep, narrow, winding trail. Here they found a dispirited people, doomed to wear out their lives in isolation, devoid of hope for happiness or fulfillment here, except as they might find it within themselves through mental and spiritual exertion. Elder Lee endeavored to feed that glimmer of hope at a meeting he and President Murphy held with members of the Kalaupapa Branch.

The mournful and hopeless condition found in the leper colony stood in contrast to the happiness and joviality Elder Lee found at luaus given in his honor at Laie and Kauai. The menus at these feasts were impressive to the visitor, so much so that he took time to record them in his diary. They included poi, roast pig, chicken, bananas, pineapple, coconut cake, and mounds of other food he could not describe or spell. Draped with fragrant leis as he ate and was entertained with song and dance, Elder Lee seemingly had never before felt so fully feted. "The genuine love and adoration of these people," wrote he of his Hawaiian friends, "is almost unbelievable."

The main purpose of the apostle's visit to Hawaii was to attend the quarterly conference of the Honolulu Stake. At the morning session, almost fifteen hundred crowded into the stake center. Elder Lee had never before seen such a mix of different cultures and races as was represented in the audience. It was pleasing to note that there were apparent harmony and good feelings among them, despite their differences. He was especially pleased to see that there were no apparent lingering antagonisms toward the Church members of Japanese origin because of the attack on Pearl Harbor. In an effort to cement these good feelings, and to forestall a backlash of enmity toward the Japanese, Elder Lee had dinner with the president of the Japanese

*Elder Harold B. Lee
at a luau*

Branch and some of his co-workers. He also inspected the temple at Laie before leaving the islands, counselling with the temple presidency about some of their challenges.

Not anxious to spend another week in a smoke-filled cabin aboard a cargo ship, Elder Lee was elated when the local brethren were able to arrange passage for him on a clipper flight from Honolulu on July 31. With a transit stop and a change of planes at Mills Field in San Mateo, California, the apostle arrived home on August 3 where he was warmly welcomed by Fern and the girls and other members of the family.

Along with everyone else, Elder Lee's enthusiasm mounted later when the war in the Pacific ended as suddenly as it had commenced. The atomic bombs dropped on Hiroshima and Nagasaki revealed to Japan the futility of continuing the fight. With the signing of the articles of peace aboard the battleship *Missouri,* a new era was ushered in for the world and for the Church. Because of his role as the chairman of the servicemen's committee, a main concern of Elder Lee was the orderly demobilization of the Latter-day Saints who were in the service and their smooth transition to civilian life. So in September 1945, he went to Washington, D.C., to confer with government officials. As always, stake conference and other assignments were clustered around the main purpose of the trip in order to conserve on time and expense. From September 7 to 9, Elder Lee presided at a stake conference in Chicago where the prominent attorney John K. Edmunds was installed as the new stake president. The following weekend found the apostle in New York where he presided over a stake conference there. The time between these two conferences was spent in the nation's capital. There, with the assistance of J. Willard Marriott, he was able to confer with various government officials, including the Chief of Chaplains. "Found them very cooperative," he reported. On the twelfth, Elder Lee spent the day with Ernest L. Wilkinson, a future president of the Brigham Young University, who was then a counselor in the stake presidency and a prominent Washington attorney. At the request of the stake presidency, Elder Lee agreed to hold a meeting with priesthood leaders that evening. He was surprised to find that it convened in the cultural hall instead of in the adjacent, air-conditioned chapel. He was even more surprised when, during the meeting, he was asked to keep his voice down so as not to disturb the organ recital in the chapel. The incident, while inconsequential, reflects an attitude that was prevalent at the time, an attitude that relegated priesthood functions to a subordinate position in the Church's order of priorities. In the years ahead, through the revolutionary correlation program, Harold B. Lee would play the major role in altering these attitudes.

Elder Lee returned from the East just in time to participate in the dedication of the Idaho Falls Temple. Twenty-five thousand members participated in the eight sessions. Since this was the first time President George Albert Smith had presided at a significant occasion since his ordination in May, the Brethren were anxious for his success. In recapping the event, Elder Lee noted, with apparent gratitude, how well the prophet had acquitted himself. "The outstanding feature of the services," he wrote, "were the inspired addresses of President George Albert Smith, who rose to the occasion in a wonderful way. The spirit of inspiration and leadership was upon him. The dedicatory prayer was most impressive and covered every conceivable interest of the church for blessing and guidance." One significant source of the deep spiritual stirrings Elder Lee felt during these services is suggested by his diary entry of September 24. Wrote he, "Both President Clark and President McKay declared that we had an unseen audience made up of our leaders of the past and worthy saints who had passed on before."

The spiritual feelings generated by the temple dedication carried forward and permeated the October general conference, which followed soon after. These were especially pronounced at the Solemn Assembly session where George Albert Smith was sustained as the eighth president of the Church and where Matthew Cowley was sustained as the newest member of the Twelve. Circumstances surrounding Elder Cowley's call illustrate the way in which prophetic calls are sometimes confirmed spiritually to others. Before Elder Cowley left New Zealand earlier in 1945, a Maori leader, who was bemoaning the death of Rufus K. Hardy, whom the Maoris looked upon as "their" General Authority, predicted that Matthew Cowley would fill the next vacancy in the Twelve, which he did. And an incident that occurred after the October 1945 general conference illustrates how these special witnesses are sometimes brought to the attention of the presiding brethren years before their actual call and who, in the interim, are, in a sense, groomed for their service in the Twelve. Two days after the conference ended, President J. Reuben Clark came to Elder Lee's office to ask him to take up a labor with the "younger brethren" to urge them not to write out their conference talks. President Clark was "fearful that

Male quartet from the Twelve: Elders Mark E. Petersen, Matthew Cowley, Spencer W. Kimball, and Ezra Taft Benson, with Elder Harold B. Lee as accompanist

the next step would be for them to write their prayers." (This counsel was given, of course, before the tight strictures on timing imposed by telecasts of the conference made it mandatory to write the talks.) At the time of this visit, Delbert L. Stapley was in Elder Lee's office discussing matters about the Phoenix Stake, where he presided. Elder Lee had had many contacts with this Arizona leader, which had convinced him of his potential as a General Authority. He was pleased, therefore, that this chance meeting had given President Clark "an opportunity to become acquainted with [Delbert Stapley] for future reference." Five years would elapse before Elder Stapley was called to the Twelve, during which others were able to gauge the depth of his character and the qualities of his leadership.

In the months that followed the October 1945 general conference, Elder Lee was heavily involved in attending stake conferences. Between then and April 1946, he attended no fewer than fourteen of them in Utah, Idaho, California, Arizona, and Washington, D.C. In addition, he held several regional welfare meetings, and spoke at funerals and at other special functions. Two funerals where he spoke, for Nicholas G. Smith, Assistant to the Twelve, and Dr. Allen R. Cutler, prominent leader of Preston, Idaho, evoked many vivid memories. Elder Lee and Elder Smith were called as General Authorities the same day, socialized together in their study group, and officed side by side with the understanding that a connecting door would never be locked. Dr. Cutler was a boyhood friend from the Oneida Academy days, whose funeral drew an audience of a thousand from all over Cache Valley and beyond. The passing of contemporaries such as these reminded the speaker of his own mortality and of the fleeting and tenuous nature of life.

At a training seminar held in Provo, Utah, in late January, Elder Lee addressed the subject of "The Application of the Welfare Plan in the Solution of the After-war Problems." The most critical and complex postwar welfare problem arose out of the devastation wrought by the war in Europe. The Church responded promptly to provide emergency welfare assistance to the beleaguered European Saints. It was also decided to send a member of the Twelve to Europe to supervise the distribution of welfare commodities and to reestablish the Church organizations in the countries devastated by the war. Elder John A. Widtsoe, who was born in Norway, and who was the only native European among the Brethren, was first assigned to this task. When Elder Widtsoe later became ill, he was replaced by Elder Ezra Taft Benson. At the time of Elder Benson's appointment, President J. Reuben Clark told Elder Lee it was felt he was the logical one to go, presumably because of his long experience in welfare matters, but Elder Benson was chosen instead because Elder Lee "was needed here." That need apparently related to Elder Lee's key role in preparing for the flood of returning servicemen and to his intimate knowledge of the welfare machinery at home, which would enable him to expedite the flow of the vast quantities of welfare commodities that the European Saints would require.

The wisdom of this decision quickly became apparent. Elder Lee and his committee soon were busily engaged in preparing instructions for returning LDS servicemen who faced major challenges in the transition from military to civilian life. His interest in them was not perfunctory. He listened avidly to the reports of their military experiences and carefully recorded those he considered to be noteworthy. He was impressed with the depth of their faith, with their bravery, and with their commitment to the Church and its mission. He was specially interested, for instance, in the reports of two marines, A. Theodore Tuttle and Murray Rawson, who participated in the bloody battle at Iwo Jima and who later rendered significant Church service, Ted Tuttle as a General Authority and Murray Rawson as a mission president. Of the latter, Elder Lee wrote: "As his boat neared Iwo, he felt that there was such a power around him that no harm could befall him. He said he owed his life to the blessings of God." Of Elder Tuttle, he wrote, "He and his buddy stayed on the deck the night before they invaded Iwo. They were nervous but full of faith. They were both wounded. Tuttle insisted on returning because of a feeling of responsibility for the LDS boys of his company." When Elder Lee prepared instructions for returning servicemen, he had in mind men like these two, and many others whom he had met, whose lives had been radically changed by the war and who would be faced with major readjustments as they eased back into civilian life.

The wisdom of keeping Elder Lee home instead of sending him to Europe was also shown in the skillful way in which he supervised the production, collection, and shipping of the necessary commodities. By late February 1946, massive shipments of food and clothing were already on the way. Based upon reports received from Elder Benson and information gleaned from other sources, Elder Lee and his associates had begun to calculate the quantities of commodities that would be needed. He reported that it had been decided to ship thirteen and one-fourth cars of food and five and one-fourth cars of clothing, in addition to that already sent. These figures were periodically upgraded as the work developed on the other end.

Later, Elder Lee and his assistant, Marion G. Romney, travelled to Washington, D.C., to try to remove a bureaucratic roadblock that was barring the shipment of welfare wheat to Europe. A functionary in the Department of Agriculture had decreed that government regulations required that wheat stored in Mormon granaries had to be sold to the United States government and could not, therefore, be shipped to Europe to feed the needy. Arriving in the nation's capital, the Brethren enlisted the aid of Ernest L. Wilkinson. He accompanied them to a meeting with the honorable S. B. Hutson, an undersecretary of agriculture. When the whole matter was laid before Mr. Hutson, the offending regulation was interpreted to allow the Mormon wheat to be shipped to Europe.

Meanwhile, the wisdom of sending Elder Benson to Europe instead of Elder Lee was confirmed dramatically soon after the appointment was made. As Elder Widtsoe had begun to seek diplomatic clearance to go, the predictions were that it would take months to complete the process. But, due to his intimate knowledge of the ways of Washington and the many key contacts he had made during his work there, Elder Benson was able to cut through the red tape and to obtain his clearance, almost in a matter of days. Thus, working in tandem, with Elder Lee directing affairs at home and Elder Benson on the job in Europe, the two boyhood friends from the Oneida Academy, now grown to apostolic maturity, were the key figures in a modern drama not unlike the ancient one when Joseph fed Israel from the granaries of Egypt.

It is significant to see the tender regard this pair had for each other as they worked through the various phases of this drama. When it was first announced that a member of the Twelve would be assigned to go to Europe, Elder

Lee felt it would not be "T" Benson because of his large, young family. Then when the call came, he lent every support to Elder Benson, assisting him in his preparation to leave, seeing him off on the train as he left Salt Lake City, and providing advice and support to the family after his departure. When Flora Benson became ill while her husband was away, it was Elder Lee who gave her special blessings for her health and peace of mind.

Of the many changes that took place during this period, none was more personally significant and satisfying to Elder Lee than the one that took place on June 24, 1946. "I had the glorious experience of sealing my own baby daughter, Helen, to L. Brent Goates," he wrote on that day. "It was the greatest experience of my life." The proud father had watched the budding romance between this couple from its inception and had given his unqualified approval and encouragement to it. He saw in Brent Goates the qualities he would have wanted in a natural son, had he been blessed with one; and he also saw in him a gentleness and kindness to which he could safely entrust his baby daughter. So, when Brent had completed his tour of duty with the Merchant Marines, he and Helen made plans for their marriage. The Lees offered to host a reception at their home the night of the marriage, which the couple accepted with alacrity. The parents exhausted their imagination and ingenuity in making preparations. The lawns and flower beds were groomed to perfection, special lighting was arranged, small decorative plantings were obtained to add beauty and grace to the surroundings, and food and drink for the eight hundred invited guests were purchased. Because Plan B for the event would force the huge reception inside, the Lees became alarmed when on the twenty-first a stiff wind kicked up, bringing with it the threat of rain. It continued to the twenty-third, once knocking out the power so that the house had no electricity for three hours. The Lees' response to this threat was typical. "We laid the whole matter before the Lord," wrote the apostle, "and He tempered the elements and gave us a perfect day for our wedding reception."

A year later, Elder and Sister Lee went through the adventure of a second wedding reception when, on June 11, 1947, Maurine was married to Ernest J. Wilkins, an Arizona native who had served a mission in Argentina. They had met while attending the Brigham Young University, both graduating a week before their nuptials, Maurine with an undergraduate degree and her fiance with a graduate degree in languages. Maurine's parents repeated the procedure of the year before, sprucing up the grounds of their Eighth West home and preparing for the huge crowd the night of the temple sealing. The results, however, were quite different. An unexpected rainstorm the day of the wedding drove the reception inside where the hundreds of guests literally filled the house while they extended their best wishes to the newlyweds. Although there was some temporary and understandable upset, especially on the part of the bride, who had anticipated a magical evening on the patio and the spacious lawns of the home, once the guests began to arrive, all disappointment was submerged in the excitement and gaiety of the moment.

During the year between these two weddings, Elder Lee had an experience unlike anything he had had before or would ever have again. It arose out of an assignment he received to assist Elder Charles A. Callis in organizing a stake in Jacksonville, Florida, the first stake in the southeastern part of the United States. Elder Callis, who had served for many years as the mission president in the south, had literally lived for the day when the first stake would be created there. He seemed to look upon the event as a fitting capstone to his ministry and was as happy and as excited as a child as preparations were made to depart.

Elder and Sister Lee travelled separately from Elder Callis, planning to meet him in Jacksonville. They left Salt Lake City by train on Saturday, January 11, 1947, attended Church services in Chicago on the twelfth, and arrived in

Atlanta, Georgia, on the thirteenth. There they were met by Heber Meeks, president of the Southern States Mission, and his wife, Effie, old friends with whom the Lees had been associated for years in their Salt Lake study group. It being the Lees' first visit to Atlanta, their hosts were anxious to show them one of the city's most famous attractions, the Cyclorama, which dramatically depicts the siege of Atlanta by Union General William Tecumseh Sherman, during his famous—or infamous as the Southerners would have it—march to the sea during the Civil War. The attitude of most old-line Southerners toward the general and his campaign is reflected in the large picture of him that hangs in the foyer of the building, a picture that the organizers of the Cyclorama must have searched long to find. It shows the general dressed in a disheveled uniform, with a scruffy beard, uncombed hair, and a vacant, haggard look in his eye. At a glance, the picture seems to represent the saying General Sherman popularized, "War is Hell," and to convey the idea that he is one of the reigning monarchs there.

The Lees were moved when they viewed the Cyclorama from the platform in its center. There are seen lifelike figures of soldiers, northern and southern, engaged in combat or lying wounded or dead on the battlefield amidst their muskets, their horses, their cannon, and other weapons of war. And in the distance is seen Atlanta in flames.

There can be little doubt that on the following day during the drive from Atlanta to Jacksonville, President Meeks, a keen student of the South and the Civil War, who had lived for a while in Augusta, Georgia, before his call as mission president, briefed the Lees about the history of the South and about the growth of the Church in the Jacksonville area where the stake was to be created.

In Jacksonville, Elder and Sister Lee stayed with Archie O. Jenkins and his wife at their palatial home on the banks of the St. Johns River. The owner of the Duvall Jewelry Company, with nineteen stores throughout Florida, A. O.

Jenkins had begun a career selling watches and jewelry accessories, house-to-house, from a suitcase. Charles A. Callis was the catalyst that brought about a radical change in the Jenkinses' business future. As the president of the branch in Jacksonville, Elder Callis went to Brother Jenkins, who was semi-active, to ask him to serve as the president of the Young Men's organization. Accepting with a notable lack of enthusiasm, the new leader was surprised, if not shocked, when the branch president told him that now that he was a leader he would be expected to keep all the commandments, including the payment of tithing. Unwilling to recant on his acceptance, or to serve halfheartedly, Archie Jenkins began from that moment to pay an honest tithing. And from that moment his business began to thrive, progressing from home-to-home selling to a very small shop and then to the chain of exclusive stores he owned in 1947. Generations of Southern States missionaries heard this inspiring story related by the man who lived it. Because of the role Elder Callis played in their success, and because of the significant event that had brought him to Jacksonville, the Jenkinses would have been honored to have had their friend stay at their home with Elder and Sister Lee. However, he declined graciously, but with firmness. Instead of the luxury he would have found at the Jenkinses' home, Elder Callis opted for the spartan accommodations of a small apartment adjacent to the Jacksonville Branch chapel. He and his wife, Grace, had lived there when he served as the branch president many years before, and he wanted to stay in these humble surroundings where he could relive some of the cherished moments of their life together. It was a bittersweet time for the aged apostle. Elder Lee noted that when Elder Callis heard a rendition of "O My Father" at one of the meetings, "he broke into tears, saying 'Take care of your wives, I haven't mine. She is gone.' " Continuing with his entry, Elder Lee wrote: "I had the impression, and so expressed myself to Sister Jenkins, that Brother Callis wanted to go and had wished it could be in that room by himself."

Patterns of Change

Organization of Florida Stake, Jacksonville, Florida, January 19, 1947: Elder Harold B. Lee at the pulpit with Elder Charles A. Callis

In the organization of the stake, the two apostles went through the usual procedure of interviewing the principal leaders, and then, through inspiration, of selecting the president. The one chosen was a young native of Florida, Alvin Chase, who in turn selected as his counselors E. Coleman Madsen, an attorney whose roots were in the West, and J. M. Lindsey. In this laborious process, which later included setting apart sixty-four ward and stake officers, Elder Callis, who was then eighty-two years old and not in robust health, deferred to his young companion, being actively involved chiefly in the interviews and the selection of the president, in speaking at the conference sessions, and in a few of the settings apart.

Elder Lee reported that in the principal talk he delivered at the conference, Elder Callis said that his wife and other spiritual beings were present, that other stakes would be organized in the Southern States, that eventually a temple would be built there, and that the younger members of the Church in attendance would live to see these things happen.

Once the organization of the stake had been completed, a great sense of peace seemed to descend upon Elder Callis. Despite having had heart palpitations on January 19, the day of the organizational meetings, he was jovial and in apparent good health when, on the twentieth, Elder Lee and Fern, along with the Meekses, left for Miami, Florida, to hold other meetings. The travellers spent the night in historic St. Augustine, the oldest European settlement in the United States, which was established in 1565 by Spain. Here they visited the old slave market and the massive battlements facing the Atlantic, which the Spaniards had constructed to guard this prized outpost. Elder Lee and his party drove south along the Atlantic Coast, enjoying the sights of southern Florida with its extensive, sandy beaches, its tropical vegetation, and its mild climate, a welcome change from the cold and icy January of Salt Lake City. Just south of Vero Beach, the companionable conversation of the travellers was interrupted when their car was stopped by a highway patrolman who advised there was a death message for them and to call a telephone number in Jacksonville. When he called, Elder Lee was informed that Elder Callis had passed away suddenly. He and the others immediately returned.

On arriving back in Jacksonville, he learned about the circumstances of his companion's death. Elder Callis was riding with A. O. Jenkins in his car when, without warning, the apostle fell silent and slumped forward, unconscious. Unable to rouse him, but finding a pulse, Brother Jenkins drove speedily to the hospital where Elder Callis passed away without regaining consciousness.

With the assistance of President Meeks and the local brethren, Elder Lee laid plans for the funeral which was held Thursday, January 23, 1947. The speakers, in addition to the apostle and President Meeks, who had served as a missionary under Elder Callis, were A. O. Jenkins and D. Homer Yarn of Atlanta, Georgia, the patriarch of a prominent Mormon family in the South who had been associated with Elder Callis for many years. As Elder Lee rose to conduct the service shortly after noon, he was so filled with emotion as to be unable to speak coherently. Motioning to President Meeks to take over, he sat down to compose himself. It was an extraordinary reaction since Harold B. Lee was known for self-control in the pulpit as, over the years, he had spoken at numberless funerals and other meetings. As Elder Lee described the incident to the author, a great sense of peace came over him after a while, and he was able to continue without further difficulty. He later learned that at about the same time in Salt Lake City, the First Presidency and the Twelve had joined in their weekly Thursday prayer circle where President David O. McKay, who was voice at the altar, especially remembered Elder Lee and prayed that he would be strengthened and inspired as he presided at the funeral services of Elder Callis in Jacksonville. Elder Lee later referred to this incident to illustrate the spiritual power generated by the prayers offered at the altar in the upper room of the temple.

Following the funeral service, Elder and Sister Lee accompanied the body of Elder Callis on the return trip to Salt Lake City. At the depot to meet them were President George Albert Smith and several other General Authorities and the son and daughter of Elder Callis. Later that day, Elder Lee met privately with the Callis family to brief them about the extraordinary circumstances surrounding their parent's death, which served as a fitting climax to his ministry. The following day, funeral services for Elder Callis were held in the Salt Lake Tabernacle.

Chapter Sixteen

The Centennial Year

The striking events connected with the creation of the Jacksonville Stake and the sudden death of Elder Charles A. Callis were the prelude to an unusual year in the history of the Church and in the life of Harold B. Lee and his family. For many months, numerous committees had been hard at work to plan for the centennial celebration of the arrival of the Mormon pioneers in the Salt Lake Valley. The official celebration, which would last for five-and-a-half months, was commenced on May 1 with a special meeting in the Tabernacle, the lighting of the Brigham Young Monument, and the hoisting of a flag atop Ensign Peak north of downtown Salt Lake City. As a member of the Twelve, Elder Lee was an interested participant in these events. Earlier, on March 8, he had participated in another event, which, though not part of the formal celebration, had symbolic relevance to the centennial. On that day, Elder Lee travelled to Fillmore, Utah, where he addressed a joint session of the Utah legislature that had convened in the old State House, which was used during the time Fillmore was Utah's capital. Elder

The Centennial Year

Lee was selected to represent the Church on this occasion because of his interest in politics, his previous involvement in Salt Lake City government, and because of the repeated efforts of Utah politicians to get him to run for governor or the United States Senate. Elder Lee routinely referred to the First Presidency any delegation that sought to persuade him to run for political office. He enjoyed political activity, but his Church responsibilities took precedence over all else and would continue to do so unless his leaders decreed otherwise.

The day after Elder Lee returned from Fillmore, his entire family gathered for dinner, an event which now occurred only infrequently. "The opportunities now to visit with our family are rare, and we appreciated this day very much," Elder Lee wrote on this occasion. These family gatherings would soon include Ernest Wilkins who was then dating Maurine regularly. Later in the month while Elder Lee was attending the conference in the Palmyra Stake, he saw them together and noted that his daughter "seemed very happy in the company of Ernest Wilkins." And during the April general conference, which followed soon after, that relationship assumed new dimensions when Maurine's suitor was invited to stay at the Lee home.

This was a busy time for Elder Lee, not only because of the pressures attending his preparation to speak at the conference and to accommodate the numerous requests for interviews by conference visitors, but because of a special assignment he received from President Clark. This was to visit Henry D. Moyle at his home, who had been called to the Twelve, to counsel him about his response. It was suggested that Elder Moyle not attempt to deliver a sermon, but that he merely bear his testimony. While at the Moyle home, Elder Lee responded to his friend's request to kneel in prayer with the family. A few days after the general conference, Elder Lee, accompanied by Henry D. Moyle, presided at the conference of the Cottonwood Stake, where Elder Moyle had served as stake president. It was Brother Moyle's first stake conference in his new role as a General Authority. He had been assigned to accompany Elder Lee, both for training in his new duties and to allow his many friends to congratulate him personally on his call. After watching the outpouring of love and friendship toward his colleague, Elder Lee noted in his diary: "Henry very much enjoyed the reunion with the saints over (whom) he formerly presided."

The April general conference where Elder Moyle was sustained as a member of the Twelve also saw other important changes in the general leadership of the Church. Because of the death of Marvin O. Ashton, first counselor in the Presiding Bishopric, the previous October, Joseph L. Wirthlin, former second counselor, was sustained in his place and Thorpe B. Isaacson was approved as the new second counselor. Also, due to the release for illness of Joseph F. Smith, Patriarch to the Church, the previous October, Eldred G. Smith was sustained to replace him. Both of these Patriarchs were direct descendants of Hyrum Smith, although Brother Eldred Smith descended through John Smith, Hyrum's oldest son, while Joseph F. descended through his grandfather, President Joseph F. Smith, who was Hyrum's son by his second wife, Mary Fielding. Elder Lee reported on April 3, the day the Brethren approved Eldred G. Smith as the Patriarch, that although he descended through John Smith's line, it was the understanding that the Patriarch to the Church could come from any of the direct descendants of Hyrum Smith. A week later, Elder Lee reported this was confirmed by George Richards who advised Eldred G. Smith "that the First Presidency and the Twelve had decided that any direct descendant of Hyrum would qualify."

The changes made at this conference, viewed in retrospect, reveal again the shifting patterns of Church leadership. In twelve years, Henry D. Moyle, six years junior to Harold B. Lee in apostolic seniority, would be elevated to the First Presidency where he would exercise presiding authority over his friend; and eighteen years later, Thorpe B. Isaacson would be elevated to the First Presidency, with similar presiding authority over Elder Lee, even though he was never ordained to the apostleship. Judging from his diary entries, these shifts were a matter of indifference to Elder Lee. Position meant little to him. Performance meant everything. Tutored by his mentor, President J. Reuben Clark, he believed the *how* not the *where* of service was all important.

Two events that occurred shortly after the April general conference effected important changes in the Lee family. One of these, Maurine's marriage, has already been mentioned. The other was the death of Elder Lee's father, who passed away on May 9, 1947. Samuel Lee, who had been ailing for some time, became worse in early May. Concerned about his father's condition, Harold spent long hours with him; and on the night of the seventh, was at his bedside until 3:00 A.M. The next day, aware that the end was near, Elder Lee made arrangements to be excused from a stake conference in Palo Alto, California. Later that evening, the son, accompanied by President J. Reuben Clark, administered to the father. Since it was apparent the illness was terminal, the blessing was one of comfort, not healing. The father passed away quietly the next morning, May 9.

Harold B. Lee loved his father fervently. That love was demonstrated by the way he lived and by the treatment accorded to his parents. The son could never forget how they had sacrificed to raise a large family under stressful economic conditions and how they had scrimped to keep him in the mission field. In turn, the parents idolized the son who had more than achieved the "big things" they anticipated for him when he entered the mission field. It is undoubtedly true that Samuel Marion Lee, Jr., the child of promise, died a happy man, surrounded by a loving family, one member of whom had already been elevated to a place of high honor and who, potentially, might become God's earthly mouthpiece.

The funeral was held on Monday, May 12, in the North Twentieth Ward chapel, located at Second Avenue and G

Street in Salt Lake City. (The funeral of the father's last surviving child, Verda Lee Ross, was held in the same chapel on August 29, 1991.) Relatives and friends flocked in from Panaca and Clifton to attend the services. The speakers were President J. Reuben Clark, who regularly attended worship services in this building, and Harold H. Bennett, the president of ZCMI, where Samuel had worked for so many years and where Verda would work for so many years in the future.

The father's death came in the midst of the preparations for Maurine's wedding. Three days later, arrangements were made to have the wedding announcements printed; and there were in progress numerous preparations at the house, with various painting, decorating, pruning, and planting projects going on. Meanwhile, Elder Lee had to float a temporary loan to pay for all this. And amidst these exertions, he continued to fulfill his weekend assignments with stake conferences at Morgan, Utah; Manassa, Colorado; and Davis County, north of Salt Lake City.

The havoc wrought by the weather at Maurine's reception has already been noted. Elder Lee found soon afterward that this was part of a blustery, long-term meteorological system that had settled over most of the intermountain area. Three days after the reception, he left for a three-week tour of the Western States Mission, during which he was intermittently troubled by heavy winds and rain, presumably part of this weather pattern. He travelled to Denver, Colorado, by train on June 14, where he was met by Mission President Francis A. Child. They left immediately by automobile for southwestern New Mexico, holding meetings along the way. The following day found them in Bluewater, New Mexico, in the northwest part of the state, four hundred miles from Denver. There the little branch was "rejoicing" over a new Hammond organ it had acquired, which was played "proudly" at the meeting the visitors held. Later that evening, they travelled to nearby Gallup, where another meeting was held. Here there were some nonmembers present who were accompanied by the missionaries working in the area.

In this place, where the travellers spent the night, they were figuratively ringed by Indian reservations: the Navajo, the Hopi, and the Zuni reservations being nearby. The long trip the following day would take them near the Apache Indian Reservation. This day's trip, covering another 350 miles, would also take them through the bleak Petrified Forest and through the verdant and stunningly beautiful Gila National Forest in eastern Arizona. This route through the Gila, over a twisting, turning road, which was then unsurfaced, is called the Coronado Trail and generally follows the route of the Spanish explorer and conquistador. After making this trip, Elder Lee, while acknowledging the magnificence of the scenery, admitted that it "was very tiring." Despite their weariness, the travellers held a good meeting that night in Silver City, New Mexico, where there were ninety in attendance. The next night at Alamogordo, the site where the atomic bomb was tested, the Brethren encountered heavy winds that knocked out the electricity so that the last fifteen minutes of Elder Lee's talk was delivered in the dark. The next day found the tourists at Carlsbad, New Mexico, where, after visiting the spectacular caverns, they held a meeting in a schoolhouse where seventy-five were present. The next day, June 19, they travelled 505 miles to La Junta, Colorado, in a steady rain that assumed cloudburst proportions at Las Vegas, New Mexico. Notwithstanding the long distance travelled this day, the Brethren paused long enough at Las Vegas to hold a meeting. And before leaving La Junta the morning of the twentieth for Denver, the Brethren held a three-and-a-half-hour meeting with the missionaries, which included the usual instruction period followed by a period of testimony bearing.

Marking the halfway point of the tour, Elder Lee spent the morning of the twenty-first examining the mission records in the Denver office before driving to Grand Island, Nebraska, with the mission president. "The storm constantly with us," he reported. At Omaha the next day, the travellers held a "delightful" instruction and testimony meeting with thirty-five missionaries. But an open-air meeting scheduled that evening at the old Winter Quarters Cemetery was "washed out" because of torrential rain. The trip to North Platte the next day was made in rain so heavy that at one point water a foot deep covered the highway where stakes had been set alongside the roadbed to guide the motorists.

At North Platte, Elder Lee reported "one of the rarest stories of courage" he had ever heard. It related to a girl who had dwarfism, Mary Lou Danks. She played piano accompaniment for the singing. Despite her handicap, this girl was valedictorian of her high school graduating class, planned to go on to the university, and was popular with her classmates. Elder Lee, being a professional teacher, was impressed with the way in which the girl's mother had trained her to be optimistic and outgoing despite her handicap.

From North Platte, the tourists veered northward into the Dakotas, visiting Mt. Rushmore in the Black Hills and holding meetings at Belle Fourche, South Dakota, and at other towns along the way. Then bending westward, they went into Wyoming, where meetings were held at Casper and Sheridan. Apparently reminded of the recent death of his father, Elder Lee spoke there about heritage and about the blessing of being well born. Turning southward, the Brethren reentered Colorado via Rawlings, Wyoming, where meetings were held at Craig, Baggs, Rifle, Grand Junction, Salida, and Colorado Springs. "Although very weary and hungry," he wrote of the meeting in Colorado Springs on July 1, "the Spirit of the Lord picked us up and I felt the greatest freedom I have had yet on this tour in sharing the value of testimony and how, through faith, the work of the Lord has progressed." Back in Denver the next day, Elder Lee met with his old friend and counselor Charles Hyde, who was conducting an audit of the mission records, was taken on a tour of the new Crestmoor resi-

The Centennial Year

dential district of the city, and in the afternoon, met with the twenty missionaries laboring in Denver, including the office staff. Here, and at the last meeting of the tour held at Ft. Lupton the next day, the apostle gave instructions to help the missionaries in working with students at the University of Colorado in nearby Boulder and about relationships with administrative officers of the mission.

In appraising the status of the Western States Mission during this tour, compared with its condition twenty-five years earlier when he was a young missionary, Elder Lee was impressed with the progress that had been made. In the Denver area, where earlier there was but a single branch, he now found a thriving stake that had been organized in 1940. While this was the only stake in the vast area covered by the mission, except for the Lyman Stake in the Star Valley of Wyoming, settled very early by the Latter-day Saints, there were strong branches that would be the nucleus for many other stakes in the future.

Elder Lee returned home in time to celebrate the Fourth of July with his family. "I cooked hamburgers for the crowd out in the back yard," he reported, a service he had rendered for many years and at which he had become very adept. That afternoon he and Brent—who was a frequent companion of his at sporting events—went to the Forest Dale Tennis Club to watch the finals of the National Tennis Championship between Frankie Parker and Ted Schroeder. This was but one of several special athletic events that had been scheduled in Utah this year as part of the state's centennial celebration. Later in the summer, for instance, the National Track-and-Field Championships were held in the University of Utah stadium, which attracted most of the top track-and-field athletes.

Another centennial event was a banquet for most of the governors of the United States held in the Hotel Utah on July 14, where Elder Lee offered the invocation and blessing on the food. Three days later, the Lees personally entered into the spirit of the centennial by hosting a party at home for their study group, where the guests came attired in pioneer garb and were served a traditional pioneer dinner. Two days later found the Lees at a Tanner family reunion held in the Jordan Park, where Elder Lee again presided at the hamburger grill. "Repeated a similar service in our back yard," he reported on that date, "for Irene Hales and Sheila Woodland and forty invited guests who had a dancing party on our patio."

On Monday, July 21, Elder and Sister Lee participated in one of the most novel events of the centennial celebration when they drove to Fort Bridger, Wyoming, where they joined a "Modern Pioneer Encampment," which consisted of 148 persons travelling in seventy-two automobiles, simulating the westward trek of Brigham Young's pioneer company of 1847. They then accompanied the caravan to the Pioneer Park in Salt Lake City, where a program was presented that featured talks by Elder Lee, Elder Spencer W. Kimball, and President David O. McKay. The speakers traced the history of the Mormon Exodus and the founding of the Church in the Salt Lake Valley. The event was specially significant to Elder Lee due to his earlier role in Salt Lake City government and because the park lay within the boundaries of the Pioneer Stake where he had presided.

On Thursday, July 24, 1947, Elder Lee joined other leaders at the mouth of Emigration Canyon for the dedication of the new "This Is the Place" monument. Assembled, in addition to high Mormon leaders, were the governor and the mayor and representatives of the Catholic, Protestant, and Jewish clergy. Thousands of spectators had also gathered under a hot, summer sun, amidst the dust and the scruffy vegetation surrounding the monument. For weeks before the twenty-fourth, seeds had been strewn around the base of the monument each morning at the hour of the dedication, so that at the moment the monument was unveiled, the air was filled with seagulls who had come for breakfast.

The next day, the traditional Pioneer Parade was staged. It featured dozens of theme floats, bands, and marching and horseback units. "It was the most artistic

The Centennial Year

and finished of any in the history of Salt Lake," wrote Elder Lee. "Everyone seemed to be thrilled with the result." He was equally enthusiastic about the play "Promised Valley," which he and Fern saw a few days later at the University of Utah stadium. This production was written and composed by Arnold Sundgaard and Crawford Gates especially for the centennial celebration.

Later in the summer, the Lees enjoyed a break in their schedule with two brief outings. The first was an overnight stay at the Judd cabin in Brighton, where the Lees, their daughters, and sons-in-law enjoyed games, good food, and unlimited conversation, the most enjoyable activity of all. The second was an outing at the Thousand Peak Ranch on the upper Weber River. Here for four days, the Lees "enjoyed to the full (a) complete rest." One day they rode to the top of the mountain on horseback, from where they had a spectacular view of the rugged, verdant terrain spread below, through which the river, looking now like a silver thread, gushed and gurgled its way toward the distant lake. On Sunday, thirty-seven neighbors from up and down the river gathered in the Lee cabin for a worship service. Here the apostle, dressed in leisure clothes, joined the others in partaking of the sacrament and in sharing testimony in a relaxed, rustic setting. Unlike gatherings in a chapel, Elder Lee did not feel like he was "on stage" here, so that the meeting was characterized by a restful, slow-paced informality that had a soothing, calming effect upon him.

Refreshed by this brief interlude, the Lees returned home, ready to resume the hectic tempo of their lives. Soon afterward, Elder Lee presided at conferences in the Ogden and Box Elder Stakes, the latter entailing a reorganization of the stake presidency. These were always time-consuming and sometimes stressful affairs as the qualifications of the various candidates were carefully weighed and analyzed. It was a matter of great consequence to select a man who would have the responsibility for the spiritual and temporal welfare of several thousand

Latter-day Saints. Therefore, it was not something that could be decided in an offhand manner but required the most diligent and concentrated effort of which he was capable. Once the critical decision about the identity of the new stake president had been made, there followed the meeting where the president and the new slate of officers were presented, which necessarily included instruction and sermonizing from the presiding officer, all to be followed by the setting apart of the numerous officers sustained by the conference. Elder Lee never completed one of these weekends but that he felt emotionally drained from the tensions to which it subjected him.

In late August, Elder Lee attended funeral services for the wife of Elder Clifford E. Young, Edith Grant Young, who was one of the daughters of President Heber J. Grant. Elder Lee and Elder Young had been sustained as General Authorities on the same day, six years before, which had created a special bond between them, notwithstanding a significant difference in their ages. Actually, that bond had been forged first some time before when Elder Young was a stake president and banker in American Fork, Utah, and Elder Lee was the managing director of Church welfare. Due to that relationship, Elder Lee was anxious to mourn with his friend and was asked to dedicate Sister Young's grave.

Through this summer, following their June marriage, Maurine and her husband had lived with the Lees in their spacious home to save money for Ernie's education. He had been accepted in a doctoral program at Stanford University in California. The newlyweds left Salt Lake City early Thursday morning, September 5, for Palo Alto where they would live. With them was family friend Mabel Hickman, Elder Lee's first convert, who owned a home there. The same day, the apostle left by train for San Francisco, where he had a series of welfare and servicemen's meetings scheduled. He learned later that the brakes had failed on Ernie's car at Battle Mountain, Nevada, where he had remained while Maurine and Mabel went on by bus. After

The Centennial Year

his meetings in the city, Elder Lee drove to Palo Alto to spend the weekend with the Wilkinses. He inspected the home where they were to live at 1680 College Avenue and attended a meeting in the Palo Alto Ward, where he found a large group of "married couples with whom Ernie and Maurine should be happily associated." The next day was special and would always stand out in memory. "I had a delightful day with my wonderful little girl," the proud father wrote of it. "Together we went to her new home to water the lawns and then for a walk through the Stanford University Campus where we had a lovely lunch at the University Cafeteria." Ernie arrived that evening after a twelve-hour drive from Battle Mountain, and the next morning, at 4:00 A.M., moved their belongings into the new home. While things were being straightened around, "Fern called to announce the birth of a baby to our Helen." That evening, Elder Lee and the Wilkinses "ate dinner in honor of my new grandson."

The Wilkinses' move to Palo Alto created a magnet that repeatedly drew the Lees to the Bay Area during the next three years while Ernie was working on his Ph.D. Whenever Elder Lee had an assignment in the general area of Palo Alto, he would arrange to spend an extra day or two there visiting his "little family." These visits became more frequent and urgent after the Wilkinses' first child, Alan, was born. The doting grandfather, as he did with all his grandchildren, showered Alan with all manner of gifts and gewgaws for the child's entertainment. And whenever Grandpa was near, he usually usurped the privilege of holding and cuddling the baby. In this, Elder Lee revealed the deeply tender and loving quality in his makeup that instinctively attracted people to him and caused them to feel a special relationship with him. Typical of the unnumbered people who, attracted by this quality, felt a special rapport with Elder Lee is Russell Holt, who has prepared a film documentary of the apostle, but who "knew" him only from a passing handshake following a Church meeting where the apostle had spoken many years before. Such was the impact created by that chance encounter that the filmmaker was impelled to make the documentary after Elder Lee's death in celebration of the mysterious bond of love that bound them together.

Elder Lee's frequent visits to Palo Alto did more than to cement family relationships. Here he frequently met and counselled with local leaders, and out of these contacts came future associations in Church leadership. Here, among others, he met Stake President Claude Petersen, who would later become the secretary to the Council of the Twelve Apostles; Bishop Richard B. Sonne, who would later become the president of the Oakland Temple; and David B. Haight, a fellow Idahoan and alumnus of Albion College, who would later become a stake president, mission president, Assistant to the Twelve, and a member of the Twelve. Moreover, during these visits, the apostle exerted a lasting influence upon a wide circle of friends of Maurine and Ernie who were occasional guests in the Wilkins home during Elder Lee's stays there. Informal gatherings in the home, sitting in a circle with the apostle, who freely shared his testimony and gospel scholarship, provided a rare opportunity for young Stanford students and their spouses to gain special insights into the Church, its inner workings, and into the character and spiritual depth of the man who would later become the president of the Church. Among the Stanford students so affected were Lee Valentine, a future mission president in South America; Mitchell Hunt, who would later become a prominent California real-estate developer and also a key player in a vast Church cattle-feeding operation in the southern United States; Terry Hansen, a future mission president in Guatemala and a future director of the missionary training center at BYU, a position son-in-law Ernest Wilkins would also occupy; and the author.

Ernest Wilkins, unlike Brent Goates, had come lately on the scene. An Arizonan, he was unknown to the Lees until only a short while before he and Maurine were married. Brent, on the other hand, a native of Salt Lake, had

The Centennial Year

been well known to the Lee family for some time before his marriage to Helen. Indeed, George R. Hill of the Seventy, once a bishop of Elder Lee's ward, was told by the apostle that he had "chosen" Brent as his son-in-law. In not too long a time after his marriage to Maurine, Ernie Wilkins, the newcomer, also earned a special place in the hearts of his wife's parents. Elder Lee was impressed by the desire of his newest son-in-law for higher education and by his energetic efforts to finance it. Elder Lee was pleased, if not somewhat surprised, that the day after his arrival in Palo Alto found Ernie applying for a part-time position to teach foreign languages at a boys school in nearby Menlo Park. And as the apostle had more opportunity to observe this young man, to visit with him, and to gauge the quality of his mind and the depth of his spirituality, he soon came to love him as a son as he had loved Brent Goates from the beginning. So, in early November 1947, during a short stay in Palo Alto, Elder Lee noted that Ernie Wilkins was "growing in my affection." The next several days revealed a close father-son relationship between them when Ernie took Brother Lee to the Stanford campus to hear a lecture by the noted educator Robert M. Hutchins and later chauffeured him to Berkeley, where Elder Lee presided at a stake conference. An entry made later in the month while the Wilkinses were in Salt Lake City for Thanksgiving clearly demonstrated that Ernest J. Wilkins had been accepted into the heart of the Lee family with unqualified enthusiasm. "We enjoyed with righteous pride our family," wrote Elder Lee on November 28, "and we find ourselves wholly satisfied with our two sons as we have always been with our girls." Another evidence of the bonding that had taken place between Elder Lee and his two "sons" is that the three of them went together to see the Thanksgiving Day football game between the University of Utah and Utah State.

The October general conference was, in reality, the concluding event of the Church's centennial celebration. The pioneer theme was interwoven throughout many of the talks delivered by the Brethren. One of these, in particular, prompted special comments from Elder Lee. "The conference was climaxed by the closing address of President Clark," he wrote, "paying tribute to the unsung heroes of the pioneers who, as he styled it, were in the last wagon." In his analysis of the talk, which he apparently had discussed with the speaker, Elder Lee had this to say: "It was a protest to the church aristocracy that some *name* families in the church have seemed to feel." This reflected a concern of Elder Lee, which was shared by President Clark, that the descendants of some of the early Mormon leaders might succumb to the folly of the Jews at the time of Christ who asserted superiority over others merely because they were descendants of Abraham.

It was during the centennial year that the first faltering steps were taken toward the correlation of priesthood and auxiliary functions in the Church. At this early period, Elder Lee's role was a subordinate one. He had been appointed to serve on a committee of the Twelve assigned to study and to make recommendations about the problem. It was a committee of three, chaired by Elder Stephen L. Richards, with Elder Albert E. Bowen as the other member. The committee had begun its work in the forepart of the centennial year and by late summer had prepared a report of its findings and recommendations. The findings focused on the way in which the auxiliaries had become so powerful as almost to be separate, independent entities, functioning alone without reference to the priesthood or to each other. Each of them prepared, approved, and published its own instructional materials. All of them had their own budgets, which fostered the image of separate autonomy. All of them had large general boards, comprised of some of the most able and creative leaders in the Church. And members of these boards travelled extensively throughout the Church, holding separate training sessions with local auxiliary leaders. Usually, these training sessions were held independent of any input from or involvement of the local priesthood leaders. Moreover, the status and image of the auxiliaries had been greatly enhanced over the years because, with the exception of the Young Women organization, they had been directly presided over by members of the Twelve or by the president of the Church. The basic recommendations of the committee were to bring all the auxiliaries at Church headquarters under the umbrella of priesthood control and direction and in the field to give local priesthood leaders greater authority and responsibility for auxiliary activities and the training of auxiliary leaders. The inevitable effect of adopting the committee's recommendations would have been, of course, to greatly diminish the authority and status of the general auxiliary executives and their boards. Given this reality, we can assume that the committee moved with caution, and not a little trepidation, as they sought to introduce proposals of such revolutionary impact. Elder Lee noted that the committee first surfaced its report "on a simplification of our present priesthood—auxiliary programs" at a temple meeting on September 11, 1947. At that time it was decided only that the Brethren would study the report looking toward a future discussion of it. Eleven days later the committee met to compare notes about the reaction they had received to their report. The results were not promising. "It seems doubtful the time is here," noted Elder Lee, "for much modification in our present programs because of sentimental objections." Notwithstanding this unpromising appraisal, the committee pressed forward with its study. Four days later they decided to "ask permission to get with the executives of the general boards of Sunday School and MIA to consider methods of simplifying the present overburdened and overlapping priesthood and auxiliary programs." At the quarterly meeting of the Twelve held on October 1, Elder Lee reported that "the chief topic of discussion was our proposed simplification program, emphasizing greater priesthood responsibility." Encouraged by the positive reaction of the Twelve, the members of the committee decided to seek an audience with the First Presidency in order to present it to them.

The request was granted and on December 8, 1947, Elders Stephen L. Richards and Harold B. Lee met with the First Presidency for this purpose, Elder Albert E. Bowen not being available. The Brethren learned later that Presidents J. Reuben Clark and David O. McKay thought they were "headed in the right direction." That view, however, was not shared by the one whose opinion counted most, President George Albert Smith, who emerged as the one who entertained the "sentimental objections" Elder Lee had previously referred to. Three days after their meeting with the First Presidency, Elder Richards confided to Elder Lee his feeling that their proposals for simplification had little chance for acceptance at the moment "because of the opposition of President George Albert Smith."

The reasons for the opposition of the prophet are apparent. For many years he had been the president of the Young Men organization of the Church. In that capacity, he had also exerted a strong influence over the Young Women organization through a system of regular meetings and interchanges between the two organizations. As the Young Men president, President Smith had organized and directed an unusual group of leaders whose talent and energy had created an extraordinary program of activities and instruction for the youth of the Church. The dance, the drama, and a host of athletic events and competitions had flourished under their direction. Moreover, a strong esprit de corps had developed throughout the Church among the youth and their leaders, which, it was feared, might be lost were the MIA to lose its autonomous status and to be placed under the more direct and controlling priesthood leadership. During the remainder of his life, President George Albert Smith never changed his views on the subject. And once the Brethren learned about his fixed attitude toward it, they never raised the issue with him again.

Chapter Seventeen

A Peaceful Interlude

Despite the customary stresses and strains, the years 1948 to 1950 marked a period of relative peace and prosperity for Elder Lee, his family, and the Church. It witnessed the addition of three new Lee grandchildren, two in the Wilkins family, Alan and Larry, and one in the Goates family, Harold Lee Goates. Prior to the birth of Alan Wilkins, Maurine's first child, prenatal complications of the mother created concern in the family. Elder Lee responded to the uncertainty in a typical way. He had returned from St. George, Utah, "very much worn out with the strain of the conference and long drive," when, on March 22, 1948, he had a special fast for Maurine and "went to the temple where [he] had a prayer for her." The following night brought the heartening news that she had given birth naturally to a healthy seven-pound, twelve-ounce boy. "I had little sleep afterwards," the proud and grateful grandfather wrote later.

Fern had gone to Palo Alto earlier to be with Maurine at the time of the birth, and Elder Lee urgently sought an opportunity to join her there. He found it on April 19, when, following a series of welfare meetings at Stockton, California, and prior to a stake conference there, he drove to Palo Alto to see the newest addition to his "little family." Because of the crowded conditions in the Wilkinses' small home, Elder and Sister Lee spent their nights in the President Hotel in Palo Alto. He returned to Stockton, where he and Elder Albert E. Bowen installed Wendell B. Mendenhall as the new stake president. In the future, Elder Lee would have a close association with President Mendenhall over a period of many years, after the latter's appointment to head the Church building committee. Following the stake conference, Elder Lee returned to Palo Alto for another short visit with the Wilkinses and especially with the new baby. "Our train left (from San Francisco) at 7:00 P.M.," Elder Lee wrote the next day, "and we were left with the beautiful picture of our little family as they left to return to Palo Alto."

The long train ride home was the first time Elder Lee had been able to truly relax for a month. After learning about Alan's birth the night of March 23, he began preparing for the general conference, which was only nine days away. "Spent several hours through last night," he wrote the morning of March 24, "in some profitable study of the scriptures in contemplation of what the spirit might direct me to say at the coming general conference." Soon after, he had to leave for a series of meetings in Logan, Utah, and Pocatello, Idaho. At Logan on the twenty-sixth, following meetings in the Logan Fourth Ward, he was up until midnight, visiting in the home of Theodore M. Burton with members of the bishopric and the stake presidency and their wives. He left early the next morning for Pocatello, where, over the weekend, he held a series of meetings in connection with their stake conference. The normal tensions of a conference were heightened when Elder Lee found it necessary to publicly correct one of the speakers who had implied the stake would be unfairly deprived unless it received a new building. He was concerned lest what he had said might cause offense. Yet, he could not

A Peaceful Interlude

let the remarks go unanswered as his silence could have been misinterpreted as agreement with what was said. It was hardly a satisfying experience.

Back in Salt Lake City, Elder Lee immediately became involved in the events connected with the April general conference. An inspiring meeting with the mission presidents somewhat mitigated his unpleasant experience in Pocatello. "It was the most spiritual meeting with mission presidents I have yet attended," he wrote. "Some of the most remarkable testimonies of the power of healing given to the elders were related by the presidents." At the Primary conference on April 2, Elder Lee spoke on "Spiritual Guidance the Year Round," and two days later, he addressed a general session of the conference on the subject of "The Gathering of Israel." He was buoyed up in delivering this address by a telephone call he received the night before. "Fern called last night from Palo Alto," wrote he, "to tell me of her love and her faith in my behalf tomorrow as I am called upon to speak." The impact of the love and faith of Fern Lee upon her husband cannot be measured. It is clear, however, they were vital to him and accounted, in large part, for the success and spiritual stature he attained.

After the conference, which included a special meeting where the General Authorities administered the sacrament, the apostle attended a Lee family reunion, where he agreed to be the president of the organization "until I can get it going." Meanwhile, on the two weekends following the the general conference, he attended conferences in the Kolob and Huntington Park stakes. In his "spare time" between these conferences, he did the spring housecleaning. "Worked far into the night to get our house cleaning done before I leave for California." His tight schedule at the Huntington Park stake conference the following weekend was typical. On Sunday, in addition to two general sessions, he instructed the high council, spoke at a fireside, performed many ordinations and settings apart, and interviewed several prospective missionaries. "I was going until 10:30 P.M.," he wrote, "with hardly time for a sandwich." He was then "taken to a down town hotel to sleep." This preceded the midweek welfare meetings and the stake conference in Stockton, already mentioned, between which, as noted, he travelled to and from Palo Alto, and then after the conference ended, he travelled back there again.

Thus, Elder Lee enjoyed the leisurely train ride from San Francisco to Salt Lake City, when he alternately rested, visited with Fern, studied, or contemplated past or future events. While sometimes there was a tedium in train travel, which was eliminated in later years when air travel became the norm, Elder Lee sometimes missed the leisurely hours aboard a train of the kind he enjoyed while returning to Salt Lake City on this occasion.

At home, Elder Lee had a brief respite before beginning another marathon of meetings. The month of May found him successively in Logan, Utah; St. David, Arizona; and Sacramento, California, on stake conference assignments. In between, he comforted and blessed his colleague, Spencer W. Kimball, who had recently suffered two separate heart attacks. These were part of a whole compendium of ailments that afflicted Elder Kimball over the years, ailments that nearly everyone thought would cut short his ministry. No one, it seems, believed Elder Kimball, who was four years older than he, could conceivably outlive Harold B. Lee, who seemed so strong and robust. Elder Lee blessed his friend Friday night, May 28, 1948; and the next morning, he and Fern left for the East where they were to conduct a three-week tour of the New England States Mission. Elder S. Dilworth Young of the First Council of the Seventy was the mission president. En route to the mission field, the Lees stopped in New York City, where their good friends Gordon Affleck and his wife hosted them at a dinner and a Broadway show. Gordon Affleck, who was a member of a prestigious Wall Street law firm, would later move back to Salt Lake City, where

A Peaceful Interlude

he would become a close confidant and advisor to Elder Lee during the years he served in the First Presidency.

The tour commenced with a missionary meeting in Bridgeport, Connecticut, on the first of June. Here Elder Lee was in his element, counselling, instructing, and motivating young missionaries, some of whom would have been previously exposed to him at one of his question-and-answer sessions in the Salt Lake Temple, during their training in the mission home. Whenever it was feasible to do so, Elder Lee used the Socratic method of instruction, responding to the questions and concerns of his audience. In this way, he was able to get at the heart of the challenges facing his listeners and to help them to confront and to overcome them.

A chief challenge some of these missionaries faced was working in nearby New Haven, the home of Yale University. Some felt that those who worked in an intellectual community such as this ought to alter their proselyting methods. Elder Lee disagreed. He taught that conversion comes through the Spirit and that missionaries should approach their contacts at that level. At the same time, he urged that those who worked among people of high intellect and training should be sure of their facts and the doctrine but should not aim merely at intellectual assent. Spiritual conversion was the goal. Yet, he realized that not all converts would receive a spiritual witness by the Holy Ghost. As to these, he counselled a patient acceptance of a secondary testimony, based on the witness of others, confidently awaiting the time when the primary testimony, imparted by the Holy Ghost, would come. Elder Lee's usual admonition to young friends was that if they had not yet received a primary testimony, through the Spirit, that they "use" his for a while. Still, he was quick to acknowledge that either kind of testimony was valid. (See D&C 46:11–14.)

Following the meeting in Bridgeport, the touring party went to nearby New Haven to visit the Yale University campus, founded almost two hundred and fifty years before. Of special interest was the main library, with its hushed atmosphere, and the Jonathon Edwards College Yard, over whose rooftops could be seen the imposing Harkness Memorial Tower. Elder Lee's academic background, his intimate connection with the Brigham Young University as a member of its Board of Trustees, and his son-in-law's current attendance at Stanford University lent special significance to this visit, as they did to his later visit to the campus of Harvard University at Cambridge, Massachusetts.

This mission tour was the first time Elder and Sister Lee had been exposed to the rich heritage of the New England states. Knowing this, Elder Young had included in the tour visits to places of historic interest, places whose names evoke memories of the dawn of American independence, places like Lexington, Concord, Faneuil Hall, the Old North Church, and Bunker Hill. While in the Boston area, the party also visited the homes of some of the pillars of early New England society, including those of Henry Wadsworth Longfellow, Nathaniel Hawthorne, and Ralph Waldo Emerson. All these things, and many others that they saw, were brought into clearer focus when they spent several hours examining the displays in the Harvard Museum. While in Cambridge, Elder Lee and his party were also the guests of George Albert Smith, Jr., the prophet's son, who was a well-respected professor at Harvard's school of business administration.

Leaving the Boston area, the party visited Plymouth Rock, which commemorates the landing of the Pilgrim Fathers, and Gloucester Rock, reputed to be the place where the Massachusetts Bay Colony landed. There followed a visit to Salem, Massachusetts, the Atlantic seaport that loomed large in America's early maritime trade when her wharves burgeoned with commodities from around the world, but which is chiefly remembered in the American psyche as the site of the infamous witch trials.

Leaving Massachusetts, the party travelled into Vermont, where the apostle was intrigued to visit Sharon,

A Peaceful Interlude

Windsor County, where the Prophet Joseph Smith was born. In the cottage near the granite shaft that commemorates the Prophet's birth and death, Elder Lee and his party held a three-hour meeting, attended by the missionaries working in the area and by some of the local leaders and members. Elder Lee capped the meeting with a fervent testimony about the divine calling of Joseph Smith, about the global destiny of the Church, and about the key role and responsibility of missionaries in its fulfillment.

Lest this recital of the historic places visited be misunderstood, it should be emphasized that all along the way, meetings were held intermittently with missionaries, where Elder Lee received reports about their work and where he gave instruction about improving the quality of it. Special emphasis was given to the discipline, the worthiness, and the spirituality of the missionaries. Elder Lee learned that the most success was being had by the missionaries who worked in rural areas without purse or scrip. Aside from the conversions this work produced, it also brought a commendable sense of humility and dedication to those who engaged in it. Still, Elder Lee and his brethren had reservations about this kind of proselyting, although they did not take steps to curtail or to discontinue it. The drawback was that these converts, living as they did in isolated areas, lacked the opportunity to associate with other Latter-day Saints in the full program of the Church. This increased the risk that, left alone, they would drift into spiritual inertia, lacking the drive toward personal development fostered by this type of situation. On this account, Elder Lee and his associates would later discourage this kind of proselyting, opting instead for growth from centers of strength. This strategy depends for its success upon the active involvement of Church members in the conversion process through the neighborly nurturing of potential investigators. Obviously, this strategy fails when neighbors live miles apart. The result was to focus on urban instead of rural proselyting.

From Vermont, the party travelled to Maine, where

missionary and member meetings were held in Bangor. Here Elder Lee found missionaries who functioned as he had done in Denver a quarter of a century before, having responsibility for both proselyting and directing the local branch.

Crossing the border, they travelled into Canada, where they spent nine days, repeating the procedures followed in New England. Here, in turn, they visited St. Johns, Halifax, and the French Provinces of Acadia, which provided the setting for Longfellow's "Evangeline." At Sydney, on the Island of Cape Breton, they inspected the crumbling fortifications that had survived the French and Indian Wars, then visited Emma Marr Petersen's aunt, Sister Ferguson. This doughty lady, whose sister, Emma Marr Petersen's mother, was once reported by a deacon in the Salt Lake First Ward to be his "bishop," had earlier fought the missionaries for having converted her sister, Mrs. McDonald, causing her to move to Salt Lake City. Later, after her own conversion, Sister Ferguson became the most avid champion of the missionaries, defending them vigorously against criticism, and providing them unstintingly with food, shelter, and motherly encouragement.

Elder Lee was struck by the almost ethereal quality of Prince Edward Island, "The Beautiful Garden Island," and the rural charm of the area around Borden prompted this poetic comment: "We saw the most picturesque farm country, with lakes which mirrored the red soil, the green foliage, and the light blue sky." Returning to the United States, the party held meetings at Portland, Maine, and concluded the tour with special meetings in Cambridge with the missionaries and with students who were attending Harvard.

Though it was inspiring and educational, the tour was exhausting. This, added to nervous tensions Elder Lee had suffered in March prior to the birth of Maurine's baby, pointed to the need for a break in his schedule. It came during the first part of July when he and Fern, accompanied

A Peaceful Interlude

Elder Harold B. Lee with daughter Helen, about 1948

by Helen, Brent, and grandson David, spent a relaxing week at the Thousand Peaks Ranch. Intermingling hikes with horseback riding, visiting, reading, snoozing, and leisurely study, the apostle was able to revive his energies for the full season ahead. Especially pleasing to Elder Lee were the carefree and spontaneous antics of his grandson. There was a special bond between him and the boy, both resembling each other so much in both appearance and temperament. And as David matured, the physical resemblance became almost startling. Not long after his birth, Elder Lee conferred the name "Skipper" on David, a pet name that mirrored the affection he had for him. The grandfather lavished gifts and special attention on David, as he did on the other grandchildren as they came along. So, a few days before the family went to the Thousand Peaks Ranch, Elder Lee drove out in the late evening "to cool baby David off so he could sleep."

Two weeks after returning from the ranch, Fern accompanied her husband to San Francisco, where he held a series of welfare meetings. They then stayed on in nearby Palo Alto for eleven days, helping the Wilkinses move into a larger home. "Cleaned the house on Waverly to be occupied by Maurine and Ernie," wrote Elder Lee on August 4. The next day, he "bought a crib for Alan," and the day after that found him "house cleaning." He was still at it three days later when he noted optimistically, "beginning to see the end." Later, his optimism dimmed. "There are some doubts," wrote he, "as to a satisfactory arrangement being worked out for our family this winter." But things looked up again two days later when the Lees returned home. They did so with the satisfying feeling that their "little family" would be comfortable and happy.

This typified the caring concern Elder and Sister Lee had for the families of their two daughters. Later when they moved into homes they had purchased, the parents not only provided menial help, as they had done in Palo Alto, but also helped in locating suitable homes and with some of the financial arrangements.

The weekend after returning from Palo Alto found Elder Lee in Green River, Wyoming, for a stake conference. Although he did not arrive home until 2:00 A.M. the Monday morning after the conference, he was at his desk a few hours later to handle matters that had accumulated during the previous week and to prepare for the schedule ahead. From August 18 to August 25, Elder Lee performed twenty-three marriages in the Salt Lake Temple and over the weekend, presided at a conference in the Sevier South Stake at Monroe, Utah, where he was joined by Elder Marion G. Romney.

Elder Lee and Fern left Salt Lake City on Wednesday, August 25, for Western Canada, where he had several assignments. The first was a stake conference in Lethbridge the following weekend. Here Elder Lee found many descendants of the old-line Mormon families who had come to Canada many decades before at the behest of the Church leaders. He felt a special kinship with these people who reminded him so much of the sturdy Latter-day Saints with

A Peaceful Interlude

whom he had grown up in Clifton. At conferences held in Calgary and Cardston on the two succeeding weekends, he found more of the same, people of faith and integrity who could be relied upon in any emergency.

A touch of early autumn lay upon the Canadian Rockies as the Lees took advantage of several free days between the Lethbridge and Calgary conferences to travel to Banff and Lake Louise. At the lake, one of the most picturesque settings in western Canada, they stayed at the large hotel, which commands a spectacular view of the lake and the towering peaks of the Rockies that surround it. As they walked along the footpath that borders the lake, Elder and Sister Lee enjoyed the nip in the air and the first showing of early fall colors. It was a delightful and restful interlude for them.

During the week between the Calgary and Cardston conferences, Elder Lee met President George Albert Smith at Lethbridge and accompanied him to Cardston. There he was pleased to assist the prophet in installing a new presidency of the Cardston Temple. Released was President E. S. Wood, a stalwart among the Mormon leaders in Canada, and a man of extraordinary spiritual sensitivity. He was replaced by Willard L. Smith, also a man of commanding stature. It was upon men such as these, whose counterparts could be found in Mormon communities reaching from the Canadian Rockies to Old Mexico, that the leaders in Salt Lake City relied for the effective administration of the Church.

During the weekend following the installation of the new temple presidency, Elder Lee was personally exposed to all of the key leaders in Cardston as he conducted the usual interviews in connection with the reorganization of the stake presidency, which took place on Sunday. After setting the new leaders apart and giving general instructions to them, he and Fern returned to Salt Lake City.

Not long after returning from Canada, Elder Lee received a telephone call from President Clark, who asked about the woman seen getting out of his car a short while before. It was a neighbor Elder Lee had seen waiting for the bus and to whom he had given a ride to work. "He warned me against giving a lone woman a ride," wrote Elder Lee. President Clark reinforced his counsel by suggesting the dilemma he would have faced had there been an accident, an investigation, and an official report stating Elder Harold B. Lee had had an automobile accident and that a woman not his wife was in the car alone with him. The counsel took. Afterward he refrained from giving lone women rides in his car. He also routinely followed the practice of leaving a crack in the door when a woman, other than a member of his family, was alone with him in the office. Sometimes, he would ask that a secretary join him inside the office if a lone woman were there with him. These precautions were a safeguard against any false accusations of improper conduct being made against him.

This incident typified the close relationship between Elder Lee and President Clark. The older man frequently imparted counsel on both official and personal matters, whether sought for or not. Periodically he briefed Elder Lee on policy matters outside the scope of his responsibility in the expectation the data would be helpful when he rose to "higher position." And, fatherlike, he gave unsolicited advice about personal matters, as when after the Lees sold their home on the west side President Clark admonished him not to live in an apartment but to buy another home. The mentor never gave reasons for this advice. That was irrelevant to Elder Lee, who never lived in an apartment, except for a short time between homes.

President Clark occasionally used Elder Lee to float ideas in committee meetings, which ideas he did not want to have seen as originating with him. We have already seen how he used this device in advancing the idea of acquiring an old warehouse where members who lived in overcrowded houses could store their year supply of food. In addition, he used him occasionally to pass on words of "counsel" to some of the Brethren, or to headquarters personnel, in cases where it was felt inappropriate for such to come directly from him.

Elder Lee never complained or balked whenever his mentor asked him to perform such a service. In fact, he seemed to regard it as an honor that the older man took him into his confidence and used him in this way. But, there was a fine line between this kind of a confidential, cooperative relationship and any action by the mentor that intruded on Elder Lee's sense of dignity or independence. President Clark's innate adroitness and diplomacy assured that this line would seldom be crossed and, if crossed, would not be done deliberately. An exception occurred in late November 1948, when President Clark criticized Elder Lee for having gone to the hospital to visit one of the Brethren. He asked whether Elder Lee didn't realize that people go to the hospital to recuperate and should not be intruded upon. The criticism did not set well with Elder Lee, especially because he had been asked to go there. Later in a meeting President Clark said something that Elder Lee interpreted as a criticism of the extent of his participation in a discussion. These incidents caused Elder Lee to become withdrawn in his attitude toward President Clark, something that the older man sensed. To clear the air, President Clark invited Elder Lee to his office, where he mentioned the negative attitude toward him he had detected. "He pleaded that there be no coolness between us," Elder Lee wrote. "He said it wouldn't be long before the younger brethren would rise to the leadership of the church and he must do all he can to see that there is unity." This bridged over the misunderstanding that had developed between them, a misunderstanding that, if left to fester, could have created a serious rift in their relationship. As it was, the effect of it was to bring the two men closer together and to promote a greater sensitivity in their relationship.

During 1949, Elder Lee conducted two mission tours, the California Mission in the spring and the East Central States Mission in the autumn. On March 14, the day before beginning the California Mission tour, he wrote discouragingly: "I seem weary and hardly in the mood; but I am hoping to feel better as the visit progresses." His weariness traced to a tiring trip into a remote part of Arizona for a stake conference the previous weekend; to a hurried trip to Palo Alto afterward where he helped Maurine prepare a nursery school she and a friend had organized, and to a special welfare meeting held in Los Angeles after returning from Palo Alto. Moreover, Elder Lee was concerned about the condition of President George Albert Smith, who was then convalescing at Laguna Beach from a mild stroke he had suffered in February. On the way to his stake conference in Arizona, Elder Lee, joined by Elder Spencer W. Kimball, had gone to Laguna Beach to administer to the ailing prophet. Besides all this, he had already been away from home for eight days and now faced eighteen more grueling days on the road touring the mission. But, as it always happened in such cases, Elder Lee's hopes were realized, and once he got under way on the tour, things looked up.

His companion was the mission president, Oscar W. McConkie, Sr., whose son, Bruce R. McConkie, had been called as a member of the First Council of Seventy in October 1946. Widely known as "Judge" McConkie, the mission president had ended his legal career on the bench, serving for many years in the Third Judicial District Court in Salt Lake City. He was a man of deep spirituality, learned in the law and the scriptures, who spoke with authority and conviction. The depth of his spirituality is seen in an experience he had with Bruce when the son was a little boy growing up in Monticello, Utah. As the father sat reading on the porch one day, he sprang from his chair and raced toward the field in response to a spiritual prompting to get up and run. There he found the boy, one foot caught in a stirrup, being dragged by his pony. The father's prompt response to the spiritual whispering doubtless saved the future apostle from serious injury, or even death. Such spiritual sensitivity was something with which

A Peaceful Interlude

Elder Lee could readily relate. This, and President McConkie's perceptive knowledge of the scriptures, provided the grist for many enlightening gospel conversations between them during the course of the tour.

The first meetings of members and missionaries were held in Blythe, California, near the Colorado River east of the Salton Sea. This "sea," which under ordinary conditions is a salt marsh covered in places by shallow lakes, is, second to Death Valley, the lowest point in the United States, being more than 235 feet below sea level. Here the Brethren found a thriving branch, whose growth had justified a new chapel that Elder Lee dedicated at a meeting held on Sunday, March 16. In recounting the service, Elder Lee commented on the vigor and power of the mission president's pulpit style, which, in some ways, was mirrored in the style of his well-known son. Elder Lee also noted the uniform kindness President McConkie showed toward the members and the missionaries and the "marked deference" he showed toward the apostle, which evidenced "a depth of humility."

Retracing their steps, the Brethren returned to Cathedral City and Hemet, California, not far from Palm Springs, where meetings were held. Then, returning to the coast, they held meetings at Carlsbad, San Juan Capistrano, and Laguna Beach. At Laguna, Elder Lee stopped to see President George Albert Smith again, who was still ailing and seemingly unable to throw off the effects of the mild stroke he had suffered.

Elder Lee and his companion travelled southeasterly to Brawley, California, in the heart of the Imperial Valley, whose lush fields, nourished by the waters of the Colorado River, reminded Judge McConkie of the continuing legal battle between the upper basin and lower basin states over water rights in the river. At the moment, however, the Imperial Valley was the recipient of surplus waters in the river, which the upper basin states were unable to utilize through the lack of sufficient impounding facilities. The Brethren found a thriving economy here, with ample jobs for all, including many field workers from across the border in Mexico. Some of these workers had joined the Church and were in attendance at the public meetings. However, they were merely a trickle compared to the flood of Hispanic converts who would come into the Church in the years ahead.

Leaving California, the party travelled into Arizona, where meetings were held at Ajo, Prescott, and Cottonwood. At Ajo, Elder Lee received a telephone call from Arthur Haycock, President Smith's secretary, asking if he could come and again administer to the prophet who had taken a turn for the worse. However, when Brother Haycock learned about the long distance from Laguna Beach and the remoteness of Ajo, he decided to look elsewhere for someone to come and bless President Smith.

At Prescott, Arizona, Elder Lee was impressed with the dedication and productivity of a group of missionaries, among whom was a young elder named Ray L. White. Several decades later, Elder White would become the president of the mission headquartered in Dallas, Texas.

In California, meetings were held in Needles, Barstow, and Death Valley. En route to Death Valley, the lowest point in the United States at 282 feet below sea level, President McConkie told about a vivid dream he had had in which Satan had appeared to him. After mulling it over, Elder Lee offered his interpretation of the dream. It reminded him of an experience he had had with a woman possessed of an evil spirit who had said to him, "You are the head of the Church." In response, "President McConkie said he thought that the evil spirit in her had spoken, not of that which I now was, but of that which Satan knew I was ordained to become."

The tour ended with meetings in Ridgecrest, Mohave, Bakersfield, San Luis Obispo, Santa Barbara, and Ventura, California. In all of these cities, Elder Lee found small but thriving branches, most of which would ultimately grow into stakes. He also found a corps of dedicated missionaries who, motivated by their president, had learned to rely on

A Peaceful Interlude

the promptings of the Spirit in their work, which was reflected in special experiences they had. "We had time to hear faith promoting experiences," Elder Lee reported of a meeting held with eight missionaries at Mohave, "which included conversions of those who had been shown in dreams the coming of the elders and instant healings, etc."

On his last day with President McConkie, Elder Lee joined in welcoming and instructing eight new missionaries who had just arrived in the mission field. The counsel he gave on this occasion reflects a proselyting initiative that he and his brethren would promote in the future with success. "I was impressed," he wrote of the incident, "to show how one could overcome opposition of a person by bringing him within the power of the Holy Ghost, operating through a faithful member of the Church who was keeping the commandments." Herein is the essence of the "Every Member a Missionary" program that would be developed in the future.

Less than a month after completing the tour of his mission, Elder Lee spent several hours with two of President McConkie's sons, Bruce R. McConkie and Oscar W. McConkie, Jr. Elder Lee rode with them from Salt Lake City to Richmond, Utah, where he had a stake conference assignment. This incident, taken with his recent tour of the father's mission, gave Elder Lee insight into the McConkie family he had not had before. During the first week in November of the following year, Elder Lee received another important insight into the ability and character of Bruce R. McConkie when they joined in reorganizing the Gridley California Stake. It was the first time they had shared such an assignment. Working together as companions, they conducted the usual personal interviews of the leaders of the stake, following which H. E. McLure was selected as the new stake president. After the new leaders had been set apart and instructed, they also participated in the dedication of a new chapel at Yuba City from which they entrained for Salt Lake City. Of the trip home, Elder Lee reported: "I had a delightful visit with

Bruce McConkie on the way home and found him entirely responsive to my suggestions relative to the work of the First Council of the Seventy and missionary work." Twenty-two years later, Harold B. Lee, as the president of the Church, would call Bruce R. McConkie to the Twelve, the only man he would call to that position during his short tenure.

As already noted, Elder Lee's second mission tour of 1949 took him to the Central States, where Thomas W. Richards presided. He left Salt Lake City on October 6 by train with Louisville, Kentucky, as his immediate destination. On board in their private car were two high officials of the Denver & Rio Grande Railroad Company, E. A. West and Willard Richards, who invited Elder Lee to have breakfast with them. Afterward, in his own car, he made the acquaintance of an elderly man "who was nearly ready for baptism" when they parted. With this positive missionary experience in mind, he was primed for the sixteen-day tour that would take him into the states of Kentucky, West Virginia, and Tennessee.

Elder Lee was met at the Louisville depot by President Richards and Elder Stanfield and was driven to the mission home, where he was greeted by Sister Richards. He found her still agitated over the brutal murder of her daughter, which had occurred in Palo Alto, California, a few months before. This tragic event had destroyed the mother's peace of mind, interfered with her work, and cast a pall of gloom over everything she did. This cloud hung over the entire party until the last day of the tour when an unusual incident dispelled it.

The procedure followed on this tour corresponded with that of other tours. Meetings were held with members and missionaries, including personal interviews Elder Lee held with each missionary. He also spent time alone with President Richards, reviewing his proselyting techniques, the supervision of his missionaries, the management of the mission home and office, and the relationships in his family.

A Peaceful Interlude

The tour commenced with a training and testimony meeting held with twenty-two missionaries in Huntington, West Virginia, on October 8. Here, following instructions given by President Richards and Elder Lee, each missionary had the opportunity to bear testimony without restriction either as to time or subject matter. It was in this context, where the missionaries spoke extemporaneously, that the visitor was able to gauge the status of the work and the missionaries in ways a statistical report could not reveal. In Huntington the next day, Elder Lee spoke over the radio in addition to holding the other usual meetings. During the next week, a similar routine was followed in six different cities: Fairmont, Clarksburg, and Charleston, West Virginia; Martin, Kentucky; and Knoxville and Nashville, Tennessee. At Knoxville, the general meeting was held in a "stuffy basement," although Elder Lee reported optimistically that "the spirit was splendid . . . and some excellent friends and investigators were in attendance." By contrast, the meeting in Nashville was held in the ornate ballroom of the Hermitage Hotel. Here he was pleased to report that among the missionaries were elders from Clifton, Oxford, and Preston, another generation of Idaho farm boys who were enjoying the same kind of experiences he had enjoyed almost thirty years before.

En route to Memphis, Tennessee, the next day, the party stopped at Cane Creek in Lewis County to visit the site of the murder of Elders William S. Berry and John H. Gibbs, who were shot to death by a masked mob on Sunday morning, August 10, 1884. Killed during the same assault were Martin Condor and James R. Hudson, son and stepson of James Condor, at whose home the dead elders were to have held a worship service that morning. The host's wife, Mrs. Condor, was seriously wounded during the attack. The details of the tragedy came alive for the visitors when they were retold by a seventy-three-year-old man, Bud Talley, who was an eyewitness. After the killings, B. H. Roberts, the General Authority who set Elder Lee apart for his mission, prepared the bodies for shipment home. The experience revealed how time had altered public attitudes toward the Church, its message, and its missionaries.

After holding the usual meetings in Memphis and Clarksville, Tennessee, the party returned to Kentucky, where additional meetings were held at Greenville and Bowling Green. Near Bowling Green, another meeting was held in a "little backwoods schoolhouse, lighted by kerosene lamps."

En route to Lexington, Kentucky, the party travelled through Hardin County, visiting the birthplace of Abraham Lincoln. It was a rustic cabin, reportedly built by President Lincoln's father of logs hewn from nearby woods and fashioned according to his own design. Nearer to Lexington, the party also visited the home of the composer Stephen Foster, whose song "My Old Kentucky Home" is traditionally played before the annual running of the Kentucky Derby. This is the heart of Kentucky's bluegrass country, famous as a breeding place for thoroughbred horses. Knowing this, President Richards was anxious that Elder Lee visit Calumet Farms, the best known of the local fraternity of horse breeders. Here the visitor was shown Whirlaway and Bull Lea, two Derby winners who had been turned out to stud.

That night, a public meeting was held in an old barracks being used temporarily while a new chapel was being constructed for the branch in Lexington. The next day, October 22, was spent quietly at the mission home in Louisville, interrupted only by a brief visit to Churchill Downs, the home of the Kentucky Derby. This was a day of prayer and fasting for Elder Lee in preparation to give a special blessing to Sister Richards, who continued to anguish over the death of her daughter. A quiet calmness pervaded the home as he pronounced the blessing. Afterward, he made this record of it: "I had the distinct impression that Marriner W. Merrill, her father, was giving her a blessing through us. She said a remarkable peace came over her, the first since the tragedy of her daughter's murder."

A Peaceful Interlude

Elder Lee returned home via St. Louis, Missouri, grateful to be able to spend a few days relaxing with his family. His relaxation included two days of vigorous physical activity helping Helen and Brent move into their new home at 1022 McFarland Avenue in Salt Lake's Rose Park subdivision. He also accompanied Fern to a dinner party with their study group hosted by Joseph and Norma Anderson. Also present were President and Sister J. Reuben Clark. In commenting on the evening, Elder Lee wrote: "President Clark described Joseph as the finest man he had ever worked with," a noteworthy compliment given President Clark's long career in the Church and his government and professional involvements. Later President Clark said of Brother Anderson: "His merit should be rewarded by an appointment in the higher councils of the church." That recognition came to Elder Anderson twenty-one years later when, in 1970, he was called as an Assistant to the Twelve. In describing his call, which came when Brother Anderson was eighty years old, Elder Lee said the Brethren knew "instinctively" that Elder Anderson was to be called as a General Authority. In setting him apart as an Assistant to the Twelve, President Lee said in part, "Joseph is like unto Moses of old; his eye shall never be dimmed nor his natural force abated." At this writing (January 1992) Elder Anderson, now an emeritus member of the Seventy, is over 102 years old; his mind is sharp and uncluttered; he remembers with equal precision things that happened yesterday or long ago; he continues to walk regularly when the weather permits; and until a few years ago, he swam regularly to keep trim. Joseph Anderson stands as a testimony to the rewards of merit, perseverance, and diligence, to the favorable influences of friends and associates, and to the blessings of heaven pronounced by apostolic authority.

The year 1950 saw more significant changes in Elder Lee's family and in the evolution of his ministry. The new year found the Lees in Palo Alto, where they had gone to spend the holidays with the Wilkinses. Maurine was expecting again and in February gave birth to her second child, a boy, whom the parents named Larry. Numerically this childbirth, which was much easier than Maurine's first, evened the score with Helen, who, several months before, had given birth to her second son, Harold Lee Goates, named in honor of his grandfather. At this point, providence seemed to be compensating for Elder Lee's lack of sons by blessing him with an abundance of grandsons. In reality, the sex of his children and grandchildren seemed irrelevant to him. Only their physical, mental, and spiritual health and their conduct had relevance for him.

This would be the Lees' last lengthy visit to Palo Alto. Ernie's studies at Stanford were winding down, although he was gearing up for his doctoral exams. As they approached, his father-in-law, as was Elder Lee's habit in matters of family crisis, conducted a special fast and prayer in his behalf. The son-in-law later confided that during the lengthy and searching oral examinations conducted by his doctoral committee of Stanford professors, answers to obscure questions came to him with effortless ease. He attributed this to spiritual insights given to him in answer to prayers offered in his behalf.

Later in the year, the Wilkinses moved to Provo, Utah, where Ernest Wilkins had been accepted as a member of the faculty of the Brigham Young University. Typically, Elder and Sister Lee were involved in helping their "little family" to locate suitable housing, to make financial arrangements, and to move their belongings into the new quarters.

The day after returning home from Palo Alto following the holiday visit, Elder Lee received the disquieting news that Aldredge Evans, whom he had recently installed as the president of the Ensign Stake, had died unexpectedly. Of the funeral service held shortly afterward, where he was the principal speaker, Elder Lee wrote: "Many had seemingly questioned the inspiration in calling a man to the presidency if he was soon to be taken in death. I sought to allay their anxieties on this question." President Lee wanted the questioners to understand that calls such as this one confirm foreordained calls given in the premortal existence and that the quality, not the length of service, is the crucial thing. Moreover, man's limited and often skewed view of things can seldom comprehend the designs of an omniscient God, who, during a limited time, through a chosen servant, can set in motion things that will have vast, eternal consequences. What person, therefore, lacking omniscience, would presume to question the inspiration of calling this man to serve for only a few weeks, or, had it been the case, for only a few days? Conceivably, his particular combination of skills and experience could have initiated, either through personal contacts or projects he commenced, vital actions that no one else could have achieved. Three weeks later, Elder Lee presided at a special conference in the Ensign Stake where David E. Judd was called to succeed Aldredge Evans.

As if to contrast Aldredge Evans's short tenure in office, three of Elder Lee's long-time associates in welfare work, Wm. E. Ryberg, Stringham Stevens, and Roscoe Eardley, passed away in the early months of 1950. Joining Elder Lee in eulogizing these men for their service in helping to lay the foundations of Church welfare, and in mourning with their families, was Elder Henry D. Moyle. A few days after the funeral of Brother Eardley, the last of the three, Elder Lee and Elder Moyle left Salt Lake City by train on a three-week trip that would take them to Washington, D. C., and then to Florida on Church business. It would be the longest trip they would take together. En route to Washington, they held a stake conference in Chicago. "It was an enjoyable experience to be with Brother Moyle," wrote Elder Lee, "and I appreciated his wise counsel and able address." They travelled to Milwaukee Sunday evening, where they dedicated a new chapel, and the next day went with David M. Kennedy, a member of the Chicago stake presidency, to look at an experimental dairy farm. Although he was a suave and successful banker, David Kennedy was no novice when it came to cows and farms since he was born and raised in the small, rural town of Randolph, Utah, where these things were a way of life. So, in talking with the Brethren about this dairy farm, he spoke with a voice of authority and experience, as he would speak authoritatively in the future about international finance and diplomacy when he became the United States Secretary of the Treasury and later the United States Ambassador at large. Still later, these skills would qualify Brother Kennedy to serve as a special assistant to the First Presidency, advising about matters of international diplomacy, as the Church mounted a major, global missionary effort.

The next day in Washington, D.C., the two apostles met with the chief of the Bureau of Internal Revenue and his staff attorneys, at which time they successfully negotiated a tax exemption for Deseret Industries facilities in California. Travelling to New York, they consulted with local Church leaders about the purchase of an expensive chapel site. This entailed a review of the local demographics, the patterns of Church growth, and the accessibility of the proposed site to transportation facilities. Predictably, during the discussions, the Brethren inquired about the status of the welfare plan in the area. Elder Lee expressed "considerable anxiety" about the lack of enthusiasm for welfare work in the stake. This quality, or the lack of it, almost became a litmus test for Elder Lee and his associates in welfare in determining the qualifications of a person to serve in key positions of leadership.

On May 12, the two apostles flew to Jacksonville, Florida, and then motored to Deer Park near Orlando where the Church had acquired large acreages of ranch and farmland. In charge of this development was Heber Meeks, President Lee's close friend and former president of the Southern States Mission. "It is a pioneer venture of great magnitude," wrote Elder Lee of the Florida ranch, "which, when completed, will have about 180,000 acres of the best ranch land in Florida." At this time, the involvement of the Church in the ownership of the ranch was generally unknown. And since Elder Moyle and Joseph L. Wirthlin of the Presiding Bishopric were the ones who had been most prominently involved in acquiring the property and in managing the ranch, the local public perception was that they owned it. This misconception, and the failure of nonmembers of the Church to understand the significance of apostolic seniority, created a comic situation when the Brethren conferred with a local businessman about the possibility of purchasing some of his land. This man, whom Elder Lee characterized as "something of a drunken sot," was "insulting" to him "as he tried to play up to Brother Moyle whom he thought was the man with the money to play up to."

When the Brethren were taken on a tour of the ranch, they, like the local businessman, also learned that things are not always what they seem to be. As they drove along a side road, which seemed perfectly safe, they became mired in the sand. The efforts of the driver to get unstuck, which were made more anxious by the knowledge that a special luncheon with local business and civic leaders awaited them in Orlando, only served to worsen the situation. They were finally rescued, but not before the motor on Heber Meeks's vehicle was almost burned out. They were three hours late for the luncheon.

Returning to Jacksonville, Elder Lee and his companion visited the home of the Jenkins family located on the banks of the St. Johns River, where he and Fern had happily stayed three years before when the Jacksonville Stake was organized. However, he found sadness there on this occasion. The husband, Archie O. Jenkins, had died not long before, and Sister Jenkins and her children were struggling, not only with the loss of the family patriarch but also with the myriad problems connected with his personal estate and his far-flung business holdings. There was little that could be done to help, except to give personal counsel and an apostolic blessing.

After holding a series of meetings with leaders and members in Jacksonville, Elder Lee finally succumbed to the urging of Elder Moyle to join him in a favorite pastime — deep sea fishing. Driving to the Atlantic Coast nearby, they rented a boat and, with a pilot who knew the waters, were taken to an area where success was likely. "Enjoyed the thrill of landing a great sail fish," Elder Lee wrote excitedly.

On that triumphant note, the Brethren returned home by train. Elder Lee used the time en route to prepare for future assignments, especially a commencement address he had agreed to give at one of the high schools in Ogden. Arriving home, he learned of the death of a cousin in Clifton, Irvin Davis, whose family had urgently requested that he speak at the funeral, a request he honored. "There were about 250 in attendance," he wrote of the occasion, "and [it was] one of the most satisfying visits I have made back home in meeting and renewing acquaintances with old friends." Although he never lived there after his marriage, and returned only sporadically for occasions like this, Elder Lee never seemed to lose the feeling that Clifton was home. This was the place where his roots had been planted and, despite his far-ranging travels, would always be the place where he seemed to feel more in touch with his past and his life's purpose.

For the moment, that purpose was to resume the regular round of stake conference assignments, interspersed with headquarters duties. Before the customary July break, he presided at stake conferences in Boise, Idaho; Ogden, Utah; Richland, Washington; and San Bernardino, California. "Finished the day very weary," he wrote of the Ogden conference, "after setting apart new high counselors, presidents of Seventy, etc., etc." These organizational tasks usually came at the end of two full days of instructional and motivational meetings where he had been "on stage," unable really to relax or to find time for private reflection. Because stake presidents had not yet been given authority to do some of these things, members from nearby stakes would often come for the visiting authority to do them while he was in the area. Occasionally, the conference visitor found sensitive situations that were difficult, or

A Peaceful Interlude

awkward, to resolve, thus adding to the normal tensions of the weekend. Such a situation arose at Richland, where a new stake was created out of a mission district. After completing the usual organizational procedures, it was decided to call a former counselor in the district presidency as the stake president. That the district president was passed over was, of itself, awkward, given the normal expectation that he would be called as the stake president. That awkwardness was intensified when the new stake president selected his former leader as a counselor. "Although this move was somewhat delicate," Elder Lee noted, "we were convinced it was the thing to do." Even though stressful, the best interests of the work took precedence over personal feelings.

What made it possible for Elder Lee to maintain perspective and a sense of equilibrium were the periodic breaks in the routine and occasional interludes of good humor. A lighthearted moment occurred shortly before Elder Lee left for Richland, when two women and a man from California came for counsel. They "needed someone to teach them about revelation they have been receiving," he wrote. Then added, "Apparently I did not qualify."

After the conference in San Bernardino, he returned home to celebrate the Fourth of July with his family. He bought some sparklers and shared them with Skipper and Hal Goates, whose enthusiasms were infectious. The next day, he returned to the Goates home where he shed some of his tensions by hard physical work in their yard: mowing, trimming, and pruning. A session like this was Elder Lee's best source of physical therapy from the stresses of his work. Later in the month, and extending into August, he spent long hours over many days at the Goates home, helping to construct a picket fence around their yard so Helen would be able to tend the children more easily. He also helped Brent prepare the forms and pour concrete for a patio at the rear of the home where they could enjoy the outdoors and entertain their guests. The neighbors who were unacquainted with Elder Lee must have wondered how the Goates family could afford such an able worker, over such a long period of time, whose distinguished looks could not be hidden under his rough work clothes. Meanwhile, he and Fern made several trips to Provo during the break to help the Wilkinses in finding a home.

The Lees also enjoyed several social events during the period, the most memorable, perhaps, being the party celebrating the third wedding anniversary of Elder George F. Richards and his wife, Bessie Hollings Richards. The eighty-nine-year-old apostle, who was the president of the Twelve, and his much younger bride were, according to Elder Lee, "the life of the party." At the time of their marriage, Bessie, a close friend of Fern Lee, had wondered about it because of the wide difference in their ages. In counselling with Elder Lee, she was told that if she married Elder Richards, she would have him for at least three years. As their demeanor at the anniversary party indicated, they had had three happy years together. Seventeen days later, Elder Richards passed away quietly, having told Elder Lee earlier in the day that he was tired "and that all he wanted to do was to rest." At the funeral held a few days later, Elder Lee was one of the speakers, eulogizing his friend who had been a member of the Twelve for forty-four years.

The effect of the death of Elder Richards was to elevate President David O. McKay to the position of president of the Twelve, a position he would occupy in tandem with his role as a counselor in the First Presidency. This dual role for President McKay would be short-lived since, within less than a year, he would become the president of the Church at the death of President George Albert Smith.

Two weeks after President Richards's funeral, Elder Lee resumed his usual responsibilities by touring the Northwestern States Mission, whose president, Joel Richards, was a son of George F. Richards. The tour started on August 26, 1950, in Butte, Montana, and ended in Portland, Oregon, the mission headquarters, on September 17. During that three-week period, Elder Lee held the usual missionary and member meetings in many cities in the states of Montana, Washington, and Oregon, in the course of which he encountered the usual grist of problems. At Butte, he gave kindly counsel to a branch president who had insisted that he interview and clear all prospective new members before their baptism. It was a mistake of the head, not the heart, the new and inexperienced branch president not having understood until then that he had no such authority, which rested only with the mission president and his missionaries. Later Elder Lee gave counsel about a missionary who had run up a large phone bill calling his sweetheart at home, and about another missionary whose lack of discipline in getting up on time, and in other matters, was seriously impeding the work. Cases like this gave Elder Lee the opportunity to discuss the reasons for mission rules and the need for missionaries to be disciplined in following them.

After holding meetings in Butte, Great Falls, Chinook, Cutbank, Kalispell, St. Ignatius, and Charles, Montana, Elder Lee and the touring party travelled into the state of Washington for a series of meetings in Spokane, Ephrata, and Tacoma. Here Elder Lee found an atmosphere reminiscent of World War II as the defense industries and military and naval installations were gearing up for the Korean War, which had erupted in open hostilities three months before. On September 15, 1950, only a week after the visit to Tacoma, the United States Navy landed marines and soldiers of the American Tenth Army Corps, commanded by Major General Edward M. Almond, at Inchon, Korea, in a brilliant amphibious operation. This laid the groundwork for a successful offensive of United Nations forces against the North Koreans, followed by the massive intervention of Chinese communist forces. A bloody war of attrition ensued, complicated by the United Nations decision not to attack communist troops and supply depots in their sanctuaries north of the Yalu River. These and other events connected with the Korean War would have heavy impact on the work of Elder Lee and his brethren in the months ahead as they struggled with the problems of Latter-day Saint personnel in the armed services and the radical reduction of the Church's missionary force occasioned by restrictive draft policies. While these events lay in the future, the war mentality that hung over the Pacific Northwest at this time colored the remainder of Elder Lee's mission tour in subtle, indefinable ways.

At Bend, Oregon, Elder Lee detected an attitude among the missionaries that was troubling and prompted him to speak out strongly about the need to be on guard always against sexual temptation. In doing so, he related the incident when Potiphar's wife sought to seduce Joseph. Later, one of the missionaries went to President Richards to report that not long before, he had had an experience similar to the one related by Elder Lee. That it had happened at all suggested that the elder had not been following the counsel never to be separated from his companion. This and other incidents that cropped up along the way illustrated the need, which Elder Lee sought faithfully to fill, to come back repeatedly to the basics of missionary work, outlined in the handbook, which contained the condensed wisdom gained over more than a hundred years of proselyting all around the world.

The last meeting of the tour was held with the mission staff and missionaries working in the Portland area. Elder Lee then presided over a conference of the Portland Stake before returning home on September 18. He was met at the Salt Lake train depot by Fern, both daughters, and their husbands. Hungry to be filled in about events in their separate, busy lives, the six of them stayed up for several hours until after midnight, visiting and reminiscing, while enjoying some of Fern's famous sandwiches.

The next day, Elder and Sister Lee went to Provo, Utah, with the Wilkinses to help them further in their search for suitable housing. There they conferred with Elder Lee's friend Howard McKean, who showed them a new house he had recently completed and who later gave helpful counsel that enabled Maurine and Ernie and their children to become comfortably settled in a home not far from the

A Peaceful Interlude

BYU campus. While in Provo on this occasion, Elder Lee was introduced to one of his numberless namesakes around the world, a baby named Harold Lee Ricks, the child of good friends Irene and Eldon Ricks.

Elder Lee had one last assignment before the October general conference, a conference in the Park Stake in Salt Lake City. Since this did not entail travel out of town, it was a relatively pressure-free weekend, which enabled him to prepare in a leisurely way for the general conference, where he was the concluding speaker at the Sunday morning session. "The spirit was wonderful," he wrote of the occasion, "and I found myself so much under the influence that I had difficulty controlling my feelings."

The spirit of the conference was greatly enhanced by the call of Delbert L. Stapley to fill the vacancy in the Twelve caused by the recent death of Elder George F. Richards. Once Elder Stapley had been sustained by the conference, ordained, and set apart, he was quickly integrated into the work of his new quorum. A duty he shared with all of its other members was to serve on the missionary committee of the Church. A pressing problem this committee then faced had arisen, as already mentioned, from the Korean War. By the first of December the problem had assumed major proportions as some local draft boards had begun to refuse to grant military deferments for missionaries. The issue reached the boiling point in mid-January 1951, when the selective service administration registered formal complaints about the large size of the Church's missionary groups (there was a group of 426 in early January, for instance) and when, as Elder Lee reported, a few of the local draft boards began "recalling some missionaries" from the mission field for induction into the armed services. Because the adverse publicity from these incidents reflected negatively on the Church, subjecting it to widespread criticism, the Brethren revised their policy after carefully reviewing it. "It was decided," Elder Lee recorded on January 30, 1951, "that as of February 1, 1951, no young men of draft age will be recommended for missionary service." This change in policy put a crimp in missionary work during the remainder of the Korean War. However, the shortfall in the number of missionaries, occasioned by the loss of the young elders, was compensated in part by the call of older brethren and their wives. But it took time to build up the numbers of these older missionaries; and they never equalled the totals achieved earlier. However, by the following November, Elder Lee was pleased to report that he had participated in setting apart 117 new missionaries, "mostly older 70's and their wives."

Chapter Eighteen

The Reins Change Hands

Elder Lee interrupted the usual New Year's Day celebration with his family on January 1, 1951, to pay a courtesy call on President George Albert Smith. "I found him in good spirits and looking fine," wrote he optimistically. The appearances were misleading. President Smith was notoriously secretive about his inner feelings. The outward appearances, of course, implied that all was well with the prophet as he sat cheerfully before an open fire, surrounded by members of his family, amid evidences of a joyful Christmas just passed. But, in fact, President Smith was a sick man, having suffered major illnesses during much of his adulthood. He was able to mask his physical ills stoically so that others ordinarily could not gauge his real condition from his appearance and demeanor. Therefore, when Elder Lee left his home that day, he erroneously believed that President Smith's physical condition was good, and that despite the fact his eightieth birthday was only three months away, he would be able to lead the Church for some time to come. On this account, it came as a surprise when, at a meeting on February 15, a letter was read from President Smith, "indicating that he felt his end was drawing near and that he was arranging his affairs with that prospect." Word came two weeks later that the prophet's condition had worsened. In an effort to revive his spirits, two of the Brethren took the sacrament to President Smith's home following the weekly council meeting in the temple. On March 22, Elder Lee noted in his diary: "A very discouraging report of President Smith's condition was made by President Clark. There is a suspicion that some paralysis is setting in."

During this period, Elder Lee himself was not in robust health. In the last weeks of 1950, he had suffered digestive disorders intermittently, so much so that he had declined speaking engagements when possible. Only three days before the surprising letter from President Smith was read, Elder Lee had written, following a busy weekend where he had installed new presidencies in the Grant, Granite, and Wilford stakes, "I finished the day very weary from my exertions." This weariness, which was aggravated by a throbbing sinus infection, hung on so tenaciously that on the first weekend in March, Elder Lee was excused from attending a stake conference in Idaho Falls, Idaho. It was the first time in ten years he had missed a stake conference assignment because of illness. Three weeks later, on March 26, as he returned to Salt Lake City from a stake conference in Rexburg, Idaho, Elder Lee was stricken with a sinus attack so severe that it put him in bed for several days. It was while convalescing from this attack that he wrote, under date of March 30, 1951: "The word from President Smith continues to be discouraging and hope for his recovery has been abandoned."

It was in these circumstances, with the prophet near death and Elder Lee weaker with illnesses than he had ever been, that plans were laid for the general conference, which was scheduled to begin on Friday, April 6, 1951, and to end on Sunday the eighth. However, the death of President Smith on Wednesday, April 4, his eightieth birth-

The Reins Change Hands

day, radically altered these plans. Elder Lee was notified of the prophet's death shortly after he passed away at 7:27 P.M. Wednesday evening. He immediately called Elder Albert E. Bowen, by whose side he had sat in the temple council meetings after the death of Elder Sylvester Q. Cannon in 1943, and the two of them went together to the prophet's home. There they joined with other General Authorities to extend condolences to members of the family who also had assembled at President Smith's home. As the Brethren left after having had prayer with the family, it was decided that the Quorum of the Twelve would meet the next morning to discuss what to do about the funeral and the conference. At this meeting, where President David O. McKay presided and conducted as the President of the Twelve, a question was raised about the advisability of holding the general session Friday morning as planned and then of cancelling the remainder of the conference in honor of President Smith. After discussion, it was decided not to do this, but instead to hold both Friday sessions as planned; to cancel the Saturday sessions, and in their place to hold President Smith's funeral; then to hold the usual Sunday general sessions, followed by a Solemn Assembly on Monday where the General Authorities would be presented for sustaining vote.

Following the Sunday afternoon session, the members of the Twelve convened in a special meeting. After the usual preliminaries, there was discussion whether the First Presidency should be reorganized or whether it should be deferred. After each one had expressed his views, it was decided that the reorganization should not be delayed. Then, on motion of President Joseph Fielding Smith, seconded by Elder Lee, President David O. McKay was approved as the ninth president of the Church and was then ordained and set apart by the other apostles. President McKay then nominated Stephen L. Richards as his first counselor and President Clark as his second counselor. While this action surprised the Twelve, they unanimously sustained President McKay's recommendation.

Harold B. Lee

At the Solemn Assembly the next day, President Clark delivered the classic speech in which he affirmed that performance, not position, should be the governing criterion in evaluating Church service. Of that meeting, Elder Lee wrote: "A wonderful spirit was in evidence, highlighted by the majestic conduct of President Clark who won the love and honor to himself and the Lord's work seldom equalled, and perhaps never excelled."

President Stephen L. Richards was greatly respected by all the Brethren. Following a conference in the Cottonwood Stake in early 1950, which he attended with President Richards, Elder Lee wrote: "His counsel was wise and timely and his procedure was an excellent training for me." Elder Lee had seen, and had come to admire, another aspect of President Richards's character. This was a deep spiritual sense, which occasionally seemed to be obscured by his high intellect. This side of his nature was shown to Elder Lee several weeks after the Cottonwood stake conference when they travelled to California together to divide the Pasadena Stake. On the return trip on the train, President Richards related a special experience he had had several years before when, in a vivid dream, he was "warned" about the misconduct of a man, known to both of them, before it surfaced.

Elder Lee had also seen President Richards's skills in analysis and organization when he had served with him and Elder Albert E. Bowen on the priesthood committee that had recommended changes in the relationship between the priesthood and the auxiliaries. He had also been impressed with the wise way in which President Richards had suggested that the matter be laid aside in view of President George Albert Smith's attitude toward it. In the years ahead there developed basic differences between them in welfare matters, but these never resulted in a loss of the confidence or respect they held for each other.

The day after he was sustained as the first counselor in the First Presidency, President Richards attended a meeting of the Twelve where he told the Brethren he would try to move forward the recommendations made several years before about a simplified program to give more emphasis to the priesthood; a revised priesthood ward teaching program; recommendations relative to ordaining and setting apart high counselors, bishoprics, and stake presidents; and developing a priesthood insurance program. "He promised to expedite these matters," wrote Elder Lee, "and to get us some action one way or the other." Unforeseen events, and the rolling out of President McKay's agenda, of which President Richards was unaware, prevented the implementation of the proposals as to home teaching and a change in the role of the priesthood and the auxiliaries. Indeed, action on these would be deferred for another ten years, some time following the death of President Richards.

The events President Richards did not foresee, which postponed action on these proposals, were physical problems of the prophet, his preoccupation with the demands of his new office, and the ambitious program of world travel President McKay undertook the year following his installation as the head of the Church.

On May 3 following the Solemn Assembly, President McKay entered the hospital for major surgery. Although he was hospitalized for only four days, the prophet functioned at only about half-speed for a month. Then in August, following his return from the Hill Cumorah Pageant, he was stricken with an attack of vertigo so severe it was almost impossible for him to stand without support. He was hospitalized immediately when his ailment was diagnosed as an inner ear disorder. He was in the hospital for a week and then for a month afterward he experienced difficulty and discomfort. During this period, the counselors could not take action alone on matters of such importance as those President Richards had outlined to the Twelve, and President McKay, with all the other demands on his time, was unable to get into these matters. When the prophet began the series of lengthy trips in May 1952, which would take him to many parts of the world — to Great

Britain, Europe, Africa, South America, and the islands of the Pacific—his time at home was restricted and the matters President Richards had discussed with the Twelve had to yield to other things that, at the moment, President McKay considered to be of greater importance.

The semiannual conference in October 1951, the first one following President McKay's installation, was a busy and important one. At that time, Elder Marion G. Romney was called as a member of the Twelve to fill the vacancy caused by the call of President Richards to the First Presidency. Also at that time, George Q. Morris, Stayner Richards, ElRay Christiansen, and John Longden were called as Assistants to the Twelve. The call of Marion G. Romney was a source of special satisfaction to Elder Lee. "President Clark came to my office," wrote he on October 4, "to share with me my joy in Brother Romney's appointment." Two days later, when the name of his friend was presented for sustaining vote, Elder Lee noted: "Needless to say, my joy is unbounded at his coming into the council."

But, Elder Lee's joy at the call of his friend was alloyed with a sadness caused by an enervating weariness. In an attempt to get some relief, Elder Lee asked Henry D. Moyle and Delbert Stapley to administer to him the evening of the fifth. It helped, but did not eliminate the problem. A week later, following a stake conference in Idaho, Elder Lee did something that he did repeatedly over the years when he had a difficult problem. "I went to an upper room of the temple," wrote he, "for some spiritual strength I sorely need." It seems not to be happenstance that during most of the ensuing year, no entries appear in Elder Lee's diary referring to such a problem. This experience in the temple seems to have provided the necessary spiritual strength to lift him out of the feeling of weariness he had felt for many weeks.

One thing that had contributed to Elder Lee's upset during this period was the purchase of a home at 849 Connor Street and the complications of moving into it. The move was completed only three days after his special

The Reins Change Hands

prayer in the temple. It proved to be a boon to live again in a home where he had a yard to putter in. While the Lees had a lovely, spacious apartment at 109 First Avenue, only a block from the Church Administration Building, he felt restrained there because of the lack of a yard and flower beds where he could work off his frustrations. Fern, too, felt a new sense of freedom and welcomed the opportunity to decorate and rearrange their new quarters.

The following weekend, Elder Lee travelled to Long Beach, California, for a stake conference. The Wilkinses, who had moved to Southern California, where Ernie had accepted employment with the Hughes organization, met him at the depot and took him to their home where he spent the night. When he returned to Salt Lake City, Maurine and her two little boys went back with him to give Ernie some time without interruption to work on his doctoral dissertation. Arriving at Salt Lake, Elder Lee was met at the depot by Henry D. Moyle. The two of them then left immediately for Washington, D.C., where they had an appointment to meet with officials of the United Mine Workers Union about a labor dispute, which had arisen over the Church's operation of a coal mine in Carbon County, Utah. "I enjoyed visiting throughout the day with Brother Moyle," wrote Elder Lee, "with his great faith and loyalty, his constant support and strength." At Washington, they were met by Elder Moyle's brother, Walter, who took them to his home, where they stayed as his guests.

The meeting with the second tier of union leaders the next day was a standoff. The Brethren explained the welfare program and the reasons why the mine couldn't be unionized, because of the principle of donated labor upon which it was based. The union men seemed not to be listening and countered by saying, "It is merely a matter of pure economics." After that, the Brethren felt it would be useless to try to go higher and decided not to seek an interview with the union's top man, tough and bellicose John L. Lewis.

While they were in the nation's capital, they met with

local leaders to review their welfare assignments, then travelled to New York with Walter Moyle, where they joined with him in blessing his grandson. Later, in reporting the incident, Elder Lee noted that Elder Moyle, uncharacteristically, became quite emotional while blessing the child, explaining later that during the prayer, "he felt the presence of his own father, James H. Moyle, very near." Later in New York City, Elder Lee blessed Elder Moyle's grandson, the eight-month-old son of Marie Moyle Wangeman and her husband, Frank, a prominent New York hotel executive. "It was a lovely experience," wrote Elder Lee, "and gave evidence that the son-in-law feels a growing bond to the church. Henry and Alberta were thrilled." It is inferred Elder Moyle's joy was significantly enhanced by the fact the grandson was named Henry Moyle Wangeman. On the way home, Elder Lee, perhaps caught up in the euphoria of the grandfatherhood he had witnessed recently, stopped at Marshall Field's in Chicago to buy Christmas presents for his own grandchildren.

The remainder of 1951 was an amalgam of Church chores and achievements and family trials and triumphs. At a stake conference in Oregon, Elder Lee found a woeful lack of qualified leaders in one of the branches, a problem he solved in an unconventional way. "We selected a branch president," Elder Lee explained, "on condition he would stop smoking and pay his tithing, which he humbly agreed to do after we had given him a blessing." In Colorado, his diplomatic skills were tested when he laid at rest serious frictions that had arisen when the headquarters of the San Luis Stake were moved from Manassa to La Jara. Elder Lee joined President McKay in attending the Ogden stake conference where the prophet dedicated a new chapel on November 25. "It was an enjoyable experience to be with him," Elder Lee wrote of the occasion.

The following day brought a significant change in Elder Lee's responsibilities. At a meeting of the Church board of education, the executive committee of the board was reorganized. Released were John A. Widtsoe, Joseph F.

Merrill, and Albert E. Bowen; and sustained in their places were Joseph Fielding Smith, chairman, and Harold B. Lee, Henry D. Moyle, and Marion G. Romney as members. This placed Elder Lee in a position where his influence on Church education would be powerfully felt for many years.

The Lees' trauma during this period came from the death of Fern's mother two weeks before Thanksgiving. She was buried on November 13 following beautiful services attended by numerous members of the family and friends. At the time, Fern was in the midst of completing the decoration of her new home and the arrangements for the holiday season. Two days before Thanksgiving, she was in the ZCMI department store, looking at fabrics and shopping for accessories, when suddenly she became terribly nauseated. Employees of the store took her to a rest area and called Elder Lee, whose office was just across the street. At the time he was in a meeting of the new executive committee of the Church Board of Education, its first. He hurried across the street to comfort his wife. Then he took her home. Her illness was not serious, and she was soon back to normal.

Elder and Sister Lee enjoyed a pleasant Christmas in their new home. Afterward, they and the Goateses travelled to Los Angeles to spend the New Year's holiday with the Wilkinses. With the help of Bishop Dean Olson, brother of Ruby Haight, the family obtained seats for the Rose Bowl Parade the morning of January 1; and in the afternoon, Elder Lee and his sons-in-law were Bishop Olson's guests for the annual Rose Bowl football game, following which they joined with the other members of the family for a New Year's feast. Two days later, the Lees hosted their daughters and sons-in-law at a special dinner at the exclusive Miramar Restaurant in Santa Monica.

When Elder Lee returned to Salt Lake City after the holidays, two main things claimed his attention at headquarters: Church education and Church welfare. On January 10, a lengthy meeting of the Board of Trustees of Brigham Young University was held where matters previously reviewed by the executive committee were presented for consideration—matters pertaining to attendance, budget, and proposed additions to the faculty. A few months before, Ernest L. Wilkinson had been installed as the new president of BYU, who had ambitious plans for the growth of the physical plant at the university, the improvement of the professional standing of its faculty, and the enlargement of its student body. He had been counselling with the new executive committee, which had approved some of his recommendations, modified some, and rejected others. The matters on which all agreed were presented to the full board for consideration. It was a process that went on for many years.

The university experienced a phenomenal growth during the 1950s and 1960s. The main figures contributing to that growth from among the ecclesiastical leaders were President Joseph Fielding Smith and Elder Harold B. Lee. Working as a team, they were heavily involved in every aspect of the work that caused the emergence of Brigham Young University as a major American institution of higher learning.

Elder Lee's involvement in this growth was a matter of personal satisfaction, given his background in education. And to have become involved in it at the threshold of that growth repeated, in a sense, his pioneering involvement in the development of Church welfare and later in the development of Church correlation and the restructuring of the Church's headquarters organizations.

At this time, the modern Church welfare program, then in the twilight of its second decade, was undergoing some significant reevaluations. President McKay believed some midcourse adjustments in the program were necessary. There was concern about the heavy, continuing welfare "assessments" that were imposed by the general welfare committee. There also was concern about the increasing number of complaints from LDS businessmen who protested against the sale of welfare commodities in the open market in direct competition with them. And there was a sense in some quarters that there had been an undue proliferation of welfare projects, beyond what was strictly necessary for the care of the needy, especially because the dire conditions of high unemployment and economic depression of the 1930s no longer existed. Moreover, there was a perception that the policy against the acceptance of government subsidies by the members of the Church was overly rigid, particularly in view of the heavy and constantly increasing tax burden imposed on the people. In these circumstances, an incident involving subsidies under Canadian law created widespread concern in the welfare department. It was reported that leaders of the Church in Canada had been advised that there was no Church policy that would prohibit members of the Church there from accepting these government subsidies. This ran counter to the philosophy that had been taught for many years by welfare leaders in the United States who had admonished Latter-day Saints that the Church should stand independent of all earthly agencies, and that if Church members needed assistance, they should reject government subsidies and should turn, instead, to their families and, if necessary, to their bishops who would provide assistance through the Church welfare system. This philosophy had its roots in the depression of the 1930s when Church leaders branded some U.S. relief measures as a dole whose effect created unwanted dependencies on government, robbed the recipients of dignity and independence, imposed heavy tax burdens on society, and fostered the idea of a welfare state. By contrast, it was taught, Church welfare provided a mechanism to enable the needy to obtain help in exchange for which they rendered service, thereby removing the stigma of a dole and preserving feelings of dignity and self-worth.

Lost in this equation was the reality that democratic government rests on people and that government assistance, therefore, represents assistance from the people, including those who might claim government subsidies. It was this rationale that supported the decision not to object to the Canadian Saints accepting the government subsidies should they elect to do so. But to the pioneers in Church welfare, especially President Clark, Elder Lee, and Elder Romney, the idea was surprising and disturbing.

As the pendulum swung away from emphasis on Church welfare, President Clark, Elder Lee, and others involved in the program developed a cautious approach to any proposal to expand it. They were concerned this might precipitate further cutbacks. So, on July 31, 1953, Elder Lee reported he had "counselled with President Clark who urged that any requests for welfare construction be handled wisely so as to prevent the welfare program from diminishing."

The reevaluation of Church welfare mainly occurred during the first six years of President McKay's administration, from 1951 to 1957. Throughout this period, the prophet was preoccupied with the initiatives that would distinguish his administration, initiatives that would signal the internationalization of the Church. During this period, President McKay made three lengthy trips to Europe during which he selected sites for temples in Bern, Switzerland, and London, England. On his third European tour he dedicated the temple in Bern, which underscored his message that the Church was international in character, that new members should remain in their native lands, and that all the blessings of the Church, including temple blessings, would be made available to all. During this period, President McKay also made a lengthy trip into Africa, and South and Central America; and another separate lengthy trip was made into the Pacific, during which he approved the site for a temple in New Zealand. During this period, he was also heavily involved in the completion of the temple in Los Angeles, California, and its dedication in March 1956. It is apparent, therefore, that President McKay had his mind on many things other than Church welfare during this period. While he undoubtedly was aware of and approved the positions his second counselor took on this issue, he had no intention that the welfare plan would be scrapped or seriously cut back, but only that there would be some trimming of its programs and some reining in of its growth. President McKay's heavy, enthusiastic involvement in laying the groundwork of Church welfare affirmed this; and the keynote address he delivered at the opening session of the April general conference in 1957 clearly demonstrated it. Of that address, Elder Lee reported, "He, for the first time during his presidency, made reference to the welfare program, extolling its leaders and declaring that its methods had been tested and proven sound." Elated by this unexpected praise, Elder Lee went to the prophet to thank him for it. "I told him that I felt as though the welfare program had gained a reprieve and that I had relived the feelings I had in the beginning when I was almost daily in his office as he directed me."

Yet, Elder Lee and his associates in Church welfare deplored some of the changes that had been made in the program. He was disturbed when, on September 3, 1957, Elder Delbert L. Stapley advised him that the First Presidency "had given instructions to the Presiding Bishop to provide government social security for all church employees, in addition to church insurance." The following day, Elder Lee recorded this lamentation of his associate, Marion G. Romney: "Marion Romney expressed anxiety that we had lost almost every one of our cherished principles in the welfare program, even including the question of accepting government aid. . . . Our ablest welfare men are called to preside over missions and no new committee members are approved. The Canadians are informed by telegram that they are to counsel their people to accept government dole. We are told to put money in the bank rather than in commodities for a year in home storage. City stakes are now proposing to build old folks homes in lieu of production projects; [and] government social security benefits are gradually replacing the Church employees welfare aid." Notwithstanding these and other changes in Church welfare, the plan remained essentially intact, providing an efficient mechanism to help the needy of the Church in time of want.

These changes in Church welfare were matched by significant changes in the Church hierarchy during the same six-year period. During the years 1952 and 1953, four members of the Twelve passed away: Joseph F. Merrill, John A. Widtsoe, Albert E. Bowen, and Matthew Cowley. These apostles were replaced, in order, by LeGrand Richards, Adam S. Bennion, Richard L. Evans, and George Q. Morris. The call of Elder Richards to the Twelve entailed a reorganization of the Presiding Bishopric, with Joseph L. Wirthlin being called as the new Presiding Bishop and Thorpe B. Isaacson and Carl W. Buehner as his counselors. Continuing the domino effect, Elder Evans's call created a vacancy in the First Council of the Seventy that was filled by the call of thirty-two-year-old Marion D. Hanks. At the October 1953 general conference when Elders Evans and Hanks were called, Elder Hugh B. Brown was sustained as an Assistant to the Twelve, filling the vacancy created by the death of Elder Stayner Richards, a younger brother of President Stephen L. Richards.

As with most of the other new members of the Twelve called after 1941, Elder Lee carefully briefed Adam S. Bennion about headquarters procedures prior to his induction into the quorum. However, because Elders Richards and Evans had served as General Authorities for many years before their calls, and because Elder Morris had served as the general superintendent of the YMMIA, and therefore knew his way around Church headquarters, it was unnecessary for Elder Lee to perform this service for them.

Although it involved neither a call, nor a release, nor a death, another significant change in the Twelve occurred in 1952. A few weeks after his election as the President of the United States in early November, Dwight D. Eisenhower named Ezra Taft Benson as the secretary of agriculture in his cabinet. Before accepting the appointment, Elder Benson had cleared it with President David O. McKay, knowing that acceptance would preclude him from performing his apostolic duties during the time he served in the cabinet. The prophet felt inclined to approve the appointment out of a sense of obligation to the country, and because of a perception that having an ordained apostle functioning at the center of the government of the United States would have a beneficial effect on it.

Elder Lee was pleased about this significant recognition that had come to his boyhood friend, "T" Benson. He first learned about it on November 24, while he was in the midst of dividing the Mount Ogden Stake, in Ogden, Utah, to create the new East Ogden Stake. A press release out of Washington, D.C., on that day was picked up and rebroadcast over the radio in Utah. Preoccupation with the work of the conference prevented Elder Lee from attempting to contact his friend that day to congratulate him. But, he called the next morning, and learning that Elder Benson was in the East, he talked with his wife, Flora, instead, conveying his genuine congratulations on the appointment and the recognition it had brought to Elder Benson personally and to the Church.

Neither President McKay, nor Elder Lee, nor any of the other Brethren, had any misconception about the impact this appointment would have on Elder Benson and the Church. It would cast Elder Benson in the midst of a heated political controversy that marked the end of twenty years of Democratic dominance of the White House. Not since Herbert Hoover left the executive mansion following his defeat in November 1932 had a Republican president presided over the government of the United States. During the intervening twenty years, Democratic presidents and legislators had put in place a host of economic measures designed to adjust what the policy makers considered to be inequities in the system. A key plank in this platform of economic reform was an elaborate system of price supports, which guaranteed minimum prices for farm products, irrespective of market demands or values. It was known at the time of Elder Benson's appointment that both he and President Eisenhower opposed this system, advocating instead a free market. It was known, too, that a shift in policy would entail major upheavals in the agriculture community as farmers lost the secure status that the system of price supports guaranteed. There was no doubt, therefore, that Ezra Taft Benson would occupy the hot seat in President Eisenhower's cabinet, that he would be the main target of criticism by groups and individuals who would be adversely affected by a change in policy, and consequently that he and his family would be subjected to continual upset and harassment. One aspect of this new status, which Elder Benson and his brethren knew would be especially troubling, if not galling, was that some members of the Church who disagreed with his policies would openly oppose him and would seek to have him removed from office, either by discharge or by the political defeat of the man who had appointed him. To one who held the apostolic office, whose life had been dedicated to the aims of the Savior, the Prince of Peace, and who, during the nine years of his apostolic ministry, had preached unity among the Saints, this was an unhappy prospect that would make his service in the cabinet an onerous burden. Being fully aware of this, Elder Benson's associates in the Twelve were very solicitous toward him and sought, by word and deed, to support him in the challenging assignment he had undertaken.

Among the most supportive of Elder Benson's brethren in this situation was his boyhood friend and fellow alumnus of the Oneida Stake Academy, Harold B. Lee. Elder Lee had an opportunity to give open support to his friend at a conference in the Washington, D.C., Stake to which he had been assigned, held only a few weeks after Elder Benson had taken office. Elder Lee arrived in the capital on Saturday, February 28, 1953, by train from New York City. He was met at the train depot by J. Willard Marriott, whose business, which he had started from scratch, was just beginning to take off and which, in the future, would become an international giant. After freshening up at the Marriott home, Elder Lee began the usual round of training

The Reins Change Hands

and motivational meetings with the leaders and members of the stake. Elder Benson came to the Saturday evening adult session of the conference where Elder Lee insisted that he be seated beside him on the stand and that he share the time with him at the pulpit. Afterward, obviously pleased to again be doing the thing he enjoyed doing most—preaching the gospel—the new secretary of agriculture drove "Hal" to Brother Marriott's home in his chauffeured limousine, which was one of the perks of his new office. It is undoubtedly true that the Oneida classmates of this pair scarcely could have imagined, in their wildest flights of fancy, that these two Cache Valley farm boys would rise so high, so fast. And the end was not yet.

At the general sessions on Sunday, Elder Benson was seated by his friend on the stand and again was asked to share the time at the pulpit. Of this day, Elder Lee reported: "Brother Benson was needing the uplift of the conference; and I did all I could to build him up before the people. There was a remarkable spirit with our entire congressional delegation in attendance."

Following the Sunday sessions, Elder Lee went to the home of Wallace F. Bennett, one of Utah's United States senators, and Mrs. Bennett, who was the youngest daughter of President Heber J. Grant. After dinner, these friends stayed up until midnight, discussing old times and current events as they related to the Church, the federal government, and world affairs. Because of his background in politics, and because of the efforts that had been made to persuade him to run for the Senate, or other high political office, conversations such as this were fascinating to Elder Lee. That fascination was undoubtedly enhanced, on this occasion, because of his gracious hostess, Frances Grant Bennett, whom Elder Lee had known since his early days in Church welfare in the 1930s and whose knowledge of contemporary Church leaders was unmatched. What Elder Lee learned during this lengthy visit with the Bennetts would be helpful in the future, perhaps in ways he could not then foresee.

Although he was up late the night before, Elder Lee arose early the next morning to have breakfast with Elder Benson, who also provided helpful insights about what was going on in Washington. Afterward, Elder Benson invited Elder Lee to accompany him to his office. There he took his visitor on a tour of the executive suite of the Department of the Interior, a large, almost palatial facility, from which he directed the activities of tens of thousands of employees located in offices throughout the country. During the tour, Elder Lee met two men whom he had known for many years who were serving on Elder Benson's administrative staff: D. Arthur Haycock, who had recently served as President George Albert Smith's personal secretary, and Fredrick Babbel, who had served as Elder Benson's secretary and travelling companion while he directed the relief work in Europe after World War II. Brother Haycock, of course, would later serve as his private secretary after Elder Lee became the President of the Church in July 1972. "They are showing the effect of tension in the department," Elder Lee wrote after this visit, "being lashed by their enemies because of a change of policy away from government price supports." However, there was an encouraging sign three days later when Elder Lee noted: "Had a good report on Ezra Taft Benson's talk at Des Moines where he won his audience to his viewpoint on agricultural questions." The public attitude toward Elder Benson and his policies would oscillate back and forth during his service as the secretary of agriculture. But, the support of Elder Lee and the other members of the Twelve would remain constant.

Before leaving Washington on this occasion, Elder Lee also visited Arthur V. Watkins, Utah's other United States Senator, who provided additional important insights about conditions in the capital and the directions in which the new administration was moving. Elder Lee and the senator had been closely associated in the early days of Church welfare while the senator served as a stake president in the Provo, Utah, area.

The Reins Change Hands

Elder Lee travelled home via New York City, where he was hosted by Frank Wangeman and his wife, who took him to Radio City to see "Cinerama," a new movie production that had caught the fancy of the country.

"It was good to be home again with my dear wife and my little ones," Elder Lee wrote on March 6 after returning from the East. There was no time to relax and enjoy his family, however, as the next day found him presiding at the conference of the Bear Lake Stake in northern Utah. Between then and the end of the month, he also presided at stake conferences in Tremonton, Hurricane, and Tooele, Utah. Meanwhile, on assignment from President McKay, he and Henry D. Moyle were active in monitoring "hot issues before the legislature" in which the Brethren had taken an interest. They were closeted with the prophet on March 12 for this purpose. By the end of the month, the pressure of this hectic schedule had taken a heavy toll on his health. "Came home in considerable distress in my abdominal region," he wrote on March 30 after completing the assignment to Tooele where he had divided the stake. "I went to the doctor where I spent three hours being examined" to try to find the cause of abdominal pains and recurring headaches. He returned for additional tests the two following days. Medications prescribed by the doctor provided some relief. It was in this condition that Elder Lee entered into the April general conference schedule. He spoke at the Primary conference, where he addressed the subject, "The Building of Testimonies by Primary Workers," and he was the first speaker at the afternoon session on the first day of the general conference where his subject was, "The Gates of Hell Shall Not Prevail Against My Church." Typically, he focused on spiritual things, which is somewhat of an anomaly given the fact his reputation in the Church was then founded on the temporal aspects of welfare.

When the general conference had ended, it was apparent to all that Elder Lee was not well. President Clark and President Joseph Fielding Smith intervened to cancel his assignments and to insist that he go away for a week to convalesce. In company with Fern and close relatives, Bill and Lida Prince, he obediently left Salt Lake City on April 10, headed for southern California and a week of relaxation. Judging from what happened, Elder Lee obviously had a skewed idea about what it meant to relax. On the way down, he stopped in Cedar City, Utah, to instruct a new stake presidency in their duties. Arriving in Los Angeles, he accepted the invitation to dedicate the new Westwood Ward chapel. Then, he acceded to the request of Soren Jacobsen to speak to the workers involved in building the Los Angeles Temple. Meanwhile, he could not disappoint a man who came to him pleading for a blessing. Finally, he was able to spend two quiet days at Brother Jacobsen's beach cottage on Balboa Island. "Slept last night," he wrote on April 16, "as I have never done for years. I awoke at 10:30." After a leisurely brunch and a few desultory hours watching the sea and reading, Elder Lee was jerked back to reality by a call from his secretary who advised he had just received assignments to attend stake conferences at Panguitch, Utah, and Oahu, Hawaii. "My promised vacation was immediately ended," he wrote, "as we began to keep the telephone busy making arrangements to leave Balboa." In the meantime, Salt Lake apparently became aware how Elder Lee's vacation had been short-circuited and advised that his assignment to Panguitch had been cancelled and that he could leave immediately for Hawaii. Since the assignment in Hawaii was two weeks away, this meant he would get his vacation after all.

This was Elder Lee's first trip to Hawaii since his visit more than ten years before when he had shared cramped quarters aboard a freighter with twenty-three others, including smokers. It was the first trip to Hawaii for Fern. They left San Francisco on the *Lurline* on April 21, assigned to a comfortable stateroom with a private lavatory and shower. Elder Lee characterized the *Lurline* as "a floating hotel with recreational facilities, sumptuous dining rooms

The Reins Change Hands

and continuing activities throughout the day or night, suited to all kinds of travellers." And, he also noted, the Lees "proved to be good travellers" with no signs of nausea, helped undoubtedly by dosages of Dramamine, the motion sickness pills that friends had given them at San Francisco.

The casual ambience aboard ship had a soothing effect on the apostle. He settled into an unstructured routine, sleeping as long as he wanted, walking the decks for exercise, reading and writing when the urge came, and in between, gazing at the sea and the marine life that abounded there. On the last night aboard ship, the Lees joined other passengers at the traditional Captain's Dinner, a formal affair with "paper hats and balloons to spice the occasion." Harold Lee had not enjoyed such carefree frivolity since his school days. And, the fact he was on assignment from his leaders, was insulated from all telephone calls and visitors and had no meetings to attend or sermons to deliver, removed any sense of guilt or self-reproach.

The *Lurline* was destined, first, for Hilo, on the big island, where it would remain for a few hours before going on to Honolulu on the smaller, but better known, island of Oahu. Elder Lee apparently did not learn about this scheduling until late in the voyage. "We regretted that we did not know soon enough," he explained to his diary, "to have notified our missionaries there so that we could have the day with them and our Saints in Hilo inasmuch as we would be there from 8:00 A.M. to 6:00 P.M." In these circumstances, he resorted to the only means of communication then available to him: "In our prayers," he explained, "we asked the Lord to alert them somehow to our coming so that our day could be profitably spent with them." The next day's entry, April 26, 1953, reported the outcome. "As we saw the crowd assembled on the pier, we noted a distinctive group of about fifty whom we recognized as our Latter-day Saints. Our prayers had been answered. They greeted us with a profusion of flower leis and took us to a priesthood and Relief Society meeting in our branch."

Elder Lee was impressed by stories told there about how the Saints had been blessed during the devastating tidal wave in 1946, "when 35-foot waves washed away a number of buildings at the waterfront, leaving one lone building which had housed some of the missionaries." A sister also told how she had been washed to sea, but was saved by clinging to a door, and who testified that her temple garments had protected her body from mutilation by sharks. And later in Honolulu, Sister Mary Kaliki told Elder Lee how the tidal wave had receded when she 'commanded' it 'to spare her home.' Such stories confirmed the tradition of Polynesian faith that Matthew Cowley had shared with Elder Lee and the Brethren.

The outpouring of love and leis showered on the Lees at Hilo was repeated when they arrived at Honolulu. The unpretentious affection shown the visitors captivated them and created in them a lasting love for these whole-souled people. That love grew and intensified during the thirteen days they spent on Oahu, days during which they were feted at luaus and shown places of interest, in between which they attended stake conference and missionary meetings, as well as a session at the Laie Temple. The Lees also did some shopping for gifts to take home to the family, made plans to go deep sea fishing, but had to give it up because of rough seas, and had dinner with several different families, among whom was Joseph F. Smith who, several years before, had been released as the Patriarch to the Church. At this time, Brother Smith was on the faculty at the University of Hawaii and was anxious to visit with Elder and Sister Lee to be briefed about their mutual friends. At his request, Elder Lee also gave a special blessing to their host, who, the next day, showed the visitors around the campus. As he had a free day, Elder Lee spent most of it in the university library, "seeking for some ideas which might [be suitable] for the baccalaureate sermon at the USAC on May 31." That night, the Lees "had dinner with the Woolleys [Ralph and wife] at their lovely home atop 'Tantalua.'" Thoroughly rested, the travellers boarded the *Lurline* on May 9, cleared customs on the fourteenth, and arrived home on the sixteenth, ready to resume their normal schedules.

Before delivering the baccalaureate address at the USAC in Logan, which he had prepared while in Hawaii, Elder Lee presided at stake conferences in Davis County, Utah, and Star Valley, Wyoming. He also attended a special meeting in Clifton, where, as the town's favorite son, he dedicated an addition to their newly remodeled chapel. In order to perpetuate the connection between him and the community, local leaders later erected a monument on the chapel grounds, bearing a plaque with key data about Elder Lee and identifying Clifton as his birthplace.

Elder Lee's baccalaureate address at Logan a few days later, and the events which followed it, were another effort to pay homage to a Cache Valley boy who had made good and had brought distinction to his neighborhood. His address bore the title, "I Dare You to Believe," in which he discussed the fundamental concepts of true religion. At the graduation exercises the following day, he was awarded an honorary doctor of humanities degree, one of several such recognitions that would come to him.

Two days after receiving his honorary degree, Elder Lee joined with the other General Authorities in paying their respects to Elder Stayner Richards, Assistant to the Twelve, who had passed away on May 28. Elder Richards's unexpected death at age sixty-seven, after only two years of service as a General Authority, prompted discussions about the need for some help at the general level to handle the ever-increasing load of work. It also precipitated one of the "brainstorming" sessions that President Clark and Elder Lee engaged in from time to time as they considered various ways in which the work could be facilitated. "President Clark came to the office," Elder Lee noted on June 12, 1953, "to make an observation related to the supervision of wards and stakes as the Church grows." What the president had in mind was to appoint three men in each region on a Church service basis who could train and motivate stake and ward leaders within their respective regions and who, in turn, would report periodically to "the Twelve, or those whom they designate." An interesting feature of President Clark's proposal was the personalities of the three men who would comprise the regional teams he envisioned. He speculated one would be "hard headed or hard boiled," another would be "suave or easy going," and the third would be "of a practical turn of mind." But, all three of them were to be "sound in doctrine and loyal and true." Elder Lee noted that this idea coincided, to an extent, with one he had had about organizing the general priesthood committee, which he chaired, into three groups: children, youth, and adult, "with one of the full time assistants as the executive secretary." In this we see the germ of several ideas that, in the years ahead, would become incorporated in the organizational structure of the Church, the concepts of regional training and supervision, of priesthood coordination and correlation at the general level, and even of area presidencies who would oversee groups of regions, and their constituent stakes, wards, and missions. In instances such as this, we also see the dynamics of Church growth and supervision at work, within the general framework of the priesthood, directed and controlled by apostolic authority.

After the summer break in 1953, Elder Lee was introduced to another phase of Church work when, on August 27, he was appointed to the temple committee, which was chaired by President Joseph Fielding Smith. Elder Spencer W. Kimball was the other member of this three-man committee. This opened a new vista of Church work for Elder Lee and marked the beginning of an intensive study of the origins, the purposes, and the implications of the temple ordinances. In a sense, it was an extension and an intensification of his interest in the temple ordinances that was kindled shortly after his call to the Twelve when he began to instruct groups of missionaries in the Salt Lake Temple.

The Reins Change Hands

Now, however, his involvement would be much broader and would extend beyond theory to matters of supervision and administration.

In the wake of this appointment came other temple related assignments. In September of that year, he was given the responsibility to make arrangements for a Solemn Assembly in the Logan Temple; and a year later, he performed the same function as to a Solemn Assembly in the St. George Temple. He also chaired the committee that made the arrangements for the cornerstone laying ceremony at the Los Angeles Temple. Afterward, he played a key role in making the final arrangements for the dedication of that temple. Moreover, in connection with his stake conference and other assignments, he began to take care of temple matters while in outlying areas. In mid-October 1953 during an assignment in Alberta, Canada, he visited the Cardston Temple "to make some inquiries [he] had been asked to make by the First Presidency."

The main reason for this trip to Canada was to preside at a quarterly conference of the Lethbridge Stake. With Elder Lee on this occasion was Elder Hugh B. Brown, who, the previous weekend, had been sustained as an Assistant to the Twelve. Having lived in Canada for many years, Elder Brown was almost regarded as a native son, and that perception was enhanced by his marriage to Zina Card, the daughter of one of the Church's most noted pioneers in Canada, and by the death of his son, who was killed in World War II while flying in a Canadian contingent of the Royal Air Force. These things, added to the fact that this was Elder Brown's first assignment as a General Authority, created an air of expectancy in the conference toward what he might say during his public addresses. What he said was electrifying to the Lethbridge Saints, as it was to others when Elder Brown repeated it later on other occasions. Elder Lee summarized what his companion said: "He bore a remarkable testimony," wrote Elder Lee in his diary on October 11, "of a power that tried to crush him and overcome him by a terrible despondency. This came on Friday night before he was notified by telephone late Saturday night by President McKay that he would be named as an Assistant to the Council of the Twelve." Two days later at a special meeting in Edmonton, Elder Lee again shared the pulpit with his companion when he wrote of Elder Brown: "Hugh was very nervous and in distress, possibly due to the strains and tensions of the past week." It may also be that Elder Brown was overwhelmed with the prospect of what lay ahead, having learned by personal acquaintance with many of the Brethren over the years the demands made on the time and energies of the General Authorities. At this time, Elder Brown was within a few days of his seventieth birthday, an age when most men would already have been in retirement for several years. Ahead for him, however, lay the most active, the most demanding, the most stressful, albeit the most productive and enjoyable years of his life, which would extend into his ninety-third year. Indeed, Elder Brown, although sixteen years older than Elder Lee, would outlive him by a year. And the remaining years of their lives would see them switching leadership roles as Elder Brown would be elevated to the Twelve, then to the First Presidency, then returned to the Twelve at the same time Elder Lee would become the first counselor in the First Presidency, and then the president of the Church.

The day after this special meeting in Edmonton, Elder Lee dedicated a Church institute building to be used by the LDS students attending the University of Edmonton. Sharing the rostrum with him on this occasion were Elder Brown, Andrew Stewart, the president of the university, and prominent local Latter-day Saint political, business, and church leader N. Eldon Tanner. Eldon Tanner, a distant cousin of Fern Tanner Lee, would play a significant role in the future leadership of the Church, both at the local and the general levels, serving ultimately as a counselor to four presidents of the Church: David O. McKay, Joseph Fielding Smith, Harold B. Lee, and Spencer W. Kimball.

The Reins Change Hands

Brother Tanner's meteoric rise to the highest echelons of Church leadership began a month after the dedication of the Edmonton Institute Building when the Lethbridge Stake was divided to create the new Calgary Stake. Elder Lee was assigned to effect the division, assisted by Elder Mark E. Petersen. The two apostles went by automobile to Great Falls, Montana, the first day in clear autumn weather. On the second day, November 13, 1953, they drove to Calgary, Alberta, Canada, where the headquarters of the new stake were to be established. There they had dinner with N. Eldon Tanner "to get better acquainted as he was being considered as a leader in the new stake," wrote Elder Lee. The apostles apparently wanted to see the candidate in his home setting to determine whether his family and his personal life-style were of a kind they could urge the local members to emulate. Brother Tanner had already received strong endorsement from people who knew him well, including his uncle, Hugh B. Brown, who had known Eldon since he was a boy. Elder Lee had seen him in action a month before at the dedication ceremony in Edmonton and had been favorably impressed. But he and Elder Petersen still wanted to go behind the curtain of his public life and reputation to see him in the place where he lived.

Elder Lee's diary entry of the next day reveals that N. Eldon Tanner had met every test. "We went into a series of interviews throughout the day," wrote he, "and particularly with Eldon Tanner who for years has been one of the strongest leaders in the Social Credit Party of Alberta, having served as the Minister of Lands and Mines. We satisfied ourselves as to his soundness and his loyalty to church principles and leadership." Another entry in the diary indicates one of the special "church principles" Elder Lee felt the candidate should accept without qualification. "He told us," wrote Elder Lee, "that neither he, nor any of his children, had accepted the 'Family Allowance' paid by the Dominion Government. He said he valued his freedom too much to sell it for so little." Having learned that, the conclusion seemed inevitable. "We finally selected him for our stake president." It is apparent that although Salt Lake had indicated its approval for Church members in Canada to accept the "Family Allowance," if they elected, Elder Lee wanted to be certain that the stake president he installed in Calgary did not accept the allowance and, in principle, was opposed to it.

It is an interesting commentary on the fluid nature of leadership in the Mormon church to note that in less than ten years from the date he was called at age fifty-five, as the Church's newest stake president, of a new remote stake, hundreds of miles from Church headquarters, N. Eldon Tanner would be catapulted into the First Presidency where he would have supervisory responsibilities over Elder Harold B. Lee, the apostle who called him as stake president. These leadership roles would, of course, be reversed in 1970 when Elder Lee became President Joseph Fielding Smith's first counselor, with Brother Tanner as the second counselor, and in 1972 when President Lee became the president of the Church.

It is anomalous that alongside the fluidity in Church leadership, reflected in N. Eldon Tanner's rapid rise to the First Presidency, stands a bedrock stability in the members of the Quorum of the Twelve Apostles and the First Presidency, who, once called, serve for life, conditioned on their faithfulness.

The strain of travel and the pressures of events in Canada caused a recurrence of the nervous tension and headaches that had troubled Elder Lee in recent years. He was bedridden a few days before Thanksgiving, but was sufficiently recovered to go to the football game on Thanksgiving Day with son-in-law Ernie Wilkins. It was a nationally televised game between the University of Utah and Brigham Young University, which Utah won thirty-three to thirty-two. It was a tonic to Elder Lee to spend several hours in the brisk autumn air, enjoying the excitement of the close, hard-fought game and the companionship of his son-in-law.

Chapter Nineteen

The Cycle Continues

Elder Lee loved this young man, Ernie Wilkins, who with Maurine had struggled to complete his formal education at Stanford, but for lack of time and means had not completed his doctoral dissertation. Lacking his Ph.D., he had first accepted a low entry position on the BYU faculty, then had given that up to accept employment in industry in southern California and later had returned to Utah after stressful experiences in business convinced him that he wanted to pursue an academic career, despite the slim financial rewards it offered. Meanwhile, he and Maurine had provided the Lees with their first granddaughter, Marlee, who had been born the previous June. Now the Wilkinses were in the process of sinking deep family roots in Provo, much to the happiness of Elder and Sister Lee. The security of the Wilkins family was significantly enhanced by an event that occurred a few months after the Thanksgiving celebration in 1953. "Today," Elder Lee wrote on April 2, 1954, "our dear son-in-law, Ernest J. Wilkins, was awarded his doctors degree at the Stanford University in languages. I believe

I am even more thrilled than he, not because of the honor thus conferred, but because of the victory won and the assurance and security it will give."

The joy this incident brought was muted by a serious injury Fern had suffered a few days before. While climbing the stairs in their home, she had fallen and fractured her left hip. Because of low blood pressure, an operation had been postponed. By April 2, however, she was strong enough to undergo the needed surgery, which consisted of knitting the fracture together with a metal plate. This serious accident and his wife's natural frailty had been a cause of concern to Elder Lee. The relief he felt once the delicate surgery had been successfully completed is mirrored in this entry of April 5: "The love and faith of the First Presidency and the Twelve and Bishop Wirthlin was never in greater evidence. Fern has undoubtedly been [blessed] by the wonderful prayers and faith offered by so many." And the next day, during which George Q. Morris was sustained as a member of the Twelve, and Sterling W. Sill was sustained as an Assistant to the Twelve, Elder Lee wrote: "While seated in the tabernacle, in the closing service of conference, I seemed to have been bathed in Heavenly peace which assured me that the Lord had given my beloved Fern back to me."

Sister Lee's recovery was steady, although marked by occasional setbacks. "Fern took a turn for the worse," Elder Lee wrote on April 8. During the three following days, he spent long hours at the hospital, comforting his wife. Afterward, he was "weary" and his nerves were "somewhat unstrung," which brought on a "nervous stomach disorder." In this condition, he drove to Pocatello, Idaho, the following weekend for a stake conference. While there, he suffered a severe attack of sinusitis which was temporarily alleviated by a blessing given by the local brethren. Indeed, he felt so much better the next day after returning to Salt Lake that he cancelled an appointment at a laboratory for "allergy tests."

Elder Lee brought Fern home from the hospital on April

20. "She was revived by the smell of the yard and the feel of home," he wrote. "I brought my mattress and slept on the floor by her throughout the night." During the ensuing week, Elder Lee's sinus problem flared up again. After consultation, it was decided surgery was necessary; so on April 27, a week after Fern returned home, Dr. Leroy Smith operated to "remove some growths" from his nose, "which had been causing difficulty in breathing." This surgery, and minor follow-up surgery in July, seems to have effected a significant improvement in Elder Lee's health. For several years afterward, his diary is devoid of references to physical problems, except once, about eighteen months after the surgeries, he noted he had suffered some "nervous tension."

The dawning of May, with the colorful display of flowers in their tidy yards, seemed to infuse the Lees with new enthusiasm. They were both on the mend and looked forward to resuming their normal routines. Both daughters, with their husbands and children, lived nearby, which enabled them to enjoy the nurturing of these two "little families." On the first Sunday in May, Helen and Brent brought their six-week-old daughter, Elizabeth Jane, to visit her Lee grandparents. Elder Lee had just returned from a stake conference in Moroni, Utah, and with his wife, enjoyed holding and cuddling this their second granddaughter.

Later in the month, the Lees' horizons were broadened when President McKay asked them to tour the Orient. They were given latitude to leave when Fern had regained her strength. By August, she felt well enough to go. Meanwhile, Elder Lee was involved during much of the summer directing a course on the Bible for seminary and institute teachers given for credit at Brigham Young University. He gave some of the weekly lessons and assigned the remainder to other General Authorities, whom he accompanied to Provo where he introduced them. Among those who assisted him were President J. Reuben Clark, who spoke twice, President Joseph Fielding Smith, and Elders

Henry D. Moyle, Marion G. Romney, and Adam S. Bennion of the Twelve. It was a stimulating and enjoyable experience for Elder Lee, which was reminiscent of the past when he regularly taught in an academic setting. The benefit to the students was attested by the many favorable reports received during and after the course.

But the experience had its downside. At the outset, he learned secondhand of grumbling among members of the faculty that the one directing the course, Elder Lee, not only did not have a bona fide Ph.D., but did not even have an undergraduate degree from an accredited four-year university. In the view of these critics, the honorary Ph.D. awarded to Elder Lee the previous year by the Utah State University was insufficient to remove the academic stigma they feared his directing a "for credit" class would bring to BYU. This situation understandably created the awkward and anomalous feeling in Elder Lee that he was unwelcome there, although he served on the executive committee of the Board of Trustees that directed the university and controlled its administration, including the hiring and firing of its faculty. These feelings were intensified when, during the course, a member of the faculty confronted him following a lecture, to criticize his citation of scriptures in the Doctrine and Covenants, something he felt was inappropriate in a study of the Bible and he said might endanger the university's accreditation.

Having received a series of vaccinations during the summer, and later having received special blessings from President McKay, Elder and Sister Lee left Salt Lake City on the *California Zephyr* on August 3 destined first for San Francisco. Two days later, they boarded the SS *Cleveland*, bound first for Hawaii, then Yokohama, Japan. Aboard the *Cleveland* were BYU President Ernest L. Wilkinson and his wife, who were going to Honolulu where President Wilkinson would study the feasibility of establishing a junior college there. Elder Lee's position on the executive committee of the Board of Trustees of BYU brought him into frequent contact with President Wilkinson to discuss university policies. So, during the five-day voyage to Hawaii, they spent many hours together, talking about matters of mutual interest. The thing that seemed uppermost in President Wilkinson's mind was his relationship with the First Presidency, all of whom were members of the Board of Trustees of the university, but none of whom served on the executive committee. Obviously he did not want to violate protocol, either by failing to keep these brethren fully advised about his administration or by intruding unduly on their time. Elder Lee, who by this time had been intimately connected with the First Presidency for almost twenty years, was able to give President Wilkinson counsel that, in the future, would help him to avoid needless embarrassments.

Waiting to greet Elder and Sister Lee at the pier in Pearl Harbor were the temple president, the stake president, and the mission president and their wives, the latter being D. Arthur Haycock and his wife, Maurine. In addition, of course, there were many Polynesian Saints present who welcomed the visitors in traditional fashion with song, dance, and a profusion of fragrant leis.

The Lees made the mission home their headquarters during the two-day layover in Honolulu. This enabled Elder Lee to counsel his friend Arthur Haycock, who had been called to Hawaii from Elder Ezra Taft Benson's staff in the Department of Agriculture. Elder Lee also spent some time with Henry Aki and Colonel Gillette of the Oahu Stake high council, to be briefed about conditions in the Orient.

The travellers boarded their ship at 10:30 P.M., August 13, for the six-day voyage to Yokohama. Unlike the smooth passage from San Francisco to Hawaii, this leg of their trip was marked by heavy storms and much seasickness. This limited their enjoyment of the elaborate cuisine, which was available to them on request, night or day, and the host of other amenities to be found aboard a luxury liner.

The Lees' ship eased into Yokohama Bay on the nineteenth after the submarine net guarding the mouth of the bay had been lifted. This protective measure was considered necessary because of the tensions in the Orient arising out of the Korean War and its aftermath. Shortly after the ship dropped anchor, the passengers were surprised to hear the announcement over the ship's PA system, "The port of Yokohama is closed until further orders. The time of docking will depend solely upon weather conditions." This was a major disappointment as they had anticipated quitting the ship and its constant movements immediately upon their arrival, movements that, though not nearly as pronounced in port as in the open sea, still were noticeable as she rode at anchor.

The wait ended on the twenty-first when their ship eased into the Yokohama dock to disgorge its passengers and cargo. The pier teemed with longshoremen who, with typical Japanese dispatch, unloaded the baggage of the passengers along with the extra cargo the ship carried. Waiting on the pier to greet the Lees were Mission President Hilton A. Robertson and his wife and several missionaries and servicemen, including Colonel Reed Richards and Colonel Vasco Laub. After clearing customs, a usually complex procedure that had been simplified through the help of President Robertson and his staff, the travellers were taken directly to the Eighth Army Base. There they were greeted by the commanding general of the Eighth Army, Lt. General Thomas B. Hickey, and Chaplain Wilson, who supervised all chaplains in the area. After the usual pleasantries, Elder Lee was outfitted with army clothing and insignia that would enable him to visit army camps as a VIP with all the privileges normally accorded to a major general. After an elaborate meal at the officers club, the Lees were taken to the mission home, where they made preparations for meetings to be held the next day, a Sunday.

Separate priesthood and Relief Society meetings were held in Yokohama on August 22, followed by a sacrament meeting attended by a congregation of two hundred, twenty-five of whom were investigators. Among the mem-

The Cycle Continues

bers present was a Korean convert, Lt. Commander S. Lee, an officer in the Korean Navy, who, Elder Lee was surprised to learn, travelled three hours each way on Sunday to meet with two other members of the Church. He also found other similar examples of dedication among the converts whom he would meet during the five-week tour that lay ahead. That tour would take him to many cities and military bases in Japan, Korea, China, Taiwan, the Philippines, Okinawa, Guam, and Wake Island. Fern spoke at many meetings. Her qualities of spirituality and loving concern increased the impact of her husband's words. His report of her participation in the Yokohama meetings illustrates the quality of her influence. "Fern's motherly talk to the boys," wrote he on August 23, "brought almost universal requests from the servicemen to contact their mothers, wives, and sweethearts."

The next day the visitors flew to Sapporo on the island of Hokkaido, where they met with a group of servicemen at Camp Crawford. Here Elder Lee focused on chastity, a theme that was interwoven throughout the talks he gave to servicemen during the tour. He referred to reports that in a nearby city, classified as one of the most wicked cities in the world, there were four thousand prostitutes and their purveyors. In contrast, he cited the example of a serviceman who contributed over half of his monthly allotment to help finance his brother in the mission field.

Then followed meetings in Tokyo, Itazuki, and Osaka, Japan, before the visitors were flown to Seoul, Korea, in a Globemaster military craft. The Lees were met at the Seoul airport by five LDS chaplains and were then driven to U.S. Army headquarters in a staff car, where they were welcomed by General Oates, the divisional chief of staff. Here they were given ID cards and were outfitted in fatigues before being taken on a tour to see the city and the ravages it had suffered during the war. That it had changed hands four times during the bitter fighting was evident from the many gutted and blackened buildings that still remained standing.

The next day the visitors were briefed on the history of Korea. Elder Lee was interested to learn that of over two thousand Korean clan names, the four predominant ones were Kim, Yi, Chang, and Lee. His name, therefore, opened many doors and provided the grist for many friendly conversations. Given his name, it seems altogether fitting that Harold B. Lee was the first General Authority of the Church to visit Korea.

A conference was held at the Seoul army post chapel on Sunday, September 2. There were 325 in attendance at the morning session and 338 in the afternoon. Those attending included military personnel, thirty Korean converts, and some nonmembers, both from the military and from the Korean population. The speakers, in addition to Elder and Sister Lee, included LDS chaplains, group leaders from the military camps, and Dr. H. Kim, a graduate of Cornell University. Elder Lee found later that the ratio of Ph.D.'s to the total population is perhaps higher in Korea than in any other country.

During the following three days, Elder Lee flew to army camps located some distance from Seoul, identified as camps Abel 2 and Abel 143, where worship services were held. On the flight to Abel 143, the pilot of the F-19 was Captain Daniel Lewis who had been a student at the Woodrow Wilson grammar school in Salt Lake City when Elder Lee was its principal. Captain Lewis flew his passengers up the Chun Haun Valley where hundreds of ROK troops had been annihilated and across the demilitarized zone where, Elder Lee wrote, "We could see the smoke from the Chinese camps."

At Abel 143, Elder Lee was briefed by General McLure, the commander of the Twenty-fourth Division. "In this valley," Elder Lee reported, "we got a glimpse of what total war can do. Two entire villages, one with a population of forty thousand, were completely wiped out."

Returning to Seoul, Elder Lee was introduced to General Maxwell D. Taylor, chief of the Far Eastern command of the US Armed Forces. He gained many helpful insights from this seasoned military leader who was two years younger than he. A graduate of West Point, General Taylor was a skilled linguist who had taught French and Spanish at the academy and who had studied Japanese in Tokyo in the 1930s. He also had commanded the 101st Airborne Division in its airborne landings in France and the Netherlands in 1944 and had been commander of the American military government in Berlin. The year following Elder Lee's visit to Korea, General Taylor became the chief of staff of the United States Army.

The next day, the Lees witnessed the baptism of a Korean convert, Ho Nam Rhee, one of many investigators who were then being taught the gospel by returned missionaries among the United States servicemen. Afterward, Elder Lee talked at length with Dr. H. Kim, asking for suggestions about how proselyting work could be carried on effectively in Korea. Many of Dr. Kim's suggestions were utilized when, the next year, Korea became part of the Northern Far East Mission under President Hilton A. Robertson. And in 1962, a separate Korean mission was organized with Gail E. Carr as its president. Brother Carr, who intermittently visited Korea as a serviceman in the early 1950s, served in the Korea district of the Northern Far East Mission from 1956 to 1958 when he learned the language that enabled him to serve as the first mission president in Korea. These events, which preceded or followed Elder Lee's trailbreaking visit in 1954, reveal the evolutionary process by which Church growth expands following the initial planting of Latter-day Saint influences.

The day after witnessing the baptism in Seoul, Elder Lee was scheduled to fly to Pusan, Korea, for a series of meetings. However, foul weather socked in the Seoul airport, which required a switch to the train. Chaplain Palmer was stressed by this change because, unknown to Elder Lee, he and others had planned a surprise dinner in Pusan honoring the Lees and General Richard E. Whitcomb, which was scheduled hours before the train would arrive. When Elder Lee was informed of the dilemma, he told the

Harold B. Lee

Brigadier General Richard S. Whitcomb (right) and the Pusan Military Post Chaplain (left) greet Elder Harold B. Lee in Pusan, Korea, September 6, 1954

chaplain "not to worry, that if it was vital, the way would be opened to attend." That afternoon, the storm let up briefly to allow a military plane to take off. Hurried arrangements were made for Elder and Sister Lee to board it, but not until they had donned parachutes and Mae West jackets and had been given a crash course in how to bail out of a crippled plane and how to survive in the water should they land at sea. Luckily, they had no need to use this riveting information and arrived safely in Pusan in time to prepare to look surprised at the dinner. It was encouraging to learn that at the meeting the next day, there were eighty-seven nonmember Koreans in attendance.

The travellers flew directly to Tokyo from Pusan, arriving in time to enable Elder Lee to meet with the leaders of fifteen religious denominations on September 11. The plan was for him to speak for an hour and to respond to questions for half an hour. However, the interest in what he said was so intense, they kept him at the lectern for three hours during which he discussed, among other things, the organization of the Church, the restoration, authority in the priesthood, temple work, tithing, missionary work, and the Word of Wisdom. Elder Lee spoke through his interpreter, Brother Sato. "They were most cordial and attentive," he wrote of his hosts.

The visitors travelled by train from Tokyo to Sendai and Nikko, where special worship services were held; and on September 15, Elder Lee met in Tokyo with eighty missionaries in a report and testimony meeting that lasted from 6:00 A.M. to 12:30 P.M. Even then, the missionaries were reluctant to see it end, so sweet and powerful was the Spirit that attended it. It was reported that thirty-two converts had been baptized during the year and that others were in line for baptism in the future. Obviously, new attitudes were stirring in Japan. Fifty years before when Heber J. Grant presided there, only two Japanese joined the Church during his two-year tenure; and they fell away. Elder Lee gained an insight into a main reason for this change through the testimony of Elder Aki. "He thanked the Lord for the war, despite its terrors because through it, the LDS servicemen [came among them]."

From Tokyo, the travellers flew to Okinawa, the site of the last major battle of World War II. Here Elder Lee was introduced to generals Fay Upthegrove and David D. Ogden, who hosted him on a tour of the island while they described the bloody battles that took the lives of nineteen thousand Americans, ninety thousand Japanese, and one hundred thousand Okinawans. Worship services were conducted in a chapel just off the beaches where the first amphibious landings were made nine years before. Outside the pounding surf, devoid of tongue, was mute to tell of deaths the war had won. Inside the Seer, endowed with golden speech, explained unending life within man's reach.

Leaving Okinawa, the party flew to Kowloon with a

brief stop in Taipei. A meeting was held with members of the small Kowloon branch on September 22. The next day, they were taken on a tour of Kowloon, with its narrow streets lined with shops whose merchandise spilled on to the sidewalks and where customers and shopkeepers talked animatedly. It is said strangers who buy at the listed amounts deprive Kowloon shopkeepers of a chief joy, that of trade-haggling over the price of their goods.

The visitors were then ferried to Hong Kong across the harbor where they were the honored guests at a dinner hosted by George Liu and his sister, Eva, and her husband. It was a typical Chinese feast, served in fourteen courses with friendly conversation. During the dinner, President Robertson presented Elder Lee with a Rolex watch and Sister Lee with a beautiful painted ivory piece, both gifts to the Lees from Wendell Mendenhall. Two days later, the visitors were the guests of Daniel F. Y. Chan at another elaborate Chinese dinner.

Before leaving the area, Elder Lee visited the spot where, on July 24, 1949, Elder Matthew Cowley dedicated the land of China for the preaching of the gospel. While they were there, Elder Lee, at the request of President Robertson, also offered a prayer in behalf of the Chinese people and of the missionary work to be performed among them in the future.

From Hong Kong, the party flew to the Philippine Islands where they were shown around Manila by a wealthy nonmember businessman, Peter Grimm, who later joined the Church, and his Latter-day Saint wife, Maxine Tate Grimm of Tooele, Utah. Elder Lee also held a meeting with servicemen at Clark Field where he met General Wm. L. Lee, who gave him the name of a Lee relative in North Carolina who would be able to provide genealogical information that might show a family tie between them.

Leaving the Philippines, the Lees headed eastward toward home with brief stops at Guam and Wake Islands and Hawaii. They arrived in Salt Lake City on October 3 in time to enable Elder Lee to be the last speaker at the

The Cycle Continues

general conference where he reported on his recent tour of the Orient.

This tour opened Elder Lee's mind to the proselyting prospects in the Far East. It also gave him insights into the attitudes of orientals, their qualities of character and their receptivity to the gospel. Moreover, it revealed the interactions between orientals and visitors from the West and the potential for future leadership of the oriental converts. All these and other insights gleaned from the tour would be important in the future as Elder Lee's voice would be heard in the inner councils of the Church, advocating an acceleration of the work in that part of the world. The tour also gave Elder Lee a better understanding of the needs and mentality of LDS servicemen, which would be important in his continuing role as the chairman of the servicemen's committee; and it enhanced the image and status of the Church in the eyes of military leaders as Elder Lee had been hosted and assisted by army and air force generals all along the way. These contacts would prove valuable in the future as the Church sought greater consideration for LDS chaplains.

Soon after returning from the Orient, Elder Lee received the frightening assignment to give the Church of the Air address at the coming April general conference. It was frightening because he would have a nationwide audience, comprised overwhelmingly of nonmembers. Because the talk would be given near Easter, he decided on an Easter theme. His text was taken from the "Hosanna Shout," found in Zechariah 9:9, "Blessed be the King that cometh in the name of the Lord. Hosanna, to the Son of David." The main focus of the talk, which was given at the Sunday morning session of the conference on April 3, 1955, was the ministry of the early apostles who came in the name of the Lord. After tracing their calls to the apostleship and the beginning of their ministry, Elder Lee asked rhetorically: "How was it possible that a handful of apostles, who as fishermen and publicans could engage the learned and the mighty as well as the simple and those of low degree to forsake their religion and embrace a new religion?" In answering his own question, Elder Lee said: "There were undoubted marks of celestial power, perpetually attending their ministry. There was in their very language," he said, quoting Mosheim, " 'an incredible energy or amazing power of sending light into the understanding and convictions of the heart.' " (Conference Report, April 1955, p. 19.) He characterized these early apostles as "God's engineers," who "by following a blueprint made in heaven have charted the course for safest and happiest passage [through life] and have forewarned us of the danger areas." Then, after alluding to the Savior's triumphant entry into Jerusalem and to his later triumph over death through the Crucifixion and Resurrection, Elder Lee, speaking in the spirit and authority of his own apostolic calling, concluded by saying: "Today, as did they in past generations, we declare boldly, that 'The fundamental principles of our religion are the testimony of the Apostles and Prophets concerning Jesus Christ, that He died, was buried, and rose again the third day, and ascended into heaven; and all other things which pertain to our religion are only appendages to it.' O that the inhabitants of an unrepentant world would humble themselves and with faith in the Redeemer of mankind join in the chorus of the multitude who welcomed the Master into the Holy City. . . . For that I pray humbly." (Ibid., p. 20.)

Elder Lee was touched when, at 7:30 the morning he delivered this talk, President J. Reuben Clark came to his office "to be with me [and] to give personal support and uplift." This gracious act was appreciated all the more because President Clark was recuperating from a bad fall he had suffered and was still mourning the death of his brother, Ted. A few days later, the Lees and several others were dinner guests at President Clark's home. "We were shocked," Elder Lee wrote of the occasion, "at the realization that he was failing in health. He was unsteady on his feet and was obviously not his usual self. When he wanted to relate an incident, he usually would refer it to me and ask me to tell it." President Clark, who was eighty-four years old at the time, would later throw off the effects of this temporary despondency and would live for six more years.

Two days after the dinner at President Clark's home, Elder Lee left by train to tour the Central States Mission, where Alvin R. Dyer presided. The apostle had become well acquainted with the mission president after he moved to the home on Connor Street. President Dyer was the bishop of the Monument Park Ward in which the Lees then lived and had enjoyed unusual success in motivating the priests in the ward to fill missions and in creating enthusiasm in the ward. Because there had been favorable reports about Brother Dyer's service in the mission field, Elder Lee noted on April 15, 1955, following their first meeting of the tour, held in Dodge City, Kansas, "I am pleased to be able to inquire into the work of a 'master craftsman of human engineering.'" President Dyer's good work as a mission president would be acknowledged three years later when, in 1958, he was called as an Assistant to the Twelve. Several years after that, he was ordained an apostle, although he was never inducted into the Twelve, and later still he was called as a counselor to the First Presidency, where he had some supervisory responsibilities over Elder Lee.

Oblivious to these future events, the touring party left Dodge City, reputed in pioneer days to be one of the wildest cities in America, to drive to Wichita, Kansas. This took them through a major wheat growing area, then in its third year of a serious drouth, which had created havoc with the local economy, crippling the wheat farmers and the flour and feed mills that were dependent on them. At Wichita, they were the guests in the luxurious home of prominent local businessman T. Bowring Woodbury and his wife. Brother Woodbury, called "By" by his friends, was a counselor to President Dyer in the mission presidency. The training he received in this position and his exposure to Elder Lee and other general Church leaders resulted in By Woodbury being recommended as a mission president, a recommendation that the prophet later followed when Brother Woodbury was called as a mission president in Great Britain. It was under the leadership of men like Brother Woodbury that a massive increase in convert baptisms occurred in Great Britain in the late 1950s and early 1960s. And the harvest from that effort produced many of the staunch leaders of the Church in Great Britain a few decades later.

After holding meetings with missionaries and members in Wichita, the party travelled into Oklahoma. Here Elder Lee met another man who would later render significant service in the Church. "One of the outstanding men of the mission is James Cullimore," wrote Elder Lee on April 19, 1955. "He owns three furniture stores." James A. Cullimore would later serve as a mission president in Great Britain during the period of rapid growth there and, in 1966, would be called as an Assistant to the Twelve.

At this point of the tour, Elder Lee received word of the death of Howard McKean, chairman of the Church building department. Since Elder Lee had previously agreed to speak at his friend's funeral, he flew home for this purpose and then returned immediately to complete the tour. District conferences and missionary meetings were then held in St. Louis, Independence, Columbia, and Springfield, Missouri. Also meetings with servicemen were held at the Scott Air Force Base near Bellville, Illinois, and at Fort Leonard Wood. At this last base, Elder Lee was pleased to hear the commanding officer, Major General Frank Bowman, say "that the boys [Latter-day Saints] did not forget the church and the church did not forget the boys."

Elder Lee took three days after the tour ended to visit places of Church historic interest in Independence, Richmond, Liberty, Far West, and Adam-ondi-Ahman, Missouri. At Independence, in addition to inspecting the temple site, he paid a courtesy call on the two counselors in the first presidency of the Reorganized church: Francis

Henry Edwards, a fifty-seven-year-old convert from England, and W. Wallace Smith, fifty-five-year-old brother of Israel Smith. Elder Lee was interested to learn that President Edwards had followed President David O. McKay around during his recent tour in the Pacific and that President Smith planned to follow Elder Spencer W. Kimball around during his coming tour of Europe. Their reasons for doing this were not made clear.

President Dyer was helpful in briefing Elder Lee about the historic sites in Missouri. He had made a detailed study of the area and had a special interest in the events that had taken place there and those that were predicted to occur in the future. Their first stop north of Independence was at Richmond, where the Prophet Joseph Smith and Hyrum were imprisoned for a while in 1838 in an old house that was later torn down. Here they saw the grave sites of David Whitmer and Oliver Cowdery and a monument erected in memory of the three witnesses of the Book of Mormon. At nearby Liberty, they inspected the old jail where the Smith brothers had been incarcerated. At Far West, they walked around the temple site; and at Adam-ondi-Ahman, they examined the remains of the ancient altar. Elder Lee was amazed that at all these sites, and at places in between, there were no buildings standing that had been constructed by the Latter-day Saints, except a small house built by Lyman Wight, which stood on the side of the hill below the altar at Adam-ondi-Ahman. In contrast, there were numerous buildings standing in both Kirtland, Ohio, and Nauvoo, Illinois, constructed by the Mormon people, places where they had lived for a shorter period of time than in Missouri.

Elder Lee boarded the *City of St. Louis* at Kansas City at 9:30 P.M. on May 1955 for the long trip home. He was startled to find that Fern had suffered hemorrhaging in one of her eyes while he was gone, which had produced a red blotch in it. "As usual, her courage and faith were great," he noted, "but my heart melted as I contemplated the possibility of her failing health." The major concern for her health was high blood pressure, which ranged from 200 to 230. This and medication the doctor prescribed limited her activity. The help of a German sister hired by Elder Lee, who lived in a basement apartment with her young daughter, and assistance from Maurine and Helen, who were nearby, eased Fern's household duties and made it possible for things at home to function smoothly. And counsel given by President McKay at the last meeting of the Brethren in June proved to be providential to the Lees. The prophet then instructed the Brethren to take full advantage of the summer break to spend time with their families and to take care of personal affairs. Following that counsel, Elder Lee spent July and part of August close to home, working in the yards, quietly studying and visiting with Fern. With help from the German sister and her daughter, Fern planned and hosted a dinner party during the month in honor of President and Sister Joseph Fielding Smith, prior to their departure for the Far East. The guests included President David O. McKay, who, when he was introduced to the Lees' grandson, David Goates, said to him, "David, let's you and I keep that name honorable, what do you say?" The only other interruption to the Lees' peaceful summer break was during three days over the Twenty-fourth of July celebration. With his sons-in-law and grandsons, Elder Lee went to Treasure Mountain Scout Camp near Driggs, Idaho, where about a thousand Scouts and their leaders and families had gathered for an encampment. There the title "Chief Friend of the Forest" was conferred upon him. In response, Elder Lee spoke to the group, focusing mainly on the Scouts, whom he admonished to live worthily. It was a significant privilege to be in this ruggedly beautiful setting with his young grandsons. It was fortuitous, too, that their fathers were along so that when Grandpa was through visiting or playing with them, Brent and Ernie could take over to feed and supervise them. While the men and boys were thus employed, Fern and her daughters and granddaughters were enjoying each other at the Lee home in Salt Lake City. Two months later,

The Cycle Continues

Maurine added to the treasure trove of Lee grandchildren when she gave birth to another son, Jay, who was born on the same day that "Skipper," the oldest grandchild, was baptized.

Toward the end of summer, Elder Lee was assigned by President McKay to lead out in making and executing final plans for the dedication of the Los Angeles Temple. This brought them into frequent contact as the arrangements were finalized. In late February 1956, Elder Lee had a vivid dream about President McKay in which the prophet gave instructions about the love of God and its relationship to the command that we love our neighbors as ourselves. When President McKay offered the prayer dedicating the Los Angeles Temple on March 11, 1956, Elder Lee was startled that the prayer's ending essentially repeated what he had seen and heard in the dream. "I was deeply moved as the dedicatory prayer was read," he explained in his diary under that date, "because of a dream I had two weeks ago, in which President McKay was impressing me with the meaning of the love of God, as it relates to the love of our fellowmen and of His service. The dedicatory prayer closed with similar instructions to those I had heard in my dream two weeks before." The impact of this dream upon Elder Lee, and the dedicatory prayer that followed it, seems to have been profound and lasting.

Several weeks after the Los Angeles Temple dedication, President McKay assigned Elder Lee to travel to Mexico to create a new mission. Elder Spencer W. Kimball was assigned to accompany him. They would be together for three weeks, during which their relationship, which had always been cordial and close, would be firmly cemented. Elder Lee had loved and admired Spencer Kimball from the time they first met. He was amazed at his friend's brimming energy, his thoroughness, and his nonstop activity. He marvelled at the enthusiasm with which he undertook any assigned task and the persistent way in which he pursued it to conclusion.

These feelings of love and admiration toward him were

reciprocated by Elder Kimball. He regarded Harold B. Lee as one of the greatest men of his generation. While he was four years older than Elder Lee and a member of one of the most distinguished families in the Church, he was always subordinate to his friend and anxious to do his bidding. Because of the age differential and his seeming poorer health, Elder Kimball never expected to become the President of the Church and, therefore, had reconciled himself to the idea that throughout his apostolic ministry he would follow the lead of Harold B. Lee.

The two apostles left Salt Lake City by train on June 3, 1956. With them were Sister Kimball and Brother and Sister Joseph T. Bentley, who were to lead the new mission. Fern's frail health dictated that she not go. Given her high blood pressure, the doctors feared that the altitude in Mexico and the heat of a Mexican summer could seriously impair her health or could even be life threatening.

The party travelled by rail to El Paso, Texas, via Los Angeles, Phoenix, and Tucson. En route, the two apostles spent time instructing Brother Bentley about his duties as a mission president, whose headquarters would be in Monterrey. Crossing the border at El Paso, the party headed for Monterrey. Brother Bentley, who was fluent in Spanish and whose family roots were deep in the Mormon colonies in northern Mexico, served as translator and as advisor about Mexican protocol. Arriving safely in Monterrey, after a hot and dusty two-day trip, the party was met by Harold A. Pratt, president of the Spanish American Mission. With the assistance of President Pratt, and the concurrence of President Bentley, the brethren rented facilities in Monterrey that would serve as the headquarters of the Northern Mexican Mission.

The members of the Church in Monterrey were in awe to have two members of the Twelve in their midst. This seems never to have happened before. Although the brethren were on a tight schedule, they met briefly with the members and leaders there, speaking to them through brothers Pratt and Bentley, their interpreters. Here Elder

The Cycle Continues

Lee was pleased to meet his son-in-law Ernest Wilkins, who was serving as a guide and translator for a group touring in Mexico.

On June 8, the party drove the six hundred miles from Monterrey to Mexico City over high mountain passes and through country of wild, picturesque beauty. After spending a day to prepare, to recuperate from their tiring trip, and to adjust to the higher elevation, the apostles held a meeting in Mexico City on June 10 with members and missionaries where the Mexican Mission was officially divided, creating the Northern Mexican Mission, the forty-fifth mission in the Church.

The day after this organizational meeting, the visiting apostles held a ten-and-a-half hour testimony meeting with the seventy-nine missionaries who were to remain in the Mexican Mission. "President Bentley seems to have his eye fixed on a young Elder Lee," wrote Brother Harold B. Lee, "a great-grandson of John D. Lee, as his second counselor, provided President Bowman will consent." He didn't consent. "We talked with President Bowman," wrote the apostle, "about the possibility of allowing President Bentley to take Elder Rex Lee as a counselor from this mission to the new mission; but, we found him adamant in his determination to keep Elder Lee as a prospective new leader here." The special qualities of intelligence and character the two mission presidents saw in this young elder flowered in the years ahead to see him successively become a prominent Phoenix, Arizona, attorney, the first dean of the Brigham Young University law school, solicitor general of the United States, and the president of the Brigham Young University.

Having completed the work that brought them to Mexico, the visitors spent a week visiting historic sites southeast of Mexico City in Vera Cruz, Palenque, Mérida, on the Yucatán peninsula, Chichén Itzá, and Oaxaca. Elder Lee noted that some scholars had speculated that the Savior had made his appearance to the Nephites near Palanque and that some had speculated that the state of Oaxaca was the area settled by the Mulekites. While the brethren realized that such conclusions were highly speculative, they were interesting and provocative.

Returning to Mexico City from Oaxaca on June 25, Elder Lee became ill with an intestinal ailment. The following day, he returned to Salt Lake City, via Los Angeles, still suffering stomach upset. When it hadn't cleared up four days later, he consulted Dr. Leroy Kimball, who prescribed some medication that seemed to do the trick.

Elder Lee enjoyed a variety of family activities during the July break. There was a relaxing outing at Fish Lake. Less relaxing, but perhaps more enjoyable, were activities with some of Elder Lee's grandchildren. Maurine had accompanied Ernie on a tour of Central America, and the two older Wilkins children, Alan and Larry, had come to stay with their grandparents for a while. Shortly afterward, Elder Lee, accompanied by Brent and his sons, took his charges on an overnight trip near Huntsville, Utah. It seems to have been a nonstop affair. A few days later, he decided on some urban entertainment for his grandsons. "Took Helen's and Maurine's older boys with me to a cowboy show," he wrote on July 30, "which took much of the afternoon. That, preceded by some shopping and followed by refreshments at Keeleys, was about all the energy and patience I had."

Elder Lee ended his diversions during the summer break with an outing at Yellowstone Park for some fishing with bishops Joseph L. Wirthlin and Carl W. Beuhner. A few days later, he and Fern hosted a party at their home for several General Authorities and their wives. The honored guests were Elder and Sister Henry D. Moyle, who had just returned from a lengthy tour of South and Central America.

Refreshed, Elder Lee returned to his normal routine. A few days after the dinner party, he conducted the graduation exercises at BYU. This was followed in quick succession by a stake conference in Orem, Utah, with Eldred G. Smith; an assignment to speak at a banquet honoring the participants in a softball tournament; and an appointment with Elder Hugh B. Brown to divide the Oakland and Berkley, California, stakes to create the new Walnut Creek Stake. Elder Lee called this last assignment "one of the most difficult and yet most satisfying experiences I have yet had as a member of the Twelve. There was unmistakable evidence of divine direction which could not be denied."

The month leading up to the October general conference was equally busy. On successive weekends, he presided at conferences in the Oneida, Idaho; Pasadena, California; East Rigby, Idaho; Smithfield, Utah; and Spanish Fork, Utah, stakes. At Oneida, he reported that "many of those present were old friends," and at Pasadena he was impressed by the thoughtfulness of Stake President Howard W. Hunter, who had invited Fern's relatives, Bill Tanner and his wife, to have breakfast at the Hunter home so Elder Lee could visit with them. In three years, President Hunter would join Elder Lee as a member of the Twelve.

As usual, the Saints poured in to Salt Lake City from around the Church for the October general conference, filling up the hotels, overcrowding the restaurants, and giving downtown stores a welcome surge of business. They were a cosmopolitan lot, representing every culture where the Church was located and speaking a score of different languages. As usual, Elder Lee was involved not only in the formal meetings but in counselling with many from outlying areas who came to see him.

He delivered a talk of major importance at the beginning of the last session of the conference, Sunday afternoon, October 7. His subject was "The Preparation of the People for the Beginning of the Millennial Reign." While the talk did not presume to say precisely when the millennial reign would begin, it acknowledged the reality of it and the need for the wise to be prepared.

During the remainder of the year, stake conferences occupied most of his time. Two of them stood out. At Rexburg, he and Elder Moyle "found the usual wavering between sentiment and good judgment as to the qualities of leadership." Most of those interviewed recommended the incumbent counselors, even though others appeared to be better qualified. Seemingly they felt it would be an act of disloyalty to nominate anyone else.

The following weekend, he and Elder Mark E. Petersen organized a new stake in Independence, Missouri, carved out of the mission. They found high excitement among some members who believed the apostles were there to create "the center stake of Zion," which would foreshadow the Second Coming. Perhaps some of them saw confirming evidence of this in the subject of Elder Lee's recent conference talk, "The Preparation of the People for the Beginning of the Millennial Reign." Whatever the reason for the excitement, the visiting brethren sought to quell it. They named the new stake the Kansas City Stake rather than the Independence, Missouri, Stake.

Chapter Twenty

Signs of Growing Influence

Elder and Sister Lee enjoyed a quiet Christmas holiday, which included several gatherings with members of their family. One of these was an evening spent with Maurine and Ernie Wilkins, who had driven up from Provo. "It was a joy to have them with us," Elder Lee noted on December 29, "and we talked late into the night before a roaring fire."

It is safe to assume two of the subjects discussed around the fire that night related to recent happenings affecting Ernie Wilkins and Elder Lee. The son-in-law, a recently called bishop, had been long enough in office by this time to have gained insight into the scope and the complexity of his duties. Given Elder Lee's extensive knowledge about these matters and the son-in-law's penchant to seek his advice, it is not unlikely there were comments about the bishop's role in Church administration. As to Elder Lee, the thing most likely discussed was an invitation extended to him on November 24, 1956, to become a member of the board of directors of the Union Pacific Railroad Company. This occurred while he was in New York on an assignment to attend a stake conference. Since he had no inkling it was coming, the invitation stunned Elder Lee. Union Pacific was one of the most powerful companies in the United States. It counted among its officers and directors men of the first rank among American businessmen. Not only was the company a giant in transportation, but its assets and land holdings represented one of the major pools of potential wealth in the country. When the company constructed its portion of the Transcontinental Railroad in the 1860s, it received as a government subsidy alternate sections of land within a certain distance on either side of the tracks along the 1,086 miles of its line, extending from Omaha, Nebraska, to Promontory Point, Utah. Later consolidation with other railroads had, by 1957, increased its trackage almost tenfold, and through reciprocal agreements with still other companies, it had extended its transportation outreach from midcontinent to the West Coast and northwesterly into Canada. Meanwhile, it had become involved in mineral development in several western states as the direct result of the extensive landholdings it had acquired by subsidy from the United States government. As a member of the board of directors of this company, Elder Lee would have an important voice in its management, giving him an influence in temporal affairs far beyond the influence of the Church. Moreover, the men with whom he would become closely associated on the UP board, drawn as they were from among the leaders of other major companies or institutions in the country, would provide another rich source of information and of networking influence that would extend deep into the fabric of American affairs.

While the invitation to become a member of this board of directors was flattering to Elder Lee, he did not look on it as a means of personal benefit or aggrandizement but as a means of extending the influence of the Church. It was in this spirit he was prepared to accept. When he consulted his mentor about it, however, President Clark threw cold water on the idea and advised him to decline.

Signs of Growing Influence

Elder Lee, seemingly, was almost as shocked at this as he was when he received the invitation. President Clark did not elaborate on the reasons supporting his advice, but implied that acceptance might interfere with Elder Lee's Church duties or would unduly increase his responsibilities or time commitments. President Clark later changed this advice, but his original opposition weighed heavily on Elder Lee.

On December 20, 1956, the invitation to join the UP board was confirmed by A. E. Stoddard, president of the company, who was passing through Salt Lake City in the company's private car. He invited Elder Lee to join him at the UP depot, where the car had been put on a siding. During their conversation, Mr. Stoddard advised that Elder Lee's appointment, which had been approved by E. Roland Harriman, chairman of the board, and Mr. Lovett, chairman of the executive committee, would be made official at the meeting of the board scheduled on January 24, 1957, in New York City. "He indicated that he had thoroughly inquired about me," Elder Lee noted in his diary, "and that such an appointment would have been made much earlier had it not been that he had been advised by someone whom he thought knew that such an appointment could only be given to one of the First Presidency among the general authorities." In reflecting on this interview, Elder Lee wrote that he "was left with overpowering conflicting emotions." The first was a sense of elation at the recognition, which thus had come to him and the Church. The second was a sense of sadness because of the seeming lack of an unqualified endorsement by the First Presidency. This sense of sadness was largely mitigated by two subsequent events. First, at a meeting on January 31, 1957, President Stephen L. Richards announced approvingly that Elder Lee "had been elected to the board of one of the great corporations of the world." Second, on February 6, the First Presidency and Elder Lee were the luncheon guests of A. E. Stoddard in the company's private car, where there was a discussion of Elder Lee's appointment with apparent good feelings all around.

Elder Lee left for New York on January 21 to attend the meeting where he was to be formally inducted into the UP board. He stopped in Chicago on the twenty-second to visit with David M. Kennedy and to congratulate him on his recent appointment as the president of the Continental Bank. He arrived in New York the next day, where he was met at the airport by Theodore C. Jacobsen, president of the Eastern States Mission, who later drove him to the Waldorf Astoria where reservations had been made for him by his friend, Hilton Hotel executive Frank Wangeman, Elder Henry D. Moyle's son-in-law. During the years ahead when Elder Lee made monthly trips to New York to attend UP board meetings, and later the Equitable Life board meetings, he usually stayed at the Waldorf where he always received royal treatment.

The day before his induction, Elder Lee engaged in a special fast and prayer. He did so because he believed he had been appointed as a representative of the Church. At the meeting, three other new board members were also inducted: Eldredge Gerry of New York, Oscar Lawler of Los Angeles, and George S. Eccles, a Salt Lake City banker. Later, Elder Lee had lunch with Mr. Harriman in his private dining room, and that night he had dinner in the mission home with the Jacobsens.

It is obvious why the Union Pacific brass invited Elder Lee to join them on their board. He had seniority among the leaders of the Church, yet was a comparatively young man. His key role in the development of the Church's welfare program had proven him to be both creative and persistent. And his work on the boards of directors of Church-owned and controlled companies had given him broad business perceptions that would be valuable as Union Pacific charted its future strategies. Moreover, his political experience and his prominent position in the administration of the Brigham Young University would provide the board with vital insights. All things consid-

Dedication of Timpanogos Region Storehouse, 1957. Left to right: Mark B. Garff, Elders Clifford E. Young and Harold B. Lee, President J. Reuben Clark, Jr., and Alpine Stake President Phil W. Jensen

ered, Harold B. Lee brought more to this board than he received from it.

On his way home, Elder Lee stopped in Kansas City to conduct a stake conference, where he was able to check on the progress of this new stake and to counsel its members and leaders. This assignment set a pattern that would be followed during the many years Elder Lee travelled regularly to New York for board meetings. He would usually have a stake conference or other special assignment on the weekend before or after the board meeting, or sometimes on both weekends in order to economize on time and travel expense.

After returning from New York, Elder Lee received from the First Presidency a copy of a report prepared by the financial secretary to the First Presidency, which proposed that the responsibility for welfare be transferred to the Presiding Bishopric. He took a dim view of some aspects of the report. He was not necessarily opposed to transferring welfare responsibility back to the Bishopric, but he was concerned that Bishop Joseph L. Wirthlin was not well and that a transfer at the time might impose such an additional heavy burden as to require his release. Moreover, he wanted to correct any misunderstandings about the program. He received that opportunity when on March 22, he and Elders Henry D. Moyle and Marion G. Romney were invited to meet with the First Presidency, where these matters were fully aired. As a result the action to transfer responsibility for Church welfare back to the Presiding Bishopric was deferred until April 1963, eighteen months after John H. Vandenburg succeeded Joseph L. Wirthlin as the Presiding Bishop.

During this period, Elder Lee and other members of the council were concerned about the condition of Elder Spencer W. Kimball, who had suffered a recurrence of the hoarseness that had troubled him several years before. While he was in New York to attend a stake conference in late February 1957, it was decided Elder Kimball would consult a specialist. At home, the Brethren joined in prayer, pleading with the Lord to bless him. After a meeting in the temple, Elder Lee wrote to Brother Kimball in New York, telling him of their prayers that the Lord would heal him "if necessary by His miraculous power." In conclusion, he added: "All I know, Spencer, after what we experienced today, is that if He does not listen to that plea, it will be an evidence that He has plans for a greater mission that we know nothing about. Somehow there seemed to be expressed with all the brethren a feeling that because of the magnificence of your service, and because of the greatness of the mission you are now performing, that as measured by all human understanding, that mission is still uncompleted." The New York doctors performed an extensive biopsy on Elder Kimball to determine whether a malignancy had caused the hoarseness. Instructing him that he should not try to speak for at least thirty days, they sent him home to be monitored by his Salt Lake doctor, pending a decision about the need for major surgery. He arrived at Salt Lake's Union Pacific depot on March 16, where he and Sister Kimball were met by Elder Lee and Fern, who accompanied them to their home. Five days later at the weekly council meeting, Elder Kimball, rendered mute by the doctor's decree, had Elder Lee read his report.

The following weekend, Elder Lee presided at a stake conference in Denver, Colorado. Since Fern accompanied him, it proved to be a nostalgic treat for them. "There was an opportunity," wrote he, "for us to meet many of our old friends from our missionary days in the Western States Mission." Afterward, the Lees travelled by train to New York City, where Elder Lee attended the monthly UP board meeting on March 28. At that time he was elected as a member of the boards of UP's three subsidiary companies: the Oregon Short Line Railroad, the Oregon Washington Railroad and Navigation company, and the Los Angeles and Salt Lake Railroad. Reflecting on the significance of the day, he confided to his diary: "It was my fifty-eighth birthday with a realization that advancing years bring increased problems and anxieties."

Because of scheduling problems, the Lees flew from New York to Salt Lake City rather than going by train. It was the first time Elder Lee had flown cross-country and marked the beginning of a new mode of travel for him. In time, Elder Lee and the other brethren travelled by train only in cases of emergency.

A few weeks later, Elder Lee returned to New York in company with President Clark, who was going there to attend a meeting of the Equitable Life board. While they were in the city together, President Clark arranged to introduce Elder Lee to the chairman of the board and the president of Equitable Life, Ray D. Murphy and James F. Ostler. "It was a pleasant meeting," wrote Elder Lee, "and for a purpose which at present does not seem clear but may later have meaning." As we shall see, that purpose became clear the following year when Elder Lee was appointed to the Equitable Life board to replace President Clark when he retired.

Because the UP board meeting was scheduled the following week, Elder Lee flew to Jacksonville, Florida, to hold a stake conference over the weekend of June 23 and 24. After the Jacksonville conference, he flew to Washington, D.C., where he conferred with local leaders and had lunch with Elder Benson and his family in the executive dining room of his suite. Following the UP board meeting he flew to Norfolk, Virginia, where he met Fern, who had travelled there from Salt Lake with Elder and Sister Delbert L. Stapley. The two apostles had been assigned to create a new stake, assisted by Mission President Henry A. Smith. Following the usual procedure, the brethren selected Cashell Donahoe, Sr., as the stake president. Afterward, the Lees and Stapleys accompanied Henry A. Smith and his wife to Newport News, where a two-day conference was held with 160 missionaries. The usual instruction and testimony meetings were held, interspersed with personal interviews by the visitors.

Travelling to Williamsburg, the party attended a pageant on July 4, which portrayed the struggle for independence. "A most fitting way to celebrate the Fourth of July," noted Elder Lee.

The following day, the party visited Monticello, Thomas Jefferson's home. Nearby, in the family burial plot, they saw Jefferson's tomb, surmounted by an obelisk on which is inscribed the epitaph he composed for himself: "Here was buried Thomas Jefferson, author of the Declaration of American Independence, of the statute of Virginia for religious freedom, and the father of the University of Virginia." Conspicuous by their absence were his roles as Governor of Virginia and President of the United States.

The party then drove to Washington, D.C., through the scenic Blue Ridge Mountains. Nearby in the Shenandoah Valley, many notable battles of the Civil War were fought. The names of nearby towns or places along the route they followed brought memories of the war that

Signs of Growing Influence

defined the American character—Staunton, Manassas, and Bull Run being a few.

Elders Lee and Stapley had also received an assignment to represent the Church at the Scout jamboree at Valley Forge, Pennsylvania, later in July. As they had several extra days, they decided to spend them in the capital. They were hosted by J. Willard Marriott and his wife, who took them to see a professional baseball game between the Washington Senators and the New York Yankees Saturday afternoon, then accompanied them to church on Sunday. On Monday the two apostles paid courtesy calls on senators Arthur V. Watkins and Wallace F. Bennett of Utah and the two senators from Arizona, Carl Hayden and Barry Goldwater. Then on Tuesday, the visitors were hosted on a tour of the area, especially for the benefit of the wives who had never had this experience. Among other things, they were shown through the White House, visited the Lincoln Memorial, and attended part of a session of the United States Senate where, according to Elder Lee, they were "just introducing the debate on the proposed civil rights legislation."

Elder Lee would see the revolutionary effect of this legislation, once it had been enacted into law after long, and sometimes acrimonious, debate.

The following day in Philadelphia, the brethren attended a banquet for Scout executives, where Henry Cabot Lodge gave what Elder Lee called an "impressive address." At Valley Forge, the party found fifty thousand Boy Scouts and their leaders encamped for the jamboree. This included twenty-five hundred LDS Boy Scouts with their leaders, among whom were Elbert R. Curtis, YMMIA superintendent, Lavern Parmley, president of the Primary, and T. C. Jacobsen, mission president. An impressive pageant was followed by remarks from Vice-President Richard M. Nixon and by what Elder Lee said was a "stupendous" fireworks show.

Returning to New York City, the Lees and the Stapleys parted, the Stapleys returning to Salt Lake City and the

Lees remaining in the East, where Elder Lee had several other assignments. During a break of several days, he and Fern went to Laconia, New Hampshire, where they were guests of the Marriotts at their summer home. On returning to New York, Elder Lee attended his Union Pacific board meeting and on July 26, with Fern, met Elder Spencer W. Kimball and his wife Camilla at the train depot. Elder Kimball had an appointment with the cancer specialists and asked Elder Lee to accompany him there. "After a careful examination by Doctor Martin and his two assistants," wrote Elder Lee, "he told Spencer that further surgery was imperative immediately to check the cancerous growth that had advanced on the other vocal cord. . . . Both Spencer and I impressed the necessity of preserving his voice if at all possible because his voice in his present position was his very life. . . . He then said that it seemed likely that by an immediate operation that he might be able to save one vocal cord, although he would insist upon an understanding that he must be left free to decide when he operated and also . . . to determine" the extent of the surgery. The doctor was hopeful he would be able to leave Elder Kimball with some voice, although he warned it might not be "even as good as at present." After lengthy discussion and prayer, the decision was made to go forward with the surgery. "It seemed the only thing to do," wrote Elder Lee, "and arrangements were made to admit Spencer to the . . . hospital Sunday afternoon in preparation for an operation on Monday."

Since Elder Lee had a commitment in New Haven, Connecticut, over the weekend, he and Fern left the Kimballs on Saturday, but returned in time Monday for Elder Lee and Roy Fugal to give Brother Kimball a blessing before the surgery. Elder Lee reported the results the following day: "They removed completely the left vocal cord and trimmed off a portion of the right where the two join. They also removed a portion of the larynx which also was malignant." The following day, Elder Lee visited Elder Kimball in the hospital and then called President David O.

McKay in Salt Lake City to brief him about the surgery and its aftermath.

Having done all that he could to help Elder Kimball and his wife, Camilla, the Lees went to Palmyra, New York, where they attended the annual pageant staged on the Hill Cumorah. While there, Elder Lee and President Jacobsen held two separate meetings in the sacred grove with the missionaries and other guests. Here Elder Lee alluded to the extraordinary events that had occurred in the grove when the Father and the Son appeared in open vision to young Joseph Smith, and to other significant events in Church history that had occurred nearby. Later the Lees were taken on a tour of the area where they saw many sites connected with early Church history, including the Joseph Smith, Sr., home, the Peter Whitmer home, and the Martin Harris home. They also had lunch at the bureau of information at the Hill Cumorah, hosted by Brother Joseph Olsen and his wife, who were the directors. Brother Olsen was a teacher at the Oneida Stake Academy when Elder Lee attended there.

Leaving Palmyra, the Lees were driven to Rochester, where they caught the plane home. They arrived in Salt Lake on August 4, 1957. After an absence of seven weeks, it was good to be back.

On the three successive days following his return, Elder Lee was confronted with issues that were stressful and controversial. On August 5, President Ernest L. Wilkinson came to express dismay at a decision made by the Church Board of Education to leave Ricks Junior College at Rexburg, Idaho. President Wilkinson, and others, had made a determined effort to have the school moved to Idaho Falls, where they thought it would better serve the people in the southeast part of the state. At one point, it looked as if they had won their point. More mature consideration, however, dictated that it remain in Rexburg. President Wilkinson came to Elder Lee because of his role on the executive committee of the board, hoping, perhaps, that he could revive the issue. It remained for Elder Lee to divert him and to endeavor to convince him of the wisdom of the board's decision and to cause him to accept it. Given President Wilkinson's determined personality, this was not an easy thing to do. However, he yielded at length and let the matter lie. It was hardly a restful way for Elder Lee to resume his headquarters duties after a seven-week absence.

The issue raised the next day was even more troubling for him. It was whether the Church should provide social security insurance for the employees at the Deseret Clothing Factory. Elder Lee was adamant in voting no. He felt a yes vote would be "a step away from the welfare program," which he believed would provide every benefit the employees needed, free of government interference or control. There were powerful voices among the leaders of the Church that opposed Elder Lee on this issue, and his negative vote unavoidably created tension. As we shall see, time and circumstances would moderate Elder Lee's views toward social security; but at the moment, it was an issue fraught with emotional dynamite.

On August 7, Elder Lee had a visit with Ted Tuttle and Boyd Packer, "seminary supervisors, who came to talk over problems for beginning their year's work." For some time, Elder Lee had been dissatisfied with the way the seminary and institute program had been administered. He believed that there were some on the staff and among the teachers who held unorthodox views on doctrine and on the mission of the Church, and who were, therefore, creating confusion and, in some instances, apostasy among the students. When, following World War II, Ted Tuttle and Boyd Packer were employed by the Church Educational System, Elder Lee saw in them the kind of young men whose character and outlook had been tempered by spiritual conversion and the discipline of war, who could provide the leadership he believed the system required. So, he had encouraged and counselled them over the years, while promoting their advancement in the system and receiving their recommendations. This had brought the three of them close together, providing the younger men with wise counsel and a role model while enabling Elder Lee to gauge the leadership potential of his associates. It would not be long before these young men would have a broader field in which to exercise their abilities. In less than eight months after this meeting, A. Theodore Tuttle was called as a member of the First Council of Seventy; and three and a half years after that, Boyd K. Packer was called as an Assistant to the Twelve, to be followed in 1970 with a call as a member of the Twelve. Meanwhile, in the fall of 1958, both Brother Tuttle and Brother Packer were appointed as members of an administrative council for seminaries and institutes chaired by Ernest L. Wilkinson, and in September 1962, they both became members of the Church Board of Education and the Board of Trustees of Brigham Young University. In these positions, Elder Lee's two protégés, in concert with him, were able to exert a strong influence on the policies governing church schools, altering the deficiencies in the administration of seminaries and institutes as Elder Lee had perceived them.

As Elder Lee resumed his schedule of stake conference assignments, he encountered a headstrong attitude in one stake president, a condition he found from time to time. Apparently exasperated by the man's obstinate refusal to follow counsel, Elder Lee took refuge in his diary. "Here is an able business executive as stake president," wrote he, "who sets out to change every program he receives to suit his own ideas of how it should be administered. There is little to be done to change his thinking."

The October general conference was cancelled this year because of a widespread flu epidemic. It was one of the few times such an action had been taken. Since the main danger in spreading the epidemic lay in bringing people together in large numbers from around the world, there was no restriction on holding ward and stake meetings. So on the first Sunday in October, when he ordinarily would have been in general conference, Elder Lee accepted the invitation of Ernest Wilkins to speak in the ward where the son-in-law served as bishop. Commenting on the occasion with evident pleasure, Elder Lee noted that "Ernie was emotional" in introducing him, stating that Elder Lee was "like a father to him."

Aside from the never-ending stake conferences, Elder Lee's last assignment of 1957 was to tour the Southern States Mission in company with the mission president, Berkley Bunker. Elder Lee flew to Atlanta, Georgia, November 1, 1957, from New York City, where he had attended the monthly Union Pacific board meeting. After inspecting the mission office facilities and interviewing the members of the staff, Elder Lee and the touring party travelled to Birmingham, Alabama, on the second where the first zone meeting was held with fourteen missionaries. While in Birmingham, Elder Lee also met with local leaders and members in a district conference. The small branches he found there would be organized into a stake within a decade.

Leaving Birmingham, the party drove south through Montgomery, Alabama, the site of the first capital of the Confederacy, and into northwest Florida and southwest Georgia where meetings were held at Pensacola and Marianna, Florida, and Moultrie, Georgia. Being in the heart of the "Old South," some in this area were agitated by the debate over civil rights, which had commenced in Washington. The more extreme of these had begun again to use time-tested tactics of terror, designed to keep the African Americans "in their place." "The local people are worried about the Ku Klux Klan," wrote Elder Lee on November 6 during his visit in Moultrie. While at this time Church policy precluded male African Americans from holding the priesthood, Church membership was open to all who met the scriptural standards. Therefore, Elder Lee and the other leaders deplored any attempts to use terror, force, or undue influence to prevent these people from asserting their rights, or from enjoying the privileges of Church membership. This volatile issue would trouble members of the

Church in the South for many years, especially after the issue was taken to the streets.

Leaving Moultrie, the party travelled through Orlando and Deer Park, Florida, where the large Church ranch is located, and thence to Miami, holding meetings along the way. At Miami, Elder Lee and President Bunker caught a flight to Puerto Rico, where meetings were held with the servicemen stationed there and their families. Other members also attended these meetings, among whom was businessman Gardner Russell, an acquaintance of Ernest Wilkins from their missionary days in Argentina and their school days at Stanford University. Almost thirty years later, more than a decade after Elder Lee's death, Gardner Russell would be called to the Seventy.

The brethren then flew from Puerto Rico to Atlanta, where they picked up the mission car that members of the staff had driven there from Miami. The tour was then concluded by automobile with missionary and member meetings in Aiken and Moncks Corner, South Carolina, Savannah, Georgia, and Orlando and Tampa, Florida. In these and other cities in the South, Elder Lee found conditions and attitudes that foreshadowed the fierce struggle over civil rights that would take place there in the years ahead. At Savannah, for instance, he noted that "color lines are strictly observed on buses [and in] restaurants, toilets and theatres."

On the way home, Elder Lee stopped in New York to attend the monthly meeting of the Union Pacific board of directors and arrived in Salt Lake City on November 28. He had been gone for five weeks, having missed Thanksgiving with his family. The next day his mother called to chide him for trying to do too much and to admonish him to guard his time and his health. "No one else will do it for you," she warned. Then she asked him to speak at their Christmas program.

Chapter Twenty-one

Grinding It Out

After a few days of respite with his family between Christmas and New Year's, Elder Lee was ready for another round. He started it with a stake conference in Bountiful, Utah, north of Salt Lake City, where, in addition to the usual duties, he dedicated an addition to a chapel. Three days later, he left on the train with Elder Spencer W. Kimball to organize new stakes in San Antonio, Texas, and Shreveport, Louisiana. This was the second speaking assignment Elder Kimball had received since the operation on his throat six months before. The first was a stake conference in the Gila Valley of Arizona in December with Elder Delbert L. Stapley. He had spoken briefly three times during that conference. This assignment with Elder Lee, however, was to be the acid test for Elder Kimball since there would be numerous meetings and interviews before the organizational sessions. En route to their assignment, Elder Lee wrote of his companion: "It is remarkable how diligently Brother Kimball struggles to use his remaining voice which is greatly hampered by noise interference, as on the train." Elder Lee reported that during the first three days of their work together after they reached Texas, "Brother Kimball did his share of the speaking, although his voice was little more than a hoarse whisper; but a sensitive microphone around his neck gave him needed volume." Unknown to Elder Lee, his companion had been suffering from diarrhea, nosebleeds caused by two boils that had started in his nose, and from excruciating back pain. Finally, at three in the morning, the night of the eighteenth, he decided to awaken Elder Lee to tell him about his condition. "Brother Kimball . . . had refrained from telling me," Elder Lee wrote, "for fear I would . . . curtail his activities. I had some tablets in my grip and administered to him. He declared he had no return of the pain he had suffered."

In preparation for the organizational meetings of the new stake in Shreveport, the brethren held meetings in several small branches that were to be brought into the stake. "Brother Kimball excused himself from speaking because of soreness in his throat which gave him a little anxiety, lest it be the result of overtaxing his voice so soon after the operation." Seemingly, this concern prompted Elder Kimball to go to New York with Elder Lee, instead of returning to Salt Lake, "to get some clinical training to help him in his speaking." In the city, Elder Lee accompanied his friend to a special clinic where he made arrangements for a series of lessons. These were helpful and enabled Elder Kimball to resume the full scope of his duties more speedily. By the end of March when they were again assigned together, this time to reorganize the Houston Texas Stake, Elder Lee noted a distinct improvement in his companion's voice, his physical condition, and his mental outlook. "Brother Kimball is a wonderful travelling companion," wrote he, "and is full of zeal and devotion to the work." These qualities seemed evident a few days later when Elder Kimball delivered his first sermon in general conference after his throat surgery. "Spencer Kimball's talk touched the heart of everyone," wrote Elder Lee.

The camaraderie created between Elder Lee and Elder

Kimball in fulfilling these stake conference assignments was duplicated, in varying degrees, with other General Authorities as they travelled and worked together over the years. While in a sense all stake conferences were alike in the uniformity of the meeting schedule and often in the content of the instruction, yet each one was different because of differences in the personalities and the abilities of the local leaders and in the nature and the gravity of the problems encountered. A frequent problem raised was how to handle transgressors. Many local leaders wanted Elder Lee to tell them how to decide specific cases. He would never do that but, instead, would teach principles to assist them in their decision making. Typical of his responses to such questions is this: "I counselled the bishop," he wrote on May 21, 1958, "to proceed as he felt he should and be guided by the inspiration to which he is entitled as a common judge in Israel."

In reality, this is the essence of the counsel Elder Lee gave to any leader or member, counsel which laid on the individual the responsibility to obtain spiritual direction for himself. At a stake conference held in Washington, D.C., in September 1958, Elder Lee admonished the members "to prayerfully [seek] for spiritual solutions to personal problems," and at an evening meeting with young people, he talked about "being fortified against the wiles of the devil." And what Elder Lee preached, he lived. He constantly sought spiritual guidance in reaching decisions affecting his personal life or his ministry. Typical was his experience in seeking guidance in the call of a patriarch during a stake division. "I awoke early this morning," he wrote on February 26, 1961, "with an impression as to the calling of John D. Hill as a patriarch in the new stake." Typical also was his experience in reorganizing the Detroit Michigan Stake in January 1963, made necessary by the election of Stake President George Romney as governor of Michigan. "I stayed in the O'Hare Inn for the night," wrote he. "The storms were closing in and on Saturday there seemed to be doubt that the plane could land at Detroit, even if we could leave Chicago. After talking to the Lord about the importance of my Detroit assignment, I went to the airport with full faith that He would control the weather. Just as we were loading, the word came that the plane would proceed to Detroit but no further. Our prayer had been answered."

Elder Lee believed unquestioningly in the divine origin of the decisions he made by spiritual means and in the harmonious impact of them. In the reorganization of a Salt Lake City stake presidency, for instance, he passed over the first counselor as the new president in preference for another, calling the first counselor as a patriarch. Apparently sensing a feeling of disappointment in him, Elder Lee suggested, on an impulse, that the first counselor review his patriarchal blessing, something he had not done for many years. "He found," wrote Elder Lee, on August 17, 1958, "that this new calling gave him a fulfillment of one part of his blessing which he had previously overlooked." This knowledge cast new light on the significance of the call to the new patriarch, revealing a prophetic pattern. Moreover, in the scale of comparative importance, Elder Lee placed the office of patriarch above that of stake president. To him a patriarch was "the fountainhead of spirituality" in a stake. Stake presidents came and went; patriarchs remained. A stake president was called for years; a patriarch for life.

A role often played by Elder Lee in filling stake conference assignments was to train new General Authorities. He took special delight in playing that role for Elder Thomas S. Monson, who was called to the Twelve in October 1963. Elder Lee viewed Thomas Monson as a protégé, a promising young man, reared in the Pioneer Stake, who was called as a bishop at age twenty-two, reportedly the youngest bishop in the Church. He had watched Brother Monson mature as a bishop and as a counselor in a stake presidency while struggling to rear a family and to complete his education. Later, Brother Monson distinguished himself as a mission president in Eastern Canada and as general manager of Deseret Press. This protégé looked on Elder Lee as a mentor, who provided crucial counsel on matters of key importance pertaining to his Church callings and his career path. So, by apparent design, Elder Lee was assigned to accompany Elder Monson on his first stake conference assignment after his call to the Twelve. It was a conference in Edmonton, Canada, over the weekend of October 11–13, 1963. "The presence of the newest apostle brought out a near record attendance," wrote Elder Lee of the occasion. The next month, Elder Monson accompanied Elder Lee to Portland, Oregon, where they divided the Columbia River Stake to create the North Columbia River Stake. "Brother Monson was a great help," wrote Elder Lee, a significant compliment given Elder Lee's terse, factual writing style.

His style in making diary entries was also marked by an absence of humor, except in rare cases when someone made comments that amused him. Such an occasion occurred during a conference in the Jacksonville Florida Stake. "At the evening service," wrote Elder Lee on May 23, 1959, "thirteen year old Jinx Jenkins was speaking when she stopped and said 'Brothers and Sisters, I am very scared standing here before you all. If you all will say a prayer for me, I will be able to give my talk.' She bowed her head, as did the whole audience, then she said: 'Now I will start all over again.' This time she did perfectly."

The day before Jinx Jenkins gave her talk, Elder Lee attended funeral services for President Stephen L. Richards, who died unexpectedly on May 19, 1959. Elder Lee was in New York City on business when he learned of President Richards's death. He cut short his stay in the city to return home for the funeral and then left immediately for Jacksonville. Following the stake conference, Elder Lee went to Deer Park, Florida, to confer about affairs on the ranch, flew to New York for the monthly Union Pacific board meeting, and returned to Salt Lake City in time to attend the quarterly conference of the Cottonwood Stake on May 30 and 31, where James E. Faust presided. Fourteen years later, Brother Lee, then the president of the Church, would call James E. Faust as an Assistant to the Twelve. Meanwhile, Elder Faust would play a key role in the leadership training program as it developed in the 1960s and eventually would be called to the Twelve.

On June 12, 1959, President McKay convened a special meeting of the apostles, where he announced he had selected President J. Reuben Clark as his first counselor and Elder Henry D. Moyle as the second counselor. "It seemed almost too good to be true," wrote Elder Lee of these actions. Perhaps his elation was prompted by the assumption that another favorable voice within the First Presidency would bolster the welfare program. While that was an evident result of these changes, another was the need to restructure the welfare organization as Brother Moyle's new duties would prevent him from continuing to serve as the chairman of the general welfare committee. Moreover, the increasing burden upon Elder Lee, both from his church and outside responsibilities, militated against his appointment as the chairman of the committee, or against his continuing to serve as the managing director. Accordingly, it was decided after consultation that Elder Marion G. Romney would become the chairman of the general welfare committee and that Elder Henry D. Taylor, who had been called as an Assistant to the Twelve the year before, would become the managing director of welfare.

Among Elder Lee's major nonecclesiastical responsibilities was a new one that had come to him during 1958. On June 26 of that year, while he was in New York City for his monthly Union Pacific board meeting, he received a call from James F. Oates, Jr., president of Equitable Life, requesting an interview. When they met, Mr. Oates asked Elder Lee to become a member of Equitable's board of directors, filling the vacancy to be created by President Clark's retirement from the board. Elder Lee accepted, reflecting perhaps on the occasion a few months before when President Clark, unaccountably, had gone out of his way to introduce him to some of Equitable's chief executives. Elder Lee's appointment was ratified by the Equitable Life Board of Directors at their meeting held in New York on July 17, 1958.

This began a thirteen-year association with the Equitable Life board, on which sat some of America's most able and influential business and professional leaders. These men came from different parts of the country and were connected with other influential companies or organizations whose impact extended into most of the vital aspects of American society. Regular association with these men opened a new window of understanding for Elder Lee, broadening his perceptions of society in general, increasing his knowledge of management strategies and skills, and enlarging his network of influence, both personally and for the Church. As with his appointment to the Union Pacific board, Elder Lee considered the Equitable Life appointment to be a recognition of the Church as much as a recognition for himself personally. Moreover, he endorsed the concept of insurance and therefore approved the aims of Equitable Life, aims that paralleled those of Church welfare—to help provide security and independence for the individual.

As a director of Equitable Life, Elder Lee was required to obtain a large life insurance policy with the company, something he was pleased to do. Indeed, this coincided with action he had taken several months before to provide added security for Fern. "Spent time studying the question of taking steps to be covered by social security under the category of a self-employed minister," he wrote on March 4, 1958. "This, it appears, will offer some additional security and insurance for Fern after I am gone." Aside from revealing the anxious concern he had for his wife's welfare, this entry also reveals a shift in Elder Lee's thinking about the comparative roles of social security and Church welfare.

Apparent feelings of lassitude caused Elder Lee to seek medical help a week after he was invited to join the Equitable Life board. It is possible, but only conjectural, that this explains his earlier steps to obtain protection for Fern under social security. "I spent the morning at the Memorial Clinic," he wrote on July 3, "being examined to discover the cause of internal bleeding. . . . They came to the conclusion that I had hemorrhoids in my lower colon causing intermittent bleeding, and an ulcer in the duodenal canal. Doctor Jos. F. Orme has placed me on an ulcer diet for a month." This diet seems to have been effective as Elder Lee was free from illness during the ensuing year. This was fortunate because of a heavy assignment he received the next month. On August 15, President David O. McKay informed Elder Lee he was to tour the South African Mission with Sister Lee "as soon as arrangements can be made." Two trips to New York, several stake conferences, headquarter assignments, and a series of shots delayed the Lees' departure until September 16. Before leaving for the airport, Elder Lee was able to talk by phone with President McKay, who had just returned home from dedicating the London Temple. President Clark, who had given them blessings of health, protection, and discernment two days before, accompanied the Lees to the airport, suppressing for the moment his repugnance toward flying. "President Clark's legs were shaky," Elder Lee noted. "He said he was glad he didn't have to think with his legs."

In a sense, this was a false start since the Lees would spend ten days in New York and Washington, D.C., before finally getting under way. During that time, Elder Lee attended Equitable Life and Union Pacific meetings, held a stake conference in Washington, and visited various officials to obtain letters of reference to be used while they travelled abroad.

Elder Ezra Taft Benson and his son Reed met the Lees at the Washington, D.C., airport with a chauffeured limousine. With the help of Elder Benson and his staff, the required visas were obtained for the Lees and their flight schedules were confirmed. Back in New York after the stake conference in Washington, Elder Lee met President Joseph Fielding Smith and Elder Henry D. Moyle, who were on their way to Salt Lake City following the dedication of the London Temple. They were unable to return with President McKay and his party because of a crisis in the French mission, which had resulted in the excommunication of several missionaries. "Henry seemed almost obsessed" with this matter, reported Elder Lee. While they were together, Elder Lee took Elder Moyle with him to the Manhattan Ward where they ordained and set apart John Q. Cannon as the bishop. Bishop Cannon was the secretary of the Radio Corporation of America and a long-time associate of General Sarnoff, one of the founders of this communications giant.

A final chore for Elder Lee in New York was to visit Abba S. Eban, Israeli ambassador to the United Nations. "He and his chief aide," reported Elder Lee, "gave me the names of Jewish officials to contact when we arrive in Israel next month on our way home."

The following day, September 27, 1958, Elder and Sister Lee boarded a London flight at La Guardia airport, which, following a refueling stop at Shannon, Ireland, arrived at Heathrow on the twenty-eighth. There they were met by the mission president and his wife, President and Sister Woodley, helped through customs, and driven to the mission home where lunch awaited them. After checking into their hotel, the Grosvenor House, and freshening up, they returned to the mission home to spend the afternoon and evening with missionaries who had been invited there from nearby districts. Also present were Brother and Sister T. Bowring Woodbury, who had arrived to preside over their assigned mission, and President and Sister Kerr, who had completed their mission and were on the way home. "We had many fine testimonies," Elder Lee wrote of this gathering.

During the next two days, the travellers visited the London Temple, which was just beginning to function efficiently following its recent dedication, and various historical sites in and around London. Westminster Abbey, Buckingham Palace with its flashy, tradition laden changing of the guard, and the Parliament Building were special targets of interest.

The Lees flew to Brussels on the afternoon of the thirtieth where they were met by Mission President Milton Christensen and his wife, who skillfully shepherded them through customs and chauffeured them to the Palace Hotel, where fortunately they had confirmed reservations. Accommodations were scarce in Brussels at the time because of the World Fair, which was then in progress. Elder and Sister Lee attended the fair the next day, where they were especially interested in the contrasting pavilions of the Soviet Union and the United States, which had attracted much attention. "The first displayed the power and might of the Russians and ours depicted the life of the American people, including the culture, dress, technical equipment, social life, etc."

The Lees flew to Rome via Amsterdam on October 2. While waiting for clearance of their flight reservations, they spent a few hours visiting some of Rome's ruins and antiquities. However, a more detailed sampling of the historic treasures this ancient city has to offer would have to await their return.

Leaving Rome's International Airport, they flew to Johannesburg, South Africa, almost the full length of the continent, with intermediate stops in North Africa, Nairobi in Kenya, and Salisbury in Rhodesia. In South Africa, the Lees were in a country with perhaps the most complex racial structures of any country in the world. Before leaving Salt Lake City, President Clark, the skilled international lawyer, had briefed Elder Lee about racial and political problems that beset South Africa and had counselled him to use wisdom in discussing them. He also cautioned him about making any direct or implied statements about a temple in that country. Later, during the course of the tour, Elder Lee spent several hours with Dr. Helm, a professor at the University of Rhodesia, who sketched South Africa's cultural, political, and racial history, explaining issues that were essential for him to understand in formulating strategies for proselyting in that country and in directing missionary work. The issues of race, language, and religious preference predominated. Native Africans, people of mixed blood, and Asiatics outnumbered whites four to one. But, restrictive policies of apartheid helped enforce political control by the white minority. This had aroused bitter enmities within the country and international pressures for change from without it. As to language, the majority of whites spoke Afrikaans and the remainder spoke English. The natives spoke several different Bantu languages. Afrikaans, a derivative of Dutch with some French and German overtones, was adopted as South Africa's official language in 1924. As to religious preference, most whites were Dutch Reformed or Episcopalians, although other Christian sects were represented, as were Hindu and Muslim among the Asiatics. There was a small Jewish population.

By the time Elder Lee arrived in October 1958, the Latter-day Saints had been proselyting in South Africa for many decades with good results. There were active districts and branches throughout the mission, the strongest being in Johannesburg and Cape Town. All were directed by President Fisher, who, with his wife and a group of Saints, met Elder and Sister Lee at the airport after dark on October 4. Anxious to get a running start on the mission tour, President Fisher had scheduled a gala Gold and Green Ball that night, which was to double as a welcoming reception for the visitors. Because of a delay in the arrival of their flight, Elder and Sister Lee did not arrive at the dance until 11:00 P.M. With introductions, welcoming and acknowledging remarks, and handshaking afterward, they did not reach the hotel until well after midnight. The long flight, interrupted by the several landings, the disorientation caused by the change in time zones, and the excitement of the ball had given Sister Lee a throbbing sinus headache. A blessing given by Elder Lee and President Fisher brought relief and a few hours of peaceful rest before the full schedule of Sunday meetings the next day.

Grinding It Out

Like most successful mission presidents, President Fisher wanted to utilize the visitors to the maximum extent in bolstering his work. So, on Sunday, the first full day of the tour, there were two general sessions for the members, an instruction and testimony meeting for the missionaries, and a ceremony to dedicate a new chapel. Monday morning, the party drove to Pretoria, the administrative capital of the Republic of South Africa, and the provincial capital of Transvaal, which is one of four provinces in the Republic, the other three being Cape of Good Hope (called the Cape province), Orange Free State, and Natal. This was Elder Lee's introduction to the complexities of the government of South Africa and the inertia of its bureaucracy. While Pretoria is the country's administrative capital, its legislative capital is in Cape Town, some eight hundred miles southwest, and its judicial capital is at Bloemfontein, which is also the provincial capital of the Orange Free State. The main purpose in visiting Pretoria was to attempt to obtain an increase in the quota of American missionaries. The secretary of the interior, whom Elder Lee visited for this purpose, greeted the request with icy disdain. Not only did he suggest that the request be abandoned but seemed to hint that pressing it might even result in a reduction of the quota. Knowing that any future approval for an increase must come from this office, and grasping, perhaps for the first time, the vast distances involved in administering the affairs of the mission, Elder Lee became more sympathetic to President Fisher's recommendation that the mission headquarters be moved from Cape Town to either Johannesburg or Pretoria.

Given the crowded schedule President Fisher had arranged for the first day of the tour, it must have surprised the Lees when, at this point, he suggested that they take off for three days to visit Kruger Park, the world's largest wildlife sanctuary. The reason for this timing became apparent when it was learned that the park would close for the season on October 15. The party drove there on the seventh, a distance of over two hundred miles northeast of Pretoria. We gain some insight into Elder Lee's excitement in visiting the park from this graphic diary entry: "As we drove slowly through the area," he wrote, "we saw animals of great variety and took many pictures, the most exciting of which was the great African bull elephant whom we surprised. He turned quickly as I took his picture, and for a moment seemed ready to charge us as intruders." Being two hundred miles long and forty miles wide with some one thousand miles of roads and numerous rest camps, the park is readily accessible by automobile from which visitors can see great numbers of animals living in a natural state.

On October 10, five days before the park closed, the party drove south three hundred miles to Durban on the coast of the Indian Ocean, which is the commercial center and the largest city of Natal and the third largest city and chief eastern seaport of the Republic. Here Elder Lee found the largest concentration of Asiatics in South Africa, mostly Indians, whose ancestors had migrated as indentured labor beginning almost a century before Elder Lee's visit and continuing for many decades thereafter. It was here in Durban that Mahatma Gandhi had laid the groundwork for his mass, nonviolent civil disobedience campaign, which advanced the cause of racial equality in South Africa.

In Durban, Elder Lee found "unrest" among the members "because of uncertainty about the political situation." Gandhi's legacy, which was inherited only by the Asiatic population, and which, at best, was but a minor victory, had practically no effect upon the overwhelming numbers of African blacks among the population. And these, who were agitated by outside communistic influences and by the indigenous stirrings for equality, were becoming more and more vocal and sometimes violent in their opposition to apartheid. So, the members here who were already living in stressful turmoil and who could see nothing but increased turmoil ahead, were understandably stressed and anxious about their future. It is likely that these attitudes contributed heavily to an unusual incident that occurred at the evening session held in Durban on October 12. When Elder Lee had finished speaking, and the meeting had ended with song and prayer, the audience sat motionless and quiet, showing no intention of stirring, let alone of leaving. After an awkward pause, the branch president arose and asked if they wanted to hear more. They answered "yes" in unison. "I arose again," wrote Elder Lee, "and bore my testimony and gave them my blessing. It was a most impressive demonstration of a people seemingly overcome by the spirit. Some came later to confess their sins and to declare their determination to live more perfectly."

In four days, beginning on October 13, Elder Lee and his party travelled a thousand miles and more paralleling the coast of South Africa, extending from Durban on the Indian Ocean to Cape Town at the southwestern tip of the continent, bordering the South Atlantic Ocean. In between, they stayed at East London, Port Elizabeth, and George, coastal cities whose names signify South Africa's colonial past. At East London, a meeting was held with a small group of members and nonmembers numbering less than fifty, and at Port Elizabeth, Elder Lee dedicated a new chapel and counselled with eight missionaries and with local leaders.

It was the Portuguese navigator Bartholemeu Dias who discovered the cape in 1488, five years before Columbus made his first landing in the new world. Originally it was called *O Cabo Tormentoso,* the Cape of Storms, but was later named *O Cabo da Boa Esperanca,* the Cape of Good Hope, by King John II of Portugal. Arriving at the cape more than four hundred and fifty years after Dias's discovery, and three hundred years after its founding as a ship-victualing station by the Dutch as part of their trade route to the Dutch East Indies, Elder Lee found Cape Town to be a modern city of several hundred thousand population, situated on Table Bay at the foot of Table Mountain. This was the leading export point for South African diamond and gold fields and for a rich agricultural region producing fruit, grain, wine, wool, and flowers. Here was found a thriving Latter-day Saint colony and a corps of able and successful missionaries. During his three-day stay in Cape Town, Elder Lee participated in a musical program, a Gold and Green Ball, two general sessions of a district conference, and a training and testimony session with the missionaries. After the morning general session on Sunday, Mr. Jacob Coopman, a diamond merchant, came to Elder Lee to say "I was so filled when you spoke that I could hardly keep from crying." Also, several came to discuss the problem of mixed blood. "I gave them assurance," wrote he, "of their eternal blessings if they would live up to all they are permitted in their present state."

During a break in their schedule at Cape Town, the Lees visited a diamond cutting plant where Elder Lee purchased a diamond ring for Fern, having the diamond in the old ring she had worn for years made into an earring. Unknown to Elder Lee at the time, Fern had mixed emotions about this transaction, being grateful for the new gem, while regretting the loss of the old diamond setting on her finger to which she attached such sentimental significance.

The party flew to Salisbury, Rhodesia, on October 20, with an intermediate stop in Johannesburg. Here in the midst of the southern hemisphere's spring, with its brilliant show of flowers, a "delightful meeting" was held in a small chapel where sixty were in attendance. The next day found the party across the border into northern Rhodesia, now Zambia, where in Ndola another meeting was held.

On the way back to Johannesburg, they stopped in Livingstone from where they drove seven miles south to the Victoria Falls on the Zambesi River at the border of Rhodesia and Zambia. Elder Lee's words seemed inadequate to describe the impact of the sight of the falls, over a mile wide, and the roaring sounds they produced as the cascading water fell over three hundred and fifty feet into the chasm below. That inadequacy was compensated for by the many pictures he took of the falls, one of which later graced the cover of an issue of the *Ensign*.

Elder Lee ended his tour of the South African Mission with a public meeting at Springs, near Johannesburg, where 261 were in attendance, and a series of personal interviews with the missionaries who were laboring in that part of the mission. He and Sister Lee bid good-bye to President and Sister Fisher at the Johannesburg airport on October 15, boarding a plane whose ultimate destination was Cairo, Egypt. It landed in Nairobi briefly to drop off some passengers and board others, before taking off for another intermediate stop at Khartoum in the Sudan, which lies at the confluence of the White Nile and the Blue Nile rivers. Some time after it was airborne, the passengers received the disquieting news that the plane had engine trouble, which would require a return to Nairobi. Here they put up at the Spread Eagle Hotel and the next morning boarded their plane again, which arrived safely in Cairo on the twenty-sixth.

They registered at the Shepherds Hotel, fronting on the Nile, from where they could see the almost constant procession of crafts of different sizes and shapes, plying the waters of this fabled river, whose story is bound up with the earliest chapters of recorded history. It was in Cairo that Elder Lee's New York connections first came into play to smooth the way for him and Fern. Here Bill Landry of the United Press and his wife, Luby, made themselves available to host a trip into the desert to see the Sphinx and the Pyramids, two of Egypt's most famous attractions. Back in Cairo, the Lees coincidentally met young Elder Gardner, from Cedar City, Utah, who was on his way home after having served as a missionary in New Zealand. On Sunday, they invited the grateful and astonished young man to join them for a sacrament service in the privacy of their hotel room. They would encounter Elder Gardner again.

At Beirut the next day, the Lees were shepherded through customs by representatives of American Express, though they did not have passport clearance, and were taken to the St. George Hotel where they had a room fronting on the Mediterranean. In this place, reminiscent of the "Cedars of Lebanon" mentioned in the Old Testament, Elder Lee seems to have begun to feel the biblical influences that would surround him during his stay in the Middle East. These feelings were heightened the next day when they flew over ancient Damascus and arrived in Jerusalem. Here, with the aid of other American Express representatives, they were registered at the National Hotel and put in touch with a guide who had a good automobile and who was fluent in English.

Then began a memorable tour that brought to life scenes and events of biblical history that the Lees had read and heard about since infancy. They visited Bethany, the Tomb of Lazarus, Jericho, the Dead Sea, the place of the Ascension, Gethsemane, the supposed location of King Solomon's Temple, the supposed location of the judgment before Pilate, the Via Dolorosa, the Garden Tomb, Golgotha, and the places of the Nativity and Shepherds' Field at Bethlehem. They realized that many of the places shown them may not have been the actual places where the historic events occurred. In this they were sometimes governed by their own feelings rather than by what their guide told them. The place identified by the guide as Golgotha "seemed right" to the Lees, while another supposed location "did not at all satisfy" them.

After seeing Tel Aviv and some of the surrounding areas, Elder Lee noted: "The Jews are making the desert blossom as a rose." Flying from Tel Aviv to Athens, Greece, the travellers were met by a representative of Pan American Airlines, ushered through customs, and driven to their hotel. After freshening up, Elder Lee went to the American Embassy where he met with Mr. Riddleburger, the U.S. Ambassador to Greece, to discuss the problems of establishing a proselyting mission of the Church in Greece. The Ambassador did not hold out much hope of that happening within the near future. Elder Lee then rented a car to enable him and Fern to visit the Pantheon, the Acropolis, and Mars Hill where the Apostle Paul delivered his famous speech to the people of Athens. At one stop, Elder Lee opened his car door to get out and an inattentive driver struck the door from behind, shearing it off. This somewhat took the edge off the visit to Athens.

Arriving at Rome on November 1, Elder and Sister Lee made their headquarters at the Excelsior Hotel. During three days, they visited museums, shops, and historic sites in the city. They also visited the Vatican on Sunday the second, where preparations were under way for the coronation of the new Pope, which was scheduled the following Wednesday. They were struck by the beauty of the ornate chapel. Having encountered him earlier, the Lees spent most of this Sunday with Elder Gardner and invited him to their hotel room for another sacrament service.

After leaving Rome, Elder and Sister Lee travelled to Switzerland, where they visited the temple at Bern; to Frankfurt, Germany, where they were impressed with the "splendid work" of Theodore M. Burton as the president of the West German Mission; to Paris where they toured the city and saw *La Traviata* at the Paris Opera House; to Glasgow and Edinburgh, Scotland, where Fern made arrangements to obtain genealogical information about some of her Scottish ancestors; to London where Elder Lee visited Sir Oliver Franks, the head of Lloyds of London, and Mr. Ogburn, the head actuary of Equitable in London; and to Southampton where, on November 15, they boarded the *Queen Elizabeth* bound for New York City. During the four-day voyage, they enjoyed a belated celebration of their thirty-fifth wedding anniversary and of Fern's sixty-third birthday, when Elder Lee gave his bride the diamond earring he had had reset in Cape Town and one to match.

An absence of fifty-four days from her shores had enriched the Lees' allurement for America. Though still two thousand miles from Salt Lake City, busy, bustling New York was "home" to the travellers. They were met at the pier by an agent of the Plaza Hotel, who took charge of their luggage, steered them adroitly through customs without delay, and led them to a waiting limousine. A restful night at the Plaza restored the travellers' land legs. While Fern busied herself at the hotel checking and readjusting their luggage, now encumbered with mounds of mementoes and gifts for the family, calling friends and making notes and lists of things to do in Salt Lake, Elder Lee attended a meeting of the Equitable Board where he briefed them on his trip, especially his contacts with Sir Oliver Franks and their London actuary. Returning to the hotel early, he and Fern enjoyed another good night's rest before travelling home the next day. President and Sister Jacobsen picked them up early at the Plaza on the twenty-first and drove them across the river to Newark, New Jersey, where they caught their flight home.

We now discern a pattern in Elder Lee's travels, whether accidental or designed, which had taken him throughout the United States, the Pacific, the Far East, the Middle East, Great Britain, Europe, Mexico, and Africa. Its effect was to acquaint him with the Church and its people around the world, providing knowledge and insight, invaluable were he to become the head of the Church with global responsibilities. Returning from the African trip, the only major areas he had not visited, where the Church was actively proselyting, were South America and the South Pacific. This lack would be remedied within the next two and a half years.

Chapter Twenty-two

Family and Personal Trauma — South America

Meanwhile, the regular rhythms of the work and his personal affairs continued unabated. During February 1959, while in New York for his board meetings, he and President Jacobsen flew to Bermuda, where they spent several days meeting with members and with servicemen and military leaders at the air base. In mid-May, accompanied by Gerald G. Smith, who had replaced T. C. Jacobsen as the president of the Eastern States Mission, Elder Lee spoke at services in Harmony, Pennsylvania, commemorating the restoration of the Aaronic Priesthood. Here Elder Lee bore convincing testimony about the reality of the unusual event that had occurred there when John the Baptist appeared in resurrected form to confer the Aaronic Priesthood on Joseph Smith and Oliver Cowdery.

During the summer, as he planned the South America trip, Elder Lee suffered serious physical setbacks. In late June, en route to New York for his board meeting, he became "deathly sick" from abdominal upset. He recuperated enough to attend the Union Pacific board meeting by resting in his room at the Waldorf all the next day. It was an important meeting where the board, constituted as the trustees of the Union Pacific Foundation, approved guidelines for making annual grants to deserving institutions. BYU would later be a recipient of some of these grants.

President Gerald Smith, look-alike son of Elder Lee's special friend Nicholas G. Smith, picked him up after the meeting, took him to the mission home for lunch, then drove him to La Guardia where he enplaned for Chicago. There Elder Lee caught a Pullman sleeper for Salt Lake. "My whole digestive system seemed out of order," he wrote aboard the train, "and I suffered constantly from a headache." While the intensity of this attack subsided, it did not disappear entirely but lingered like a vague, gnawing presence, which interrupted his sleep and shadowed his working hours. Meanwhile, there was work to do, a stake conference in Holladay and a speech to summer school students at the University in Logan, Utah. Amidst these, the already mentioned shake-up in the welfare department took place, changes which prompted Elder Lee's mother to ask him confidentially what it all meant and why he had been "demoted."

On July 8, the illness, which had been relatively dormant for twelve days, flared up, this time producing nauseous vertigo that prevented him from standing alone and, while he was lying prone, caused everything to turn and tumble in a whirl. Tests conducted in the hospital revealed Elder Lee suffered from a bleeding ulcer in the duodenal canal. The doctors gave him a transfusion of three pints of blood, prescribed medication, and decreed a lengthy convalescence.

Then came his close associates Henry D. Moyle and Marion G. Romney to bless him. Brother Moyle, newly called to the First Presidency, who served as voice, promised Elder Lee that his "ministry would not be interrupted." After a few days in the hospital, he returned home to convalesce. There he received several more visits from

Family and Personal Trauma—South America

President Moyle, who shared insights about new initiatives being considered by the First Presidency—about a restructuring of missionary work and about plans to appoint members of the Twelve to the executive committees of the Church's financial and business institutions. After digesting these revelations and the manner in which they were presented, Elder Lee wrote: "It is becoming increasingly clear that Brother Moyle is going to become an aggressive mover of plans representing the First Presidency." Time would confirm this.

Elder Lee was strong enough to attend Equitable's centennial celebration in late July. Fern accompanied him to New York for this purpose. The centennial program included attendance at an athletic competition in Madison Square Garden the evening of July 28. During the event, an announcement came over the public address system that Harold B. Lee had an emergency call. Salt Lake was on the line to advise that his mother had suffered a heart attack. She died that night. The mother had lived a long, exemplary, and fruitful life and had slipped away quietly without undue pain.

Members of the family and President Moyle met the Lees at the Salt Lake airport on the twenty-ninth. The funeral, low-key but impressive, was held the next day. President Moyle and Lee Palmer were the speakers. "Afterward at the home," wrote Elder Lee, "Verda said she had a heavenly peace, more wonderful than she had ever known before."

A final family trauma for the summer occurred on August 7 when Perry Lee was hospitalized with an apparent heart attack. The next day, Elder Lee and President Moyle administered to him, a service they repeated a few days later. Perry, buoyed up by the blessings, soon recovered.

When Perry's illness first arose, Elder and Sister Lee had only eleven days to complete preparations for the tour of South America. Meanwhile, there was a stake conference in Bountiful, Utah, a meeting with Elder Henry D. Taylor, who, overwhelmed by his new appointment in

Church welfare, sought counsel, a blessing, and a conference with President J. Reuben Clark, who wanted to give fatherly advice and to share important information "for the future."

Elder Lee left the Salt Lake airport alone on Monday, August 17, 1959. Fern would join him later in New York. There to see him off were President David O. McKay and President Henry D. Moyle. After extending his love and blessing, the prophet reminded Elder Lee that his main responsibility during the tour was to create the new Brazil South and Andes missions. As to the latter, President McKay said that while Elder Lee had discretion in the matter, he hoped he would "get the inspiration of the spirit to have Lima, Peru as the headquarters." Elder Lee responded that "as far as [he] was concerned, that the spirit had already spoken." Later, Elder Lee confided to his diary that "it was, indeed, an unlooked for thrill to have the president come to see me off."

Elder Lee's arrival at the Idlewild Airport in New York was his most dramatic ever. One of the motors on his plane caught fire on landing, which brought "the whole fire department." The passengers were hurriedly evacuated to prevent injury or death should the fire ignite the plane's highly flammable fuel. Elder Lee was unscathed.

He would remain in New York City eleven days. During that time, he presided at a conference of the New York stake; attended Union Pacific and Equitable board meetings; met with President Gerald G. Smith and Elder Delbert L. Stapley, who were in the midst of a mission tour; and counselled with Elder Ezra Taft Benson, who flew up from Washington, D.C., for this purpose. Only a little more than a year remained of Elder Benson's service as the secretary of agriculture, and he wanted counsel about invitations he had received from three different corporations to join their boards of directors once his government service had ended.

Fern arrived on August 22 in company with Helen and with Brent, who, the next day, was inducted into the college of hospital administrators at services held in the Met-

Elder Harold B. Lee, about 1959

ropolitan Opera House. It was a significant recognition for their son-in-law, in celebration of which the Lees treated him and Helen to some of the sights and excitement of Manhattan during the next several days. There was the customary tour of the city and attendance at the current Broadway hits, *Music Man* and *My Fair Lady*. They also attended a show at Radio City, which "was alright" according to Elder Lee, "despite the usual overtones and undertones of immorality which are usually dramatized in the shows of today." This was a trend Elder Lee spoke out against pointedly, a trend, he felt, that cheapened and vulgarized society.

Elder and Sister Lee boarded their ship, the SS *Brazil*, on Saturday, August 29, 1959. They were joined there by Asael Sorenson and his wife and their six children. Brother Sorenson, who had been released as the president of the Brazil mission only a few months before, had been called as the president of the new Brazil South Mission, whose headquarters would be in Curitiba. Since the travellers did not board their ship until 5:00 P.M., dark had begun to fall by the time it maneuvered slowly away from its pier, out into the river, past the battery at the tip of Manhattan Island, past the Statue of Liberty, which guards the entrance to New York Harbor, and out into the open sea. Except for a brief stop at "steamy" Bridgetown on Barbados Island, the travellers would be at sea for nine days.

Since the SS *Brazil*, which had accommodations for four hundred, had only two hundred passengers, the travellers had free run of the ship. On the first day at sea, a Sunday, the Lees and Sorensons joined for their own worship service. They did the same thing a week later. The other days followed the usual, relaxed shipboard routine, with plenty of time for reading, writing, walking the decks and visiting, and, perhaps, with too much food. Elder Lee also spent many hours with Brother Sorenson, being briefed about Brazil and the status of the members and the missionaries.

As their ship crossed the equator and moved further into the Southern Hemisphere, the travellers could detect a marked change in the weather. Here winter was merging into spring. There was that sense in the air as their ship docked at Rio de Janeiro on September 7, Brazil's national holiday. Because the dock workers were off duty celebrating, the travellers were unable to check their large bags through customs until the next day.

At dockside to greet the Lees were Mission President W. Grant Bangerter, a future General Authority of the Church, his wife, Geraldine, several missionaries, and about fifty members of the Church. Here the visitors had their first exposure to the exuberant and loving nature of the Brazilian people. And here Sister Lee was introduced to the charming Brazilian custom of *abracos*, as the sisters among the welcoming party each gave her a hug and a kiss on the cheek. During the three weeks she would spend among these warm and affectionate people, she probably got more hugs and kisses than she had received over a period of years among her more restrained sisters in the United States.

Elder Lee began his work in South America the day after arriving in Rio de Janeiro when he ferried across the bay to Niterói. There he met with seventeen missionaries with whom he held an instructional and testimony meeting. Afterward, he conducted personal interviews with each one. This set a pattern he would follow in meeting with missionaries throughout Brazil and the other South American countries he visited.

The next day, Elder Lee held a public meeting in his hotel in Rio where two hundred members and investigators had assembled. "They were a brilliant and intelligent congregation," wrote he, "and wholly responsive to all that was said." Then, looking to the future, he added, "Here, surely, is the seedbed for great future possibilities."

At Rio, President Sorenson left the party to go south to lay the groundwork for the new mission. Accompanied by President and Sister Bangerter, the Lees then travelled to Juiz de Fora by way of Petrópolis, known as the "Summer Capital" when Brazil was part of the Portuguese Empire. After holding a public meeting in Juiz de Fora, the party went on to São Paulo. Here, in the commercial capital of Brazil, Elder Lee found a strong district, comprised of six branches, which formed the nucleus of the stake created there in 1966, the first stake in South America.

Among the promising new leaders Elder Lee met in São Paulo were "three Methodist ministers" who had been baptized recently, Helio da Rocha Camargo, Walter Queroz, and Saul Messias. These converts were part of the harvest of a special proselyting effort President Asael Sorenson undertook before his release. During that special effort, President Sorenson and his missionaries, through fasting and fervent prayer, focused on the conversion of Brazilians who could provide leadership in the future. All three of these converts later served as stake presidents and mission presidents, while Elder Camargo became the first native Brazilian to serve as a General Authority of the Church.

Elder Lee spent six days in São Paulo, holding missionary and member meetings, including a district conference where five hundred were in attendance at the Sunday morning session. One of the features of the conference was an MIA festival titled "Praise Ye the Lord," which, Elder Lee noted, was presented "in a masterful way." Also, on Sunday afternoon following the conference, he presided at a ground-breaking ceremony for the first LDS chapel to be built in São Paulo.

During most of three days, Elder Lee closeted with President Bangerter, working out the details for the division of the mission. It was decided that forty missionaries would be assigned to the Brazil South Mission, plus members of the office staff. Districts and branches were divided on a geographical basis.

Leaving the city of São Paulo, Elder Lee and President Bangerter held meetings in Rio Claro and Bauru, cities located in the interior of the state of São Paulo, and then flew to Londrina in the state of Paraná where they met President Sorenson. After holding a public meeting in Londrina, where 115 were in attendance, the party travelled to Curitiba. There, on Sunday, September 20, 1959, the Brazil South Mission was formally organized, the forty-ninth mission in the Church.

Elder and Sister Lee spent nine days touring in the new Brazil South Mission with President and Sister Sorenson. Meetings were held in the states of Paraná, Santa Catarina, and Rio Grande do Sul. In addition to the already mentioned meetings in Londrina and Curitiba, Paraná, meetings were also held in Ponta Grossa, Paraná. The main center of strength in Santa Catarina was at Joinville and in Rio Grande do Sul, at Pôrto Alegre. Successful meetings were held in both cities.

In Ponta Grossa, Elder Lee was impressed by the way in which one family, the Gaertners, could "leaven" an entire community. Comprised of the parents, six sons, and a daughter, the influence of this family had been the chief impetus for the growth of the Church in this city. Elder Lee learned that when Elder Henry D. Moyle had visited Brazil several years before, he found that the father in the Gaertner family had not been advanced in the priesthood because he smoked. "Henry took him in a room," wrote Elder Lee, "and after exacting a promise to keep the word of wisdom, ordained him an elder. He has not smoked since."

Of German extraction, the Gaertners were part of a significant migration of Germanic people to Brazil, beginning in the 1870s. Elder Lee found the largest concentration of members of German descent in Joinville, a city whose architecture gives it the appearance of having been lifted from its native locale on the Rhine and transported to Brazil intact. The German tongue was heard on the streets of Joinville almost as often as Portuguese. Elder Lee learned that the Church had begun proselyting in Brazil, here in Joinville, in September 1928, when Reinhold Stoof, president of the South American Mission, headquartered in Buenos Aires, Argentina, brought with him two elders who spoke German, Elders William F. Heinz and Emil A. J. Schindler, and set them to work. President Stoof had visited Joinville the year before, and, impressed with the reception he had received, had decided to begin the work there. For several years afterward, LDS missionaries worked exclusively among the German-speaking people in Brazil. Only later did they begin to proselyte Brazilians who spoke Portuguese.

At a meeting held in Pôrto Alegre on September 26, 1959, Elder Lee had an experience that was repeated several times during his South American tour. A young Brazilian sister who was present reported that "suddenly" during Elder Lee's sermon, "she was understanding without translation." The experience was but one more incident, in a long line of others, when the gift of tongues was manifested.

After finishing the mission tour at Pôrto Alegre, the

Lees and Sorensons flew to Curitiba and then drove to Uguacu Falls near the border of Argentina and Paraguay. Here they were met by President and Sister Bangerter, President and Sister Arthur Jensen of the Uruguayan Mission, and Brother Robert E. Wells. Brother Wells, who also would become a General Authority in the years ahead, was an American banker and businessman then living in Asunción, Paraguay.

While here, Elder Lee counselled with the three mission presidents about their work, also finding time to visit the massive falls that compared favorably with the Victoria Falls he had seen in Africa the previous year. During this time, Sister Lee suffered severe hemorrhaging in one of her eyes, which inflamed it a fiery red and interfered with her sight. Assisted by the brethren, Elder Lee gave her a blessing, "asking for miraculous intervention."

The Lees and Jensens, accompanied by Brother Wells, travelled to Asunción by bus on September 30, a distance of two hundred miles "over red dirt roads, through jungle country." They arrived in time for Elder Lee to counsel with and to interview the missionaries. That night, a general meeting was held in the branch chapel where 163 assembled to hear the apostle. The following night, "Bob Wells had arranged for some natives with harps and guitars and singers and dancers to serenade us while we ate a late supper under the patio trees for a touch of Paraguayan culture." Many years later, one of the Wells's daughters, Sharlene, became Miss America, playing the Paraguayan harp in the talent competition.

The next day, the Lees and Jensens flew to Montevideo, Uruguay, the headquarters of the Uruguay Mission. They were met by officials from the U.S. Embassy staff and several elders, among whom was Elder Douglas McKay, one of President David O. McKay's grandsons. Here in Montevideo, Elder Lee found another thriving LDS community. The following weekend, the members of the Church assembled for a conference in their own chapel where crowds of six hundred and seven hundred fifty,

Family and Personal Trauma—South America

respectively, attended the morning and afternoon sessions. At the last session, the gift of tongues was again manifested.

Elder Lee spent a week touring in Uruguay. Meetings were held in Treinta Tres, Paysandú, Salto, and Rivera. At Paysandú, Elder Lee was startled to see how thin Richard Moyle was. He was concerned enough about the health of this missionary, who was a son of President Henry D. Moyle, that he sent him to another city for a check up. Later, he arranged to have him transferred to Lima, Peru. Much of the travel in Uruguay was by bus, which enabled the Lees to see the countryside, made picturesque by the many gauchos on horseback with their ponchos to protect them from the intermittent rains.

Elder and Sister Lee flew to Buenos Aires, Argentina, on October 13, where they were met by Mission President Lorin Pace and over two hundred members of the Church. The twelve-day tour of the mission began the same day with a zone conference at Rio Cuarto. There followed missionary and member meetings at Mendoza, at the foot of the Andes, La Plata, Rosario (where son-in-law Ernest Wilkins had served as a young missionary and where he was remembered by some of the members), Bahía Blanca, Tres Arroyos, and Mar del Plata. At this last city, Elder Lee gave the missionaries a three-step formula for approaching the Lord for his blessings: First, keep the commandments. Second, do everything possible to solve one's own personal problems. Third, "pray to the Lord with real intent and desire."

Elder Lee received more media attention in Argentina than in any other South American country. At a press conference held in Buenos Aires, representatives of the four leading newspapers were present to question the apostle from the north. It was only thirty-four years before that when another apostle from the north, Elder Melvin J. Ballard, had come to Buenos Aires to dedicate South America for the preaching of the gospel. Unknown and unnoticed, he and his companions, Rulon S. Wells and

Rey L. Pratt, went to the Tres de Febrero Park near the banks of the La Plata River on Christmas Day, 1925, when Elder Ballard dedicated the continent of South America for the preaching of the gospel. After serving for nine months, during which there were only six conversions, Elder Ballard predicted, "The work will go forth slowly for a time just as the oak grows slowly from an acorn," but, ultimately, "thousands will join here." (*From Acorn to Oak Tree*, p. 30.) From what he had seen in Brazil, Paraguay, Uruguay, and Argentina, and from what he would see later in the tour, Elder Lee could attest to the accuracy of Elder Ballard's prediction as there were then almost twenty thousand members in South America.

Elder and Sister Lee flew over the towering Andes to Santiago, Chile, on October 26 where they were met by J. Vernon Sharp, who had been called as the president of the new Andes Mission, whose headquarters would be in Lima, Peru. Elder Lee found several branches of the Church in Santiago, Chile, the first of which had been organized by President Henry D. Moyle when he toured South America in 1956. While in Chile, Elder Lee travelled south to Concepción, paralleling all the way the Andes, which loom up to the east like enormous sky caps. He also travelled west to the coastal cities of Valparaiso and Viña del Mar, the area in which Elder Parley P. Pratt spent several months during the early 1850s. Here, in an unidentified grave, lie the remains of one of Elder Pratt's daughters, to whom his wife gave birth after the Pratts arrived in Chile, the first child of Latter-day Saint parents to be buried in South America.

On October 29, Elder Lee presided at a meeting in Santiago where the organization of the Andes Mission was presented for sustaining vote. After holding an eight-hour instruction and testimony meeting with the missionaries the next day, Elder Lee and his party flew north to Lima, Peru, where, on November 1, the Andes Mission was formally organized. At the time, there were several branches

Family and Personal Trauma — South America

of the Church in Peru, including the one at Lima, which President Moyle also organized in 1956.

Elder Lee's translator at these services in Lima was Frederick S. Williams, one of the first missionaries in South America in the 1920s, a former president of two missions in South America and the first president of the first Lima branch. At the time of Elder Lee's visit to Lima in November 1959, Brother Williams was the general manager of TAPSA, a Peruvian airline. He reported that during his address to the Lima Saints on this occasion, Elder Lee alluded to Elder Ballard's prophecy. "Standing at his side as interpreter," reported Brother Williams, "I felt the deep spiritual context of his words. He stated that the time would soon come when Father Lehi's children would be inspired to accept the Book of Mormon and enter the Church in great numbers. "Soon," he quoted Elder Lee as saying, "the Pacific coast of the Americas will become the most fertile proselyting field of the church." (Ibid., p. 303.) A Church membership of 571,000 by 1989 in the countries of Chile, Peru, Ecuador, and Colombia; 570,000 in Mexico; and 191,000 in Central America demonstrates the accuracy of this prediction. No other area of the world came near to matching the explosive Church growth in these countries that front on "the Pacific coast of the Americas."

Before leaving Peru, the Lees flew to Cuzco in an unpressurized plane, receiving supplements of oxygen through tubes held between their teeth. The high altitude at Cuzco — 11,300 feet — temporarily gave them the *soroche*, an altitude sickness, which gradually left as they became acclimated. Here on the upper reaches of the Amazon River system, the visitors were treated to the novel combination of Inca and Spanish architecture. The foundations of most buildings are Incan, constructed before 1200 A.D. But above the first floor are the Spanish constructions of masonry and adobe, featuring carved woodwork that is most prominently displayed in the Spanish style balconies that overhang Cuzco's narrow, winding streets. From Cuzco, they travelled fifty miles northwest on a narrow gauge railroad to Machu Picchu, an Incan fortress city constructed on a narrow ridge between two mountain heights. Known as the last citadel of the Incas after the Spanish conquest, Machu Picchu's massive buildings are constructed of mortarless white granite. The city is said to have been abandoned after the death of the last Incan monarch. Retracing their route, the travellers returned to "mist covered Lima" on November 5; and during the two following days, travelled into southern Peru, holding meetings at Tacna and at Toquepala, the latter being the headquarters of a copper mining company that, according to Elder Lee, was an affiliate of the American Smelting and Refining Company.

During the following week, Elder and Sister Lee, in quick succession, touched down, and, in some instances, held meetings in Panama City, San Juan, Costa Rica, Managua, Nicaragua, Tegucigalpa, Honduras, San Salvador, and Guatemala City.

On November 15, sixteen hundred members of the Church from the five districts in Guatemala met in Guatemala City, the largest congregation during the three-month tour. "This is among the most distinctive Lamanite people I have yet been among," Elder Lee wrote of the occasion. Moreover, he had "a strong feeling that this place is without question the Lamanite capital of North America and that a temple for the Latin American people should be built here." That impression saw fruition on December 14, 1984, when a beautiful temple was dedicated in Guatemala City.

Elder Lee's last stop was in Mexico City where he and Sister Lee arrived on the seventeenth. After holding meetings with missionaries and members, he wrote: "The remarkable improvement in the appearance and performance of our Mexican Saints never ceases to amaze me."

The Lees arrived home on November 19 after an absence of three months. It took several days for them to unpack their things, to distribute gifts to the members of the family, and to reset their inner clocks, which had been scrambled by their frequent movement into different time zones. Elder Lee was then on his way to New York for board meetings. He ended the year with conferences in the Mount Logan and Temple View stakes, a quiet Christmas with his family, still another trip to New York for more board meetings, and, on the last day of December, with a funeral honoring his friend Charles S. Hyde. "Charlie's passing," Elder Lee wrote, "recalled [the] delightful but strenuous seven years . . . presiding over the Pioneer stake, along with Paul C. Child."

Chapter Twenty-three

New Duties, Changes, and Challenges

As if he lacked something to do, Elder Lee was appointed to the board of Zions First National Bank on January 6, 1960, and then to the executive committee of the board. Apparently fearful his protégé was overextended, President Clark urged that if he accepted these appointments, he should resign from the boards of Union Pacific and Equitable Life. When Elder Lee insisted he could carry the extra load, President Clark conceded. Later Elder Lee became the vice-chairman and then the chairman of this board, which further increased his responsibilities and time commitments.

Meanwhile there were major changes in the First Presidency and among the other General Authorities of the Church. At the October 1960 general conference, three new Assistants to the Twelve were sustained: N. Eldon Tanner, Franklin D. Richards, and Theodore M. Burton. In a major change in policy, these assistants were given the apostolic authority that was later defined to mean they could do anything out in the world the members of the Twelve could do, with two exceptions. So authorized, these men could

New Duties, Changes, and Challenges

Elders Harold B. Lee, Howard W. Hunter, Marion D. Hanks, and Spencer W. Kimball, early in 1960

help lift the ever-increasing burden that rested on the Twelve and the First Presidency.

At the moment, President J. Reuben Clark, who had turned eighty-nine the previous month, was seriously disabled and unable to carry his share of the load. "President Clark," wrote Elder Lee on October 9, "who had not attended the other meetings, came on Sunday. He can hardly walk now. He thrilled the audience." Not only was he physically impaired, but he was overwhelmed with a deep sense of depression, which seriously reduced his ability to function effectively. "Marion Romney and I went to see President Clark," Elder Lee reported on October 28, "who is still in a very depressed state and has apparently ruled himself out of much future activity. He seems obsessed by the idea that a man in his 90th year has nothing to which he can look forward." Twelve days later, they visited President Clark again, this time taking President Moyle with them. "We found him waiting to talk about the three of us being speakers at his funeral," reported Elder Lee, "the handling of his personal library; the possibility of disposing of his Grantsville ranch to some stake as a welfare project; and for Marion Romney to move up on the obtaining of someone to write his biography after his passing."

Given this background, it is not surprising that on June 22, 1961, Elder Hugh B. Brown was called as a Third Counselor in the First Presidency to help shoulder the burden President Clark was no longer able to carry. Elder Brown's call created a vacancy in the Twelve, which was filled by Elder Gordon B. Hinckley, who was sustained as a member of the Twelve on September 30, 1961. At the same time, Thorpe B. Isaacson and Boyd K. Packer were sustained as Assistants to the Twelve, and John H. Vandenburg, Robert L. Simpson, and Victor L. Brown were sustained as the new Presiding Bishopric. Six days later, President J. Reuben Clark passed away quietly, age ninety years, thirty-six days. Thus passed from the scene one of the most powerful and influential men of his generation. His funeral was held on October 10 in the Salt Lake Tabernacle. President McKay conducted the services and offered a eulogy. In addition to the three whom President Clark had selected and instructed, President Joseph Fielding Smith was one of the speakers. The prayers were offered by President Hugh B. Brown and Elder Mark E. Petersen. Following the funeral sermon, Elder Lee paid another tribute to President Clark at a meeting of the Equitable board in New York on November 16, 1961. There he read a eulogy of his mentor, which was incorporated into the minutes of the meeting to become part of the permanent records of the company. It was the final act of a dutiful son toward his surrogate father.

During this time, Elder and Sister Lee sold their home on Connor Street and moved into a one-level home at 1436 Penrose Drive in Salt Lake City. This became necessary because of Fern's deteriorating health. Following the exhausting trip through South America, she had slowly gone downhill, unable to regain her strength. After an operation in January 1961, she fell at home, tearing some of the stitches. She was then returned to the hospital. By this time, it was apparent that it would be necessary for the Lees to move to a home on one level where Fern would not have steps to climb. This recognition had set in motion the events that culminated in the sale of their Connor Street home and the purchase of the one on Penrose Drive. They moved in on October 20, 1961. "Fern said she was so happy and couldn't sleep," wrote Elder Lee on that day, "so I am happy too."

During this period, significant steps were taken to implement the vision Elder Lee had had about correlating and coordinating the work of the Church since the 1940s. The first move was to introduce system and control into the Church's curriculum, which, until then, had been fragmented, with each organization independently preparing its own instructional materials. "Conducted a lengthy meeting of the general priesthood committee," wrote Elder Lee on May 19, 1960, "who are now instructed to undertake a study of the whole curriculum of church organizations and to recommend some correlation in the meeting in the temple." The committee worked steadily on this assignment throughout the following year. Meanwhile it expanded the scope of its study to consider matters other than curriculum involved in the overall subject of correlation. "At the meeting of the general priesthood committee," Elder Lee wrote on March 22, 1961, "the principal item of business was to consider the final draft of a proposed overhaul of the ward teaching program of the past under the title 'Priesthood Correlation Program' with those participating [to be designated] as 'Priesthood Watchmen.' Twelve or fourteen stakes will be selected for the experiment before launching it as a church wide operation." Two weeks later, following the April general conference, Elder Lee and his committee "met with the presidents of the fourteen stakes across the church who have been chosen for an experimental launching of a priesthood correlation program which will give impetus to ward teaching." As reports filtered in from these stakes, Elder Lee and his committee analyzed them, making such adjustments in the program that experience in the field suggested. Meanwhile, Elder Lee gave periodic reports to the Twelve and the First Presidency to keep them fully apprised of new developments. Two weeks before the October 1961 general conference, Elder Lee again met with President McKay for this purpose. "In meeting with President McKay," he wrote on September 16, "he said he awoke at 6:30 A.M. with a clear impression as to the proper theme for the general priesthood meeting and that he was impressed that the newly approved correlation program should be the theme. He asked me and Richard L. Evans to speak on this subject." Elder Lee was pleased with the way the correlation program was formally launched during the conference. "President McKay announced the newly approved correlation program," wrote he on October 1, 1961, five days before President Clark passed away, "and requested Richard L. Evans and Harold B. Lee to explain the proposed church coordinating council, with associated correlation committees for the adults, the youth and the children, each headed by a member of the Twelve. He has named me as the chairman of the all church coordinating council." Within days after President McKay made this announcement, Elder Lee met with Marion G. Romney, Richard L. Evans, and Gordon B. Hinckley of the Twelve, who, according to Elder Lee, were "to head up the three divisions of the correlation program." A week later, Elder Lee convened the first meeting of the All Church Coordinating Council, with all the General Authorities present, except the First Presidency, and "with all heads of all church [headquarters] units in attendance." Thereafter, Elder Lee met periodically with this council to help everyone understand his role in the scheme of correlation, to encourage its members to carry the message into the field, and to promote unity and cooperation between the priesthood and the auxiliaries.

New Duties, Changes, and Challenges

Meanwhile, he and the general priesthood committee realized that this was but a first important step toward the correlation of all priesthood and auxiliary activities throughout the Church. So, with the authorization and encouragement of President McKay, Elder Lee and his committee worked behind the scenes during the next sixteen months, designing a comprehensive plan of priesthood directed correlation. By February 1963, it was ready. When it was presented to the Brethren for consideration, it proposed a general priesthood board of a hundred nonpaid men, divided into four priesthood correlation committees of twenty-five each: missionary, priesthood (later designated the home teaching committee), genealogical, and welfare. It was also provided that at the outset, these four committees would be chaired, respectively, by President Joseph Fielding Smith, Elder Marion G. Romney, Elder N. Eldon Tanner, and Bishop John H. Vandenburg. At first, this proposal was approved as presented. Then later, when questions were raised about creating a separate general priesthood board, it was decided that the General Authorities would constitute the general priesthood board, under which the four named groups would function as subcommittees. With this organization in place, the groundwork had been laid to accomplish the major task of teaching the principles of priesthood correlation.

Before this new program could be effectively implemented throughout the Church, it was essential that all headquarters personnel be trained. Steps toward that goal were taken on May 27, 1963. On that day, Elder Lee met first with the priesthood missionary committee, where he outlined "the programs they are to carry to stake conferences throughout the year." Later, he "assembled all general board members, all correlation workers and most of the general authorities in a five hour presentation of the entire program which will be carried to the stakes during the third and fourth quarters by the missionary committee, the home teaching committee, the Sunday school and the MIA." Appraising the effect of this training, Elder Lee concluded: "There was a remarkable response as the total program was unfolded to them."

Afterward, members of these four subcommittees and auxiliary representatives accompanied General Authorities to stake conferences where training sessions were held and where they were called on to speak at the general sessions of stake conference. This program, directed by the general priesthood board, obviated the need for a general priesthood committee, which was formally discontinued on May 22, 1963.

Once the Brethren began to implement the priesthood correlation program throughout the Church, Elder Lee saw a repetition of some of the difficulties he had experienced when the welfare program was first rolled out. Some whose authority and prerogatives had been restricted or infringed upon were slow to respond. But, the great majority of the membership was supportive and cooperative. Later, as we shall see, the cause of correlation was greatly enhanced when Regional Representatives were called who devoted their entire Church service time to training local leaders in correlation and other principles.

Chapter Twenty-four

The Ultimate Trauma Followed by Healing

Though they did not know it at the time, when the Lees moved into their new home on Penrose Drive in October 1961, Sister Lee had less than a year to live. Fern was happy in this new environment. Her home, equipped with every modern convenience, beautifully decorated and furnished, and with treasured mementoes of her worldwide travels, was a place of culture, refinement, and comfort. Among her treasured keepsakes were those obtained during the tour of New Zealand and Australia she had undertaken with her husband the previous May and June. It was the last international tour they would take together.

They had spent five weeks in the South Pacific, holding stake conferences in Hamilton and Hawkes Bay, New Zealand, and Melbourne and Sydney, Australia. Also, at Hamilton, Elder Lee installed Wendell H. Weiser as the new head of the Church college, replacing Clifton D. Boyack. Along the way, other meetings had been held with members and missionaries. Like the other tours she had taken with her husband, this one was both tiring and exciting.

*Elder Harold B. Lee
and Fern Tanner Lee*

She had enjoyed mingling with the Saints and speaking in many of the meetings. But, it was so good to be home, and once the move had been made to their new place, Fern had a supreme sense of peace and contentment that was enhanced by the nearness of her daughters and their families. We gain an insight into the love and joy that pervaded this home from the diary entry Elder Lee made the day after Christmas 1961. "Marlee [Wilkins] came home to spend a few days with us and Jane [Goates]," wrote he on that day. "It was like having our own two little girls of 'yesterday.'"

Only eleven days after this sweet experience, Sister Lee's frail health took a startling turn for the worse. On Saturday, January 6, 1962, she fainted three times during the night. Understandably alarmed, Elder Lee arranged to have his stake conference assignment cancelled. With medication to help neutralize her high blood pressure and solicitous care from Elder Lee and the family, she seemed to bounce back. But three months later, she had a recurrence of the fainting spells, suffering a slight concussion when she fell. Hospitalized for ten days, she was released with the doctor's warning that it could happen again because of the persistent high blood pressure she had suffered over the years. Her condition was such that Sister Lee was able to attend the ground-breaking ceremonies for the Oakland Temple the last week in May, and on the Fourth of July, she hosted a dinner on her lovely patio, honoring the Lees' Hawaiian friends Jay and Virginia Quealy, who had been called to preside over the Southern Far East Mission.

By now, Fern was living on raw nerve. Later diagnosis revealed that her fainting spells were caused by small, intermittent blood clots in the brain. It was likely true that in some instances, this clotting occurred without causing her to lose consciousness but was severe enough to cause pain, nausea, and feelings of despondency.

By September, her condition had deteriorated to the point that hospitalization was again necessary. On the fourteenth, she suffered "intense nausea and vomiting," accompanied by severe pain. Medication prescribed by her doctors and injections for the pain provided little relief. Elder Lee and Fern's sister, Emily, spent the night near her bedside. When an episode during the night almost took her off, special duty nurses around the clock were arranged for, and two of her former physicians were brought back on the case to provide consultation and more comfort for the patient.

Surprisingly, she made a strong recovery in the days which followed until, by the twentieth, there was talk about releasing her from the hospital. It was in these circumstances that Elder Lee, with the concurrence of the doctors and the encouragement of his wife, went to Nevada to attend the conference of the Lake Mead Stake. However, on Saturday night, she suffered a massive cerebral hemorrhage. Notified at 12:30 A.M., Elder Lee was able to return home on a chartered flight, arriving in Salt Lake on Sunday at 4:00 A.M. Then, with solicitous care, he watched over her sick bed for thirty hours, only leaving at intervals to care for personal needs. At first, he prayed for her recovery; then, sensing her precarious physical state, he yielded to God's will, foregoing his own. Kneeling at her bedside, he whispered words of love and testimony, the funeral sermon she had asked him to give, but which he could not bring himself to speak in public. Then, she slipped away, quietly. It was mid-morning, Monday, September 24, 1962.

The funeral, held three days later, was preceded by a public viewing in the mortuary and a private viewing in the home for family and close associates. The spoken word by members of the First Presidency, the music by friends from the Tabernacle Choir, and the prayers by family members were appropriate and impressive, calculated to honor the deceased and to bring solace to family and friends. Yet, at day's end, when all had gone, and Elder Lee was left alone, the full impact of his loss struck home. No conviction of a reunion in the afterlife, nor glowing memories of past joys, could erase the sense of present loss and deprivation. Aware of this, Elder Lee's sister, Verda, and her husband, Charles Ross, now stepped forward, offering to move into the home, there to assume the responsibility of maintaining it while providing some semblance of family life for him. Avidly accepting this unexpected offer, Elder Lee, to his death, could never adequately express his gratitude for this loving gesture. With the Rosses in the home and with his daughters and their families nearby, he had all the support one could hope for to adjust to life without Fern.

It still was not easy. One does not sever a loving relationship of forty years without major trauma. He mechanically went about to pick up the threads of his shattered life, performing, as if by rote, his daily tasks at headquarters and in the field. Thinking, perhaps, a change of scene would speed the adjustment, President McKay assigned Elder Lee to attend conferences in Europe. Walter Stover, a member of the priesthood welfare committee, who was fluent in the Germanic languages, accompanied him. They left Salt Lake November 9, 1962, and during the following two weeks, held a series of meetings in Germany, Austria, and Switzerland. On balance, the trip helped Elder Lee to refocus his life. But it had a down side. November 14, Fern's birthday and their wedding anniversary, far from home, in a foreign land, was "a most difficult day of memories." Later, he suffered spells of nervous tension and depression, sometimes accompanied by tears. At Berlin, he was unable to attend a large public meeting because of his emotional state.

Back home, he endeavored to recreate the atmosphere that had always brought joy at Christmas time, clearing the yards, trimming the shrubs, and putting up lights. He added a new touch by having an artificial gas log installed in the fireplace. It didn't work. The celebration was cold and meaningless without his companion. Nor could he find peace in public gatherings. It was necessary for him to leave a testimonial dinner honoring President McKay because of an agitation in his "nervous system," which, he wrote, increased when he was "too long confined and in an idle mood." For the same reason, he refrained from attending Sunday School in his own ward over the holidays.

These feelings dominated Elder Lee's waking hours and troubled his dreams until mid-January 1963, when help came from an unexpected source. Following an Equitable meeting in New York, board member John A. Sibley, Atlanta banker, took him aside to share his experience in losing his own wife. "This is the most severe test you will ever be confronted with in your life," said his friend. "If you can meet and surmount this test, there will be nothing else in life you cannot meet and surmount." This thought seemed to infuse him with a new vitality and sense of purpose. It also seemed to bring into focus counsel given by Fern before she died and events of the past two weeks.

When death seemed imminent for her, Fern, ever sensitive to his needs, had urged Harold to remarry when she passed on, and not to delay unduly. She also shared this advice with Helen and Maurine. For three months after Fern's death, Elder Lee, caught up in mourning, had given no apparent thought to his wife's counsel. But during the Christmas season in 1962, conscious of the loneliness of single life and the potential hazards of remaining unmarried, he began to take Fern's advice to heart. He then formulated general criteria of what to look for in a second companion. Preferably, she should be near his own age; someone whom Fern had known and admired; and someone who had not been sealed to another. The one who fit these criteria perfectly was Freda Joan Jensen, a well-known educator, who for years had been the supervisor of primary education in the Jordan School District. She was well known to the Lees as she had served on the general boards of both the Primary and the YWMIA and, being about their age, had been involved in social and other activities with that age group. She had never married, although Elder Lee learned later she had been engaged to be married to a widower who died unexpectedly two weeks before the planned nuptials. Given these circumstances, there remained the delicate task of how to open up a dialogue with her, to determine her feelings and whether the personal chemistry between them was such as to give hope of a happy and successful marriage. Elder Lee's task was simplified when Sister Jensen was among those who called at the Lee home during the holidays to pay their respects. Following up on that fortuitous contact, he chose a means of furthering their acquaintance that was ideal for two professional teachers. He gave her a book. It was a copy of President J. Reuben Clark's most recent book to which Elder Lee had written the foreword. Calling in advance, he went to her home on January 2, 1963, to deliver it in person. From the beginning of their relationship, both seemed to know intuitively that they were destined to be man and wife. There was the circumstance of Joan's (the name she preferred Elder Lee to use instead of Freda, which was used by most others) aborted marriage. There was the special blessing she had received years before in Alberta, Canada, from temple President Edward James Wood, who told her that in the future she would occupy a place of high distinction, such that she could then hardly imagine. As for Elder Lee, his prophetic sense whispered that this was the woman whom the Lord had raised up to stand by his side in matrimony and to help assuage the grief caused by Fern's death.

Over a period of months, Elder Lee and Joan Jensen became better acquainted through personal and telephone contact, and by correspondence when Elder Lee was away on assignment. As their courtship progressed, they realized the need to smooth Joan's entrance into the family so as to preserve the unity that existed there. So, Elder Lee met privately with Maurine and Helen to explain his relationship with Joan Jensen and their plans to marry. As expected, he found both of them to be wholly supportive and in favor. Meanwhile, Joan wrote personal letters to the girls, expressing the love she had for both of their parents. Then on March 25, 1963, the entire family was brought together for the first time to meet Joan and to have Elder Lee explain the coming marriage. A month later, he invited Joan to carefully inspect the home to decide what changes, if any, she wanted to make in it and what items of furniture she wanted to bring from her own home. Later, when all his personal and family arrangements for the marriage had been completed, Elder Lee went to President McKay to consult with him about his plans. The prophet heartily approved them, citing the scripture that "it is not good for man to be alone." Then, at his request, Elder Lee took Joan to meet President McKay. Sister McKay was present. Both were impressed with Joan's dignified but friendly charm and gave their unqualified endorsement of the marriage.

The ceremony was performed in the Salt Lake Temple by President McKay on June 17, 1963, in the presence of members of the families, a few choice friends, and the two official witnesses, President Henry D. Moyle and Elder Marion G. Romney. Afterward, a wedding breakfast arranged by friends Lou and Geraldine Callister was held in the Hotel Utah, and at 2:00 P.M., the newlyweds boarded a plane for New York. There they checked into the "palatial" bridal suite of the Waldorf Astoria. They remained in the city four days. Except for a meeting with the Equitable board and checking on preliminary plans for the Church's World Fair pavilion, Elder Lee spent the time with Joan, acquainting her with the city that had almost become his second home. In the months ahead, he would visit there even more often because of his assignment as the chairman of the committee planning the Church's World Fair exhibit. "My days with Joan were glorious," he wrote of this abbreviated honeymoon. "Each night we sat up talking, sometimes until 1–2 A.M., talking about things we had little opportunity before to say."

Later, in Chicago, the private car of Union Pacific's president was made available to them. "This was travel deluxe," Elder Lee wrote of the trip from Chicago to Salt Lake City. Still later, they took the private car on a trip to California. With them were Verda and Charlie Ross and Lou and Geraldine Callister, "for a little diversion and as an expression of our gratitude for all they have done."

Thus, at age sixty-six, Joan Jensen Lee was fully launched on her career as the wife of the man who was destined to become the president of The Church of Jesus Christ of Latter-day Saints. She never ceased to marvel at the extraordinary turn of events that had brought this about, nor at the spiritual sensitivity of President E. J. Wood who had predicted it, even though in veiled terms. And both she and Elder Lee were struck by the way in which Joan, over the years, had slowly and faithfully acquired the talents, the qualities of character, and the spirituality that equipped her to fill this niche. Later, she would become a role model for many Latter-day Saint women who, deprived of the opportunity to marry worthy men in their youth, were encouraged to continue to grow and mature as individuals, to develop professional and other skills, and to live happy, productive lives, not with any idea of marrying a great man like Elder Lee later in life, but with the idea of making the most of the circumstances and opportunities that each life affords.

During the remainder of 1963, Joan was introduced to the somewhat nomadic life she would live during the next ten years. In September she and Elder Lee took their first overseas trip together when they spent ten days in Hawaii. They flew to Honolulu on the seventh, where they were met by local leaders and members and were treated to the customary Polynesian welcome with song and dance and flowers in profusion. It was an eye-opener to Joan, who had not before been exposed to the unfeigned love of the Polynesian Saints. That night, they were dinner guests at the luxurious home of the Wong family, prominent and wealthy members of the Church.

During the following week, the visitors went to Maui. There they visited the old church where missionary work began in the islands more than a century before. They then flew to Hilo on the big island of Hawaii, from where they drove to the Hawaii Volcanoes National Park. Here the visitors saw the driving mechanism that had built up these volcanic islands in the Pacific.

Back in Oahu over the weekend, Elder Lee presided at a stake conference in Laie. Joining him in giving instructions were D. Arthur Haycock of the missionary committee and Harry Brooks of the home teaching committee. Joan was called on to bear her testimony at the general sessions in which she focused her remarks, as she usually did, on the children in the audience, with whom she had a great rapport.

The plan to hold a stake conference the following weekend in Honolulu was cancelled when, on the eighteenth, Elder Lee received word that President Henry D. Moyle had died earlier in the day at Deer Park, Florida, while visiting the Church ranch. The Lees returned to Salt Lake

City immediately, where Elder Lee was appointed to the committee to arrange for the funeral, which was held on the twenty-first. He was one of the speakers, lauding his friend for his fine qualities of character and for his years of effective service in the Church, his profession, and his businesses.

Following the October 1963 general conference, when N. Eldon Tanner was sustained as second counselor in the First Presidency and Hugh B. Brown as the first counselor, Elder and Sister Lee travelled to Washington and New York and then to England and Europe. They were gone for twenty-four days, leaving the Salt Lake City airport on October 25. They travelled first to Washington, D.C., where Elder Lee attended a meeting of the board of governors of the American Red Cross. Elder Lee had been appointed to this board some time before, an appointment that further expanded his ability to serve and enlarged his sphere of influence among business, professional, educational, and political leaders throughout the country.

After spending a day as the guests of J. Willard Marriott and his wife at their ranch near the capital, the Lees travelled to New York where Elder Lee attended Equitable board meetings. They also spent a day with Alberta Moyle, President Moyle's widow, who was staying with her son-in-law and daughter, Mr. and Mrs. Frank Wangeman. Still in deep mourning over the death of her husband, Elder and Sister Lee tried to persuade her to accompany them abroad, thinking this might speed the process of healing. But, she did not feel up to going with them.

The Lees flew out of New York on the morning of November 1. Waiting to meet them at Heathrow, outside London, were Elder Marion D. Hanks and his wife, Maxine, who were directing the mission. They checked into the Grosvenor Hotel, which they made headquarters during their three-day stay. It being Joan's first trip to London, the Hankses arranged for her to see the usual places of historic interest. Elder Lee counselled with Elder Hanks, who was then a member of the First Council of Seventy,

The Ultimate Trauma Followed by Healing

and with Selvoy J. Boyer, the president of the London Temple. Elder Lee also inspected the temple, its grounds, and the church-owned buildings nearby.

The travellers flew to Munich, Germany, on November 4. The following day Elder Lee attended a conference for servicemen and their dependents at a site near Munich, after which, in turn, he and Joan went to Zurich and Bern, Switzerland. At Bern, Elder Lee inspected the temple and counselled with the temple president. After a hurried trip to the Alps, the Lees returned to Zurich from where, on November 12, they flew to Paris, checking in at the Grand Hotel, which was their headquarters during a three-day stay in the French capital. Here Elder Lee treated his new bride to some of the cultural riches of this renowned city. They attended the ballet at the Royal Opera House, visited the Louvre, had lunch in the Eiffel Tower, and visited government buildings and monuments, including Napoleon's tomb. He then accompanied Joan on a shopping tour, buying her some French perfume, a pair of fine leather gloves, and a dainty handkerchief for which Paris is famous.

The travellers went from Paris to Amsterdam, where Elder Lee held a meeting with the missionaries working there, then to The Hague, where they attended Sunday School on the seventeenth, and, finally, to Rotterdam, from where they caught a flight to New York City, arriving in time to enable Elder Lee to attend his monthly Equitable meetings. During that time, Joan visited with Sister Moyle. "Alberta seems lonely," Elder Lee noted later, "and so much alone. How well I know her hurt and the intensity of her loss." So, despite the happy adjustment Elder Lee had made in his marriage to Joan, and despite the love and the gratitude he had for her, he could never forget, nor could he cease to love and to long for, his first love, the mother of his children.

Chapter Twenty-five

A Family in Transition

For years before her death, Fern had been frail and fragile in health. The high blood pressure had limited her activities and had interfered with her enjoyment of everyday life. In later years, the many operations, falls, and confinements she experienced had cast doubt on her ability to survive to an old age. So, while her passing created a great sadness and and sense of loss in the family, it did not come unexpectedly or with violent shock. Such was not the case with the sudden, unexpected death of Maurine Lee Wilkins on August 27, 1965, at age forty. This bright, vivacious, friendly woman, whom her father called "Sunshine," was carrying her fifth child when she died. At the time, Elder Lee was in Hawaii with Elder Paul H. Dunn for some meetings they had planned to hold in the Pacific. He returned home immediately. "My heart is broken as I contemplate the passing of my darling 'Sunshine,' " wrote he, "and the great need of Ernie and her little family." After the sadness of the funeral, he wrote disconsolately, "Somehow, I seem unable to shake off this latest, shattering blow. Only God can help me."

A Family in Transition

In time, the shock and sadness subsided as Elder Lee picked up his burden and moved on. But, now and again, memories of the loss of his loved ones evoked poignant feelings, as they did on November 14, 1965, Fern's birthday and their wedding anniversary, when he had a bad day. On the fourth anniversary of her death, in September 1966, he was "yearning" for his departed mate. Meanwhile, in December 1965, four months after Maurine's death, he became concerned about Joan, who had lost twenty pounds and who occasionally was heard to cry out in her sleep as Fern had sometimes done in the months before she died. "The horror of having the possibility of a similar loss," wrote he, "has shaken me to the limit." Fortunately, Joan regained her strength and retained it throughout the remainder of Elder Lee's life and beyond, providing comfort and encouragement during the infirmities and trials he was yet to endure. The only physical impediment she suffered before her husband passed on was reduced vision, which was corrected by cataract surgery.

Meanwhile, the third generation was reaching maturity. In 1967, Elder Lee's two oldest grandsons were called into the mission field, David Goates and Alan Wilkins. David was called to serve in England, and when his grandfather was there during November of that year, they spent a day together in Leeds. The next day, when Elder Lee and the mission president drove to Sunderland to hold missionary meetings, Elder David Goates was at the wheel of the mission car. No doubt, the grandparent was neither irritated nor annoyed when the mission president told him that David was the "most outstanding of his missionaries," and that he was "thinking of him as an assistant."

Three months before Elder Lee saw David in England, he attended Alan's missionary farewell in Provo. Ironically, it was on August 27, the second anniversary of Maurine's death. On this account, Alan was very tender in his feelings, and as he sat on the stand beside Elder Lee, he whispered to him: "Oh, Grandfather, Mother would have wanted so much to be here. I have prayed constantly that the Lord would permit her to come."

The third grandson to enter the mission field was Elder Lee's namesake, Harold Lee Goates, who was called to the South Africa Mission in March 1968. Elder Lee accompanied Hal Goates to the temple when he received his endowment on March 19, 1968, commenting that, "Perhaps heaven was very close; a proud grandmother and Auntie Marr." The grandfather was no less proud of this grandson, and his other grandchildren, than was Fern, although on attending David's homecoming, he was quick to explain that he was "righteously" proud. On December 19, 1969, when he performed David's temple marriage to Patsy Hewlett, he referred to it as "a historic occasion for our family."

With ten grandchildren, four of Maurine's (Alan, Marlee, Larry, and Jay Wilkins) and six of Helen's (David, Jane, Hal, Drew, Jonathon, and Timothy), Elder Lee felt rich indeed. The aspirations he had for them were succinctly stated in a diary entry he made after seeing a group of them together at Aspen Grove during a family vacation in July 1965. "As the older ones reach their maturity," wrote he, "we are prayerfully hoping that we can [help them to be] clean, get their schooling, and fill missions, and marry in the temple." In aid of these objectives, Elder Lee set up trust funds for his grandchildren on January 5, 1968.

During this period of vibrant growth and activity of his family, Elder Lee passed through a series of illnesses that tested his patience and his staying power. During the first week in January 1966, he was hospitalized. There he underwent extensive tests of his intestinal tract and received a blood transfusion. The following week, he had to be excused from a stake conference assignment in Rexburg, Idaho, and returned to the hospital to see if the doctors could give him some relief from the "persistent headaches" he suffered. Nothing they prescribed was of lasting benefit. He entered the hospital again in March 1967 for more tests to try to determine the cause of his headaches and feelings of inertia. The only outcome was another blood transfusion, some iron shots, and an admonition to guard his health and to slow down. Elder Lee's response was to leave the next day for Jacksonville, Florida, where on March 17, 1967, he began a mission tour with his friend Glen Rudd. During a whirlwind week, Elder Lee dedicated chapels in Live Oak, Tilton, DeFuniak Springs, and Tallahassee, Florida, and Mobile, Alabama. Missionary meetings were held along the way. At Pensacola, Florida, where another public meeting was held, he commented on the "exhausting pace." The tour ended in Orlando, Florida, the mission headquarters, where he held an instruction and testimony meeting with forty missionaries, followed by personal interviews.

Elder Lee flew from Orlando to New York on Friday, March 24, where, over the weekend, he and Elder Franklin D. Richards were scheduled to divide the New Jersey Stake. He spent a miserable night Saturday, "in a cold sweat," and Sunday morning, while in the shower, he became faint. Joan called Mission President Jay Eldredge, who came with two elders to administer to him. "They blessed me to be able to attend the conference, which I did, and participated in the division of the New Jersey stake and the creation of the New Jersey Central stake." When on Monday morning he again felt faint, Elder Lee cancelled plans to remain in New York until Thursday and returned home immediately. There, the next day, he entered the hospital where he was given a massive blood transfusion, iron shots, and gamma globulin shots. Then, over a period of several days, a team of four doctors conducted extensive tests, which resulted in the decision to operate. The surgery was performed April 11, 1967, in a marathon operation from 8:00 A.M. to 11:30 P.M. The doctors later explained that the source of the bleeding was "from a large ulcer in the duodenal bulb where it had not been possible to x-ray." They also told him they had removed about a half to two thirds of his stomach "in that portion most susceptible to over-acidity." They found no malignancy. Elder Lee seemed to feel that his life had been miraculously preserved for a purpose. "One can only suppose," wrote he, "that the Almighty has it in hand to give or to take, and He alone keeps the time table. To the thoroughness and the skill of the doctors I owe much; but I am not unmindful of the spiritual power which has been in evidence in the events leading up to the operation, as well as the circumstances resulting."

By April 27, the patient had recovered from the surgery and was ready to return to work. "I am amazed," he recorded, "at no pain in my digestive system and my headaches [have been] reduced to a minimum. The Lord, indeed, has been good to me." As he prepared to gear up again, Dr. Orme gave Elder Lee parting instructions "to do only half a man's work rather than the work of ten men," instructions that, as we shall see, he did not follow with exactitude.

This surgery seemed to solve Elder Lee's current physical problems. He was in good health during the next year. However, following the April 1968 general conference, he became ill again and was unable to attend a stake conference in Boston. In the hospital, x-rays "showed signs of infection" in his lower right lung, which was later diagnosed as pleural pneumonia. After recovering from this ailment, there followed another year during which Elder Lee was in comparatively good health. Like a good juggler, he was able to keep all the balls in the air without dropping them. It was a continual round of headquarters duties, chiefly correlation matters at the moment, stake conferences, mission tours, and board meetings, always more board meetings. Following the April 1969 general conference, however, he was overcome with "extreme weariness." Consulting his lead doctor, Joseph F. Orme, he underwent a three-hour examination. "Seemingly, he found nothing irregular," noted Elder Lee, and, so saying, he boarded a plane for New York for some more board meetings.

But, like the ghost of Banquo, Elder Lee's sense of

weariness would not down merely by a doctor's finding that there was nothing irregular about him. "Went to the LDS Hospital x-ray laboratory," he noted on September 2, 1969, "for further exploration of some possible causes for my digestive problems and weariness." The following weekend, Elder Lee's assignment to attend the Norfolk stake conference was cancelled. Instead, he entered the LDS Hospital, exhausted, where he underwent another extensive series of tests over a period of three days. They revealed nothing, so he returned home and for a week worked there, holding committee meetings and dictating to his secretary. Elder Thomas S. Monson and his leadership team came one day to discuss plans for the coming Regional Representatives seminar. Before leaving, the brethren administered to him. Elder Monson, who was to leave for Germany that night, pronounced the blessing to seal the anointing. "I awoke in the early morning hours," Elder Lee wrote the next day, "feeling that somehow I was being 'cleansed,' as nearly I could describe the feeling."

After the week at home, he reentered the hospital for more x-rays and tests. These revealed a large stone in the left kidney. At this point a specialist, Dr. Hal Bourne, was brought into the picture to help determine what to do. This led to the decision to remove the stone by surgery, it being too large to remove by other means. At 5:00 A.M., September 22, an orderly came to Elder Lee's room to prepare him for the operation. Always on duty, he responded to the orderly, who plied him "with many questions and particularly as to how he could keep himself free from the temptations of Satan." Following the surgery, which proved to be successful, the patient was in intensive care for two days. During that time, he was visited by President N. Eldon Tanner and Elders Spencer W. Kimball, Marion G. Romney, and Thomas S. Monson, who wanted counsel about work he had shifted to them. "While somewhat tiring," noted he, "I felt mentally alive as I tried to respond with such counsel and direction as I was able to give." We gain understanding about his interior world at this time from a diary entry made September 25, 1969, a Thursday. Elder Lee remembered those attending the temple meeting who had prayed for him "as [he] struggled to rise above pain and discomfort and worrisome anxieties as to the ultimate results of this surgery."

During the next three weeks, these "worrisome anxieties" subsided as he convalesced and regained his strength. He was uplifted when on October 2 Elders Spencer W. Kimball and Thomas S. Monson came to report on the successful outcome of the Regional Representatives seminar.

It took more than a month for Elder Lee to recover from this surgery and its aftermath. By November 9, 1969, he seems to have regained his strength and was prepared to move forward. "I am now about ready," he wrote on that date, "to take my first steps into a full scale activity if I have not already achieved that in fact." Elder Lee then resumed his duties with a vigor and enthusiasm he had not shown for some time. The deadening weariness he had suffered for so long was gone, so were the splitting headaches. His renewed health at this time was fortuitous, for in two months a burden heavier than any he had borne before would be thrust upon him when, in January 1970, President Joseph Fielding Smith called him as the first counselor in the First Presidency.

Chapter Twenty-six

The Church in Transition

Transitions in the Church during the years from 1965 to 1970 matched those in the personal and family life of Elder Lee. In October 1965, President David O. McKay, faced with diminished physical strength and increased administrative burdens as the Church grew worldwide, called two additional counselors to help shoulder the load, Joseph Fielding Smith and Thorpe B. Isaacson. Since President Smith was not released from his duties in the Twelve, he had to share more of them with Elder Lee because of the new demands on his time that service in the First Presidency entailed. President Isaacson, whose wide and varied experience qualified him to counsel the prophet in business and educational matters, served effectively for only three months. On February 7, 1966, he suffered a massive stroke that severely impaired his speech and his ability to move about and to care for himself. From then until President McKay's death in January 1970, he was unable to render the service for which he had been called. Later, President McKay began to look to Elder Alvin R. Dyer for counsel as to the matters President Isaacson had handled, first unofficially and then officially when he was sustained as a counselor in the First Presidency at the April 1968 general conference. At that same conference, Elder Marion D. Hanks was sustained as an Assistant to the Twelve, and Elders Hartman Rector, Jr., and Loren C. Dunn were sustained as members of the First Council of the Seventy. Eighteen months later, Elder Marvin J. Ashton was sustained as an Assistant to the Twelve. There would be no other changes among the General Authorities of the Church until January 1970 following President McKay's death.

Meanwhile, there were significant changes among headquarters personnel below the General Authority level. These had to do mainly with staffing the three correlation committees and the four priesthood committees, and developing and implementing the concepts of Regional Representatives and the training committee. The first major change in the composition of the correlation committees occurred on March 13, 1965, when Elder Thomas S. Monson was appointed as the chairman of the adult correlation committee, replacing Elder Marion G. Romney, who continued as the chairman of the priesthood home teaching committee, assisted by Elder Boyd K. Packer.

The organization of the three correlation committees and the four priesthood committees effected major, far-reaching, changes in the administration of the Church. They were not implemented overnight. It took time and patience to put them into effect. So long had the auxiliaries been accustomed to preparing their own instructional materials that it was difficult and sometimes frustrating for them to go through the correlation process to get a new manual written and approved. And, if a General Authority, for instance, wanted a particular lesson included in a manual, he also had to go through correlation in the usual way and could no longer go directly to the auxiliary involved and request that it be inserted. This issue was joined in December 1965 when a ranking General Authority sought and obtained permission directly from President McKay

The Church in Transition

to have a special set of lessons prepared, bypassing the correlation process. Elder Lee protested vigorously, stating that were this procedure to be allowed, "We might as well close out correlation." The new and somewhat revolutionary procedure survived, of course, and in time became firmly established, accepted by all, and immune from indirect attack, as in this case.

As the correlation program was rolled out, with representatives of the four priesthood committees accompanying General Authorities to stake conferences to give instructions, there developed a perceived need to have a corps of teachers and trainers in the field, constantly on duty, to see that the policies and procedures adopted by the General Authorities were fully understood and implemented. The role of the Regional Representatives of the Twelve arose out of this perceived need. As the Brethren prayerfully considered the creation of such an office, they were careful to define the scope of the authority of a Regional Representative. He was not to be an officer in the priesthood line but was to serve merely in a staff capacity, teaching and training local leaders in matters as directed by the Twelve. Regional Representatives were to serve without compensation for a period of years. Concurrent with this development emerged the need for a training committee whose role would be to help structure training seminars for the Regional Representatives and instructional programs to be taken into the field as part of stake or regional conferences.

By July 1967, final decisions had been made about the role of the Regional Representatives and steps were being taken to identify, call, and train them. "Spent today reviewing brethren to be appointed as regional representatives," wrote Elder Lee on July 7. "This is a laborious task, but of vital importance to see, if possible, that the most qualified are put in their positions to teach other leaders to be effective to the utmost of their ability. I was delighted as I became aware of the splendid leadership available to us now." As the process of identifying the Regional Representatives went forward, Elder Lee was working behind the scenes with Elder Thomas S. Monson about plans for the training committee. On August 9, they and other members of the correlation executive committee met with the First Presidency in President McKay's Hotel Utah apartment, where the plans for training the Regional Representatives were approved. Also, "the names of proposed regional representatives were approved, with few exceptions." Afterward, Neal A. Maxwell, a future member of the Twelve, and Wendell J. Ashton, a future publisher of the *Deseret News* and mission president in England, were appointed to work with Elder Monson on the training committee.

Between this date and September 27, 1967, when the first meetings with Regional Representatives were held, all those identified and approved were called to serve and detailed plans for their training had been developed by Elder Monson and his committee. The day before these first meetings with the Regional Representatives were held, Elder Lee met with Elder Monson and his committee to make certain everything was in readiness. Wrote Elder Lee of this meeting: "Thomas S. Monson and his associates, Neal A. Maxwell and Wendell Ashton, have done a tremendous job in expediting and planning for all the details."

The first training sessions for Regional Representatives on the twenty-seventh were held in the Seventeenth Ward chapel located on First North near West Temple. Elder Lee spoke for an hour and a half, presenting an overview of the correlation program and outlining the duties of the Regional Representatives. Afterward, he introduced the sixty-nine men who had been selected to serve in this new office. During the next two days, additional meetings were held with these men, including a devotional session in the temple under the direction of the First Presidency where all the other General Authorities were also present. "Our meetings in the Seventeenth Ward," wrote Elder Lee, "were wonderfully developed according to an outlined plan. I was particularly blessed in closing instructions on the subject 'How to use the Scriptures in our Teaching.' " Friday night, the twenty-ninth, a dinner was held for the General Authorities, Regional Representatives, and correlation workers and their companions. At the general priesthood meeting Saturday evening, Elder Lee presented "the new regional representatives program" in a forty-five minute address, and the day after the conference ended, a final question-and-answer session was held with these new leaders.

Thus was formally launched one of the most significant changes in Church administration during the twentieth century. It provided an effective means for training and supervising local leaders as the Church expanded and intensified its global operations. It demonstrated the flexible yet unchangeable nature of the Church organization with these new officers being engrafted on the basic Church structure to help the Quorum of the Twelve Apostles to discharge its responsibility of supervising and setting in order the affairs of the Church around the world. While many people were involved in formulating and launching this far-reaching initiative, and while it all was done under the authority and the direction of the prophet, it is clear that the most conspicuous contributor to the event was Elder Harold B. Lee. It was something he had anticipated and sought for since almost the inception of his apostolic career. His intricate knowledge of Church administration at the ward, stake, and mission level soon made it apparent, after his induction into the Twelve, that an organizational change such as this would be essential as the Church expanded worldwide. That vision became a reality because of his inherent skills in organizing and motivating people, skills which were honed by his world travels in the interests of the Church, by his association with distinguished business and professional leaders, and because of his tenacity and discipline. Given the numerous delays, setbacks, and reversals that occurred along the road leading to a correlated church, the role played by Elder Lee was not for one of faint heart or weak will. Nor was it for one easily deterred by opposition or criticism. As one reflects on what occurred in bringing correlation into being, the conclusion seems inescapable that the key player, Elder Harold B. Lee, was raised up by the Lord and placed in circumstances where his character, skill, and intelligence coalesced to produce this extraordinary result.

A year after the Regional Representatives were put in place, the training committee was enlarged by the addition of James E. Faust and Hugh W. Pinnock. At the same time, Antone Romney, J. Thomas Fyans, and Doyle L. Green were called on by Elder Lee to consider and to make recommendations about the mechanics of preparing and distributing instructional materials.

It is interesting and significant how several of those who worked closely with Elder Lee in correlation during this period later became General Authorities of the Church: James E. Faust and Neal A. Maxwell were ultimately inducted into the Twelve, and J. Thomas Fyans and Hugh W. Pinnock became presidents of the Seventy. Also, during the period correlation became established, Elder Lee was exposed to other leaders who, in the years ahead, were added to the ranks of the General Authorities. So, in June 1965, when Elder Lee reorganized the presidency of the Los Angeles Stake, a promising young attorney, John Carmack, who later became a Seventy, was sustained as a counselor in the stake presidency. During a period of nine months, in 1968 and 1969, Elder Lee installed three men as stake presidents who also later became members of the Seventy: Waldo Pratt Call, installed as the president of the Juarez Stake in November 1968; Devere Harris, installed as the president of the Malad Idaho Stake in June 1969; and J. Ballard Washburn, installed as the president of the Kanab Utah Stake in August 1969. Three months after installing J. Ballard Washburn in Kanab, Elder Lee attended the conference of the Midvale Stake in company with Regional Representative Rex C. Reeve, Sr., of whom he wrote: "Rex added a great spiritual tone to the meeting." A few years later, Elder Reeve also was called as a member of the Seventy.

A week after the Midvale stake conference, Elder Lee and Elder Marion D. Hanks met with a group of young adults packed into the Salt Lake Tabernacle. "This was one of the most responsive audiences I have ever faced," he reported. Two weeks later, Elder Lee and Elder Hanks met with student association leaders from all over the United States. The meeting was held at the institute of religion near the campus of the University of Utah. Elder Lee spoke for forty-five minutes at the end of the meeting, bearing his testimony and sharing some choice spiritual experiences. From the report of the meeting, there was an almost electric feeling among the audience as he finished speaking. The closing song was "I Walked Today Where Jesus Walked," followed by a benediction. "As the meeting closed," Elder Lee wrote, "no one moved to leave, so great was the spirit, until after several minutes. When we arose to leave the chapel, someone commenced to sing 'The Spirit of God Like a Fire is Burning.' Many were in tears. Marion D. Hanks said 'This is a night those present will never forget. Nor will I.' It has been the greatest spiritual experience I have ever had, also." Some of those present were heard to say that the mantle of the prophet fell on Elder Lee at the time. That would not actually occur for two and a half years. But, the following month, he would be called into the First Presidency, which would be an important prelude to his call as the president of the Church.

This meeting was held during a time of considerable upset in the Church. Not long before, the administration of Stanford University had announced that it would no longer schedule athletic events with Brigham Young University because of the Church's policy against conferring the priesthood on blacks. This touched off another round of debates as to whether this policy was based on principle or was merely a practice. This was really nothing new because that issue had been debated for many years. The debate heated up following President McKay's visit to

South America in 1954 when it was reported he had said that the policy was based on a practice. This doubtless arose from a misinterpretation of a change made at that time in the procedure for issuing temple recommends. Under the changed procedure, an applicant was deemed qualified to receive a temple recommend if he met the worthiness standards and if there was no positive evidence of disqualification due to lineage. Moreover, in the early 1960s when pressures were exerted by blacks in West Africa that the Church proselyte there, President McKay affirmed that the policy as to priesthood would change only if it were based on revelation from God. In this posture, the flap within the Church, which followed the announcement of Stanford's policy, would have died soon had it not been for an article that appeared in the *San Francisco Chronicle* a few days before Christmas 1969. That article quoted President Hugh B. Brown as saying that the Church policy on priesthood would "change in the not too distant future." The *Salt Lake Tribune* picked the story up and published it on Christmas Day. Because the news accounts were garbled and incomplete, a letter was sent to priesthood leaders, reaffirming the Church policy on priesthood. Again, that ordinarily would have ended the matter as to the Church's position had not the *Tribune* reported in its January 1, 1970, issue that this statement to Church leaders had been "sent out by Elder Harold B. Lee." Because of the thoroughly confused status of the record at this point, the Brethren decided that the statement to priesthood leaders, reaffirming the Church policy on priesthood, signed by the First Presidency, be published in its entirety in the *Deseret News*. This was done on January 10, 1970. The publication of this letter settled the question about the Church's current position on blacks and the priesthood. Unsettled, however, was the external turmoil that had been stirred up by the Stanford policy. And, as we shall see, that turmoil, with all its ramifications, would snowball in the weeks ahead, creating one of the major problems to face the administration of President Joseph Fielding Smith.

Chapter Twenty-seven

Counselor in the First Presidency

The publication of the statement on priesthood occurred only eight days before President David O. McKay passed away on Sunday, January 18, 1970, at age ninety-six. He had been ailing for some time, having suffered a series of mild strokes in recent years. However, with the assistance of the additional counselors he had called, the members of the Twelve, his staff, members of his family, and others, he had been able to carry on effectively despite his advanced age. He died in the early morning hours of that day. "At 6:00 A.M., I had a call from the wife of Joseph Fielding Smith," Elder Lee wrote on that day, "to tell me that President David O. McKay had just passed away and that the president wanted me to meet him at the Hotel Utah [where the prophet had died in his apartment] as soon as possible." Arriving there soon after, Elder Lee found President Smith and all of President McKay's family, except son Llewelyn, who had recently suffered a stroke, and daughter Lou Jean, who was in Chicago. After counselling with the family for two hours, it was decided to hold the funeral the following

Thursday, and the general outline of the services was agreed upon. The next day, the Twelve met when Elder Lee was appointed to chair the committee on arrangements for the funeral with Elders Spencer W. Kimball, Ezra Taft Benson, and N. Eldon Tanner as members.

On the day before President McKay's funeral, President Smith visited Elder Lee in his office. He said that if, in the natural course of events, he became the head of the Church, he wanted Elder Lee "by his side."

When the Smiths left his office, Elder Lee realized that if what President Smith had proposed materialized, he would become both a counselor in the First Presidency and the president of the Quorum of the Twelve Apostles. These reflections "brought an overwhelming sense of obligation and responsibility," wrote Elder Lee, "which could not be assumed, except by the Lord's help."

Before the funeral, President McKay's body lay in state in the main foyer of the Church Administration Building as thousands, both members and friends of the Church, filed by his casket. Elder Lee was amazed by this show of respect for the great man. "As I look out of my windows," wrote he, "I see thousands lined up all the way down to Main Street, all the way around the block, in order to get a glimpse of the president."

Because of the worldwide commitments and holdings of the Church, it was important that there be no unnecessary delay in reorganizing the First Presidency. So, the members of the Twelve, which at this point also included President McKay's former counselors, Hugh B. Brown and N. Eldon Tanner, met in the upper room of the Salt Lake Temple on January 23, 1970, for this purpose. "There was an air of expectancy and some tension," wrote Elder Lee, "as each spoke, beginning with the junior member of the Twelve," who at the time was Elder Thomas S. Monson. When it was his turn, Elder Lee, conscious of the rumors Joseph Fielding Smith's wife Jessie had heard, read a letter Wilford Woodruff had written to Heber J. Grant following the death of President John Taylor. The letter was prompted by "rumors" that an effort might be made to bypass Wilford Woodruff, who was then the president of the Quorum of the Twelve, in favor of a younger man. The letter merely affirmed the principle, already mentioned, that at the death of a president of the Church, the president of the Twelve simultaneously becomes the "acting" president of the Church and that under well established principles of priesthood leadership, nothing would be done without his approval and authorization. After reading this letter, Elder Lee moved that Joseph Fielding Smith be named as the president of the Church. Elder Spencer W. Kimball seconded the motion, which was carried unanimously. With all the apostles present joining, and with Elder Lee acting as voice, Joseph Fielding Smith was then ordained and set apart as the president—the prophet, seer, and revelator—and the trustee-in-trust of The Church of Jesus Christ of Latter-day Saints. President Smith then named Harold B. Lee and N. Eldon Tanner as his first and second counselors, respectively, who, being approved by the council, were set apart. During the same meeting, Elder Lee was sustained and set apart as the president of the Quorum of the Twelve Apostles and Elder Spencer W. Kimball was sustained and set apart as the acting president of the quorum. "The following day," wrote Elder Lee, "a press conference was conducted in the church [administration] building where about twenty men and one woman representing all the news, radio and TV networks were permitted, for an hour, to record our answers to written questions which had been previously submitted."

With these formalities behind them, the new First Presidency was prepared to move forward toward goals that had not yet been clearly defined. They had entered office with the avowed purpose of being directed by the spiritual promptings that would come to them. In this, they recognized their subordinate role to the one who is the actual head of the Church that bears His name.

At the outset, there were various organizational matters to handle. As among themselves, it was decided that temple and related matters would be directly under President Smith, assisted by President Lee. Other administrative matters at the First Presidency level were delegated to the counselors, subject to overview and to any necessary revisions by the prophet. President Lee's chief responsibilities were to be in education, budgeting, finance (shared with President Tanner), management systems (computer technology), and communications (KSL radio and TV, Bonneville International Corporation, and *Deseret News*). Also, he was to have executive responsibilities in certain Church-owned or controlled corporations: Zions Securities Corporation, ZCMI, Utah Idaho Sugar Company, Hotel Utah, Beneficial Life, Deseret Book Company, and Deseret Management Corporation, a holding company. In addition, Elder Lee would be the first contact in the First Presidency for the Primary and Relief Society auxiliaries, Church personnel, and Church correlation. These responsibilities were in addition to those in corporations not controlled by the Church: Union Pacific, Equitable Life, and Zions First National Bank.

Because the First Presidency met together several times each week, there was ample opportunity for President Smith to receive the reports of his counselors and to give any necessary advice or direction. Because of the confidence he had in them, the prophet gave his counselors wide latitude to function in the matters over which they had been given responsibility.

At the moment, correlation was the work for which President Lee had the greatest concern. While the mechanism was working satisfactorily, especially since the Regional Representatives had been put in place, there still was a need for constant surveillance and follow through. Elder Thomas S. Monson became the principal one upon whom President Lee depended "for attending to the many details of the total correlation effort." As a means of educating and motivating all the General Authorities in correlation principles and procedures, President Lee soon began to invite various correlation workers to the monthly meetings of all General Authorities in the upper room of the Salt Lake Temple, to explain various aspects of the work. Moreover, President Lee took advantage of every opportunity to explain correlation principles, whether in small, private gatherings or in public meetings, a technique he had learned well during the years Church welfare became established as one of the foundational organizations of the Church.

A major concern that faced the new First Presidency grew out of the Church's policy on priesthood. The Stanford action was only one manifestation of the problems it created. There were others. On February 5, 1970, there was a near riot at a basketball game in Fort Collins, Colorado, between Brigham Young University and Colorado State University. It was triggered by a group of militant black students from CSU who used this means of protesting the Mormon Church's policy on priesthood. These militants were permitted to offer an invocation before the game, which was little more than a broad indictment of the Church. There also was an overt show of protest during the warm-ups when a group of blacks massed beneath the BYU basket, shouting threats at the players. At halftime vulgar insults were made against the BYU Cougarettes and the players, eggs were thrown onto the playing floor, and an iron object and a lighted torch were thrown toward the floor. Finally, fights broke out in the arena. Order was restored only when the city police were called in.

A few days after this incident in Fort Collins, a militant activist named Jerry Rubin, who was then under indictment for rioting in Chicago, spoke on the campus of the University of Utah in Salt Lake City. During his incendiary remarks, the speaker bitterly berated the Latter-day Saints, warning, "We will either integrate the Mormon Church, or we will destroy it." These incidents were symptomatic of broad-based attacks being made on the Church around the country by its enemies and detractors. Adding to the turmoil this created was the upheaval caused by America's involvement in the Vietnam War. At the time, a member of the Church, a Vietnam War veteran, had been speaking in Church meetings, "arousing people to fever pitch," according to President Lee, "with scare stories about impending doom."

In such a hostile environment, the Brethren began taking steps to provide necessary security. On February 14, the First Presidency met with the Presiding Bishopric to discuss "the need to provide sufficient security for the Church headquarters buildings." The next day, President Lee met with Salt Lake City Commissioner James Barker and other officials to discuss the coordination between Church security personnel and the city police in handling any emergencies that might arise.

At this time, the Church was ill-prepared to guard against the kind of assault that the rhetoric of the militants threatened. There was not so much as a receptionist in the outer foyer of the Church Administration Building. Anyone, regardless of his intentions, could enter the building and roam at will. The only physical protection the General Authorities had against an intruder was the shield of their secretaries, most of whom were women. The Church's security force at the time consisted of a few men, practically all of whom lacked professional security training, and some of whom were little more than night watchmen. The unsettled times demanded more than this. So, beginning with the meeting on February 14, the Presiding Bishopric, who had the main responsibility for security, began to take positive steps to make the headquarters secure and to provide necessary protection for the Brethren, especially the president. It was the philosophy of the First Presidency that if they did all within their power to provide adequate security, the Lord would intervene to provide any protection, the need for which their ingenuity did not foresee. "If ye are prepared, ye shall not fear," was a scripture President Lee was heard to quote occasionally during this period.

The preparations made were extensive. Many meetings

were held with the Presiding Bishopric to review and to discuss their proposals. Two weeks after the Presiding Bishopric were first charged with the responsibility, they met with the First Presidency "about plans for improved security against possible riots from enemies from the outside and from Judases within the church." Soon, the size of the security force was augmented with men who had had professional training in law enforcement work. Television scanners were placed in strategic places in the Church headquarters buildings, and security personnel were equipped with communication devices. Also, a male receptionist, who was part of the security force, was positioned in the front foyer of the Church Administration Building to screen out those who did not have a legitimate reason for being there. In not too long a time, riot-proof glass was installed in the windows on the main floor of the administration building to guard against the kind of violence that had flared up in Fort Collins and in the civil upheavals spawned by opposition to the Vietnam War.

Meanwhile, President Lee took steps to try to forestall, or to minimize, opposition to the Church arising from a misunderstanding of its teachings or objectives. In a word, he sought to put the Church on the offensive in the arena of public opinion. He felt that for too long the Church had merely reacted to news events, or had silently watched emerging groundswells of anti-Mormon sentiment, without any effort to stop or to mitigate them. In this effort, one of the most significant of his long and distinguished career, President Lee brought into play all of the skills and know-how he had accumulated over the years as a Church leader at the local and general levels, as a teacher, as a politician, as a strategist in developing and executing plans for Church welfare and correlation, and as a high official in charting the course of major corporations.

He launched this initiative on February 18, 1970, a month after President McKay's death, while he was in New York City to attend an Equitable Life board meeting. His diary entry of that date best explains what happened and why. "We had a two and a half hour meeting in a committee room at the Waldorf with Spencer W. Kimball, Ezra Taft Benson, Richard L. Evans, Gordon B. Hinckley, Bob Barker, Lee Bickmore, George Mortimer, G. Stanley McAlister, Bob Sears, DeWitt Paul, Howard Wilkinson, and George Watkins. The purpose of the meeting was to seek counsel as to how the church could get the offensive position in public relations which, because of the negro priesthood issue, are at a low ebb." As we shall see, this meeting in the Waldorf was the formal genesis of the Church's department of public communications. Out of this also grew the idea of a department of internal communications, which was organized to simplify, expedite, and economize in the process of preparing and distributing Church instructional and other materials. This meeting also sheds important light on some of the special leadership qualities of Harold B. Lee. In the first place, he was never a one-man show. Rather, he served as a catalyst to bring together many people of talent and ability and to mold them into a team in which each played his essential role. In this process, he was meticulous in gathering the facts and in obtaining advice from the people most qualified to give it. All this was aimed toward the solution of a specific problem or the fulfillment of a vision he held. Finally, the objective, as refined by the team, was pursued with single-minded purpose, sometimes awesome in its intensity.

As noted, the objective sought in bringing this group together was to put the Church on the offensive as to public issues affecting it, rather than to react defensively. The composition of the group shows the care with which its members were selected, having in mind the objective sought. Elder Kimball, of course, was the acting president of the Twelve, and Elder Benson, who was next in seniority to him, had had vast experience in the nation's capital, first as the executive secretary of a national farm cooperative and then as a cabinet member. Elders Evans and Hinckley were members of the Church information committee. Perhaps more important, Elder Evans had been the voice of the Church on the weekly national Tabernacle Choir broadcasts for over forty years, and Elder Hinckley, as far back as the 1930s, had been heavily involved in directing radio and other media publicity for the Church. Robert Barker was an attorney from the prominent Washington law firm that represented the Church and Bonneville International Corporation on television, radio, and other media matters. Lee Bickmore was the chairman of the board of directors of the National Biscuit Company (Nabisco), a powerful international corporation. Robert Sears was the chief executive officer of Phillips Petroleum Company, and the other members of the group were prominent Latter-day Saint business and Church leaders. Out of this meeting came important suggestions, many of which would be incorporated in the final plans for the Church department of public communications, originally called the department of external communications and later called the department of public affairs.

The day after this historic meeting, President Lee accompanied President and Sister Kimball to a consultation with the cancer specialist, Dr. Martin, to discuss the need for further surgery or cobalt treatments for President Kimball. All were surprised and pleased when the doctor advised that neither would be necessary. As reported by President Lee, the doctor said that it was "just possible that Spencer could live out his years without any further surgery. He admitted that this decision defied all the rules of medical practice, but after considering all phases of the case, he was modifying his previous diagnosis and recommendations." As if to affirm the accuracy of the doctor's decision, President Kimball lived more than fifteen years afterward without the need for additional surgery or treatment on his throat, although he later underwent open-heart surgery and other surgeries.

While in New York on this occasion, President Lee also conferred with Lee Bickmore about the need for the Church to restructure its system in handling the translation and distribution of instructional and other materials around the world. It was felt that his involvement in the direction of a major international corporation better qualified Lee Bickmore for such a task. Moreover, he was nearing retirement from Nabisco, and it was believed he might be available to help the Church in this matter on a continuing basis in the future. He called President Lee on March 17 to advise that he was coming to Salt Lake City soon, as President Lee explained it, "to confer with our publicity and communications team to see if we can take the next step in moving to a coordination of public relations, communications, [and] publicity [with] translations, distribution, etc." He arrived on March 26, spending the day closeted with President Lee, members of the Church information committee, and others. Armed with organizational charts and data gleaned from his interviews, Lee Bickmore spent several months analyzing the organization of the Church at headquarters as it related to the matters discussed with President Lee on March 26. All recognized that an undertaking of this magnitude could not be accomplished overnight and that it would take time and prayerful consideration. After a year, during which he was in frequent contact with President Lee and others to obtain additional information, Lee Bickmore believed that a more in-depth analysis of the operation of the Church in these areas was necessary before meaningful recommendations could be made about organizational changes. He therefore suggested that the management consulting firm of Cresap, McCormick, and Paget Inc. be employed to make a detailed study. This suggestion was approved on March 14, 1971, when, according to President Lee, the firm was employed "to study several areas of the church to find the most accurate answers as to 'where we are now' in order to determine where 'we want to go from [here].'"

This decision posed an interesting question because the employees of the consulting firm were not members of the Church. This was not considered to be a serious problem, however, because the main focus of their study would be on the mechanical operation of the Church in the above-mentioned areas of interest and would have no real relevance to its strictly ecclesiastical or doctrinal aspects. In order to provide the members of the consulting team with some insight into the doctrinal foundation and the terminology of the Church, they were asked to study the Doctrine and Covenants before beginning their work.

The consulting team was at work for five months. During that time, its members were authorized to confer with anyone at Church headquarters, including the General Authorities. Their reports were submitted on August 11, 1971. "These reports," President Lee noted on that day, "will now be placed in the hands of Lee Bickmore and his committee to come back with recommendations."

Meanwhile, three key new members had been added to the Bickmore committee: James Conkling, an executive with Columbia Records; Roy Fugal, an executive with General Electric; and Ren Hoopes, an executive with Safeway Stores, whose expertise was in industrial engineering, know-how that would be vital in restructuring the Church's worldwide distribution system. As the members of the Bickmore committee analyzed the reports of the consulting firm in the light of their own intimate knowledge of Church doctrine and procedure, they recommended the creation of the departments of internal communications and external communications, the first to embrace the operations dealing with the translation and distribution of instructional and other materials internationally, and the second to deal with communications of the Church to the outside world through the public media and by other means.

In due course, the First Presidency approved the recommendations of the Bickmore committee, with necessary revisions. Then followed an interesting turn of events when it was decided to put the department of internal communications in place first. It was interesting because the concern about public communications first prompted President Lee to bring Lee Bickmore and the others together in New York in February 1970 to consider how the Church could go on the offensive in public relations matters. Consideration of restructuring the procedure in handling translations and distributions came as an aftermath. The apparent reason for this order of things was the ever-mounting pressure to solve the translation and distribution problem as the Church population grew worldwide, extending into countries with different languages and cultural patterns. On the other hand, the Church information service had already begun to take steps to stem the tide of anti-Mormon rhetoric in the public arena so that the formal organization of the department of external or public communications could be delayed without undue concern.

On November 13, 1971, Lee Bickmore, Ren Hoopes, G. Roy Fugal, and James Conkling spent all day in Salt Lake City interviewing men who might be used in the department of internal communications. They had narrowed the number to seven who were discussed the following day with President Lee and other General Authorities. Out of this and other discussions, J. Thomas Fyans was selected to head this new department. During the following weeks he, in consultation with President Lee and members of the Bickmore committee, selected his team, which was approved on January 4, 1972: James Paramore, administrative services; Daniel Ludlow, instructional materials; Doyle Green, editorial matters; and John Carr, translation. "They were all called," wrote President Lee on that date, "and undertook their duties under the direction of Lee Bickmore and Ren Hoopes." Nine days later, this organization was approved by all the General Authorities, when it was explained that the head of the department "would report through a committee of the Twelve comprised of Gordon B. Hinckley, Thomas S. Monson and Boyd K. Packer."

Six months later, the department of public communications was formally brought into being. On June 3, 1972, Lee Bickmore came to Salt Lake City to discuss candidates for the position of director of public communications. Wendell J. Ashton, executive in a Salt Lake based advertising and public relations firm, was selected to fill this position. "The position," wrote President Lee on June 5, "requires one in whom we can place complete confidence and loyalty and one who has the organizing ability to make his place and also has the natural ability to greatly improve public relations and to communicate appropriately whenever the occasion requires."

Thus, twenty-eight months after President Lee held his historic meeting in New York with Lee Bickmore and the others, the final step had been taken to set in motion the mechanism that would enable the Church to respond affirmatively and promptly to public issues facing it, and to anticipate and to respond to issues detrimental to it. In the meantime, growing out of that initiative had come another organization that would be vital as the Church expanded explosively throughout the world. In the years ahead, there would be changes in the structure, the personnel, and the nomenclature of the departments of internal and external communications, but the basic concepts developed in their inception would continue to apply.

There was an important spin-off from all this. The Cresap report revealed that many members of the Twelve were directly involved in administrative work at Church headquarters, a fact about which President Lee and the Brethren, of course, were already aware. This was inconsistent with their scriptural role, which invests them with broad responsibility on a global basis. So, steps were taken at this time to relieve the Twelve of direct administrative responsibility. "Spent some time," wrote President Lee on November 25, 1971, "in putting together an outline . . . restructuring the work of the Twelve, particularly in defining the staff and administrator roles of the assistants and the seventy." He worked on this during a period of four days, preparing a draft "which could be a beginning of a major overhauling of the administrative functions of the brethren." President Lee went on to explain that "some of this was a composite of ideas and suggestions from some of the brethren and from the Cresap consultants recommendations."

As part of this, Elder Howard W. Hunter was released as the Church historian, and to replace him, Elder Alvin R. Dyer, Assistant to the Twelve, was appointed as the managing director of the historical department. Under Elder Dyer, Leonard Arrington was appointed as historian and Earl Olsen as archivist. Then, establishing the "reporting through" concept, Elder Hunter was designated as the member of the Twelve through whom Elder Dyer was to report the work of his department. In like manner, Elder Theodore M. Burton, Assistant to the Twelve, was appointed as the president and managing director of the genealogical society, with Elder Hunter as the member of the Twelve through whom he would report. Changes such as these relieved the members of the Twelve of the entanglements of headquarters administrative assignments and left them free to discharge their worldwide responsibilities and to counsel with and to assist the First Presidency.

Concurrent with the changes affecting the administrative responsibilities of the Twelve, there were significant changes made in the responsibilities of the First Council of the Seventy. At a meeting of the First Presidency and the Twelve on January 13, 1972, approval was given, in concept, to the creation of a corps of officers to be known as Regional Representatives of the Twelve and the First Council of the Seventy. The matter was turned over to the Twelve for further study and recommendations. The Twelve submitted its report on March 16, 1972. It included these recommendations, which were approved: That these new Regional Representatives be appointed, effective the following June; that they serve chiefly under the direction of the First Council of the Seventy; that their main responsibility would be to give training and motivation in proselyting work in the missions; and that they also would have authority to give counsel in administrative matters in mission districts. The Regional Representatives of the Twelve were also authorized at this time to give counsel in administrative matters in mission districts where circumstances made this necessary or desirable.

At the same time, the work of the First Council of the Seventy was restructured. Elders S. Dilworth Young and Milton R. Hunter were assigned to handle quorum administrative matters; Elders Bruce R. McConkie, A. Theodore Tuttle, and Loren C. Dunn were given responsibility to work with the Regional Representatives of the Twelve and the First Council of the Seventy in training and motivating the full-time missionaries; and Elders Paul Dunn and Hartman Rector, Jr., were appointed to work with stake missionaries.

Along with these matters, other significant changes in organization and procedure took place during this period. In the summer of 1970, a program for teacher training, spearheaded by Rex Skidmore, was initiated. This resulted in a teacher training manual and a procedure followed throughout the Church to implement its instructions. At about the same time, there was a major restructuring of the Church magazines, which consolidated them all into a unified system of only three: the *Ensign*, the *New Era*, and the *Friend*. At the same time, paid advertising in the Church publications was discontinued. And a significant initiative was undertaken in 1970 when, under the direction of Doctor James Mason, a program to enlist LDS doctors and nurses in health services missions to deprived areas was commenced. On January 15, 1971, President Lee reported having heard a "thrilling" report from Doctor Mason about how doctors and nurses were being organized "on a church service basis to provide medical assistance in different countries around the world."

Shortly before Dr. Mason was called into service, Neal A. Maxwell, a future member of the Twelve, was appointed as the church commissioner of education. This initiated a series of major changes in the educational structure of the Church, including the following: In August 1970, Harvey L. Taylor and William E. Berrett retired, having served, respectively, as administrator of Church schools and administrator of seminaries and institutes. The following month, Joe J. Christensen, a future Seventy, who was then serving as a mission president in Mexico, was appointed associate commissioner of education for seminaries and institutes. Four months later, Henry B. Eyring, a future counselor in the Presiding Bishopric, was appointed president of Ricks College, and Steve Brower was appointed president of BYU Hawaii. These appointments were followed, a few weeks later, with the appointment of Dallin H. Oaks as the president of Brigham Young University, replacing Ernest L. Wilkinson. In October of that year, when the J. Reuben Clark Law School was created, Rex E. Lee, a future president of BYU, was appointed as its first dean.

Two other major organizational changes occurred during the time President Lee served as a counselor in the First Presidency. In June 1971, Russell M. Nelson replaced David Lawrence McKay as the general superintendent of the Sunday Schools of the Church. At the time, Doctor Nelson, who, along with Dallin H. Oaks, also later became a member of the Twelve, was then serving as the president of the Salt Lake Bonneville Stake. He was released as stake president the following month, being replaced by Francis M. Gibbons, the secretary to the First Presidency and a future Seventy.

The other major organizational change occurred in January 1972, when the department of church physical facilities was created. This new department combined the functions of the old building, real estate, and maintenance divisions. John H. Vandenberg, who was then the Presiding Bishop of the Church, was appointed as the first head of this new department following his call as an Assistant to the Twelve in April 1972.

Elder Vandenberg's release as the Presiding Bishop, and his simultaneous call as an Assistant to the Twelve, was only one of several changes made in the General Authorities of the Church during President Lee's tenure as a counselor in the First Presidency. At the Solemn Assembly on April 6, 1970, when President Joseph Fielding Smith and his counselors were formally sustained, Elder Boyd K. Packer was sustained as a member of the Twelve. He filled the vacancy created when President Lee was called to the First Presidency. Before this call, Elder Packer had served as an Assistant to the Twelve for eight and a half years, during which time he had also served as a mission president. At the time of his call to the Twelve, Elder Packer, who holds an Ed.D. in educational administration, was the only man among the council of the First Presidency and Quorum of the Twelve, other than President Lee, who was a professional educator. He was prophetically chosen for this position by President Smith from a long list of able and qualified men, whose names had been submitted at the prophet's request. Concurrent with Elder Packer's call to the Twelve, Elders Thorpe B. Isaacson and Alvin R. Dyer, who had served as counselors to President David O. McKay, were returned to their previously held positions as Assistants to the Twelve. Although Elder Dyer had been ordained to the apostleship, he had never been inducted into the Twelve, which accounts for his reassignment as an Assistant to the Twelve.

The ranks of Assistants to the Twelve were also augmented at this time by the addition of Elders Joseph Anderson, David B. Haight, and William H. Bennett. Elder Anderson, who was eighty years old at the time, had served for almost fifty years as the secretary to the First Presidency when he was called as a General Authority. In the blessing setting him apart, President Lee, who was voice in the blessing, said, in part: "Joseph is like unto Moses of old; his eye shall never be dimmed nor his natural force abated." Joseph Anderson lived to be a hundred and two years old. He walked daily, weather permitting. His mind was clear and precise. He spoke without repetition. On his hundredth birthday, when he was honored by his brethren of the General Authorities, he said, after he had been praised and lauded: "Brethren, I will remember this day for the rest of my life." He passed away in March 1992.

Elder David B. Haight, who would later be called to the Twelve, had served as a stake president, mission president, Regional Representative, and assistant to the president of the Brigham Young University before his call as a General Authority. He had also been a successful businessman in Palo Alto, California, having once served as the mayor of that city. Elder William H. Bennett was a well-known, admired, and accomplished university professor before his call as an Assistant to the Twelve.

The ranks of the General Authorities remained unchanged, following the Solemn Assembly in April 1970, until October 30, 1971, when Elder Richard L. Evans unexpectedly passed away. His death was a shock as he had been actively engaged in his work until only a few days prior to his passing. His loss was especially felt by President Lee since Elder Evans was playing a key role in structuring the new departments of internal and external communications. As already noted, these departments were put in place only a few months after Elder Evans died. His passing was a grievous loss, not only to his family and his associates among the General Authorities, but to the entire Church and to a host of others who were not members of the Church. Through his weekly sermonettes, given in conjunction with the Tabernacle Choir broadcasts, he had become known to a wide audience, including many who were not members of the Church, some of whom regarded him as their spiritual pastor. He would also be missed by Rotarians around the world whom he had once served as their international president.

The vacancy in the Twelve created by Elder Evans's death was filled on December 2, 1971, by the call and ordination of Elder Marvin J. Ashton, who at the time was serving as an Assistant to the Twelve. A former Utah State Senator and prominent Salt Lake businessman, Elder Ashton was serving as the managing director of the Church social services department at the time of his call to the Twelve.

Elder Ashton was formally sustained as a member of

the Twelve at the general conference in April 1972. As already indicated, at that time, John H. Vandenberg was released as the Presiding Bishop and then was sustained as an Assistant to the Twelve. His release as the Presiding Bishop entailed a reorganization of the Presiding Bishopric. Sustained to replace him as the Presiding Bishop was Victor L. Brown, who had served as Bishop Vandenberg's second counselor. Sustained as Bishop Brown's counselors were H. Burke Peterson and Vaughn J. Featherstone. Bishop Robert L. Simpson, who had served as Bishop Vandenberg's first counselor, was also sustained as an Assistant to the Twelve.

Amidst the development of the departments of internal and public communications and the changes among the General Authorities and the general auxiliaries of the Church, there was much else to occupy President Lee during the time he served as a counselor to President Joseph Fielding Smith. While, as a member of the First Presidency, he no longer filled regular stake conference assignments, as he had done for almost thirty years as a member of the Twelve, he found that this slack was more than taken up by other special speaking assignments. He soon was inundated with invitations to speak. "There has been an avalanche of speaking requests," he wrote on April 19, 1970, "[from the] University of Utah, Ricks College, Dixie Junior College, College of Southern Utah, Denver Convocation, Cambridge, Massachusetts fireside, University of Utah stake banquet, etc. etc. Of necessity, I am forced to turn down many of these in order to preserve my strength for the 'must' requirements." Do we detect a sign of bias in the fact that out of these invitations to speak, the only one President Lee accepted took him to Idaho? On May 6, 1970, he delivered the baccalaureate address at Ricks College in Rexburg, where 879 graduates gathered to receive counsel from one of Idaho's most distinguished sons. He and Joan left Salt Lake on the fourth, stopping in Logan, Utah, where, in the evening, he spoke to three hundred workers gathered in the temple. The following day, in the verdure of a burgeoning spring, they drove, in a leisurely way, through the upper Cache Valley, past the little towns so important to President Lee—Franklin, Preston, and of course, Clifton. This was his first trip back "home" since his call to the First Presidency. A few weeks later, President Lee performed a similar service at the Utah State University when he spoke at the baccalaureate services there. While this was not in Idaho, it was pretty close. Moreover, it was in Cache Valley, the northern part of which lay within Idaho. It does not seem to be happenstance that of the many invitations he received to speak at college functions after he became a member of the First Presidency, the first he accepted were at Rexburg, Idaho, and at Utah State University at Logan, Utah, which people from Clifton and Preston naturally consider to be an extension of Idaho.

There is no doubt that President Lee dearly loved and was partial to Idaho and Cache Valley. He never returned there but that he made favorable comments about the visit and mentioned old friends with whom he had renewed acquaintance. His special feelings about Logan centered around the temple there, the place where his parents had been sealed together as man and wife and where he had received his endowment before going into the mission field.

It is interesting, perhaps significant, that the meeting he held with the Logan temple workers en route to the baccalaureate services at Ricks College was the first special meeting he had held in a temple after becoming a member of the First Presidency. And a survey of his service as a counselor in the First Presidency reveals that one of his principal interests and activities during that period related to the temples. Though now a member of the First Presidency, President Lee continued to meet regularly with the newly called missionaries in the Salt Lake Temple as he had done over the years while a member of the Twelve. He would do this until within a few days of his death. He was always uplifted by his contact with these energetic

Counselor in the First Presidency

and inquisitive young people, and a session with them was always memorable, especially when one of his own was involved. So, May 3, 1971, was golden because among the outgoing missionaries was President Lee's number-five grandson, Lesley Drew Goates, who had been called to the Australia East Mission.

Soon after the new First Presidency was sustained in April 1970, steps were taken toward the construction of new temples in Ogden and Provo, Utah. In addition to the usual details of site acquisition and preparation and the architectural drawings, special arrangements were necessary to obtain and install the sophisticated equipment necessary to present the endowment on film. These two temples would be the first in the state of Utah to use endowment films. For this purpose, Armis J. Ashby was approved by the First Presidency on August 19, 1970, to work with the architects and builders of these two temples. A few weeks later, fifteen General Authorities and their wives travelled to Ogden for special cornerstone laying ceremonies. Some local members had questioned the location of the site for this temple, which was on the west side of the downtown business district in a neighborhood that was frayed at the edges. These questioners believed the temple should have been constructed on an eminence on the east side of the city where it could be seen from around the valley. The First Presidency, however, promised that the site selected by inspiration would prove to be an even greater blessing to the community by completely changing the ambience of the downtown area and thereby improving the cultural climate of the entire city, a promise which the passing of time has proven to be true. Only a week before the cornerstone laying exercises in Ogden, President Lee had accompanied President Smith to Mesa, Arizona, where the temple presidency was reorganized. Bryant Whiting, a member of a prominent pioneer family in Arizona, was installed as the new temple president, replacing President J. M. Smith. And in early November 1970, the First Presidency travelled to St.

George, Utah, where the presidency of that temple also was reorganized. A year later, in November 1971, a special Solemn Assembly was held in the upper room of the St. George Temple. The First Presidency and other General Authorities travelled there by chartered bus, stopping at Provo en route to attend the inauguration of Dallin H. Oaks as the president of the Brigham Young University. A dinner was served to the visiting brethren in a ward cultural hall on Friday, November 12, and the next morning, they met in the temple with more than a thousand local priesthood leaders from the stakes and wards in the St. George Temple district. After the sacrament had been administered to and passed by the General Authorities, several members of the Twelve were called on to discuss topics of current interest and concern, including gambling, racing, liquor by the drink, apostate sects, disciplinary procedures, and the need for family solidarity. President Lee then instructed the Brethren about temple ordinances and procedures, emphasizing the sacred nature of the building and the need to preserve its sanctity by carefully interviewing those seeking temple recommends. President Smith capped the meeting, reviewing salient historical facts about the temple, the first one in the West, which had been dedicated in 1877. He occasionally said, facetiously, that attending the St. George Temple dedication was his first Church "assignment," as he had been taken there as a babe in arms by his parents.

Meanwhile, the Ogden and Provo temples were ready for formal dedication by early 1972, the cornerstone laying ceremony for the Provo Temple having been conducted on May 21, 1971. The first of six dedicatory sessions for the Ogden Temple held over a three-day period was on Tuesday, January 18, 1972, the second anniversary of the death of President David O. McKay. When, after reading two-thirds of his dedicatory prayer, President Smith became weak from standing so long, President Lee finished reading it. President Lee also spoke at this session and led in the Hosanna Shout. A sweet, spiritual feeling pervaded all the sessions, which were attended by members who filled the celestial room of the temple, and all of its other rooms, as well as the nearby stake tabernacle, to which the proceedings were carried by television. The reports of the spiritual impact of the dedication were typified by the one given by President Lee's oldest grandchild, David Goates, who said that "when the First Presidency stood at the pulpit during the last session, he saw a special light surrounding them."

The Provo Temple was dedicated on February 9, 1972. There were only two sessions, both on the same day. The need for additional sessions was avoided by seating the participants in the Marriott Center, the George Albert Smith Fieldhouse, the Joseph Smith building, and the Fine Arts Center, in addition to the temple.

In his main address delivered at the dedication, President Lee related the spiritual experience he had had at the dedication of the Los Angeles Temple when the prayer of President David O. McKay corresponded almost exactly with a vivid dream he had had some time before. In the prayer and in the dream, the prophet admonished his listeners, an admonition President Lee felt was directed pointedly to him, about "the meaning of the love of God, as it relates to the love of our fellow men and of His service." The spirit that attended these dedicatory services at the Provo Temple was quite remarkable. One of the General Authorities later told President Lee that he clearly saw President David O. McKay in vision in the company of several men whom he could not identify. The wife of another General Authority reported that during the services, her mother appeared to her in vision, clear and distinct. "I was watching the strange look on her face," wrote President Lee of the incident, "as she probably witnessed this vision." And still another General Authority reported that during his sermon, there was opened to his mind a vision of young people seated in the Marriott Center and that thereafter he directed his remarks particularly to them. As for President Lee, he was uplifted spiritually by the dedication to a high degree. It provided an important impetus for the heavier duties that would come to him in a few months.

The experience of the wife of the General Authority who saw her mother during the Provo Temple dedication was similar to an experience President Lee had had several months before. It occurred on May 19, 1971, while President Lee sat on the stand at the funeral of Pearl Lambert. "There was a remarkable spirit [present]," wrote he of the occasion, "and I was uplifted thereby. As I was seated on the stand, I seemed to see a congregation facing me. In it was Fern in a black dress. Over her shoulder was someone who, I surmise, was Maurine." The incident kindled anew the love he had for the sweetheart of his youth, the mother of his children, feelings that in no way diminished the love he had for Joan, the noble woman who had come to him as a gift from God in his time of great loneliness and need.

On the day of the Lambert funeral, the First Presidency reviewed plans for an area conference to be held in Manchester, England, the following August, to be attended by Latter-day Saints from all over the British Isles. Since it was the first of a series of area conferences planned for the future, considerable care had been given to the preparations. Elder Boyd K. Packer of the Twelve, who had special apostolic responsibilities in Great Britain at the time, had been appointed to coordinate the preparations with a cadre of local leaders, headed by Regional Representative Derek A. Cuthbert, a future member of the Seventy. Elder Loren C. Dunn, of the First Council of the Seventy, who also had assigned responsibilities in Great Britain, had been appointed to assist Elder Packer.

The site of this first area conference had been selected with prayerful deliberation. Since a main purpose of the area conferences was to stress the international character of the Church and to cause members of the Church worldwide to feel themselves part of a global organization, it seemed appropriate to schedule the first area conference in the locality where the Church's first international proselyting effort had commenced. Near Manchester is Preston, where Elder Heber C. Kimball and his brethren opened the work in England by preaching in the chapel of the Reverend James Fielding, whose brother, Joseph Fielding, was a member of this first group of Mormon missionaries to proselyte in Great Britain. When the first baptisms by these missionaries included some of Reverend James Fielding's flock, he closed his church doors to them. But the message was out, and the work flourished, beginning with these first baptisms in the River Ribble and culminating with a great flood of converts from this area and other areas in Great Britain. Because of President Joseph Fielding Smith's connection with these historic events through his two great uncles, James and Joseph Fielding, brothers of his grandmother, Mary Fielding Smith, he and everyone connected with the coming Manchester conference were excited about it, whether at Church headquarters or in Great Britain. When on August 3, 1971, President Smith announced emphatically that he did not intend to go to Manchester, surprise and confusion reigned at Church headquarters and all plans for the area conference, scheduled to begin three weeks later, were temporarily suspended. The cause of this sudden about-face was the death of President Smith's wife, Jessie Evans Smith. The passing of this vibrant woman, who had brought such joy to him, was a shattering blow to the ninety-five-year-old prophet. She was the third wife taken from him in death. His age, his waning strength, and the bleak prospect of continuing life without her effervescent enthusiasm made the prospect of a long trip to England oppressive to him. And so, he had announced with finality that the area conference in Manchester would have to go on without him. President Lee empathized with the prophet in a way none of the other brethren could do because of the trial he had endured in Fern's passing. Yet, he knew what a shroud of disappointment would descend on the Manchester conference were it announced President Smith would not attend. He knew also that the prophet's attitude likely would change once the immediate shock of Aunt Jessie's death had subsided and once he had begun to view the decision not to go in terms of his prophetic responsibility rather than in terms of his personal feelings. So, a few days after the funeral when the Manchester conference was discussed again, President Smith, recognizing that the interests of the Church and his prophetic office must predominate, said he would go. With that, the previously laid plans rolled out with precision.

It having been decided that only President Smith and President Lee from the First Presidency would go to Manchester, it was also decided, as a matter of precaution, that they would travel separately. For his comfort and protection, arrangements were made for the prophet's son, Douglas A. Smith, to be his travelling companion, accompanied by a physician, Dr. Donald Smith, and by President Smith's personal secretary, D. Arthur Haycock. President Lee and Joan left Salt Lake City on August 30 for London, England, with planned, intermediate stops in Midland, Michigan, and New York City. In Midland, over the weekend of August 21 and 22, President Lee presided at a stake conference, in the course of which he dedicated a new stake center. In transferring from one airline to another in Detroit, Michigan, en route to New York, President Lee lost his briefcase, which contained all the papers for the area conference in Manchester. Distraught, he retraced his steps, and for an hour anxiously and vainly examined every place where he and Joan had stopped in making the transfer. "As I stepped out to get the shuttle bus," he wrote, "there was my brief case. Why I hadn't seen it before, I will never know; and why it was safeguarded for nearly an hour, I will never know. Only the good Lord could explain. It was a miracle."

President and Sister Lee flew from New York to London on August 24, landing at Heathrow airport, where they spent the night in the nearby Excelsior Hotel. The next morning, they flew to Manchester, where they were met at the airport by Elder Boyd K. Packer and J. Thomas Fyans, who would soon be appointed as the managing director of the department of internal communications and who was assisting Elder Packer in arranging for the housing and transportation of the visitors from Salt Lake City. The Lees were driven to the city center where they checked into the Piccadilly Hotel, the headquarters for the official party. President Smith arrived later in the day, Wednesday the twenty-fifth.

President Lee was closeted with the prophet the next day, reviewing the plans for the conference, scheduled to begin officially on Friday the twenty-seventh. That evening, he went to the Manchester stake center where he addressed a group of young people. After returning to the hotel, he and President Smith decided to call the General Authorities together for a special meeting to prepare for the conference. It was held in a conference room in the Piccadilly Hotel. It turned out to be the first ever official meeting of the Council of the First Presidency and Quorum of the Twelve held outside the United States. Present were two members of the First Presidency, Joseph Fielding Smith and Harold B. Lee, and seven members of the Twelve, Spencer W. Kimball, Marion G. Romney, Richard L. Evans, Howard W. Hunter, Gordon B. Hinckley, Thomas S. Monson, and Boyd K. Packer. Joining the brethren of the council were other General Authorities, Henry D. Taylor and Marion D. Hanks, Assistants to the Twelve; Paul H. Dunn and Loren C. Dunn of the First Council of the Seventy; and Bishop Victor L. Brown, along with several who were not General Authorities, Russell M. Nelson, president of the Sunday School, W. Jay Eldredge, president of the YMMIA, Joe J. Christensen, associate commissioner of education, D. Arthur Haycock, and Francis M. Gibbons. Elder Thomas S. Monson, whose arrival late in the evening provided the required number for an official council meeting, had flown in from Europe during bad weather, which had threatened the plane's ability to arrive on time.

Following the handling of matters of business and a review of the meetings scheduled during the conference by President Lee, there was a period of testimony bearing. Frequent references were made to the historic significance of the conference in the city where members of the Twelve established their headquarters during the early 1840s when proselyting in England was established on a firm foundation. During that period, the public meetings of the Twelve were held in Carpenters' Hall, which was destroyed during the German bombing of Manchester during World War II. It was in Manchester during that period that the Twelve held an official quorum meeting, the first one held outside the United States.

This unusual meeting provided a spiritual tone for the conference that commenced at 2:00 P.M. the next day in the Belle Vue Exhibition Center in Manchester, with two sessions held simultaneously: an adult session held in Kings Hall and a youth session held in the nearby Cumberland Suite. The speaker's stand in Kings Hall, a sports and entertainment arena, had been arranged to simulate the stand in the Salt Lake Tabernacle, with red carpeting and red upholstered seats for the General Authorities. At the request of President Smith, President Lee conducted the adult session as he did all the other sessions of the conference, except the youth session, which was conducted by Elder Thomas S. Monson, and the women's session Saturday evening, which was conducted by Sister Belle S. Spafford, general president of the Relief Society. All general sessions of the conference were held at the Belle Vue Exhibition Center, except the Saturday evening priesthood session, which was held at the Free Trade Hall in downtown Manchester.

As a means of tying this first area conference to the beginnings of the Church in Great Britain, the opening song at the adult session was "The Morning Breaks, the Shadows Flee." President Lee explained to the audience that "The words of this hymn, . . . written by Parley P. Pratt, . . . appeared on the front cover of the first issue of *The Millennial Star*, which was published in May of 1840." Elder Pratt, one of the original members of the Twelve, who was the editor of the *Millennial Star*, then lived in Manchester. In his keynote address, delivered at this opening session, President Joseph Fielding Smith suggested that the Manchester area conference was, in a sense, a formal recognition that the Church, growing from its struggling beginnings, had become a global organization. "We are coming of age as a church and as a people," said he. "We have attained the stature and strength that are enabling us to fulfill the commission given us by the Lord through the Prophet Joseph Smith that we should carry the glad tidings of the restoration to every nation and to all people. And not only shall we preach the gospel in every nation before the second coming of the Son of Man, but we shall make converts and establish congregations of saints among them." In commenting afterward on the prophet's keynote address, President Lee said: "I am sure that if the Saints will keep their hearts and minds attuned to what the President has said, this will indeed be a great conference." (British Area General Conference Report, Aug. 1971, pp. 5, 7.)

During the three days of the conference, all of the General Authorities spoke, as did some of the visitors and local leaders. In addition to comments he made while conducting the meetings, President Lee delivered major addresses at the Saturday evening priesthood session and the Sunday morning general session and made brief concluding remarks at the last session. At the priesthood session, his main focus was on the need for priesthood bearers to be worthy. "Are you always ready?" he asked rhetorically, after describing the qualities a priesthood bearer ought to possess. "Are you a clean vessel to exercise your priesthood?" In his Sunday morning address, President Lee commented on the growth of the Church from its beginning and on its growth in England since 1960, when he had presided at the conference in Manchester wherein the first stake in the British Isles and Europe was organized. He then sketched the first principles of the gospel and admonished his listeners to keep the commandments. "To all honest seekers after truth," he explained, "the answer has always been the same as declared in our articles of faith: 'We believe that through the atonement of Christ all mankind may be saved by obedience to the laws and ordinances of the gospel.' " In support, he cited the words of earlier prophets who had admonished the people to keep the commandments, words which offended some, but which were a comfort and solace to those who followed them. President Lee also counselled his listeners to heed the words of the living prophet, to guard against the intrusion of Satanic influences in their lives, and to conduct themselves so as always to have the Spirit of God to be with them. He then affirmed that the answers to life's complex problems could be found through adherence to the gospel and cited basic principles and programs of the Church that contributed to individual and group happiness and security — tithing, fast offerings, Church welfare, missionary work, family prayer, and family home evening. At the conclusion of this comprehensive and compelling discourse, President Lee bore a fervent testimony. "As a little boy," he said, "I had my first intimate touch with divinity." He then retold the story of having heard the voice warning him not to go near the broken-down buildings and sheds across the field. "I looked in every direction to see where the speaker was. I wondered if it was my father, but he couldn't see me. There was no one in sight. I realized that someone was warning me of an unseen danger — whether a nest of rattlesnakes or whether the rotting timbers would fall on me and crush me, I don't know. But from that time on, I accepted without question the fact that there were processes not known to man by which we can hear voices from the unseen world, by which we can have brought to us the visions of eternity." President Lee then told of the struggling events that followed his call to the Twelve and their aftermath: "After a long night of searching," he said, "and days of spiritual preparation that followed, I came to know as a witness more powerful than sight, until I could testify with a surety that defied all doubt, that I knew with every fiber of my soul that Jesus is the Christ, the Son of the living God, that he lived, he died, he was resurrected, and today he presides in the heavens, directing the affairs of this church, which bears his name because it preaches his doctrine. I bear that testimony humbly and leave you my witness and my blessing here this morning, in the name of the Lord Jesus Christ. Amen." (British Area General Conference Report, Aug. 1971, pp. 141–42.)

The impact of these words upon the audience was profound. The eloquence, the sincerity, the personal magnetism, and the stance of the speaker conveyed a sense of conviction, comfort, and spiritual confirmation to the listeners. And the spirit engendered by President Lee's talk, augmented by the words and testimonies of the other speakers, built to the climax that occurred following the last session of the conference. After the closing song, "This Is Our Place," composed especially for the occasion, and the benediction, the audience stood and quietly waited while the prophet left the hall. Then, unannounced and without direction or accompaniment, they sang "We Thank Thee, O God, for a Prophet" in its entirety. Then they sang in its entirety "God Be with You till We Meet Again." Then after a pause, the audience, almost as one, broke into applause, clapping their hands loudly. As the applause subsided, they began to disperse, slowly and quietly as if they were loath to leave or to break the spell that the conference had cast over them.

President Smith and the other visitors from Salt Lake City, except President Lee, returned home soon after the conference. President Lee had assignments in England and on the continent, which would keep him occupied there for two more weeks. On September 1, he and Joan flew to London. There he met with David Lawrence McKay and an English solicitor, Mark Sharman, to discuss a possible appeal from a decision of a local planning commission, denying permission to build a patron living complex on the temple grounds. After weighing the alternatives and consequences, it was decided not to appeal.

Before leaving England, President Lee and Joan visited Windsor Castle and that evening attended a London musical, *The Great Waltz,* the story of Johann Strauss. During the next two days, he counselled with the presidency of the London Temple and, with Joan, did some sightseeing in London, visiting, among other places, the Parliament building and Westminster Abbey.

They flew to Frankfurt, Germany, on September 4, where they were met by Kay Schwendiman. Over the weekend, President Lee, assisted by Brother Schwendiman, reorganized the presidency of the Kaiserslautern servicemen's stake. Selected as the new stake president was John Lasater, a future General Authority of whom President Lee wrote, "The new president, John Lasater, has been named as the special assistant to the commanding general who has promised him that he will endeavor to schedule his time so as not to interfere with his family or church responsibilities." President Lee was tremendously impressed with the performance of this stake, noting that it was "unsurpassed for dedication and thoroughness, with complete understanding of all programs."

President Lee spent the following week in Switzerland, conferring with Mission President Edwin J. Cannon in Zurich and with the temple presidency in Bern. At the time, consideration was being given to constructing a "Hospitality Center" near the temple, which could accommodate one hundred fifty guests at a time. Principals in these discussions were two more future General Authorities of the Church, architect Hans B. Ringger and Regional Representative Enzio Busche. Also present in Bern to discuss the installation of more modern projector equipment in the temple was Armis J. Ashby, who had been conferring with President Lee about similar matters affecting several temples.

Over the weekend of September 11 and 12, President Lee held leadership training meetings with Hans Ringger, a stake president, and Enzio Busche and dedicated the

Church's first chapel in Lucerne. He and Joan flew to New York and thence home on the fourteenth.

Before the official party left Salt Lake City for the Manchester conference, arrangements had been made for President Smith to live at the home of his daughter, Amelia, and her husband, Bruce R. McConkie. By the time the prophet returned home from England, some of his treasured things had been moved to a private room in the McConkie home, and he was taken directly there from the airport on his arrival. Here amidst members of his family who loved him, President Smith was comfortable and at peace. But there was a sense of loneliness in him because of Jessie's death. And, he was tired. Just how tired is reflected in President Lee's diary entry of September 17, three days after he arrived home from Europe. "President Smith went into a deep sleep," he wrote that day, "the second in two days." Despite this, the prophet continued to go to his office regularly, meeting with his counselors and others as the usual grist was handled and as preparations were made for the general conference, which was only two weeks away.

While he deferred to his counselors in conducting the conference sessions, President Smith participated, as usual, in speaking, delivering the keynote and concluding addresses, and speaking at the general priesthood meeting. During his concluding address, the prophet lauded his counselors. "May I express before you the profound appreciation I have for the faith, devotion and service of the two great men who stand beside me," said he. Then, referring to his first counselor, he said: "President Harold B. Lee is a spiritual giant with faith like that of Enoch. He has the spirit of revelation and magnifies his calling as a prophet, seer and revelator." President Lee never took lightly the confidence and goodwill shown toward him by President Smith and genuinely appreciated these comments and the sentiments that prompted them.

Meanwhile, the ongoing work of the Church required the constant diligence and attention of the Brethren. We have already noted the changes in the Twelve caused by the death of Elder Richard L. Evans and the call of Elder Marvin J. Ashton to replace him. The installation of the new presidents at BYU and Ricks and the Solemn Assembly at the St. George Temple also occurred during this period. And because a presidential election would take place the next year, the First Presidency was contacted by political leaders seeking support for their party or its candidates. While the Brethren remained aloof from partisan politics, they never rejected the request of prominent politicians for an audience, regardless of their political persuasion. So, on November 5, 1971, Senator Edward M. Kennedy of Massachusetts came for a visit, accompanied by local democratic leaders Oscar W. McConkie, Jr., and Wayne Owens. Previously the Brethren had been visited by members of the administration of President Richard M. Nixon, including the president himself, Vice-President Spiro Agnew, and Secretary of Labor Hodgson. Also, the Speaker of the House of Representatives, Carl Albert, had come calling.

However, political maneuvering was the least important thing on President Lee's mind as he worked under President Smith's direction to complete the organization of the departments of internal and public communications, the mission representatives of the Twelve and First Council of Seventy, and the arrangements for the dedication of the Ogden and Provo temples. And while these and other stressful and demanding things were going on, President Lee became involved in still another life-and-death decision that faced his friend Spencer W. Kimball. The most recent of President Kimball's compendium of ailments was a grave heart condition. The doctors had advised him that without open-heart surgery, his remaining days would be both drastically reduced and marked by a loss of energy. He and Sister Kimball sought an audience with President Lee on March 13, 1972, to discuss the matter. The Kimballs had already made the tentative decision to go forward with the surgery. First, however, they wanted to know whether

President Lee thought President Kimball's "position was important enough to wish for longer life." President Lee, who had been joined by President Tanner and Doctors Russell M. Nelson and Ernest L. Wilkinson, Jr., assured him it was and, indeed, was surprised that he had asked. Yet, knowing his friend as he did, President Lee assumed that the question was but another reflection of his self-deprecating humility, which increased the love he had for him. "We could counsel only," wrote President Lee, "that he follow the direction as given in D&C 9 and receive his answer. Apparently, he had already done this and felt that he would take the 25 percent risk of an operation which could be done following the April conference."

Following the last session of the conference on April 9, the council of the First Presidency and Quorum of the Twelve met with President and Sister Kimball in the upper room of the temple, where both of them received special blessings. The surgery was performed three days later, a Wednesday. The night before, Dr. Russell M. Nelson went privately to President Lee and President Tanner for a special blessing. He later reported that the surgery was "technically perfect" and that as the operation was nearly completed it was made known to him that one day President Kimball would become the president of the Church.

Because of conflicts, the weekly council meeting was held in the temple on Wednesday rather than on Thursday. During the meeting, President Lee was called to the phone when he was advised that the operation had been a success. When he returned to the council room to make the announcement, he said with emotion as his voice quavered, "The Lord has heard and answered our prayers." It was one of the few times, if not the only time, President Lee openly showed such great emotion. Following the surgery, he was very solicitous of President Kimball. On April 20, he visited the hospital to give him a blessing. "He was in a highly nervous state," wrote President Lee, "but quieted down after the blessing." Later, President Lee persuaded the patient to go to the cottage at Laguna Beach,

California, to convalesce; and in mid-June, Brother Lee travelled there "to give him a feeling of belonging and involvement," and to "brief him in many matters where he needed to be better informed." Sister Kimball later reported that the visit had effected "a marvelous transformation in him by lifting him out of his depression and making him feel that he was wanted and needed."

While President Lee was involved in this way, building up the man who, in less than two years, would succeed him as the president of the Church, he was also involved on a daily basis in working with the man whom he would succeed as the president of the Church in a few weeks. Three days before President Kimball underwent his surgery, President Joseph Fielding Smith delivered his last sermon in the Salt Lake Tabernacle. It occurred on April 9 at the last session of the general conference. The last words of this brief sermon are a fitting benediction to the life and ministry of this faithful man: "O God our Heavenly and Eternal Father," said he, "look down in love and in mercy upon this thy church and upon the members of the church who keep thy commandments. Let thy Spirit dwell in our hearts forever; and when the trials and woes of this life are over, may we return to thy presence, with our loved ones, and dwell in thy house forever, I humbly pray, in the name of Jesus Christ. Amen." (Conference Report, Apr. 1972, pp. 163-64.)

President Smith's energy level continued to decline, although he regularly attended his meetings. An occurrence on May 5 signalled the end was near for him. On that day, he blacked out while seated at the dinner table in the McConkie home. Amelia and her husband were able to revive him, using tanked oxygen they kept in the house for such an emergency. The end came at 9:25 P.M. Sunday, July 2, 1972. He was seated in the same chair in which Aunt Jessie died several months before. He had attended sacrament meeting earlier and was chatting with Amelia who was writing letters. She stepped out of the room to get an address and on her return, found him slumped over in the chair. Elder Bruce R. McConkie, whom Amelia summoned from another room, moved him to a nearby couch and administered oxygen. His pulse remained fairly strong for a while, but suddenly stopped. He died as he lived, peacefully and with no fanfare. He would have been ninety-six years old in seventeen days.

Members of the family and President Lee were informed and gathered at the McConkie home. President Lee picked up President Tanner to accompany him there. After praying with the family and conferring briefly about funeral arrangements, President Lee and President Tanner returned to their homes after deciding to convene a meeting of the Twelve the next morning. It was held in the First Presidency's council room in the administration building. All fourteen of the Brethren were there, including President Spencer W. Kimball, who was recovering nicely from the heart surgery, but who had added still another ailment, Bell's palsy, to his growing list of infirmities. He sat, uncomfortably, throughout the meeting with a handkerchief held to his face to mask the paralytic effect of the palsy on his features.

President Lee, who presided at this meeting as the president of the Twelve, was calm and subdued, reflecting the burden he carried as the de facto head of the Church. The inference drawn from his appearance was that he had slept little, if at all, the previous night as he wrestled with the intricate problems he now faced.

The agenda of the meeting was brief, but important: The Brethren were reminded of the procedure governing events connected with the death of a prophet when the minutes of a similar meeting held following the death of President David O. McKay were read; a committee was appointed to meet with the Smith family in making the funeral arrangements; it was agreed the Brethren would meet in the upper room of the temple the following Friday to consider the reorganization of the First Presidency; approval was given to issue all checks necessary to carry on the work pending the reorganization; and President Lee, acting as the president of the Twelve, was authorized to sign all correspondence and documents during the interim period, which documents ordinarily would have been signed by the First Presidency.

The next morning, July 4, President Lee awakened with severe pain on his left side. From experience, he knew it was nothing trivial and did not, therefore, resist Joan's pleading entreaty that he check in at the hospital. There a team of medics, headed by his old standby, Doctor Orme, conducted a battery of tests. These revealed several blood clots in the lungs. He remained in the hospital all day and that night, receiving injections and medication aimed at dissolving the clots and thinning his blood. These continued at intervals throughout the fifth and the morning of the sixth, before President Smith's funeral, being administered by a young intern sent to the home from the hospital.

During the period President Lee underwent these treatments, he began to give thought to the choice of counselors in the First Presidency. "I knew who I had in mind," he wrote, "but I wanted the confirmation of the Lord. I spent an hour or more in the temple and [prayed] throughout the night. When the morning came [Thursday the sixth], there was no doubt that N. Eldon Tanner was to be named as the first counselor. . . . I also was certain that Marion G. Romney should be named the other counselor; and that was likewise spiritually confirmed to my satisfaction." During this process, President Lee also decided that the selection of someone to fill the vacancy in the Twelve to be created by the call of Elder Romney to the First Presidency would be deferred until the October general conference.

The physical emergency President Lee had experienced two days before was shielded from the view of all but a few as he conducted President Joseph Fielding Smith's funeral on Thursday, July 6, 1972. The Tabernacle was filled to capacity as the assembled Saints sought to pay tribute to their departed leader. The music was provided by the Tabernacle Choir, which sang some of President Smith's favorite pieces. The speakers were President Lee, President N. Eldon Tanner, and son-in-law Elder Bruce R. McConkie. It was entirely in character when President Lee "spoke more particularly to the spiritual phases of his life," which was the angle from which he habitually viewed the affairs that daily swirled around him.

After the funeral, President Lee acutely felt the need for additional spiritual strength as he faced perhaps the most momentous day of his life. He went alone to the temple for this purpose where he spent several hours praying, planning, and reminiscing. The record he left of this illuminating interlude opens a revealing window into the heart and soul of Harold B. Lee. "As I viewed the paintings of the presidents of the church," he wrote of his visit to the upper room of the temple, "from the Prophet Joseph Smith to the present, I had brought to me the overwhelming responsibility that will rest upon me to follow where these great leaders have led. I also sat for a moment where I was joined in marriage to my darling Fern by President George F. Richards and again in the sealing room where my lovely Joan was sealed to me by President David O. McKay. I poured out my soul in gratitude for these two of the greatest women who have ever walked the earth who have been brought to me through circumstances which attest to the divine guidance of the almighty who knew my need."

Chapter Twenty-eight

President of the Church

The Brethren met in the upper room of the temple on Friday, July 7, 1972, at 8:00 A.M. to reorganize the First Presidency of the Church. The early hour was decided on because of plans to hold a press conference afterward and the need to finish in time so the results could be published in the afternoon papers. The procedure already described was followed in effecting the reorganization, with each member of the Twelve expressing himself, following which, on motion of President Kimball, President Lee was sustained, then ordained, and set apart as the eleventh president of the Church, with President Kimball acting as voice. In turn, President Lee named N. Eldon Tanner and Marion G. Romney as his counselors, who, being unanimously approved by the Brethren, were set apart by him. Finally, with similar approval, President Lee set apart Spencer W. Kimball as the president of the Twelve.

The press conference was held in the west board room on the main floor of the administration building where more than fifty representatives of the various news media were present. Flanked by his counselors, and occasionally assisted by them, President Lee fielded a barrage of questions for an hour. His wide experience in dealing with the press, gained as a member of the Twelve, as a politician, and as a high-level business executive enabled him to respond with poise and confidence. The questions focused mainly on his plans for the Church. He responded in essence that he had no plans but that he would lead wherever the Lord, by revelation, prompted him to go. When asked what would be his first message, he replied, "Keep the commandments of God. Therein will be the salvation of individuals and nations during these troublesome times."

A few days later, President Lee granted a private interview to Mr. Thorupp, religion editor of the Los Angeles *Times*. Mr. Thorupp had two main questions concerning the Church policy on priesthood and why the Church was growing so fast. As to the first question, President Lee explained that the policy traced back to the beginnings of the Church, had been affirmed and supported since by prophetic sanction, and would be changed only by revelation from God. As to the second question, he explained simply that the Church was growing while other churches were not because "of the individual testimonies of the members and the missionaries."

Significantly, the first public discourse President Lee delivered after being ordained as the president of the Church was to the leaders of the youth. On July 16, 1972, he spoke at a meeting of all the officers and teachers of the MIA in the University West Stake. "There was a remarkable spirit which prompted many tears," he wrote of the occasion. This reaction was quite typical of the response to President Lee's preaching from the beginning of his apostolic ministry. The reason seemed to derive from the spiritual intensity and sensitivity of the man and from the spiritual focus he gave to everything he did. His elevation to the prophetic office magnified this reaction. This was affirmed by an experience he had on August 11. "I had my first session in the temple with the missionaries since my present call," he wrote on that day. "This fact seemed to intensify, both in me and in the missionaries, an unusual depth of spirituality. One [missionary] standing and representing the group pledged loyalty, love and support in my new calling." President Lee received spiritual strength from these devoted young missionaries. And despite a crowded schedule, he continued to meet with the groups of new missionaries during the remainder of his life, the last one being just a few days before his death.

Before President Smith passed away, plans had been made to hold an area conference in Mexico City the last of August. It was decided to go forward with these plans. President and Sister Lee flew there on Saturday, August 26, arriving in time for four special meetings held in the evening at four different locations. The women met at the National Auditorium, the young women at the Bosque Theatre, the Melchizedek Priesthood at the Camerones stake center, and the Aaronic Priesthood at another stake center in the city. President Lee spoke at all four of these meetings, the starting times of which were staggered to make this possible. The essence of his message was the same at all four meetings—obedience to the laws and ordinances of the gospel, which translates into compliance with the first and great commandment to love God.

The conference actually commenced Friday evening with a *Folklorico,* which featured dance and choral groups from all over Mexico and Central America performing in gaily colored costumes. The following day before President Lee arrived, two general sessions were held at the National Auditorium. The first was conducted by President Marion G. Romney and the second by President N. Eldon Tanner. President Lee delayed travelling to Mexico because of imperative commitments in Salt Lake City and to avoid all three members of the First Presidency travelling on the same flight.

Over fifteen thousand Latter-day Saints, drawn from Mexico and Central America, assembled in the National Auditorium Sunday morning, August 27. As in Manchester the previous year, the place where the general sessions were held had been arranged and decorated to simulate the appearance of the Salt Lake Tabernacle. Moreover, the Salt Lake Tabernacle Choir had flown to Mexico City to add another touch to remind the local Saints of the general conferences in Salt Lake City. The choir performed its traditional weekly broadcast shortly before the Sunday morning general session and then sang at the two general sessions that followed.

It was here in Mexico City, at the Sunday morning session, that President Harold B. Lee was first sustained as the president of the Church in a public meeting. President Tanner, who conducted, presented the names of the General Authorities for sustaining vote, following the invocation and a special number by the Tabernacle Choir, "I Know That My Redeemer Lives." The General Authorities present, in addition to the First Presidency, were President Spencer W. Kimball and Elders Ezra Taft Benson, Mark E. Petersen, and Delbert L. Stapley of the Twelve; Elders Franklin D. Richards and David B. Haight, Assistants to the Twelve; Elder Bruce R. McConkie of the First Council of the Seventy; and Bishop Victor L. Brown.

In his keynote address, President Lee briefly traced the growth of the church in Mexico, noting that the membership there then stood at 115,000. He attributed this vigorous growth to the influence of the Holy Ghost brooding over the land and to the diligence of the missionaries and members. He counselled that investigators be admonished to study and to pray since true conversion comes to an individual only through the power of God. He also blessed the parents with a new resolution to keep their houses in order, to be faithful to their companions, and to promote the teaching of young people. "Teach so many good things to them," he admonished, "that they can't find time to be bad."

President Lee also delivered the concluding address of the conference at the end of the Sunday afternoon session. In it he urged the members to hold family home evening, to look after each other, and to live more perfectly. And he admonished the brethren to magnify their priesthood callings. In conclusion, he bore a fervent testimony and shared with the audience a sweet experience he had the day after he was ordained as the president of the Church. "As my wife and I kneeled in humble prayer," he said, "suddenly it seemed as though my mind and heart went out to all three million members throughout the world. I seemed to love every one of them, regardless of their nationality or their color, whether rich or poor or educated or not. I suddenly felt as though they all belonged to me, as though they were all my own brothers and sisters." In that spirit, the prophet extended his love and blessings to the audience, invoking the Spirit of the Lord to abide with them always.

The depth of feeling this experience and these words evoked are reminiscent of the spirit induced by the remarkable dream President Lee had shortly before the dedication of the Los Angeles Temple. And the overflowing love he felt for all members of the Church, as he kneeled with Sister Lee the morning following his ordination as the president of the Church, seems to have fulfilled the condition for prophetic worthiness defined by President David O. McKay in his prayer dedicating the Los Angeles Temple, which was echoed in President Lee's vivid dream. Herein lies the explanation of the true greatness of Harold B. Lee. What he did or accomplished during his remarkable career does not define or explain that greatness. It is rather what he *was* or what he *became* that does so. That he spearheaded the welfare program, nurtured and shepherded the correlation program, and was the moving force behind the restructuring of the headquarters organizations, are extraordinary achievements, not to be disparaged. But they pale in comparison to the quality of genuine, universal love that at last found lodgement in the mind and heart of this prophet. And, unlike the many things he accomplished during his life that required the exercise of his own initiative, diligence, and discipline, this premier attribute

President of the Church

came to him as a gift from God, without a conscious act of will or self-determination on his part. This quality of love was evident in every aspect of his short tenure as the president of the Church. Those who associated with him, or who heard him speak, were conscious of it and felt its influence.

Even as the pure love of the Savior did not protect him from the agony of the cross, neither did President Lee's feelings of universal love provide immunity from the hatred and threats of vicious men. Two days after the Mexico City area conference ended, an anonymous call was received at Church headquarters warning that two men, members of an apostate cult in Mexico, were in town to assassinate President Lee. Soon after, it was learned that a week before, the leader of this apostate cult had been murdered by one of the assassins reported to be in Salt Lake City, seeking the life of the prophet. Immediately on learning this, security personnel were assigned to stay constantly with President Lee until the danger had abated. The next day, the Salt Lake City police were called in to help protect him. Such was the uncertainty the threat created that on the first Sunday after returning home from Mexico, President Lee did not attend meetings in his own ward but stayed home. Meanwhile, automatic, electric locks were installed on the door leading to his office and security procedures were tightened up all around Church headquarters. The following Sunday, at the "urgent request" of President Jack Goaslind, "a splendid young leader" and a future General Authority, President Lee attended the conference of the Olympus Stake on the east bench of the Salt Lake Valley. Concerned about the appearance of being closely guarded, President Lee requested that the police and security personnel be as "inconspicuous" as possible. "Despite that," he wrote, "they had gone out the previous day to inspect the stake center," and on the way to the conference session he attended, "they had three or four cars in the lead, behind, and by the side of our car driven by Arthur Haycock." After the session, there was such a crush of people who wanted to see the prophet up close, or to touch or to shake hands with him, that he had great difficulty getting off the stand and to his car, "a circumstance," wrote President Lee, "I have thought must be prevented as much as possible."

Because of the tension and upset caused by the assassination threat, it was fortunate that President Lee had previously planned a three-week tour of Europe and the Middle East. It was hoped things would be settled down by the time he returned.

With his car protected by another cocoon of police vehicles, President Lee was driven to the Salt Lake airport on September 12, where he and Sister Lee boarded a plane for New York City. A friend told the prophet as he waited to board the plane that he "never thought he would live to see the day when the president of the church would come to the airport guarded by the police." Were the truth known, President Lee probably felt the same way. The Lees had dinner that night in New York with Mission President David Lawrence McKay, his wife, Mildred, and the office missionaries. The next morning, the McKays saw the Lees off at the Kennedy International Airport. Waiting for them when they landed at London's Heathrow airport were Elder Gordon B. Hinckley and his wife, Marjorie, who would be the Lees' travelling companions, and Mission President Milan Smith and his wife, Jessica.

The agenda for the three days spent in London was crowded. It included a meeting with U.S. Ambassador Annenberg, a luncheon hosted by British media mogul Lord Thompson of Fleet, a meeting with four hundred missionaries from the England East and England South missions, a visit to the London Temple where the prophet performed important administrative work, a press conference, and meetings connected with the London Stake conference, when the stake presidency was reorganized. Sandwiched in between was a visit to the British Museum and a tour of London in a new, chauffeured Rolls Royce that Lord Thompson made available to President and Sister Lee.

President Harold B. Lee with his wife Freda Joan Jensen Lee

On the eighteenth, the Lees and Hinckleys flew to Athens, Greece, where they were met at the airport by the U.S. Ambassador and his aide and by a group of Latter-day Saints that included Mission President Edwin Cannon, his wife, Janath, some of the missionaries, and a number of military personnel. The main reason for stopping here was to make further inquiry about obtaining official recognition for the Church. Nothing materialized. Later in the day, the prophet held a meeting with a group at the military base. Then, "as the sun set over the mediterranean," wrote President Lee, "we visited the famed Acropolis and Parthenon." During most of the day, the prophet was distracted by "a somewhat severe distress" in his lower right back, similar to the pain he suffered before President Smith's funeral. He concealed the intensity of his pain the following day when he and several others climbed Mars Hill where the Apostle Paul delivered his famous address to the men of Athens. Both the prophet and Elder Hinckley spoke on this occasion, and President Cannon offered a prayer. "It was a glorious experience," President Lee wrote.

The next day, the travellers flew to Tel Aviv, where they were met by David Galbraith, the president of the Jerusalem branch, and a group of Saints. Also present was Mr. Lourie, an assistant to the Israeli foreign minister, Abba Eban, who was then in New York. However, in token of his regret in not being able to greet President Lee in person, Mr. Eban left an inscribed copy of the book *My People*. Later in the day, the prophet met with Dr. Calbi, the minister of religion, and with Mayor Teddy Kollek, when there was a discussion about the possibility of constructing a monument on the Mount of Olives commemorating the Orson Hyde story. This project came to fruition years after President Lee's death and gave the Church an important presence in the Holy Land. Between meetings this day, President Lee and his party were taken to the Jerusalem Museum, where, among other antiquities, the Dead Sea Scrolls were displayed, along with artifacts from Lehi's Cave, which, according to President Lee, "link the Book of Mormon" to the Middle East. The next day was occupied with a round of visits and contacts, including a meeting with Rabbi Joffe, who was cordial and encouraging.

Meanwhile, the prophet continued to feel twinges of pain and a general sense of tiredness and discomfort in his back. Later he wrote: "These were exhausting days. My physical strength was at a serious low ebb. I knew something was seriously wrong. . . . Joan insisted that I have Brother Hinckley and President Cannon administer to me." Afterward, following severe coughing, he expelled two blood clots. "Immediately, my shortness of breath ceased," he noted, "the weariness was diminished and the back pains began to subside; and twenty four hours later, were entirely gone." In reflecting on this stressful experience, President Lee wrote: "I now realize I was skirting the brink of eternity, and a miracle in this land of even greater miracles was extended by a merciful God who obviously was prolonging my ministry for a longer time. I give to him, in whose service I am, all the strength of my heart, mind and soul, to indicate in some measure my gratitude for his never failing condescension to me and my loved ones."

During the next few days, President Lee saw again many of the things he saw during his first visit to the Holy Land. Now, however, he saw them through new eyes and from a different perspective. He now seemed to have a greater affinity toward the Savior and a more intense sense of the obligation he owed as his earthly representative. With David Galbraith as their guide, President Lee and his party travelled through Jericho to the Sea of Galilee, there "to walk the same shores as did the Master." Then followed visits to Capernaum, where the Savior delivered the Sermon on the Mount, to Nazareth and the valley nearby where he fed the multitude with loaves and fishes, and to Samaria and the well where Jesus requested a drink. On the evening of the twenty-first, the Israeli department of tourism hosted the prophet and his party at a banquet where Rabbi Samuel Nathan was the master of ceremonies. The following day was spent touring the usual places of historic interest in Old Jerusalem and Bethlehem.

The party flew to Rome on the twenty-third, where they visited the Vatican, held a youth conference, and met with missionaries and members of the Rome branch. During the next few days, the prophet travelled to Florence, Pisa, and Milan, intermingling member and missionary meetings with visits to places of historic or cultural importance. The final meeting held in Italy was at the Dow Chemical auditorium in Milan, where the prophet and Elder Hinckley met with Mission President Dan Jorgensen and one hundred forty of his missionaries in a training and testimony meeting.

The party flew to Zurich, Switzerland, on the twenty-sixth, then travelled to Bern by automobile. Here President Lee and Elder Hinckley met with the temple workers, then installed a new temple presidency, releasing President

Grob and his counselors and installing President Luschin and his counselors. After a stop in Geneva, where the brethren met briefly with Mission President Charles Didier, a future member of the Seventy, and some of the missionaries, the travellers flew to New York on Swiss Air, where they were met by Mission President David Lawrence McKay.

Although he was weak from his ordeal in Israel and from the stress of travel, and though he was anxious to return home to prepare for the Solemn Assembly, where he would be presented for sustaining vote as the head of the Church, President Lee remained in New York an extra day to attend two special meetings. The first was a luncheon at the Marco Polo Club attended by the newscaster Lowell Thomas, the noted minister Norman Vincent Peale, Lee Bickmore, and other prominent people from the eastern United States. This was followed by a press conference where, for an hour, President Lee responded to "searching questions" put to him by twenty-two newsmen from the major newspapers and magazines in the East. At this press conference, President Lee announced the appointment of Lee Bickmore as a "special consultant" to the First Presidency. The impact of this announcement on the sophisticated business and professional community in New York City was significant. As the chairman of the board of Nabisco, Lee Bickmore stood almost at the pinnacle of business eminence there. His new role as a special consultant to the First Presidency undoubtedly altered the perceptions many of his peers had previously held toward the Church, changes that could open doors, cultivate tolerance, and foster understanding toward the Church and its message. Though he never sought to conceal it, Lee Bickmore's polished urbanity effectively masked his rural origin in a small, nondescript Mormon town in northern Utah, located only a few miles from Clifton, Idaho, where President Lee was born.

Before leaving for the Mexico City area conference, President Lee had asked the Twelve to submit the names of men they considered to be qualified to fill the vacancy created by the call of Elder Marion G. Romney as a counselor in the First Presidency. Since then, he had given the matter prayerful consideration and had decided on Elder Bruce R. McConkie. However, he wanted spiritual confirmation of that decision. To that end, he engaged in a special fast, then went to the "most sacred room in the temple" on Sunday, October 1, 1972. "There, for an hour," he wrote, "I prayerfully considered the appointment of a new apostle. All seemed clear that Bruce R. McConkie should be the man." When the prophet shared this with his counselors, "both said that from the first they seemed to know also it was he." At the time President Lee extended the call to Elder McConkie, he learned about another spiritual confirmation of his selection. Elder McConkie told the prophet that when the General Authorities' names were read for sustaining vote in Mexico City, he heard his name spoken as the last member of the Twelve. Troubled by the experience, he "wrestled" with it in the temple for a long time when "he seemed to see a council of the brethren on the other side and they were advocating his name."

Elder McConkie was the only man President Lee called to the Twelve during his short prophetic tenure. Yet, two men whom he called as Assistants to the Twelve, James E. Faust and L. Tom Perry, were later called to the quorum. Elder McConkie and these two brethren, along with O. Leslie Stone, another new Assistant to the Twelve, and Rex D. Pinegar, a new member of the First Council of the Seventy, were presented for sustaining vote at the solemn assembly where President Lee and his counselors were sustained.

This meeting, and the others connected with the October 1972 general conference, represented a high water mark in the life of President Lee. During the conference, he delivered four major addresses, which paint a striking picture of an introspective man who was fully conscious of the magnitude of his new role and of the qualifying steps necessary to attain it, yet who seemed mildly surprised it had happened to him. They also defined the chief criterion by which he felt the success or failure of his ministry should be judged and included a comprehensive review of the essential doctrines and aims of the Church.

The deep introspections in which he had indulged were suggested in his keynote address, delivered immediately after he and the others had been sustained. He recounted how, the previous July when he was ordained, he had gone to the upper room of the temple to meditate and to pray. There he had gazed reflectively at the portraits of those who had preceded him, whose lives and characteristics he then briefly outlined for the audience. After referring to President Joseph Fielding Smith, he said, "As 'the finger of God touched him and he slept,' he seemed in that brief moment to be passing to me, as it were, a sceptre of righteousness as though to say to me, 'Go thou and do likewise.' " Then followed the prophet's own criterion by which to judge whether he had measured up to this mandate. "Now, I stood alone with my thoughts," said he. "Somehow the impressions that came to me were, simply, that the only true record that will ever be made of my service in my new calling will be the record that I may have written in the hearts and lives of those with whom I have served and labored, within and without the church." (Conference Report, Oct. 1972, p. 19.) He then shared with the audience insights into his feelings as he undertook his new duties. He prefaced this by quoting from a sermon of Orson Hyde, which described the "tribulations and trials" through which a prophet must pass to prove himself worthy of the office. He also quoted from the statement of the Prophet Joseph Smith in which he likened himself to a rough stone being polished by the buffeting experiences of his life. President Lee then added: "These thoughts now running through my mind begin to give greater meaning to some of the experiences in my own life, things that have happened which have been difficult for me to understand. At times it seemed as though I too was like a rough stone rolling down from a high mountainside, being buffeted and polished, I suppose, by experiences that I too might overcome and become a polished shaft in the quiver of the Almighty. Maybe it was necessary that I too must learn obedience by the things I might have suffered—to give me experiences that were for my good, to see if I could pass some of the various tests of mortality." (Ibid., p. 20.)

The sermons President Lee delivered at the third session Saturday morning and the general priesthood meeting Saturday evening sketched in some detail the beginnings and the purposes of the restored Church, its basic doctrines, the responsibilities of its members, especially the priesthood, the special problems facing the Church, and the blessings held out to those who will remain faithful.

It was in his concluding address at the last session of the conference, Sunday afternoon, that President Lee expressed a sense of disbelief at what had happened. "I come now to the closing moments of this session," said he, "when I have time for some sobered reflections. Somehow I have had the feeling that during the expressions here, whenever my name has been mentioned, they were talking of somebody other than myself. And I really think that is so, because one cannot go through the experiences that I have gone through these last three days and be the same as before. I am different than I was before Friday morning. I cannot go back to where I was because of the love and faith and confidence that you, the people of the Lord, have reposed in me. So you have been talking of somebody that you want me to become, which I hopefully pray God I may, with his help, become." (Ibid., pp. 175–76.)

With the close of this conference, President Harold B. Lee had been officially and finally ushered into the select company of ten other men who also had served as the president of The Church of Jesus Christ of Latter-day Saints. Of these, he would serve a shorter period of time than any of them, less than eighteen months. And of these, he would die at a younger age than any of them, with the exception of the Prophet Joseph Smith. But, despite the shortness of his prophetic tenure, his influence upon the

Harold B. Lee

President Harold B. Lee

Church ranks among the highest because of his key involvement in welfare, correlation, leadership training, headquarters organization, and because of his personal influence. It is the latter, perhaps, which in the end will be the most lasting and significant of all. A man of my acquaintance once defined the three levels of leadership: First, the leader who does the job with reasonable competence. Second, the leader who not only does the job well, but does it with flair and originality. And, third, the leader who inspires discipleship. The most noteworthy examples of the third level are the Savior and Joseph Smith. Their fame and notoriety rest largely on the efforts of disciples who made certain that knowledge of their lives and teachings was perpetuated. L. Brent Goates, who has written a fine biography of President Lee, has also compiled and has had published a collection of tributes to the prophet under the title *He Changed My Life*. These, added to numerous other testimonials expressed personally to the author about him, suggest that President Harold B. Lee was not only an incredibly competent and creative administrator and leader, but that he may well have qualified to be included within the small circle of those who inspire discipleship.

Soon after the Solemn Assembly, President Lee was inundated with messages of congratulation. "There began an avalanche of letters," he wrote on October 9, "not only from our faithful leaders and members, but from those not in the church. One of the choicest was a letter from my dear old friend, John A. Sibley, a great southerner and a former director of Equitable Life." He also made special mention of a letter from Governor Calvin L. Rampton and one from his cousin Sterling W. McMurrin, a gifted though somewhat unorthodox member of the Church, who "extended the prayers and blessings of the McMurrin family."

Predictably, President Lee was also inundated with invitations to speak at various events. The first one he accepted after the conference was from the presidency of the Oakland Temple. He and Joan travelled there over October 14 and 15, where the prophet spoke at a meeting of all the temple workers. They returned in time to attend a court of honor where grandson Jonathon Goates received his Eagle Scout award.

These pleasant, mountaintop experiences were alloyed with incidents that echoed ominous tones. On October 17, President Lee received a visit from Mr. Gray, head of the Federal Bureau of Investigation in Salt Lake City, who offered the cooperation of his office in protecting against the assassination threats made by the cult from Mexico. President Lee put him in touch with the Church security personnel who, for some time, had been working cooperatively with the Salt Lake City police force. The FBI had become involved because those making the threats were from out of state and out of the country, which involved them in violations of federal law.

On October 23, President Lee went to the hospital, where for three hours he underwent a series of tests and had x-rays taken of his lungs. The doctors were baffled by the prophet's respiratory problems and seemed unable to prescribe any treatment or medication that provided permanent relief. On November 24, 1972, he consulted Dr. Orme about a severe case of hoarseness. On the same day, he received a health blessing from his counselors. In early January 1973, President Lee's hoarseness was such that Dr. Orme strongly recommended that he not attend the inauguration of President Richard M. Nixon in Washington, D.C., out of concern that the cold, moist air would seriously aggravate his condition. During the following three months, President Lee received intermittent treatment from Dr. Orme and from Dr. Richard Snow, who treated him for a sinus condition. By mid-March, when there had been no improvement in his health, specialists, Doctors Dwayne Schmidt and Stephen L. Richards, were brought into the case. On March 19, this resulted in Dr. Richards conducting a bronchoscopy, which entailed inserting instruments down the prophet's windpipe with an attached lighting mechanism that made it possible to take pictures. "This was an ordeal," wrote President Lee, "which left me with a very sore neck." Afterward, over a period of a week, there followed a series of daily "percussion" treatments, accompanied by medications and later by visits from a physical therapist. "Naturally," wrote the patient, "this demanding schedule began to take its toll, not only on my physical, but on my nervous system." However, these extraordinary treatments proved to be beneficial, and except for a routine checkup by Dr. Orme a month later, and a temporary problem with a sciatic nerve during the summer, President Lee had no further contact with doctors until shortly before he passed away the following December.

Meanwhile, President Lee was busy with another major initiative intended to improve the ability of the Church to better serve the best interests of its single members. This contemplated the merging of the activities of the young people under the Presiding Bishopric and the creation of an organization to supervise the activities of the single adults over the age of eighteen. Formal action to implement these changes was taken by the council of the First Presidency and the Quorum of the Twelve on Thursday, October 26, 1972. At that time, the activity program for the youth was designated as the Aaronic Priesthood MIA, and the activity program for the single adults was designated as the Melchizedek Priesthood MIA. While it was provided that the activities of the youth would be under the overall direction of the Presiding Bishopric, this direction would be exercised through the presidencies of the YMMIA and YWMIA, which would continue to exist. At the same time, approval was given to call Robert L. Backman and Ruth Hardy Funk as the new presidents of these youth organizations.

The supervision of the MPMIA at the general level was placed under a managing director, Elder James E. Faust, and two associate directors, Elders Marion D. Hanks and L. Tom Perry. Later, several members, both men and women, were called to serve on an MPMIA board. For purposes of more effective administration, the single adults were divided into two groups, the young adults ages nineteen to twenty-six; and the special interests, ages twenty-seven and older. In administering the MPMIA at the local level, a member of the elders quorum presidency and a member of the Relief Society presidency were appointed in each ward to work with the ward activity director to implement the program.

As President Lee explained at the June conference in 1973, when this new program was formally presented to the Church, it did not represent a change in substance or in doctrine, but was only a change in form made necessary by special circumstances. The whole thrust of this program was to use the full facilities of the Church to reach "the one," that is, the one who had special needs.

President Lee felt keenly about these changes. As with any other step he took affecting the organization and operation of the Church, he acted only after gathering all relevant facts, analyzing them carefully, and praying fervently for spiritual confirmation of the steps he proposed to take. This was the pattern he followed here. And he made it plain that this initiative was heaven inspired and represented revelation through him as the prophet.

Confirming the experiences President Lee had had with welfare, correlation, and the previous headquarters restructuring, these changes also met with some opposition. It came mainly from those who feared that the subordination of the youth organizations to the Presiding Bishopric would stifle their creativity to the detriment of the youth. Even Sister Lee, long an exponent and leader of youth, both inside and outside the Church, shared these concerns. Forgetting for a moment the extraordinary role her husband played, Joan mildly remonstrated with him about the changes. His equally mild, yet unqualified, response made it clear that prophetic action taken in accordance with patterns set by the scriptures would not be overturned by dissent, even the dissent of his beloved companion.

We see at work here two elements that helped move President Lee toward the decision he ultimately made. The first was a desire to strengthen the Presiding Bishopric in their role in leading the Aaronic Priesthood. For many years, the activity programs of the MIA had overshadowed the priesthood functions of the Aaronic Priesthood quorums. Placing these activities and the activities of the girls under the Presiding Bishopric would strengthen their hand in leading the youth of the Church. The second was a need to focus on the plight of one of the largest, yet most neglected, groups in the Church—the single adults. The death of his wife Fern had made President Lee acutely aware of the lonely and often neglected status of this group. After her death and prior to his remarriage, he felt awkward and alone, even in the presence of married couples with whom he had been acquainted all his adult life. His later relationships with Joan and her unmarried friends gave him special insights into the thinking and the needs of these members who had never married or were divorced. As he reflected on this group and their special status, President Lee realized that every member of the Church who grows to maturity will, at some time, and for varying periods of time, be a single adult. Moreover, this is true even as to those who marry, except in the rare instance where marriage partners die at the same time. Although bishops, home teachers, Relief Society sisters, and priesthood quorums have shepherding responsibilities for the single adults, President Lee knew, because of the Church's strong emphasis on marriage and family life, and other factors, that, as a practical matter, the needs of the single adults were being largely neglected. So, as these factors provided impetus for change, President Lee gave long, prayerful thought to the steps to be taken to help solve these problems. When the changes had been effected, he said they were as far-reaching and significant as any organizational changes made in his lifetime.

It is assumed President Lee had the MPMIA chiefly in mind when he made this statement. This is so because the structuring of the APMIA merely involved the shifting of existing organizations, while the MPMIA involved the creation of an entirely new entity. The men chosen to head this new organization had been selected with great care. Two of them, Elders Faust and Perry, were called as General Authorities at the October 1972 general conference, only weeks before the creation of the MPMIA was formally approved by the Brethren. Elder Faust, who had proven himself to be a skilled administrator when he served as the president of a large stake in the Salt Lake Valley, was also one of the pioneers in correlation and leadership training. After his call as an Assistant to the Twelve, Elder Faust told President Lee of a profound spiritual experience he had had shortly before, which revealed he was to be called.

A few months before Elder Perry's call as an Assistant to the Twelve, President Lee visited the stake in the Boston area where Elder Perry served as stake president and came away greatly impressed with the way in which Elder Perry had organized to shepherd the single adults. And Elder

Hanks, who had served for almost twenty years as a General Authority, had a detailed knowledge of headquarters organization and procedure and enjoyed a special rapport with single adults around the Church as a popular speaker and a sensitive counselor.

Once these men had been called, set apart, and instructed, they ably pursued their duties assisted by a new general board and by their executive secretary, Jeffrey R. Holland. In like manner, the Presiding Bishopric, assisted by the presidencies of the YMMIA and YWMIA, energetically filled their role as leaders of the youth.

There was one other organizational change made by President Lee when on December 7, 1972, a new music department was created with Elder O. Leslie Stone as the managing director. And a year later, shortly before he died, President Lee met with Lee Bickmore when they discussed a proposed study of the health services organization, looking toward the possibility of some changes in its structure and procedure.

The many changes in organization made by President Lee have caused some to call him a great innovator. To the extent he advocated and, when he had the authority, effected changes necessary to facilitate the work, the title seems justified. However, insofar as it implies a quality of freewheeling change, it is inaccurate. From the beginning of his involvement with Church organization at the general level, President Lee was anxious to tie all organizations of the Church securely to the priesthood. This tendency was clearly shown when he struggled to devise a welfare plan for the entire Church. It was revealed then that the answer lay in using the mechanisms of the priesthood, defined in the revelations. As the welfare program evolved over the years, there were many changes in organization, designed to solve immediate problems. But, these never compromised the basic priesthood structure. So, the MPMIA was a necessary, but temporary, mechanism designed to help solve an existing problem, which was tied to the priesthood, its executive heads being Assistants to the Twelve.

President of the Church

Once he became the head of the Church, President Lee was free to choose among the Church assignments he would fill, without supervision, except as he might be spiritually prompted otherwise. Given that latitude, the assignments he accepted reveal a pattern of preference for youth meetings. Mention has already been made of his regular meetings with the new missionaries. In addition, he regularly accepted invitations to meet with other groups of young people. Indeed, it is not known he ever declined an invitation to speak to such a group.

A month after the Solemn Assembly, President Lee travelled to Mesa, Arizona, to address thirty-two hundred young people assembled in a youth conference. Joining him were Elder Marion D. Hanks and Bishop Vaughn J. Featherstone. The response to the prophet was typical. "The spiritual fervor generated," he wrote, "was almost frightening in its intensity, as to adopt, in some cases, an almost worshipful attitude which I am trying earnestly to play down to a respectful and appropriate loyalty to their leaders."

Later, President Lee went to Pocatello, Idaho, to speak to the students of the Idaho State University Stake. "It was something of a homecoming for me," he wrote, "an Idaho native now coming home." A month later found President Lee in Long Beach, California, where he addressed fourteen thousand young people, assembled in another youth conference. He spoke for an hour. The reaction was the same as at Mesa. There was little President Lee could do to prevent this, except to discontinue speaking to them. This he was unwilling to do.

The prophet took advantage of the trip to Long Beach to spend a few days in the Laguna Beach cottage. D. Arthur Haycock had accompanied President and Sister Lee there so as to be available to assist the prophet as needed. "I spent most of the day dictating to Arthur Haycock," he wrote the day after the youth meeting in Long Beach, "trying to release and be free from worries which had been troubling me." A main concern of President Lee at the time was his health. It was only a few weeks before that he had undergone the stressful percussion treatments to try to clear his lungs. While he was feeling better, his health still was not robust.

The next youth gathering the prophet attended was at Billings, Montana, a few weeks later. The young people assembled there may have lacked some of the polish among those who attended the Long Beach meeting, but President Lee seemingly felt a greater rapport with them because of a shared rural background. Despite the eminence he had gained and the cosmopolitan air his extensive international travel had given him, President Lee never lost touch with his beginnings, was proud to call Clifton his home, and always felt a special kinship with those who shared a similar background.

Not long after the Billings meeting, President Lee met with over three thousand LDS students at the Church's institute of religion near the University of Utah campus. Here he found the same support and acceptance as at other similar gatherings and the same desire for self-improvement among those in attendance. Later in the day, President Lee dedicated a new institute building for the LDS students attending the Salt Lake Valley Technical College.

A few weeks before the October 1973 general conference, the prophet spoke to the largest gathering of young people during his tenure as Church president. The occasion was a devotional held September 11 on the BYU campus, where 23,304 students filled the Marriott Center to the brim. The occasion was doubly important because President Lee was given the Exemplary Manhood Award as a token of the love and respect the young people had for him. After the October 1973 general conference, President Lee had two other opportunities to address special gatherings of young people. The first was on October 23 when he dedicated a new stake center for the LDS students at the University of Utah. Three days later found him in Rexburg, Idaho, where he addressed five thousand students gathered in a special assembly. A feature of the meeting was the rendition of a musical number composed for the occasion entitled, "Listen to a Wondrous Voice." The high point of the meeting came when the prophet was presented with a beautiful plaque from the Associated Students of Ricks College, which bore a lengthy inscription signifying the love and admiration the students had for him. "Called from the simplicity of farm and field," it said in part, "to stand in the upper rooms of the temple, where the veil is thinnest, comes such a man, whose life is a testimony that speaks the praises of God. This is a man who is more than a man, a man bearing Israel's prophetic inheritance, one of God's choicest sons. Thanks be to God that we live in a prophet's time, when his inspired leadership draws us closer to stand in those holy places where we prayerfully await Christ's second coming."

It is gatherings such as these that help inspire a spirit of discipleship. The students at Ricks came mainly from a rural environment, not unlike that of Clifton. Therefore, they had a proprietary attitude toward President Lee. He was one of them. He belonged to them. This son of Idaho had risen to the pinnacle of Church leadership and to national business prominence from a status of isolated anonymity like their own. Yet, the eminence he had achieved did not create a gulf between him and them. They were his friends. He did not shun them because of the vast differences in their status. Instead, he beckoned them to high achievement, encouraged them, expressed confidence in them, and assured them of God's loving concern for their well-being and success. Yet, young people who did not share President Lee's rural roots responded to him in the same way as did those at Billings or Rexburg. His appeal to young people was universal. There was something about the man—his stance, his attitude, his visage, and his demeanor—which naturally drew them to him. It was so from the earliest days of his teaching career.

This magnetism was not limited to the youth. Mature adults reacted to him in the same way. Marion G. Romney, for instance, who was a mature adult when he first met

President Lee, said when they first shook hands, he was "captivated by his magnetic presence." (Marion G. Romney sermon at funeral of Harold B. Lee.) "He was not only a prophet," wrote President Romney, "but also a great seer and revelator. I have never been associated with a man who drew more heavily upon the powers of heaven than Harold B. Lee." And, he added later, "We who sat with him daily were frequently amazed at the breadth of his vision and the depth of his understanding."

Many others who were first exposed to President Lee as adults had reactions similar to those of President Romney. But, as suggested, it was the youth who were especially attracted to him and who, as the reactions at the youth gathering in Mesa imply, had an almost worshipful attitude toward him. The special emphasis he gave to youth gatherings and the fact his main literary offering consists of a compilation of talks he delivered to the youth, demonstrate the reciprocal feelings of love he had for them.

Several days before the meeting at Ricks College where feelings of love prevailed, President Lee became aware once more of malignant influences that sought to do him harm. Water poured from his office pitcher had a bitter taste. Samples of the water, which were tested in laboratories in Provo, Utah, and Denver, Colorado, were shown to contain a toxic material that, when injected into mice, produced either convulsions or death, depending on the quantity injected. Given the previous death threats from the cult in Mexico, the incident produced great consternation at Church headquarters and increased concern about the prophet's safety. An extensive investigation produced no clues about the identity of the person responsible for poisoning the water in his pitcher. It was apparent, however, that there had been a serious breach of the security net that had been created to protect him. An effort was made to plug any gaps in that net when, shortly afterward, President Lee's trusted friend Gordon Affleck was appointed to supervise security for the Church Administration Building and a special office was provided for him near President Lee's office on the main floor. This, with continued cooperation from the city police and the FBI, minimized concerns about the prophet's safety.

During his short tenure as the President of the Church, President Lee retained his avid interest in the temples and temple work. In addition to the regular instruction he gave to missionaries in the temple, he also taught temple workers whenever possible. On February 11, 1973, he spoke to over thirteen hundred of them assembled in the fifth floor auditorium of the Salt Lake Temple. There he emphasized the need for the workers to be well trained and clean and to reflect, through their reverent behavior, the sanctity of the holy ordinances they were to administer. On November 18, 1973, he gave similar instructions to workers in the Manti Temple in connection with the installation of June B. Black as the new temple president.

Earlier in the year, President Lee began an initiative that was to have a profound effect on the future temple building activities of the Church. On May 3, 1973, tentative approval was given to a proposal to construct "stake center sized" temples. This was part of the plan to establish the Church on a firm international footing by making the blessings of the temple more readily available to members around the world. With the rapid expansion of the Church and the attendant ballooning of costs, it became clear the size and the cost of temples would have to be radically scaled down as the number of smaller temples was multiplied. Later in the month, the first step was taken to implement this plan when approval was given to construct a small temple in São Paulo, Brazil, the first temple in South America.

Meanwhile, President Lee and his brethren were moving forward with other plans to advance the work of the Church. Consistent with the aim to economize while increasing the efficiency of administration, President Lee began soon after his ordination to study the feasibility of using training videos to reduce the amount of travel by members of the general boards. This concept would flour-

Harold B. Lee

ish in the years ahead, leading ultimately to the installation of TV satellite receiving dishes near many stake centers, by means of which instructions could be given to many thousands from a single teaching station. He also initiated plans to construct a "meditation park" on the Mount of Olives, which later led to the construction there of a park that included a monument recognizing Orson Hyde, who had dedicated the Holy Land for the gathering of Israel.

A milestone in headquarters administration was passed in June 1973 when a three-day open house was held to commemorate the opening of the new Church Office Building. On the first evening of the open house, held June 20, President Lee and his counselors and their wives stood in a receiving line to greet business, professional, and community leaders and the official representatives of other Church denominations. With this twenty-eight story modern high rise available, it became possible to consolidate most Church staff personnel in offices on the block east of Temple Square, many of whom previously had been housed in various buildings around the city.

As the new Church Office Building neared completion, attention was focused on the condition of the Church Administration Building, which was then more than fifty years old. During its life, the building had received normal maintenance care but had now reached the point where major renovations were necessary to bring its heating, air conditioning, wiring, and plumbing equipment up to modern standards. On February 13, 1973, Emil Fetzer, the church architect, and Fred Baker, the managing director of the building department, met with the First Presidency to review the matter. "It seems imperative that we go forward as outlined," wrote President Lee of the meeting. These renovations, which were completed after President Lee passed away, took two years. During that time, the occupants of the administration building were housed temporarily in the new office building.

While the plans for the construction or renovation of these headquarters buildings progressed, President Lee was harassed by a controversy over the proposed demolition of the Eighteenth Ward chapel in Salt Lake City and an adjacent building, Whitney Hall, named after Orson F. Whitney, a longtime bishop of this ward. Because the buildings were old and disfunctional, the local leaders, and most of the members, approved of their demolition and the construction of a modern facility. A vocal minority was opposed, however, even to the point of seeking a restraining order. This was essentially a matter to be decided by the local members in accordance with established building guidelines. Because this particular chapel, out of the hundreds in the Church, was near the Church administrative complex, and was the chapel where many prominent leaders of the Church had worshipped over the years, the First Presidency unavoidably became involved. At length, the controversy was resolved, although not without some bruised feelings, when Whitney Hall was demolished, the chapel was moved to a site just south of the Utah State Capitol, and a new chapel was constructed on the old site located on A Street between Second and Third Avenues. In an effort to smooth the ruffled feathers, President Lee spoke at the dedication of the new chapel on August 14, 1973.

The day before this dedication ceremony, President Lee spoke at the funeral services of Willis J. Woodbury, which evoked nostalgic memories of the mission field. "He was a cello player," wrote the prophet of his first missionary companion, "and while I was his companion, I accompanied him many times on the piano, before church and civic groups and in many homes we had tracted." Little did the prophet know that before the year ended, he would follow his companion into another field of labor.

Before that time came, however, President Lee still had important things to do. Throughout the summer, he had worked intermittently on the plans for an area conference in Munich, Germany, in late August. President and Sister Lee, accompanied by D. Arthur Haycock and his wife, Maurine, left Salt Lake City on August 22, destined for

Munich. With intermediate stops in New York and London, they arrived there on the twenty-fourth. All of the events of the conference were held in Olympia Hall, which had been specially constructed for the 1972 Olympic Summer Games held in Munich. These included a combined dance-music festival Friday evening, the twenty-fourth, featuring groups from Germany, Italy, France, and Holland, two general sessions both Saturday and Sunday, and a priesthood session Saturday evening. President Lee keynoted the opening general session, concluded the priesthood and the Sunday afternoon sessions, and conducted all sessions. The Salt Lake Tabernacle Choir performed at the Sunday morning session. The addresses were translated into German, English, Italian, Spanish, French, and Dutch. Headsets were provided, which enabled the audience to tune to the language they understood. President Lee bore a powerful testimony to conclude the conference, which, with the closing song "God Be with You till We Meet Again," produced an almost Pentecostal outpouring of emotion. Wrote President Lee of the conference: "Never have I experienced such a response from an audience as here where all animosities of past wars were forgotten in a brotherhood which made everyone a 'kin' in the Church of Jesus Christ of Latter-day Saints."

On Monday the twenty-seventh, President and Sister Lee flew to Vienna in company with Elder and Sister Gordon B. Hinckley. This began an eight-day tour during which many meetings were held on the continent and in England. President Lee asked Elder Hinckley to join him on this his last tour because of the special rapport that existed between them. Their close acquaintance dated back to the 1930s before either of them had been called as a General Authority. At that time, President Lee was the managing director of the welfare department and Elder Hinckley was the executive secretary of the Church radio and publicity committee. Their relationship during this tour, as it had been earlier when they travelled to the Holy Land together, was that of missionary companions. Elder

Hinckley, the junior companion, assumed the responsibility of arranging the itinerary and the meetings and then joined with the prophet in sharing the pulpit. In many cases Sister Lee and Sister Hinckley joined their husbands in speaking.

In Vienna, meetings were held with Mission President Neil Schaerrer and some of his missionaries. The party then flew to London, where they counselled with several mission presidents and their wives. At the London Temple, Joseph W. Darling was installed as the new president replacing Dougald McKeown. While at the temple, the brethren instructed the officiators, then, with their wives, had lunch at the Manor House, an ancient domicile near the temple. During the next two days, the travellers held meetings with Mission Presidents Reed Reeve and Arnold Knapp and their missionaries. And afterward, they held a series of meetings with the members of the Birmingham, Bristol, and Loughborough stakes. "The spiritual response was overwhelming," wrote President Lee following the last meeting, "and many tears were shed as we bade farewell to those in attendance, after giving our testimonies and our blessings upon those assembled. Sister Hinckley and Joan both spoke, as did Gordon B. Hinckley and myself."

The area conference in Munich and the special meetings held afterward marked a high point in President Lee's ministry. The prophetic mantle he wore, and the inspired talks he delivered, enriched by the depth of his scriptural knowledge and the scope of his spiritual insight, had produced the unusual responses referred to in his diary. While these doubtless were inspiring to his listeners, they were equally uplifting to him, providing new strength and motivation to continue the course.

President Lee returned home to face a full agenda of work. High on the list was preparation for the coming general conference. Beginning with September 15, he spent many long hours outlining the several major talks he was scheduled to give, including his traditional keynote mes-

Harold B. Lee

President Harold B. Lee and President Spencer W. Kimball at the Munich, Germany Area Conference, August 1973

sage at the Regional Representatives seminar. Because of reports that some Regional Representatives misconceived their role, thinking of themselves as a sort of super stake president, he outlined remarks that clearly defined their role as teachers and trainers, functioning only in a staff capacity.

President Lee interrupted these preparations to speak at the funeral services for Sister Gladys Condie Monson, the mother of Elder Thomas S. Monson of the Twelve. President Lee had known the Monson family for many years from his service as the president of the Pioneer Stake. Young Tom Monson had been a special favorite of his, whom he had encouraged and counselled as he watched him develop under the discipline of heavy Church assignments while still young. So, he was both honored and pleased to respond to the family's request that he speak at Sister Monson's funeral.

On September 26, President Lee recorded with satisfaction an organizational change that had been under consideration for some time. "Dee Anderson was introduced as the executive secretary of the budget committee," he wrote on that day. "This will provide a constant watch over the expenditures of the church and will see to it that no new programs are launched without a full disclosure of costs, personnel and office needs. This will provide a long needed control which we have not had in the past." This device, as much as any other, would help to put a brake on the growth of bureaucracy at Church headquarters, a problem that had troubled President Lee for many years.

The first session of the 143rd semiannual conference of the Church convened in the Salt Lake Tabernacle on Friday morning, October 5, 1973. President Harold B. Lee conducted this and all other general sessions of the conference, held over a period of three days. His voice was strong. He acted with vigor. He conveyed the impression to those watching and listening that he was prepared to serve energetically for many years as the head of the Church. That his two immediate predecessors, Presidents Joseph Fielding Smith and David O. McKay, had served into their mid-nineties held the prospect this seventy-four-year-old prophet might well lead the Church for two decades. Only the prophet's doctors, a few members of his family, and a smaller number of his associates knew of the precarious condition of his health. It was only this small circle who would not have been unduly shocked had they been told that as he stood at the Tabernacle pulpit that morning, President Harold B. Lee had opened the last general conference he would be privileged to attend in life. But, such was the reality.

Following an invocation by Elder Hugh B. Brown of the Twelve, and the rendition by the Tabernacle Choir of the hymn "Lord Accept Our True Devotion," President Lee launched into the keynote address of the conference. In it, he emphasized the need for self-respect. This comes chiefly, he indicated, from a recognition that we are the offspring of God and, therefore, have the seeds of Godhood and perfection within us. These comments were prompted, in part, by "the shocking lack of self respect by so many individuals as is evidenced by their dress, their manner, and engulfing waves of permissiveness which seem to be moving over the world like an avalanche." (Conference Report, Oct. 1973, p. 3.) These conditions had been created, in large part, by the controversies stirred up by the war in Vietnam. They seemed to be tearing at the fabric of modern society and, therefore, were deserving of the special attention of a prophet. His remedy for these ills was the remedy that all prophets of God have prescribed: To honor and obey God, who has given us life, while honoring the sanctity of the bodies He has given us by keeping them pure and unsullied.

President Lee underscored the key points of his address to the priesthood brethren through this diary entry: "Saturday night at priesthood meeting," wrote he, "I *spoke plainly* to men who are over the usual marriage age and have neglected to find a wife. I also urged local leaders to give sanction and leadership to the new Melchizedek Priesthood MIA."

President Lee's concluding address at the last general session, Sunday afternoon, was an appropriate benediction to the numerous conference addresses he had delivered during almost thirty-three years of apostolic service. He expressed loving concern for the members of the Church, especially those in places of peril—the Middle East, where war raged, and in Chile, where there was serious political turmoil. He also cautioned about enemies within, mentioning those who had written disparagingly about the Church and its leaders. Referring specifically to the Prophet Joseph Smith, he quoted President George Albert Smith as saying that those who belittle the prophet "will be forgotten in the remains of mother earth, and the odor of their infamy will ever be with them, but honor, majesty and fidelity to God, exemplified by Joseph Smith, and attached to his name, will never die." He then quoted several verses from the seventy-first section of the Doctrine and Covenants, laying special emphasis upon the warnings directed to those who attempt to tear down the Church. Of these he said, "No weapon formed against the work of the Lord will ever prosper." There followed statements about the foundational importance of the Book of Mormon to the Church and lengthy quotations from the eighteenth and eighty-eighth sections of the Doctrine and Covenants about the sources and channels of revelation and from the book of Joseph Smith in the Pearl of Great Price about the signs of the second coming. As to the latter, he said: "Brothers and sisters, this is the day the Lord is speaking of. You see the signs are here. Be ye therefore ready. The Brethren have told you in this conference how to prepare to be ready. We have never had a conference when there has been so much direct instruction, so much admonition, when the problems have been defined and also the solutions to the problems have been suggested."

He ended by affirming the nearness of the Lord and His willingness to lead and protect us in times of testing and strife, by expressing thanks for the unity and the support of his brethren, by extending his love and blessings to all, and by adding this final testimony: "I know with a certainty that defies all doubt that this is His work, and that He is guiding us and directing us today, as He has done in every dispensation of the gospel." (Ibid., p. 171.)

This sermon assumes special significance because it was the last one delivered to the entire Church by this prophet, because most of it was delivered extemporaneously as President Lee was moved to speak, and because of the powerful, confirming spirit that accompanied its delivery. By way of affirmance, President Lee wrote afterward: "The afterglow of the general conference was most impressive. From the Twelve in our temple meeting there came the unanimous expression that it was something unusual. . . . There seemed to be something in my closing remarks, which came spontaneously, that seemed to some to be prophetic of the times, [stressing] the need for our people to stand in holy places and be not moved, as the Master had counselled, when the signs of His second coming were drawing near."

The day after the conference ended, the General Authorities and their wives joined in their traditional postconference dinner and social. It was held on the twenty-sixth floor of the new Church Office Building. The entertainment featured the portrayal of a meeting of the Polysophical Society. Originated by Lorenzo Snow before he became the president of the Church, this society featured gatherings where those present recited, sang, performed, or spoke at the invitation of the one presiding, who controlled the order of participation by sending written notes through a young messenger. This night, the messenger was the grandson of Francis Urry, the director of the program, who brought President Lee a note asking that he leave his blessing, and who then led the prophet to the podium. The boy's conduct was so gracious and deferential, yet so self-confident, that President Lee was instinctively drawn to him, congratulated him at the time, and later wrote a letter inviting him for a visit in the prophet's office. President Lee told the parents of this seven-year-old boy, whose name was Michael Van Harris, that he had seldom seen such an engaging spirit in one so young and said the lad had a special mission to perform. For his part, Michael expressed deep love for President Lee, while saying he knew the prophet loved him too. Michael mourned President Lee's death, then, two years later, suddenly and unaccountably took ill and quietly passed away. Michael's parents felt the deaths of President Lee and their son were spiritually linked and that the boy was called to the other side to serve a special purpose at the side of the prophet.

This touching incident seems to show the special quality of character revealed in President Harold B. Lee at the end. It was the characteristic of unfeigned love shown toward all. It was a characteristic that was an integral and dominant part of his makeup, but which, at times, was dimmed, if not obscured, by his enormous talents for organization, delegation, and motivation and by a lively temper that sometimes, though not often, led him to make critical comments. A few had felt the effect of President Lee's temper over the years. Those who did so never forgot it. What worsened the experience was the distressing sense that Brother Lee was displeased or that one had failed or disappointed him and had lost his confidence. Such was his stance and air, his personal magnetism and prophetic stature that his associates sought instinctively to please him and to obey him. Thus, any sign in the form of criticism or rebuke that one's conduct did not measure up, or was unacceptable, was cause for self-reproach. Routinely, however, the few incidents when President Lee's temper flared were invariably followed, whether immediately or in time, by a showing of increased love toward the one chastised, as the 121st section of the Doctrine and Covenants requires. In the end, as suggested, President Lee's conduct was free from any hint of harshness or any trace of temper and was marked only by a genuine, uniform attitude of love and approval shown toward all. This represented a major triumph of self-discipline over a characteristic that President Lee had struggled against all his life.

Several events President Lee attended during the last few weeks of his life illustrated the dominance of this loving quality in his makeup. On December 5, he and Sister Lee joined several hundred Deseret Industries workers for a Christmas celebration and to dedicate a new DI building in Murray, a suburb south of Salt Lake City. The prophet believed this organization was the best example of applied welfare principles of any agency within the system. Most of the workers were handicapped or aged and unable to compete in the commercial market. Here they worked to the limit of their capacity, performing important service for which they were adequately compensated in cash or commodities. Grateful to be useful and independent, they showed genuine happiness, an attitude that gave a special spark to the evening. President Lee felt uplifted, sensing among these people a spirit in full harmony with the Christmas theme.

Later that week, the prophet and Sister Lee were breakfast guests of the Cannon Stake high priests and their wives. There were fifteen hundred present. S. Perry Lee, the prophet's brother, presided over this stake, which included many of the Church units that were once in the Pioneer Stake. It was like a homecoming for the prophet. "It was a most satisfying experience," wrote he, "to recall the years gone by when I was the stake president." Then, two days later, he spoke to a group of 255 missionaries in the temple, where, for the last time, he taught some of those who would be tomorrow's leaders. He was challenged, as always, to answer their searching questions. These usually pertained to the special clothing worn during the ceremony and the sacred covenants they were asked to make. He took care to emphasize the symbolic nature of the ceremony, the need to show integrity in honoring their covenants, and the elevating effect doing this would have on their lives. He sought, also, to eliminate any false or fanciful ideas his young friends had about the endowment or the temple. He adroitly turned away questions about reported appearances of the Savior in the temple by saying that because it is His house, it would not be unusual for him to visit there, nor should one be surprised to find him there. While President Lee was aware of reliable reports of such visitations, he minimized them out of concern the missionaries would unduly focus on them to the exclusion of the vital meaning of the temple experience in their own lives.

There remained three other institutional Christmas parties President and Sister Lee would attend. The first was a dinner they shared with the employees of the Beehive Clothing Mills and their companions on December 12. The following evening, the prophet and his counselors hosted a gathering of Church employees and their families in the Salt Lake Tabernacle. A medley of Christmas carols sung by the Tabernacle Choir and a congregational hymn added a quiet, spiritual tone. President Lee's remarks celebrated the wondrous effect of the Savior's birth and His willing submission to death by crucifixion. And because December also marks the birth of the Prophet Joseph Smith, he traced similarities in their lives. The tense confrontation between Israel and Egypt, which then existed in the Middle East and which had produced shortages of food and fuel and threatened more, also prompted him to remind the audience of the counsel given since the inception of the welfare program to conserve their resources, and he pointedly asked if they had heeded it. Then, in token of the kind of charitable spirit the Christmas season engenders, he said: "I wish I could be a thousand times more understanding, to deal a thousand times more kindly, and with a thousand times more wisdom and foresight. . . . And I only want to be what you, the faithful members of the church, would wish me to be."

The last Christmas party the prophet and Sister Lee attended was one held in the LaFayette Ballroom of the Hotel Utah on December 18. It was hosted by Douglas H. Smith, the president of the Beneficial Life Insurance Company. In the brief comments President Lee made at the dinner, he referred to the violence in the Middle East and to the efforts being made by the United States to negotiate a settlement. He then asked the guests to join him in a prayer for peace. The impact of what President Lee said was described by Douglas H. Smith, who later became a member of the Seventy: "After he finished, there was total silence. Most of us were extremely hesitant to open our eyes, because we knew he was talking with the Lord. His deep, compassionate love for all of the children of the Lord—Arab, Jew and Gentile—was appealingly expressed." And as he left the auditorium, one of the senior members of the Twelve said he had never been more deeply touched by a prayer. President Lee's brief remarks were a fitting benediction not only to the evening's festivities, but to his apostolic career. He never spoke in public again.

Chapter Twenty-nine

The Prophet Passes On

When he arrived late at the Beneficial Life Christmas party, President Lee told Douglas Smith he was exhausted and would not have come were it not for the special affection he had for him. The prophet's store of energy was almost used up. He seemed to know that, although he also seemed to push the idea aside deliberately. While a few in his inner circle knew President Lee's health was fragile, they had no conception he was so near the end.

During the week before Christmas, President and Sister Lee were free from formal gatherings but had many things to do in preparation. There were gifts to be purchased not only for their large family but also for many close friends and associates. While Sister Lee assumed responsibility for most of these arrangements, the prophet inevitably was involved in some of them. Meanwhile, he had a few matters to take care of at his office. During this time, no one detected anything in his demeanor that suggested he thought the end was near. He was looking forward to the duties ahead.

The Prophet Passes On

President and Sister Lee spent Christmas morning quietly at home. They planned to join the family for dinner at Helen and Brent's. They were delayed in arriving until midafternoon because a young family had come to the house unannounced, seeking counsel and comfort for the wife and mother who had terminal cancer. The prophet's advice, which has universal application, was to live for the day, without concern or fear, confidently prepared to remain, or to pass on, as the Lord wills.

After several joyous hours with their family, President and Sister Lee returned home, where they spent a relaxed evening, visiting companionably, reflecting on the true significance of Christmas, and intermittently calling special friends and associates to extend season's greetings.

The prophet slept soundly that night, but awoke the next morning feeling tired and listless. And, during a coughing spell, there was a showing of blood. Concerned about him, Sister Lee called Doctor James Orme, who, after a cursory examination at the home, recommended that President Lee go to the hospital for further diagnosis and quiet rest. There appeared to be no cause for real concern. He was driven to the LDS Hospital, where he checked in at 3:00 P.M. Reflecting the casual circumstances surrounding his hospitalization, President Lee had asked his personal secretary, Arthur Haycock, who had come to the home, to bring along some papers he wanted to study and some letters he wanted to sign. He obviously did not regard the situation as critical and intended to go on working.

After a while, following examinations by the medical staff, Arthur called President Marion G. Romney and Brent Goates to advise them President Lee was in the hospital. They came immediately. President N. Eldon Tanner was out of the city. At the prophet's request, these three administered to him. He thanked and commended them and said he felt better. Meanwhile, a team of hospital technicians, directed by Doctor Alan H. Morris, a lung specialist, had been attending President Lee, carefully examining him and taking specimens for lab analysis. These revealed that he was anemic and, surprisingly, that he was suffering heart distress. This last diagnosis was a surprise because it had never been made before during the many examinations he had undergone. The doctor ordered that oxygen be administered, hoping this would help normalize the heart condition.

After President and Sister Lee ate a light supper together, served in the room, and there appearing to be no present emergency, she was persuaded to return home. Brent drove her there. Arthur remained in the room, reading the newspaper, while the patient rested. Suddenly, President Lee sat up in bed and removed the oxygen mask while coughing heavily. After laying him back down in bed, Arthur, concerned about the prophet's ashen color and the glazed, bulging appearance of his eyes, summoned the nurse. As there was no apparent tone of urgency in Arthur's voice, the nurse, Mrs. Nola Black, thought that since the patient was awake, it would be a good time to take him for x-rays, which the doctor had ordered. Asking for someone from inhalation therapy to accompany her and the patient to x-ray, the nurse pushed a wheelchair to President Lee's room. On entering, she saw him rise up in bed, his eyes open wide in a trancelike stare, while temporarily resting his weight on both elbows. Then he slipped back on to his pillow at about the time a resident doctor, whom Arthur also had summoned, entered the room. It required only one glance at the patient for the resident to shout "cardiac arrest." There followed an hour of the most frantic activity in room 819 in a fruitless effort to save the life of President Harold B. Lee. At the height of the drama, as many as twelve people—doctors, interns, and nurses—were crowded into the small room, along with their sophisticated and bulky equipment. Under the direction of Dr. Morris, everything within the limits of modern technology and skill was done to save this life. The effort was unavailing.

During the hour the professionals labored over the prophet, calls were made to Presidents Marion G. Romney and Spencer W. Kimball in Salt Lake City, who immediately came to the hospital. President N. Eldon Tanner was notified of the emergency in Arizona, where he had gone to spend the holidays with members of his family. Meanwhile, Brent, who had returned about the time the cardiac arrest alert was given, arranged to have Sister Lee and Helen brought to the hospital. As they waited anxiously in a nearby room, there was nothing for them to do but to pray. President Kimball, who arrived first, was asked to lead the family in prayer. Stunned by this shocking turn of events, he was hardly able to speak. Later when President Romney arrived, he also was asked to lead in prayer.

The prophet passed away shortly before 9:00 P.M. Wednesday, December 26, 1973. Word of his death was given to the family by a saddened Doctor James Orme, who had just come from room 819. Within an hour, the news had been announced over local television and radio. Everywhere it was met with a sense of incredulity. How could it be? The longevity of Mormon church presidents had become legendary. They were expected to live a very long time, at least until they were eighty years old, or older. And the public was accustomed to hearing reports of a prophet's infirmities long in advance of his death, or because of advanced age, as in the case of President Joseph Fielding Smith, the public was conditioned to the idea that he might go at any time. Neither circumstance existed here. Harold B. Lee, age seventy-four, who, as far as the public knew, was in robust health, was gone after having served less than eighteen months. No other Church president had a shorter tenure. No other Church president died so young, except the Prophet Joseph Smith, who was martyred at age thirty-eight. This would take some getting used to.

A sense of sadness and disbelief pervaded the council room when the Twelve assembled in the administration building the next morning. There, under the direction of President Spencer W. Kimball, the customary actions were taken necessary to insure the uninterrupted flow of business at Church headquarters. Also, President N. Eldon

Tanner and Elders Gordon B. Hinckley and Marvin J. Ashton were appointed to work with the family in making funeral arrangements. It was decided the services would be held in the Tabernacle Saturday, December 29, with a public viewing the day before.

More than twelve thousand filed past President Lee's casket on Friday between 8:00 A.M. and 8:00 P.M. as his body lay in state in the inner foyer of the administration building. Some of the prophet's grandsons were present during all this time. Many of the mourners were not members of the Church. Meanwhile, the family and the Church offices were flooded with messages of love and condolence.

The family and the General Authorities assembled in the foyers of the administration building Saturday morning, where the family prayer was offered by the prophet's brother, S. Perry Lee. The cortege left for the temple grounds about 11:30. The Tabernacle was crowded to capacity with overflow seating in the Assembly Hall.

President Spencer W. Kimball conducted the impressive services and delivered the main address. In it he traced the major achievements of President Lee's life and his salient characteristics. The other speakers, Presidents N. Eldon Tanner and Marion G. Romney and Elder Gordon B. Hinckley, elaborated on these, focusing on their personal relationship with the prophet. President Tanner, who seemed to look on him as a mentor from the time President Lee called him as a stake president, showed considerable emotion as he spoke, which was unusual considering his normally stoical conduct in the pulpit. President Romney, while lauding President Lee's prophetic qualities, said, "We do not mourn today for President Lee but for ourselves." Elder Hinckley, among other things, expressed the conviction that while President Lee's passing was unexpected, it was not untimely. "No righteous man dies before his time," said he. The prayers were offered by Elder Marvin J. Ashton and D. Arthur Haycock, and the music was provided by the Salt Lake Tabernacle Choir with Alexander Schreiner at the organ.

The Prophet Passes On

Funeral procession of President Harold B. Lee, December 1973 (Photo by Jed A. Clark)

Outside the weather was wet and dreary. The General Authorities stood in parallel lines north of the Tabernacle, providing a lane through which the casket was carried to the waiting hearse. It then led the way to the Salt Lake Cemetery on the north bench, followed by the family, the General Authorities and their companions, and other friends.

By the time of the interment, the drizzle had increased to a light rain, which contained some splotches of snow. This brought out the umbrellas of those who had the foresight to bring them. The mourners stood around the open grave, which was next to Fern's, while son-in-law L. Brent Goates offered the dedicatory prayer. In it he observed the propriety of the heavens weeping while a prophet was laid to rest. He also noted that President Lee's propensity of always being "ahead of schedule" was seen even in his comparatively early death.

This rung down the curtain on an extraordinary life whose salient happenings have been recorded here. But the narrative does not begin to tell the story of the impact President Harold B. Lee had on his times and his contemporaries, nor upon the organization to which he had devoted his life, The Church of Jesus Christ of Latter-day Saints. As he had said when he came to the prophetic office, the true measure of his achievements will be found only in the hearts and the minds of those touched by his ministry.

Bibliography

Primary Sources

Gibbons, Francis M., Diaries, 1950–73.

Official Reports of the General Conferences of The Church of Jesus Christ of Latter-day Saints, 1941–73.

Lee, Harold B., Diaries, 1941–73.

Lee, Harold B., Manuscripts, Archives of The Church of Jesus Christ of Latter-day Saints.

Newspapers

Church News, Salt Lake City, Utah, 1941–73.

Deseret News, Salt Lake City Utah, 1941–73.

Salt Lake Tribune, Salt Lake City, 1941–73.

Periodicals

Articles by or about Harold B. Lee

February 22, 1936. "The Glory of Man," *Church News,* 2, 7.

December 1936. "The Church Security Program in Action," *Improvement Era,* 740–41.

March 1937. "Place of the Relief Society in the Church Security Plan," *Relief Society Magazine,* 140–43.

April 1937. "Church Security—Retrospect, Introspect, Prospect," *Improvement Era,* 204–10, 260.

Bibliography

May 15, 1937. "Spirit of the Church Security Program," *Church News*, 5–6.

October 1937. "The Place of the Priesthood Quorum in the Church Security Program," *Improvement Era*, 634–35.

August 1939. "The Relief Society in the Welfare Plan," *Relief Society Magazine*, 526–27.

April 1940. "The Church Welfare Program," *Relief Society Magazine*, 458–62.

March 1, 1941. "The Welfare Plan—The Lord's Way," *Church News*, 4, 7.

May 1942. "Unity for the Welfare of the Church and the Nation," *Improvement Era*, 297, 342.

May 30, 1942. "Put on the Whole Armor of God," *Church News*, 5–6, 8.

November 1942. "Remaining Steadfast," *Improvement Era*, 713–14.

April 1942. "Hearing the Voice," *Improvement Era*, 444–47.

August 7, 1943. "What Constitutes Effective Ward Teaching," *Church News*, 4, 6.

May 1943. "Teach the Children to Use Their Hands," *Children's Friend*, 229.

August 1943. "For Every Child, His Spiritual and Cultural Heritage," *Children's Friend*, 373.

November 1943. "Wells of Living Water," *Improvement Era*, 720–22.

November 6, 1943. "As a Man Thinketh," *Church News*, 4, 12.

November 1943. "What I Read as a Boy," *Children's Friend*, 508.

February 12, 1944. "Production Increase in Church Welfare Advised," *Church News*, 7–8.

May 1944. "The Gospel Plan," *Improvement Era*, 331–32.

May 13, 1944. "Welfare," *Church News*, 9.

November 1944. "On Detecting Truth from Error," *Improvement Era*, 707–8.

May 1945. "Challenge to the Priesthood," *Improvement Era*, 319.

November 1945. "Our Responsibility Before God and Man," *Improvement Era*, 680–81.

May 1946. "Living in the Bonds of Brotherhood," *Improvement Era*, 321–22.

September 1946. "A Challenge to Youth," *Improvement Era*, 560, 561, 600.

Bibliography

December 1946. "Parents and Children in the Home at Christmas Time," *Children's Friend*, 540.

June 1949. "The Work of the Lord on Vacation," *Children's Friend*, 254–55.

August 1950. "Primary Fundamentals for Primary Workers and Parents," *Children's Friend*, 341–43.

December 1950. "Fortified by an Unshakable Testimony," *Improvement Era*, 1006–7.

February 1951. "The Primary Teacher," *Children's Friend*, 75–77.

June 1951. "Zion Must Be Strengthened," *Improvement Era*, 417–19.

June 1952. "Special Witness," *Improvement Era*, 458–60.

December 1953. "And This is My Gospel," *Improvement Era*, 937–38.

July 1953. "Harold B. Lee, Apostle of the Lord," *Improvement Era*, 504–8, 522.

December 1954. "Report on the Orient," *Improvement Era*, 926–30.

June 1955. "My Daughter Prepares for Marriage," *Relief Society Magazine*, 172–73.

December 1955. "Be Guided by the Light Within," *Improvement Era*, 935–37.

March 1956. "Put Power in Your Teaching," *Improvement Era*, 68.

June 1957. "Marriage for Eternity," *Improvement Era*, 406–8.

August 1957. "Thrift," *Improvement Era*, 566–67.

June 1959. "The Gospel, a Solid Wall of Truth," *Improvement Era*, 452–55.

June 1960. "The Work in Great Britain," *Improvement Era*, 433–36.

December 1960. "God Working With Men," *Improvement Era*, 914–17.

October 1962. "Report from the Correlation Committee," *Improvement Era*, 936–41.

December 1964. "Search Diligently, Pray Always and Be Believing," *Improvement Era*, 1104.

February 1965. "Preparing to Meet the Lord," *Improvement Era*, 121.

June 1967. "Enter a Holy Temple," *Improvement Era*, 144.

January 1968. "Woman's Glorious Purpose," *Relief Society Magazine*, 7–13.

December 1968. "Make Our Lord and Master Your Friend," *Improvement Era*, 70–73.

June 1969. "To Know God," *Improvement Era*, 103–5.

Bibliography

February 1970. "The Lighted Lamps of Faith," *Improvement Era*, 93–95.

July 1971. "Successful Sinners," *Ensign*, 2–3.

November 1971. "The Way to Eternal Life," *Ensign*, 9–17.

February 1972. "Maintain Your Place as a Woman," *Ensign*, 48–56.

April 1972. "I Walked Today Where Jesus Walked," *Ensign*, 3–7.

July 1972. "A Time of Decision," *Ensign*, 29–33.

July 12, 1972. "Harold B. Lee Named LDS President," *The Nauvoo Independent*.

January 1973. "May the Kingdom of God Go Forth," *Ensign*, 23–25.

November 1972. "President Harold B. Lee, an Appreciation," by Elder Gordon B. Hinckley, *Ensign*.

February 1974. "Diary of Action — The Life and Administration of Harold B. Lee," *Ensign*.

Unpublished Papers in Possession of the Author

A Biographical Narrative, by Mabel Hickman, Mesa, Arizona, May 28, 1975.

A Short Biography of Harold Bingham Lee — Apostle, by Paul K. Winward, Summer 1966.

"The Death of a Prophet," by Duane V. Cardall, Salt Lake Institute of Religion Devotional Speech, January 25, 1974.

Books

Allen, James B., and Glen M. Leonard. *The Story of the Latter-day Saints*. Salt Lake City: Deseret Book Company, 1976.

Anderson, Joseph. *Prophets I Have Known*. Salt Lake City: Deseret Book Company, 1973.

Arrington, Leonard J., and Davis Bitton: *The Mormon Experience*. New York: Alfred Knopf, 1979.

Barton, Peggy Petersen. *Mark E. Petersen, A Biography*. Salt Lake City: Deseret Book Company, 1985.

Berrett, William E. *The Restored Church*. Salt Lake City: Deseret Book Company, 12th edition, 1965.

Cowan, Richard O. *The Church in the Twentieth Century*. Salt Lake City: Bookcraft, 1985.

Goates, L. Brent. *Harold B. Lee, Prophet and Seer*. Salt Lake City: Bookcraft, 1985.

Goates, L. Brent. *He Changed My Life*. Salt Lake City: Bookcraft, 1988.

Bibliography

Howard, F. Burton. *Marion G. Romney, His Life and Faith.* Salt Lake City. Bookcraft, 1988.

Kimball, Edward L., and Andrew Kimball. *Spencer W. Kimball.* Salt Lake City: Bookcraft, 1977.

Williams, Frederick S., and Frederick G. Williams. *From Acorn to Oak Tree.* Fullerton, CA: Et Cetera, Et Cetera Graphics, 1987.

Index

Acropolis, 465
Adam-ondi-Ahman, 329
Affleck, Gordon, 256, 482–83
Agnew, Spiro, 452
Aki, Henry, 317
Albert, Carl, 452
Albion State Normal School, 34–37
Anderson, Dee, 489
Anderson, Norma, 273
Anderson, Joseph, 147, 152, 273, 435
Andes Mission, 382
Apartheid, 362
Apostles, importance of, 144–45
Arrington, Leonard, 432
Articles of Faith, The, 63
Ashby, Armis J., 439, 450
Ashton, Marvin J., 412, 436–37, 500
Ashton, Marvin O., 140, 238
Ashton, Wendell J., 414, 430–31
Audience won't leave, wants to hear more from HBL, 365

Austin, Mark, 129

Babbel, Fredrick, 302
Backman, Robert L., 475
Baker, Fred, 484
Ballard, Melvin J., 129, 131, 132, 140, 381–82
Ballif, Louis, 32
Bangerter, Geraldine, 376, 377, 380
Bangerter, W. Grant, 376, 377, 380
Barker, James, 424
Barker, Kate M., 136
Barker, Robert, 426, 427
Basketball, HBL injured while playing, 80
Bear Lake Stake, 303
Beesley, Wilford, 118
Bennett, Frances Grant, 301
Bennett, Harold H., 240
Bennett, Wallace F., 301, 345
Bennett, William H., 435, 436
Bennion, Adam S., 298, 316

Index

Bennion, Howard S., 187
Bennion, Mervyn, 180, 220
Bennion, Samuel O., 216
Benson, Ezra Taft: born in Whitney, 12; at Oneida with HBL, 34; helps in meeting with welfare officials, 199, 200–201; set apart as member of the Twelve, 204; helps with postwar welfare, 226; cuts through red tape to deliver wheat, 228; named Secretary of Agriculture, 298; supported by Brethren in difficult assignment, 300; takes HBL on tour of Department of the Interior, 302; helps HBL get visa, 359; counsels with HBL, 374; at meeting to improve Church's public relations, 426; attends Mexico area conference, 461
Benson, Flora, 229
Bentley, Joseph T., 332, 333
Bergeson, Vernal, 57
Berrett, William E., 433
Berry, William S., 271
Beuhner, Carl W., 298, 334
Bickmore, Lee, 426, 427–28, 429, 430, 468, 478
Bingham, Levi Perry, 10–11
Bingham, Perry Calvin, 11, 19–20
Bingham, Rachel Elvira, 11
Bingham, Sarah, 11
Black, June B., 483
Black, Nola, 498
Blacks and the priesthood, controversy over, 417–18, 423
Bonneville Stake, 197
Boud, John W., 220
Bourne, Hal, 409
Bowen, Albert E.: designated advisor to general committee, 141; as apostle, 151; visits defense facilities with HBL, 183; passes away in 1953, 205, 298; on committee to implement correlation, 250; installs new stake president, 254; called by HBL about death of prophet, 287; released as member of executive committee, 293
Bowman, Frank, 328
Boyack, Clifton D., 393
Brazil, 375, 376
Brazil South Mission, 375–79
Bronson, Edwin, 88
Brower, Steve, 434
Brown, Campbell, 126, 127, 129
Brown, Hugh B.: helps dissolve Salt Lake Stakes Associated, 118; joins Church history study group of HBL, 152; works to help servicemen, 186; sustained as Assistant to the Twelve, 187, 298; remains in Europe to help servicemen, 218; has first assignment as General Authority, 309; is uncle of N. Eldon Tanner, 311; goes with HBL to divide stake, 335; called as third counselor in First Presidency, 388; attends meeting in temple, 420; gives invocation at general conference, 489
Brown, Victor L., 437, 445, 461
Brown, Zina Card, 309
Bunker, Berkley, 350, 351
Burton, T. T., 88, 115
Burton, Theodore M., 188–90, 254, 369, 386, 432
Busche, Enzio, 450
Bybee, Lester, 22

Calbi, Dr., 466
Calgary Stake, 311
California Mission, 265–69
California Zephyr, 316
Call, Waldo Pratt, 416
Callis, Charles A., 151, 165, 205, 230, 233–35
Callister, Lou and Geraldine, 400
Camargo, Helio da Rocha, 377–78

Index

Camp Crawford, 319
Cannon, Edwin J., 450, 465
Cannon, George Q., 89
Cannon, Janath, 465
Cannon, John Q., 360
Cannon, Sylvester Q., 89, 116, 131, 140, 200
Cardston Temple, 309
Carmack, John, 416
Carr, Gail E., 321
Carr, John, 430
Central States Mission, 270–72, 327
Chaffings, Susannah, 2
Chan, Daniel F. Y., 324
Chase, Alvin, 233
Child, Paul C., 83, 91, 110, 115, 117, 126
Christensen, Joe J., 434, 445
Christensen, Milton, 361
Christiansen, ElRay, 290
Church of the Air, 325
City of St. Louis, 329
Clark, Chase, 166
Clark, J. Reuben: develops affinity for HBL, 109; unable to attend meeting, 122; speaks on role of security plan, 134; discusses revelation, 137; on opposition to welfare plan, 139; on committee reaction to plan, 140; son-in-law of, dies at Pearl Harbor, 180; goes with HBL and Fern to Arizona, 192; discusses filling apostle's vacancies, 200; invites HBL to accompany him on business, 218; speaks at funeral of father of HBL, 240; gives HBL counsel, 263–64; senses rift with HBL, 265; helps HBL teach BYU class, 315; in failing health, 326–27; advises HBL to decline offer for board of director position, 338–39; called as counselor in First Presidency, 357; in frail health, 387; passes away, 388
Clawson, Rudger, 89, 151, 200
Clayson, Merrill D., 101
Cleveland, 316
Cole, Ethel, 33
Colton, Don B., 175
Communists protest at City and County Building, 119
Condor, James, 271
Condor, Martin, 271
Conkling, James, 429
Coopman, Jacob, 366
Cowan, Clarence, 98, 106
Cowdery, Oliver, 329
Cowley, Matthew, 217, 224, 306, 324
Cullimore, James A., 328
Curtis, Elbert R., 196, 345
Cuthbert, Derek A., 442
Cutler, Allen R., 226
Cyclorama, 231

Daines, Robert, 30
Danks, Mary Lou, 242
Darling, Joseph W., 487
Davey, C. E., 111
Davies, E. C., 98, 106
Davis, Irvin, 278
Davis, Jeanette McMurrin, 10
Davis, Reese, 43
Davis, Riley, 10
Daynes, Joseph J., 119
DeBry, Theodore M., 130
Decisions for Successful Living, 214, 215
Depression, The Great, 110, 119
Deseret Industries, 141
Deseret News, 99, 120, 121, 122, 206, 418
Detroit Michigan Stake, 354
DeWitt, Paul, 426
Dias, Bartholemeu, 365
Didier, Charles, 468
Donahoe, Cashell, Sr., 344
Drury, Jesse M., 111

Index

Dunn, Loren C., 412, 433, 442, 445
Dunn, Paul H., 404, 433, 445
Dyer, Alvin R., 327, 411, 432, 435

Eardley, Roscoe, 275
East Central States Mission, 270–72
Eastern States Mission, 340, 371
Eban, Abba S., 360, 466
Eccles, George S., 340
Eccles, Parley, 106
Edmunds, John K., 223
Edwards, Francis Henry, 328–29
Eisenhower, Dwight D., 298
Eldredge, W. Jay, 407, 445
Emerson, Ralph Waldo, 1, 258
Engar, Charles A., 31
Ensign, 367, 433
Ensign Stake, 191, 275
Equitable Life, 343–44, 357–58
Erickson, A. D., 167
Evans, Aldredge, 274–75
Evans, Richard L., 205, 298, 390, 426, 436, 445
Exemplary Manhood Award, 480
Eyring, Henry B., 434

Farmer, E. G., 22
Fauntleroy, Little Lord, 18
Faust, James E., 356–57, 416, 469, 475, 477
Featherstone, Vaughn J., 437, 479
Fetzer, Emil, 484
Finck, Alfons J., 110, 111
Findling, Jack, 98
Fisher, President, 362–63, 367
Fitzpatrick, John F., 98, 107, 113
Folklorico, 460
Ford, Edsel, 121
Ford, Henry, 121
Foster, Stephen, 272
Franks, Oliver, 369
Frew, Chap, 43
Frew, Dick, 43

Friend, 433
Fugal, G. Roy, 346, 429, 430
Funk, Ruth Hardy, 475
Fyans, J. Thomas, 416, 430, 444

Gaertner Family, 378–79
Galbraith, David, 466, 467
Gandhi, Mahatma, 364
Gardner, Elder, 367
Gates, Crawford, 245
Geddes, Joseph A., 30
Gerard, Sarah, 21
Gerry, Eldredge, 340
Giant Joshua, 174
Gibbs, John H., 271
Gibbons, Francis M., 434, 445
Gibbs, Lauren W., 106
Gila Valley, 172–74
Gillette, Colonel, 317
Gleave, John P., Jr., 167
Goaslind, Jack, 463
Goates, David, 261, 330, 405, 441
Goates, Elizabeth Jane, 315
Goates, Harold Lee, 253, 274, 406
Goates, Helen Lee. *See* Lee, Helen
Goates, Jane, 394
Goates, Jonathon, 473
Goates, L. Brent: was to become director of LDS Hospital, 85; accompanies HBL to sporting events, 186; marries daughter of HBL, 229–30; loved by HBL, 248, 249; inducted into college of hospital administrators, 374; published tributes to HBL, 472; told HBL had entered hospital, 497; gives dedicatory prayer at grave of HBL, 501
Goates, Lesley Drew, 439
Gold, Oscar, 217
Goldwater, Barry, 345
Graham, James, 111
Grant, Heber J.: lives in Ensign Stake, 73; attends opening

Index

social of gymnasium, 116; attends meetings on security plan, 122, 131; calls HBL to be an apostle, 145, 147–48; delivers apostolic charge to HBL, 155; ordains Ezra Taft Benson and Spencer W. Kimball to the Twelve, 204; passes away, 216; presided over Japan Mission, 323; letter written to, by Wilford Woodruff, 420

Great Waltz, 450

Green, Doyle L., 416, 430

Greenwood, J. Fields, 106

Grimm, Maxine Tate, 324

Grimm, Peter, 324

Haight, David B., 35, 248, 435, 436, 461

Haight, Ruby, 293

Hales, Irene, 244

Hammond, D. E., 88

Hancock, J. A., 88

Hanks, Marion D.: called to First Council of the Seventy, 298; meets Lees at Heathrow, 402; sustained as Assistant to the Twelve, 412; meets with group of young adults with HBL, 417; at meeting to prepare for Manchester conference, 445; assigned to help with supervision of MPMIA, 475; travels to Arizona with HBL, 479

Hanks, Maxine, 402

Hansen, Terry, 248

Hardwick, William, 45

Hardy, Rufus K., 216, 224

Harris, Devere, 416

Harriman, E. Roland, 339

Harris, Michael Van, 492

Hatch, Walter, 45

Hawthorne, Nathaniel, 258

Haycock, D. Arthur: as seminary student of HBL, 102; served on administrative staff of Ezra Taft Benson, 302; counseled with HBL, 317; is personal secretary to Joseph Fielding Smith, 444; attends meeting to prepare for Manchester conference, 445; HBL spends day dictating to, 479; leaves for Munich with HBL, 485; asked to bring papers to hospital for HBL, 497; gives prayer at funeral of HBL, 500

Haycock, Maurine, 317, 485

Hayden, Carl, 345

He Changed My Life, 472

Heath, Fred J., 110, 115

Helm, Dr., 361

Heinz, William F., 379

Henderson, Elvira, 11

Hewlett, Lester, 126

Hewlett, Patsy, 406

Hickey, Thomas B., 318

Hickman, Mabel, 71, 146, 164, 246

Hill Cumorah, 347

Hill, George R., 249

Hill, John D., 354

Hinckley, Bryant S., 118

Hinckley, Gordon B.: becomes an apostle, 388; at meeting to discuss public relations of Church, 426; serves on committee over internal communications of Church, 430; attends meeting to plan Manchester conference, 445; meets HBL at Heathrow, 464; serves as executive secretary to publicity committee, 486–87; speaks at funeral of HBL, 500

Hinckley, Marjorie, 464

Ho Nam Rhee, 321

Holland, Jeffrey R., 478

Holt, Russell, 247

Hood, Andrew, 70

Hoopes, Ren, 429, 430

Hoover, Herbert, 116, 299

Index

Houston Texas Stake, 353
Howell, Joe, 167
Howell, Marion, 43
Hudson, James R., 271
Huff, Sparrel, 32
Hull, Cordell, 125
Hunt, Mitchell, 248
Hunter, Howard W., 432, 445
Hunter, Milton R., 216, 433
Hutchins, Robert M., 249
Hutson, S. B., 228
Hyde, Charles S., 88, 89, 91, 98, 242, 385
Hyde, Orson, 470, 484

Idaho Falls Temple, 223–24
Idaho State University Stake, 479
Improvement Era, 131, 135, 138
Irvine, Jeanette, 9
Isaacson, Thorpe B., 238, 298, 411, 435
Ivins, Anthony W., 108, 118
Ivins, Antoine R., 194

Jacksonville Florida Stake, 356
Jacobsen, Soren, 304
Jacobsen, Theodore C., 340
Jacobsen, T. C., 345, 371
Jefferson, Thomas, 344
Jenkins, Archie O., 231, 232, 277
Jenkins, Jinx, 356
Jensen, Arthur, 380
Jensen, C. O., 110
Jensen, Harriet, 60, 61, 71
Jensen, Joan. *See* Lee, Joan Jensen
Jesus the Christ, 63
Joffe, Rabbi, 466
Johnson, F. Elinor, 61
Johnson, Jane Vail, 3
Jorgensen, Dan, 467
Juarez Stake, 416
Judd, David E., 275

Kanab Utah Stake, 416
Kearns, Thomas L., 98
Kennedy, David M., 275, 340

Kennedy, Edward M., 452
Kim, H., 320, 321
Kimball, Camilla, 346, 347
Kimball, Heber C., 204
Kimball, Spencer W.: becomes official organist of the Brethren, 22; assists Gila Valley during flood, 172–74; as stake president, 192–93; President Grant suggests, as new apostle, 200; as new apostle, 201, 202, 204; speaks at Pioneer Park, 244; blessed by HBL, 256; goes with HBL to bless George Albert Smith, 266; placed on temple committee with HBL, 308; visits Mexico with HBL, 331–33; suffers recurring hoarseness, 342–43; has surgery for cancer, 346; fulfills first assignments after surgery, 352–54; seconds Joseph Fielding Smith as next president, 421; at meeting to discuss improving public relations of Church, 426; learns no need for further surgery on throat, 427; attends meeting to prepare for Manchester conference, 445; has delicate heart surgery, 452–54; attends meeting although plagued with Bell's Palsy, 455; becomes president of the Twelve, 458; attends Mexico area conference, 461; leads family of HBL in prayer, 498; conducts funeral of HBL
Kirkham, Francis W., 121, 122
Kirkham, Oscar A., 171
Knapp, Arnold, 487
Knight, John M.: called to preside over mission, 51; as a shrewd leader, 56; goes to Colorado after flood, 64–65; assigns HBL to conduct Sheridan Stake conference, 67–68;

Index

releases HBL from mission, 70; returns to Salt Lake City with HBL, 71; foresees future for HBL, 72–73; takes HBL on tour of administration building, 74; as member of Salt Lake City commission, 96; asks HBL to fill commission vacancy, 97; asked to help HBL develop welfare system, 126
Kollek, Teddy, 466
Korea, 320–23
Kruger Park, 363–64

La Traviata, 369
Laie Temple, 306
Lake, Joseph H., 97
Lambert, Pearl, 442
Landry, Bill, 367
Larson, Oscar, 119, 120
Lasater, John, 450
Laub, Vasco, 318
Lawler, Oscar, 340
Leaing, Margaret, 6
Lethbridge Stake, 309, 311
Lewis, Daniel, 320
Lewis, John L., 291
Lee, Clyde, 80
Lee, Fern Tanner (first wife): in mission with HBL, 61–62; knuckles of, turn white as HBL sustained as an apostle, 70–71; sees HBL after mission, 74–75; marries HBL, 82; two daughters born to, 85; is against HBL's remaining in education, 87; lacks enthusiasm for HBL to fill commission vacancy, 98; ideally suited for apostle's wife, 158; celebrates anniversary by riding with President and Sister Clark, 178–79; nervous about WWII, 183; goes on trip to Arizona, 192; has surgery, 207–8; daughters of, marry, 229–30; travels to Atlanta with HBL, 230–31; travels to Jacksonville with HBL, 231–34; love of, for HBL, 255; visits New England with HBL, 256–60; meets HBL at train depot, 282; loves new home, 291; mother of, dies, 293; visits Hawaii with HBL, 304; serious fall of, leads to surgery, 314–15; goes to Hawaii en route to Japan, 316–17; arrives in Japan, 318; speaks at many meetings in Japan, 319; suffers eye hemorrhage, 329; goes to South African Mission with HBL, 361–66; sad about new wedding ring, 366; seeks Scottish ancestors, 369; receives hugs from Brazilian sisters, 376; suffers eye hemorrhage in South America, 380; move to new home necessitated by ill health of, 388–89; health of, deteriorates, 394–95; passes away, 396
Lee, Francis, 3–7, 66
Lee, Francis, Jr., 6–7
Lee, Grant W., 186
Lee, Harold Bingham
—youth: faith of, 20; cuts own hair, 18–20; baptism of, 22–23; warned by voice to stay away from wood pile, 23, 448; illnesses and mishaps of, 24–25; attends general conference for first time, 27–28; goes to Oneida Academy, 29–33; attends Albion State Normal, 34–37; teaches at Silver star School, 38–40; teaches at Oxford District school, 41–42; plays in Frew Orchestra, 42–43
—mission: receives mission call, 47; leaves for mission, 50–51; gains entrance to homes

Index

through music, 52–53; becomes Denver conference president, 54–55; motivates and teaches missionaries, 57–58; meets Fern tanner, 61–62; corrected by James E. Talmage, 63; travels with President Knight, 63–65; visits Nauvoo and Carthage, 66–67; conducts Sheridan Stake Conference, 67–68; has money worries, 69; is released from mission, 70
—marriage and early responsibilities: visits Fern after release from mission, 74–75; called to preside over elders, 79; needs surgery after basketball game, 80; marries Fern, 82; called to high council, 84; leaves teaching to sell books, 86–87; called as stake president, 89–90; convenes court for former bishop, 93–94; fills vacancy in Salt Lake City commission, 99; teaches seminary, 101–2; in charge of street department, 103–4; campaigns for and achieves reelection, 105–7; begins welfare system in Pioneer Stake, 110–13; believes in delegation of duties, 114–15; asks Church support for welfare system, 118; learns of communists' assault on City and County Building, 119–20; given charge to develop Church's welfare plan, 123; forms committee to help develop welfare plan, 126–27; chosen as head of Church security plan, 129–30
—member of Twelve: felt he would be an apostle one day, 146; called to apostleship, 147–48; tells family of call, 149; recalls being sustained as apostle, 151; ordained as apostle, 153–56; influenced by Fern, 159; maintains yard and car although busy, 161–62, 185; on first assignment as apostle, 165–66; becomes close to Marion G. Romney, 168; leads Twelve in prayer, 171; travels to Gila Valley to assess flood damage, 172–74; instructs missionaries on temple ordinances, 175–76; goes for ride with President and Sister Clark, 178–79; to form air raid committee during WWII, 180; visits defense facilities, 183–84, 186; commands Theodore M. Burton to be healed, 188–90; goes on trip with Fern and President and Sister Clark to Arizona, 192–93; tours Texas-Louisiana Mission, 194–96; discusses filling vacancies in the Twelve, 200; asked to cast out evil spirit, 201; instructs Elder Benson and Elder Kimball in ordination protocol, 203; called to investigate charges against Richard R. Lyman, 205–6; concerned over Fern's ill health, 207–8; takes family on trip to Mexico, 209–13; goes to Grant home after prophet dies, 216; visits Hawaiian Islands to check on servicemen, 218–22; on dedication of Idaho Falls Temple, 223–24; talks with returning servicemen, 227; daughters of, marry, 229–30; travels to Atlanta, 230–31; travels to Jacksonville, 231–34; learns of death of Charles A. Callis, 234–35; goes with Henry D. Moyle to preside at stake conference, 237–38; father dies, 239–40; travels to Western

States Mission, 240–43; celebrates centennial, 244–45; goes to Palo Alto to see daughter, 246–47; loves his sons-in-law, 248–49; involved with Church simplification program, 250–52; fasts for Maurine, 253; visits New England Mission, 256–60; helps Wilkinses move, 262; visits Western Canada, 262–63; cautioned by President Clark, 263–64; travels to California Mission, 265–69; goes to Central States mission, 270–72; blesses woman distraught over daughter's murder, 272; learns of death of Aldredge Evans, 274–75; goes to Washington, D. C., 275–76; enjoys deep sea fishing, 278; celebrates Fourth of July, 279–80; helps Wilkinses find home, 282–83; plagued by ill health, 286; learns of death of George Albert Smith, 286–87; asks for blessing because of ill health, 290; meets with heads of mine worker's union, 291; goes to aid of Fern, 293; concerned over changes in welfare plan, 296–98; learns of Ezra Taft Benson's appointment to cabinet, 298–99; visits with Mr. and Mrs. Wallace F. Bennett, 301; again suffers with sickness, 303–4; fits in vacation to Hawaii, 304–7; goes to Canada with Hugh B. Brown, 309–12; relieved when Fern has successful surgery, 314–15; leaves for Japan, 316–17; visits Army bases in Japan, 318–19; visits Korea, 320–23; visits Okinawa, Kowloon, Taipei, and Hong Kong, 323–24; gives Church of the Air address, 325–26; goes to Central States Mission, 327–29; involved in dedication of Los Angeles Temple, 331; visits Mexico, 331–33; enjoys rest and relaxation, 334; invited to join Union Pacific Railroad board of directors, 337–40; elected as member of subsidiaries of Union Pacific, 343; meets president of Equitable Life, 343–44; attends national Scout Jamboree, 345; goes to aid of Spencer W. Kimball, 346–47; concerned over institutes and seminaries, 348–49; speaks in ward of Bishop Ernest Wilkins, 349–50; describes experience with Spencer W. Kimball, 352–54; trains Thomas S. Monson, 355–56; asked to be on board of Equitable, 357–58; travels to South Africa via several international cities, 359–61; tours South African Mission, 361–66; trip home from South Africa, 367–70; plagued once again with illness, 372; mother of, dies, 373; goes to Brazil, 375–79; tours South America, 382–84; appointed to board of Zions First National, 386; moves to new home because of Fern's health, 388–89; approves of priesthood correlation, 389–92; worried by deteriorating health of Fern, 394–95; mourns loss of Fern, 396–97; courts and marries Joan Jensen, 398–400; travels to Hawaii with Joan, 401; learns of death of Henry D. Moyle, 401–2; travels abroad, 402–3; grandsons of, go on missions, 405–6; has surgery, 407–8; has more health problems, 408–10;

Index

against bypassing correlation, 412–13; works on Regional Representative program, 413–15; learns of death of David O. McKay, 419
—counselor in First Presidency: becomes counselor in First Presidency, 421; responsibilities of, 422; begins Church public communications committee, 425–31; restructures work of Twelve, 431–32; observes many changes among General Authorities, 433–37; accepts speaking engagements in Idaho and Cache Valley, 437–38; participates in dedication of Ogden and Provo temples, 440–441; sees Fern in vision, 442; attends Manchester conference, 444–49; tours Europe after conference, 450–51; counsels with Spencer W. Kimball about heart surgery, 452–54; learns of death of Joseph Fielding Smith, 454–55; goes to hospital suffering from pain, 456; conducts funeral of Joseph Fielding Smith, 456–57
—president of the Church: becomes president of Church, 458; goes to Mexico area conference, 460–61; is threatened by apostate cult, 463; goes on tour of Europe, 464–66; becomes gravely ill during tour, 466–67; continues European tour, 467–68; goes to upper room of temple to pray, 470; receives help from FBI, 473; has severe respiratory problems, 474; plans organization for single adults, 475–78; water of, poisoned, 482; plans to use training videos, 483–84; harassed because of demolition of Whitney Hall, 485; goes to area conference in Munich, 485–86; speaks at funeral of Gladys Condie Monson, 488; speaks at his last general conference, 489–92; attends Christmas functions, 493–95; family of, comes for advice on Christmas, 497; taken to hospital for tests, 497; unexpectedly passes away at age seventy-four, 498–99; funeral of, 500–502

Lee, Helen (daughter): on father's call as apostle, 150; on days after HBL became apostle, 157–58; on Fern's influence on HBL, 159; life of, as daughter of HBL, 160; on HBL mowing quickly, 162; married to Brent Goates, 209, 229–30; travels with mother to New York, 374

Lee, Joan Jensen (second wife): courtship of, by HBL, 398–99; marries HBL, 399–400; travels to Hawaii with HBL, 401; travels abroad, 402–3; calls mission president when HBL becomes ill, 407; goes with HBL to Idaho, 437; travels to Manchester conference, 444–49; tours Europe, 450–51; insists HBL receive blessing, 466; goes to Vienna with HBL, 486–87

Lee, Louisa Bingham (mother): married, 11; industry of, as homemaker, 14; saves HBL from lightning, 16; combs hair of HBL into ringlets, 18–19; has ringlets made into watch chains, 20; saves HBL from illness and mishaps, 24–25; nurses HBL during pneumonia, 45; asks HBL not to do

518

Index

too much, 351; passes away, 373
Lee, Maurine (daughter): life of, as daughter of HBL, 160; was seventeen when HBL called to Twelve, 162; marries Ernest Wilkins, 230; dates Ernest Wilkins, 237; leaves with Ernest Wilkins for Stanford, 246; spends evening with HBL at Christmas, 337; sudden death of, 404
Lee, Perry, 373, 494, 500
Lee, Rex, 333, 434
Lee, S., 319
Lee, Samuel Chaffings, 2–3, 4
Lee, Samuel Marion, Jr. (father): goes to live with grandmother, 8; goes to live with aunt, 10; married, 11; compiles genealogy, 14; Church callings of, 15; recommends HBL to serve mission, 46; has financial difficulty while supporting HBL on mission, 77; death of, 239
Lee, Samuel Marion, Sr. (grandfather), 4, 6–8
Lee, Samuel Perry, 18
Lee, Stella, 18, 80
Lee, Verda, 18, 80
Lee, Waldo, 18, 80
Lee, William, 2
Lee, Wm. L., 324
Lightning, mother of HBL saves him from, 16
Lincoln, Abraham, 272
Lincoln, Tressie, 41
Lindsey, J. M., 233
Liu, George, 324
Lockhard, Lee M., 37
Lodge, Henry Cabot, 345
Logan Temple, 48, 309
London Temple, 360, 487
Longden, John, 290
Longfellow, Henry Wadsworth, 258

Look, 174, 175
Los Angeles Stake, 416
Los Angeles Temple, 309, 331
Loveland, Thomas, 37
Lovinger, Lee, 98
Lowe, Irel, 32
Ludlow, Daniel, 430
Lund, Anthon H., 27
Lundgren, Allen H., 102
Lundgren, Ruth Horne, 102
Lurline, 304, 305, 307
Lusk, Elizabeth, 11
Lye, HBL accidentally drinks cup of, 24–25
Lyman, Amy Brown, 136
Lyman, Richard R., 74, 84, 96, 97, 201

Madsen, E. Coleman, 233
Malad Idaho Stake, 416
Manchester conference, 444–49
Mansion House, 66
Manti Temple, 483
Market crash, 110, 119
Marriott, J. Willard, 300, 345, 402
Mars Hill, 465
Marsh Valley, 36
Martin, Dr., 427
Martin, Owen H., 51
Mason, James, 433
Maxwell, Neal A., 414, 433
McAlister, G. Stanley, 426
McConkie, Amelia Smith, 451
McConkie, Bruce R.: called as member of First Council of Seventy, 266; works with HBL to reorganize stake, 269; asked to supervise Regional Representatives, 433; Joseph Fielding Smith to live with, 451; speaks at funeral of Joseph Fielding Smith, 457; attends meeting in Mexico, 461; called to Twelve, 469
McConkie, Oscar W., Jr., 269, 452

Index

McConkie, Oscar W., Sr., 266, 267
McKay, David Lawrence, 434, 449, 464, 468
McKay, David O.: as second counselor to President Grant, 122; meets with HBL about beginning welfare plan, 126; pleased with welfare plan as proposed by HBL, 127–28; presents report, 133; on feelings about welfare plan, 134; discusses security plan, 137; prays for HBL, 235; speaks at Pioneer Park, 244; becomes president of Church, 287; has surgery, 289; makes lengthy trips, 296–97; tells David Goates to keep name honorable, 330; convenes special meeting of apostles, 357; calls two more counselors, 411; passes away, 419–20
McKay, Douglas, 380
McKay, Mildred, 464
McKay, Thomas E., 152
McKean, Howard, 282, 328
McKeown, Dougald, 487
McLure, H. E., 269
McMullen, Sarah, 2
McMurrin, Joseph W., 2, 6, 9, 10, 27
McMurrin, Margaret, 6, 8
McMurrin, Margaret Leaing, 8–10
McMurrin, Mary, 6, 8
McMurrin, Sterling W., 202, 473
McPhie, Joseph H., 112
Meeks, Effie, 231
Meeks, Heber, 153, 231, 276
Mendenhall, Wendell B., 254, 324
Merrill, Joseph F., 151, 205, 292–93, 298
Merrill, Marriner W., 11, 272
Messias, Saul, 377
Mexican Mission, 210, 333

Midvale Stake, 416
Millennial Star, 446, 447
Miller, J. E., 35
Missionaries, sister, attend fashion show, 60
Missouri, 222
Monson, Gladys Condie, 488
Monson, Thomas S.: served seven years as junior member of Twelve, 205; HBL viewed, as protégé, 355–56; comes to hospital to counsel with HBL, 409; appointed chairman of adult correlation, 412; plans for first meeting of Regional Representatives, 414; at meeting in upper room of temple, 420; depended on by HBL for correlation effort, 422; on committee to supervise internal communications, 430; at meeting to prepare for Manchester conference, 445; mother of, dies, 488
Monticello, 344
Morris, Alan H., 497
Morris, George Q., 290, 298, 314
Mortimer, George, 426
Mount Graham Stake, 192
Moyle, Alberta, 402
Moyle, Henry D.: added to security committee, 129; appointed chairman of welfare committee, 140; counsels with HBL about welfare department, 176–78; gives HBL stock for Christmas, 180; goes with HBL to Washington, D.C., 275; gives blessing to HBL, 290, 372; goes with HBL to meet with mine workers, 291; helps HBL teach BYU class, 316; returns from tour of South and Central America, 334; called as second counselor in First Presidency, 357; concerned over excommuni-

Index

cated French missionaries, 360; witnesses marriage of HBL to Joan Jensen, 400; passes away, 401–2
Moyle, James H., 292
Moyle, Walter, 292
Mr. Cox's Clifton Silver Concert Band, 22
Muir, Leo J., 189
Murphy, Castle E., 221
Murphy, Ray D., 343
Music Man, 375
My Fair Lady, 375
My People, 466

Nelson, Russell M., 434, 445, 453
Nevada, 186
New England Mission, 256–60
New Era, 433
New Jersey Central Stake, 407
Nickel, R. F. W., 111
Nixon, Richard M., 345, 452, 474
Northern Far East Mission, 321
Northern Mexican Mission, 332, 333

Oaks, Dallin H., 434, 440
Oates, General, 319
Oates, James F., Jr., 357
Ogden, David R., 323
Ogden Temple, 439, 440–41
Olsen, Earl, 432
Olsen, Joseph, 347
Olson, Dean, 293
Olympia Hall, 486
Oneida, 31, 32
Oneida Stake, 79
Oneida Stake Academy: history of, 29–30; HBL attends, 30; curriculum of, 31; HBL debates at, 32; brawl erupts at, 33–34; HBL graduates from, 34
Orme, Joseph F., 408, 456, 474
Orme, James, 497, 499
Ostler, James F., 343
Owens, Wayne, 452

Oxford Athletic Club, 42

Pace, Lorin, 381
Packer, Boyd K.: HBL sees, as man of character, 348–49; works on home teaching committee, 412; supervises department of internal communications, 430; sustained as member of Twelve, 435; coordinates preparation for Manchester conference, 442; meets the Lees at Heathrow, 444; attends meeting to prepare for Manchester conference, 445
Palmer, Chaplain, 321
Paramore, James, 430
Parker, Frankie, 243
Parmley, Lavern, 345
Parthenon, 465
Partridge, Edward, 124
Peale, Norman Vincent, 468
Pearl Harbor, 179, 181, 198, 220, 221
Penrose, Charles W., 74
Penrose, Frank, 98
Perry, L. Tom, 469, 475, 477
Petersen, Claude, 248
Petersen, Mark E., 201, 206, 311, 336, 461
Peterson, Daniel, 52
Peterson, H. Burke, 437
Pierce, Arwell L., 210
Pinegar, Rex D., 469
Pinnock, Hugh W., 416
Pioneer Stake, 82, 89, 94, 110
Pioneer Stake Gymnasium, 115
Polysophical Society, 492
Poplar Grove Ward, 82, 83, 84
Pratt, Harold A., 332
Pratt, Parley P., 382, 446
Pratt, Rey L., 381–82
Prayer circle, 171
Preece, Joseph H., 98, 106
Preston Military Band, 31
Priesthood Correlation Program, 389–91

Index

Prince, Bill and Lida, 304
Prince, William H., 146
Provo Temple, 439, 440, 441
Public Communications, Department of, 425–31

Qualey, Jay, 220, 395
Quealey, Virginia, 395
Queen Elizabeth, 369
Queroz, Walter, 377

Rampton, Calvin L., 473
Rawson, Murray, 227
Ray, L. A., 86
Rector, Hartman, Jr., 412, 433
Reeve, Reed, 487
Reeve, Rex C., Sr., 416
Regional Representatives, 413–15
Reynolds, Harold G., 74
Richards, Bessie Hollings, 280
Richards, Franklin D., 386, 461
Richards, George F., 82, 205, 217, 280, 457
Richards, Joel, 280
Richards, LeGrand, 140, 298
Richards, Reed, 318
Richards, Stayner, 290, 298
Richards, Stephen L: as youngest member of Twelve next to HBL, 151; as chairman of committee, 250; nominated as first counselor to President McKay, 287; is greatly respected by Brethren, 288; announces appointment of HBL to board of Union Pacific, 339; passes away, 356
Richards, Thomas W., 270
Richards, Willard, 270
Ricks, Eldon, 283
Ricks, Irene, 283
Riddleburger, Ambassador, 368
Ringger, Hans B., 450
Ringlets, HBL teased because of, 19
Roberts, Brigham H., 50, 271
Robertson, Hilton A., 318, 321

Robinson, J. Robert, 30
Robison, Louise Y., 136
Romney, Antone, 416
Romney, George, 354
Romney, Marion G.: feelings of, on welfare plan, 137; sustained as Assistant to Twelve, 152, 168; travels to Gila Valley with HBL, 172; goes with HBL to Washington, D.C., 228; called as member of Twelve, 290; concerned over changes in welfare plan, 297; helps HBL teach BYU class, 316; becomes chairman of general welfare committee, 357; gives HBL a blessing, 372; to chair priesthood committee, 391; witnesses marriage of HBL to Joan Jensen, 400; is chairman of home teaching committee, 412; at meeting to prepare for Manchester conference, 445; to be named second counselor in First Presidency, 456; chosen counselor to HBL, 458; conducts session of Mexico area conference, 460; leaves vacancy in Twelve, 469; captivated by HBL's magnetic presence, 481; told HBL is in hospital, 497, 498; speaks at funeral of HBL, 500
Roosevelt, Franklin D., 181
Rose Bowl, 293
Rosenvall, E. Albert, 88
Ross, Charles and Verda Lee, 163, 396, 400
Rubin, Jerry, 423
Rudd, Glen L., 22, 23, 167, 407
Russell, Gardner, 351
Ryberg, William E., 129, 217, 275

Salt Lake Bonneville Stake, 434
Salt Lake Riverside Stake, 165
San Francisco Chronicle, 418

Index

San Luis Stake, 292
Salt Lake Temple, 483
Sarnoff, General, 360
Sato, Brother, 323
Schaerrer, Neil, 487
Schindler, Emil A. J., 379
Schmidt, Dwayne, 474
Schreiner, Alexander, 500
Schroeder, Ted, 243
Schwendiman, Kay, 450
Scout Jamboree, 345
Sears, Bob, 426, 427
Security, Church's need for improvement of, 424–25
Security Plan. *See* Welfare Plan
Sharman, Mark, 449
Sharp, J. Vernon, 382
Sheridan, Philip Henry, 67
Sherman, William Tecumseh, 231
Sibley, John A., 397, 473
Sill, Sterling W., 314
Silver Star School, 38–40
Simpson, Robert L., 437
Skidmore, Rex, 433
Smith, Donald, 444
Smith, Douglas A., 444
Smith, Eldred G., 238, 334
Smith, George Albert: helps to reorganize Pioneer Stake, 89; set apart as president of Twelve, 201; rebellion quelled by, 211; approved to replace President Grant, 216; oversees dedication of Idaho Falls Temple, 223–24; opposes simplification program, 252; meets HBL in Canada, 263; recuperates from stroke, 266; death of, 286–87
Smith, George Albert, Jr., 258
Smith, Gerald G., 371, 372
Smith, Henry A., 344
Smith, Hyrum G., 50
Smith, J. M., 439
Smith, Jessica, 464
Smith, John Henry, 10
Smith, Joseph, 124, 470
Smith, Joseph F., 27, 98, 200
Smith, Joseph Fielding: introduced to HBL, 74; as former historian, 151; makes motion to sustain David O. McKay as president, 287; sustained as chairman of executive committee, 293; chairs temple committee, 308; helps HBL teach BYU class, 315; to chair missionary committee, 391; called as additional counselor to President McKay, 411; becomes president of Church, 421; at meeting to prepare for Manchester conference, 445; speaks at Manchester conference, 447; calls HBL a spiritual giant, 451; delivers last sermon, 454; passes away, 454–55
Smith, Leroy, 315
Smith, Milan, 464
Smith, Nicholas G., 152, 226
Smith, Silas, 192
Smith, W. Wallace, 329
Smith, Willard L., 263
Smith, Winslow Farr, 118
Smoot, Reed, 98, 126, 144
Snow, Lorenzo, 200
Snow, Richard, 474
Social Security, 348
Sonne, Alma, 152
Sonne, Richard B., 248
Sorenson, Asael, 377
South African Mission, 361–66, 379
Southern States Mission, 231, 350
Spafford, Belle S., 446
Spanish American Mission, 332
Sperry, Marva, 167
Sperry, Velma, 41
St. George Temple, 440
Stanford University, 417
Stapley, Delbert L., 225, 283, 290, 297, 344, 461

Index

Stevens, Stringham, 126, 129, 275
Stewart, Andrew, 310
Stoddard, A. E., 339
Stone, O. Leslie, 78, 469, 478
Stoof, Reinhold, 379
Stover, Walter, 397
Strauss, Johann, 450
Sundgaard, Arnold, 245

Tabernacle Choir, 461, 486, 489, 494, 500
Talley, Bud, 271
Talmage, James E., 62–63
Tanner, Bill, 335
Tanner, Janet, 75
Tanner, N. Eldon: meteoric rise of, to Church leadership, 310–12; sustained as Assistant to Twelve, 386; helps with David O. McKay's funeral, 420; to be counselor of HBL, 456; speaks at funeral of Joseph Fielding Smith, 457; chosen as counselor to HBL, 458; conducts session of Mexico area conference, 460; helps family of HBL with funeral, 500
Tanner, Stuart T., 75
Taylor, Harvey L., 433
Taylor, Henry D., 357, 373, 445
Taylor, John, 420
Taylor, John H., 187
Tanner, Richard, 187
Taylor, Maxwell D., 320–21
Telegram, 98
Texas-Louisiana Mission, 194–96
Third Convention, 211
Thomas, Lowell, 468
Thompson, Lord, 464
Thorupp, Mr., 459
Thousand Peak Ranch, 245
Times, Los Angeles, 459
Transcontinental Railroad, 338
Tribune, 98, 99, 113, 418
Tuttle, A., Theodore, 227, 348–49, 433

Udall, Levi S., 192
Union Pacific Railroad Company, 337
University West Stake, 459
Upper room of Salt Lake Temple, 153–54
Urry, Francis, 492
Upthegrove, Fay, 323
Uruguay Mission, 380

Valentine, Lee, 248
Vandenburg, John H., 342, 391, 434, 437
Vassal, 39, 40
Voice warns HBL not to go near woodpile, 23

Wahlquist, John, 153
Walnut Creek Stake, 335
Wangeman, Frank, 303, 340, 402
Wangeman, Henry Moyle, 292
Wangeman, Marie Moyle, 292
Warner, William L., 194
Washburn, J. Ballard, 416
Watkins, Arthur V., 302, 345
Watkins, George, 426
Weiser, Wendell H., 393
Welfare Plan: beginnings of, in Pioneer Stake, 110–13; management of, 114–15; Pioneer Stake Gymnasium built as result of, 115–16; Church members to use, not to receive government aid, 117; General Authorities pledge support for, 117–18; HBL asked to develop, for Church, 123; HBL chosen as head of, 129–30; opposition to, arises, 132, 138–39; give steps to a successful, 136; changed from security plan to, 140; Deseret Industries' part in, 141; undergoes changes, 294–95
Wells, Robert E., 380
Wells, Rulon S., 381
Wells, Sharlene, 380

524

Index

West, E. A., 270
West German Mission, 369
Western States Mission, 51–52, 240–43
Whipple, Maurine, 174
Whitcomb, Richard E., 321
White, Ray L., 268
Whiting, Bryant, 439
Whitmer, David, 329
Whitney Hall, 485
Whitney, Newel K., 124
Whitney, Orson F., 485
Widtsoe, John A.: designated advisor to general committee, 141; as former university professor, 151; dies in 1952, 205, 298; replaced by Ezra Taft Benson to oversee welfare distribution, 226; released from executive board, 292
Wight, Lyman, 329
Wilding, Thomas E., 110
Wilkins, Alan, 253, 262, 333, 405–6
Wilkins, Ernest J.: Maurine Lee married to, 230; dates Maurine regularly, 237; leaves for Stanford University, 246; known to Lees a short time before marriage to Maurine, 248–49; passes doctoral exams, 274; goes with HBL to football game, 312; gets doctorate, 313–14; serves as guide for tour group, 333; spends evening with HBL at Christmas, 337; invites HBL to speak in ward, 349–50
Wilkins, Jay, 331
Wilkins, Larry, 253, 274, 334
Wilkins, Marlee, 313, 394
Wilkins, Maurine Lee. *See* Lee, Maurine
Wilkinson, Ernest L.: spends day with HBL, 223; accompanies Brethren to discuss welfare wheat, 228; as new president of BYU, 294; aboard ship bound for Honolulu, 316; dismayed that Ricks Junior College should stay at Rexburg, 347; chairs committee over seminaries and institutes, 349; replaced by Dallin Oaks as president of BYU, 434
Wilkinson, Ernest L., Jr., 453
Wilkinson, Howard, 426
Williams, Frederick S., 383
Wilson, Chaplain, 318
Winder, John R., 27
Wirthlin, Joseph L.: as counselor to Presiding Bishop, 140; to meet with HBL, 147; becomes counselor in Presiding Bishopric, 238; involved in buying ranch land in Florida, 277; called as Presiding Bishop, 298; goes fishing with HBL, 334; succeeded as Presiding Bishop by John H. Vandenburg, 342
Woman agonizes over murder of daughter, 270, 272
Wood, E. S., 263
Wood, E. J., 400
Woodbury, T. Bowring, 327, 360
Woodbury, Willis J., 52, 68, 485
Woodland, Sheila, 244
Woodruff, Wilford, 10, 420–21
Woolley, Ralph E., 220
World War II, 179–80, 182–83

Yarn, D. Homer, 234
Young, Clifford E., 152, 246
Young, Edith Grant, 246
Young, Richard W., 51
Young, S. Dilworth, 216, 256, 433

525